# Celadon on the Seas

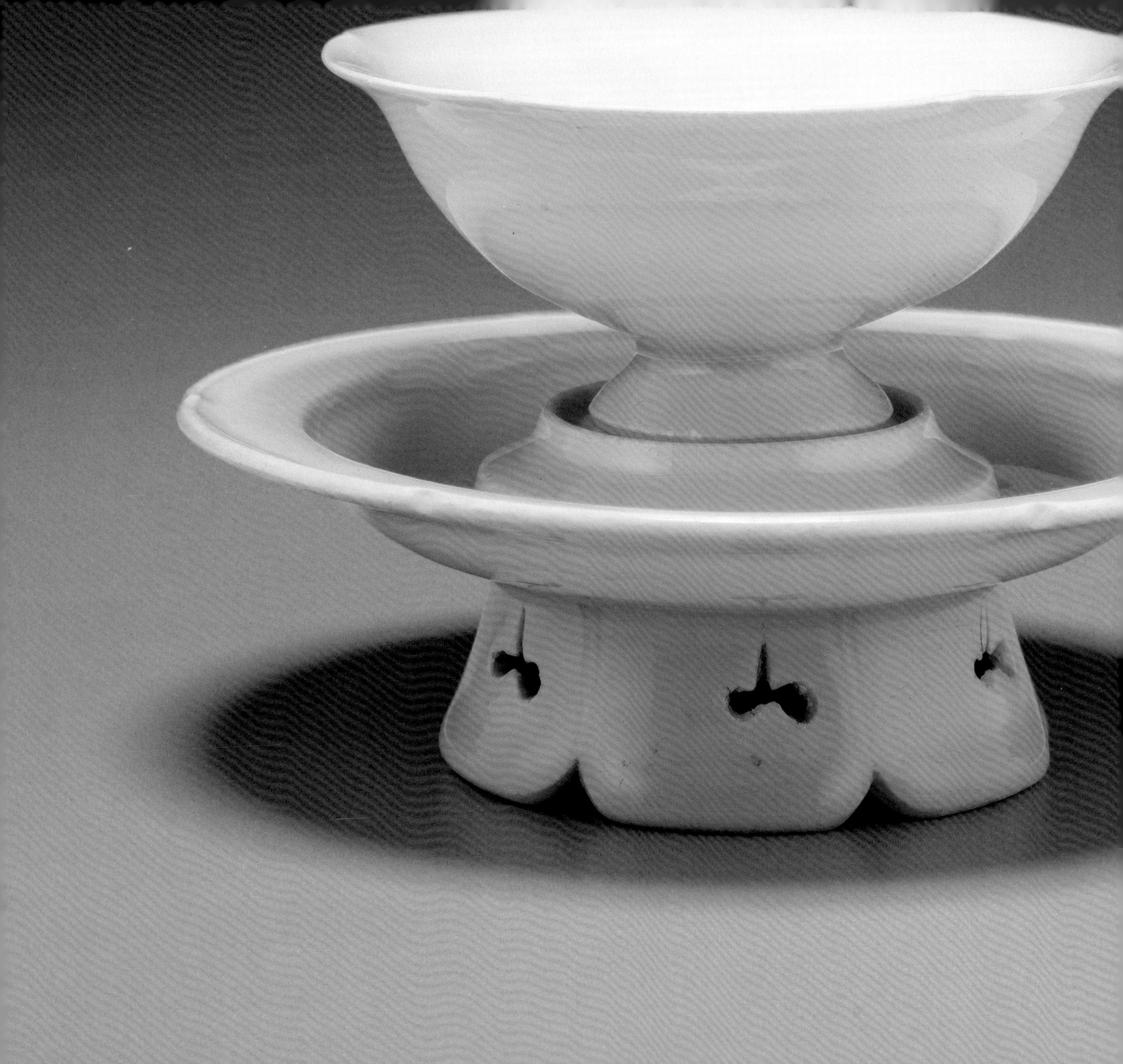

# Celadon on the Seas

CHINESE CERAMICS FROM THE 9TH TO THE 14TH CENTURY

Denise Patry Leidy

YALE UNIVERSITY ART GALLERY · NEW HAVEN

DISTRIBUTED BY YALE UNIVERSITY PRESS · NEW HAVEN AND LONDON

## YALE COLLECTIONS

Other titles in the series:
*The Naseby Cup: Coins and Medals of the English Civil War*

Publication made possible by the E. Rhodes and Leona B. Carpenter Foundation and the Andrew W. Mellon Foundation and Mary Cushing Fosburgh and James Whitney Fosburgh, B.A. 1933, M.A. 1935, Publication Fund.

First published in 2024 by the
Yale University Art Gallery
1111 Chapel Street
P.O. Box 208271
New Haven, CT 06520-8271
artgallery.yale.edu/publications

and distributed by
Yale University Press
302 Temple Street
P.O. Box 209040
New Haven, CT 06520-9040
yalebooks.com/art



Produced by the Yale University Art Gallery
Tiffany Sprague, Director of Publications and Editorial Services
Annika Fisher, Assistant Editor
Mary Ellen Wilson, Assistant Editor
Grace Zhou, Editorial and Production Assistant
Kathleen Mylen-Coulombe, Rights and Reproductions Coordinator

Project Editor: Stacey A. Wujcik
Designer: Katy Homans
Proofreader: Eric Zeidler
Mapmaker: Adrian Kitzinger

Set in Sabon and Gotham

Printed at Meridian Printing, East Greenwich, R.I.

ISBN 978-0-300-27891-0
Library of Congress Control Number: 2024933655

10 9 8 7 6 5 4 3 2 1

Cover illustration: Detail of fig. 1.22

Frontispiece: Fig. 2.4; p. 12: Fig. 2.5; p. 22: Fig. 1.17; p. 42: Fig. 2.10; p. 56: Fig. 3.11; p. 74: Fig. 4.12; p. 88: Fig. 5.14; p. 106: Fig. 6.4; p. 122: Fig. 7.17; p. 140: Fig. 1.10; p. 152: Fig. 1.20

# Contents

# Director's Foreword

Stephanie Wiles
*The Henry J. Heinz II Director*
*Yale University Art Gallery*

The term "celadon" is used to describe the exquisite and distinctive green-glazed ceramics made in East and Southeast Asia, particularly those made in southern China from the ninth to the fourteenth century. This volume begins by exploring the creation of innovative green glazes in Zhejiang and Jiangxi Provinces and traces their impact in kilns in the provinces of Hunan, Guangdong, and Fujian. The development of these lush, elegant glazes coincided with the rise of maritime trade throughout Asia. As a result, the ceramic industry in southern China would have an immense influence on its counterparts in Vietnam, Thailand, Korea, and Japan. In *Celadon on the Seas: Chinese Ceramics from the 9th to the 14th Century*, Denise Patry Leidy, the Ruth and Bruce Dayton Curator of Asian Art at the Yale University Art Gallery, expertly tells this fascinating story.

The innumerable archaeological discoveries made in China beginning in the 1960s and up to the present continue to refine our understanding of the country's history and art. In addition, ceramics—unlike more fragile materials such as aromatics or silk—have often survived in shipwrecks. Since the 1990s, underwater archaeology has provided further information regarding the development of Chinese ceramics, their staggering range of production, and their international impact as they were traded as far west as the eastern coast of Africa and as far east as Japan. These discoveries spurred Denise's examination and cataloguing of the Chinese ceramics in the Gallery's collection that are published here.

*Celadon on the Seas* is the second volume in the Gallery's *Yale Collections* series, which features important, and sometimes understudied, objects or groups of objects at the Gallery. While many Western museums collect Chinese ceramics, the Gallery has an unusually rich selection of works produced in the lesser-known kilns in Fujian, Guangdong, and Hunan. Most of these works were gifts from John Hadley Cox, B.A. 1935, who acquired them while working in Changsha, in Hunan, after his graduation from Yale. This volume reflects the generosity of many other donors, including, most recently, Molly and Walter Bareiss, B.S. 1940S; Lily L. Chu, B.A. 1982, and Gerald W. Weaver II, B.A. 1977; John Crockett; Peggy and Richard M. Danziger, LL.B. 1963; Michael de Havenon, B.A. 1962, and Georgia de Havenon; Ann and Gilbert H. Kinney, B.A. 1953, M.A. 1954; Steven M. Kossak, B.A. 1972; Robert D. Mowry; and Brian M. Salzberg, B.S. 1963; as well as the Koo Liong Bing Collection, the B. D. G. Leviton Foundation, and the Yung G. Wang Family Endowment Fund. We are grateful to them and to the Andrew W. Mellon Foundation and Mary Cushing Fosburgh and James Whitney Fosburgh, B.A. 1933, M.A. 1935, Publication Fund, as well as the E. Rhodes and Leona B. Carpenter Foundation, which has generously supported both this publication and the analysis and conservation of these remarkably beautiful Chinese ceramics from the Gallery's collection.

# Acknowledgments

Denise Patry Leidy
*The Ruth and Bruce Dayton Curator of Asian Art*
*Yale University Art Gallery*

Any project requires the goodwill and contribution of many individuals, and this volume is no exception. I am deeply grateful to both Stephanie Wiles, the Henry J. Heinz II Director of the Yale University Art Gallery, and Laurence Kanter, Chief Curator and the Lionel Goldfrank III Curator of European Art, for their encouragement and steadfast support. The commitment and generosity of many other colleagues at the Gallery are embedded in this book. Ami Potter, Museum Assistant in the Department of Asian Art, demonstrated her exemplary management skills in all aspects of the project. My research for the publication was enabled and enhanced by the cooperation of Anne Turner Gunnison, the Alan J. Dworsky Senior Associate Conservator of Objects, and, at the Yale Institute for the Preservation of Cultural Heritage Technical Studies Lab, Anikó Bezur, the Wallace S. Wilson Director; Richard Hark, Conservation Scientist; and Marcie Wiggins, Assistant Conservation Scientist. At the Gallery, Amreet Kular, former Postgraduate Associate in Objects Conservation, and Katherine (Kiki) Peters, former Pre-Program Intern in the Conservation Department, surveyed, conserved, cleaned, and sampled ceramics from the Gallery that are included in the book, as well as comparative pieces from the collection. They also authored the useful appendix. Tiffany Sprague, Director of Publications and Editorial Services, supervised all aspects of the editing, design, and production of the book. Grace Zhou, Editorial and Production Assistant, and Kathleen Mylen-Coulombe, Rights and Reproductions Coordinator, provided invaluable support. Thanks are also due to Stacey Wujcik for her thoughtful and precise editing, and for her patience; to Katy Homans for her engaging design; and to Adrian Kitzinger for creating the maps.

Most of the ceramics herein that are part of the Gallery's collection are being published for the first time. John ffrench, Director of Visual Resources, and David Whaples, Visual Resources Coordinator, shepherded their new photography, while Senior Photographers Alexander Harding and Richard House, former Senior Photographer Allaire Bartel, and Digital Photographer Milan Russell shot the delightful and elegant photographs. Thanks are also due to the staff of the Collections Department, particularly Jason DeBlock, Director of Collections, and Vicki Onofrio, Senior Museum Technician; to the Gallery's superb art handlers; and to all of the librarians at Yale University who cheerfully sourced the many publications—some relatively obscure—needed to help understand and catalogue ceramic works in the collection.

Finally, and very importantly, the publication of this volume and the conservation and analysis of the ceramics would not have been possible without the generous support and commitment of the E. Rhodes and Leona B. Carpenter Foundation.

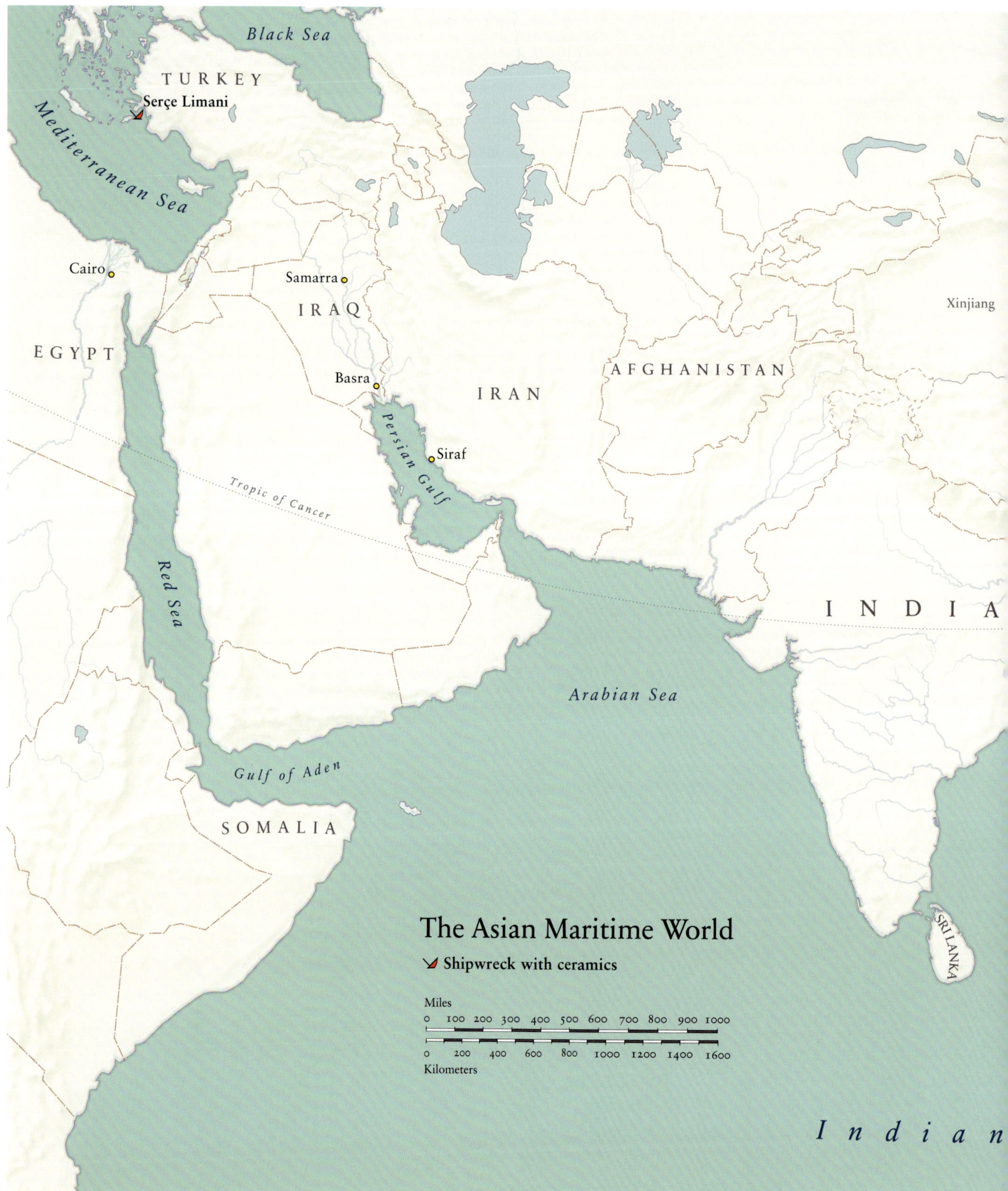
Black Sea
TURKEY
Serçe Limani
Mediterranean Sea
Cairo
Samarra
IRAQ
EGYPT
Basra
IRAN
AFGHANISTAN
Persian Gulf
Siraf
Tropic of Cancer
Xinjiang
Red Sea
INDIA
Arabian Sea
Gulf of Aden
SOMALIA
SRI LANKA
The Asian Maritime World
Shipwreck with ceramics
Miles
0 100 200 300 400 500 600 700 800 900 1000
0 200 400 600 800 1000 1200 1400 1600
Kilometers
Indian

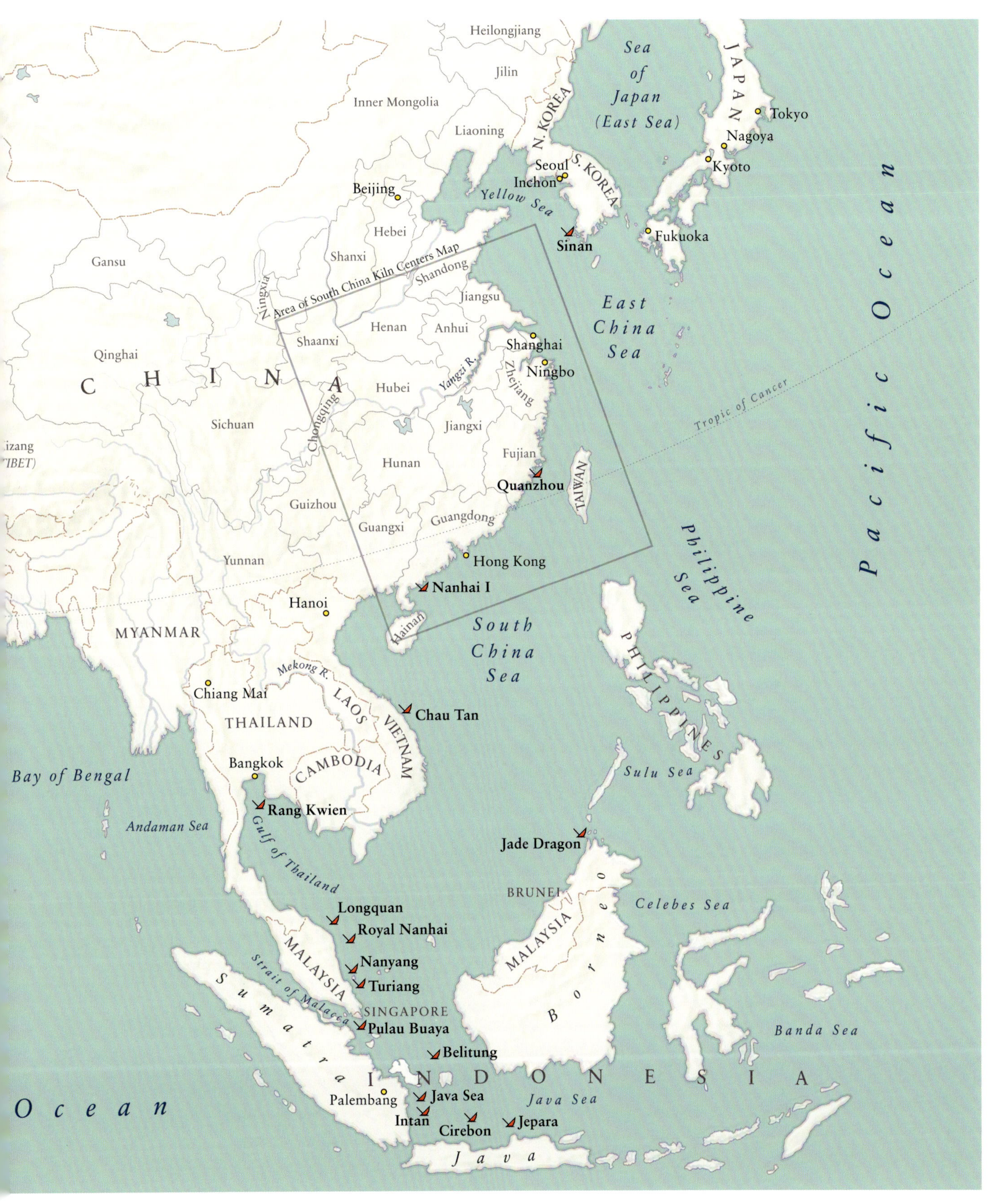

Heilongjiang
Jilin
Inner Mongolia
Liaoning
N. KOREA
S. KOREA
Seoul
Inchon
Beijing
Yellow Sea
Sea of Japan (East Sea)
JAPAN
Tokyo
Nagoya
Kyoto
Fukuoka
Sinan
Hebei
Shanxi
Gansu
Ningxia
Area of South China Kiln Centers Map
Shandong
Jiangsu
Henan
Anhui
Shaanxi
Qinghai
Shanghai
Ningbo
East China Sea
C H I N A
Hubei
Yangzi R.
Zhejiang
Chongqing
Sichuan
Jiangxi
Xizang (TIBET)
Fujian
Hunan
Quanzhou
TAIWAN
Tropic of Cancer
Pacific Ocean
Guizhou
Guangxi
Guangdong
Yunnan
Hong Kong
Philippine Sea
Nanhai I
Hanoi
MYANMAR
Hainan
South China Sea
PHILIPPINES
Mekong R.
LAOS
Chiang Mai
THAILAND
VIETNAM
Chau Tan
Bangkok
CAMBODIA
Bay of Bengal
Sulu Sea
Rang Kwien
Andaman Sea
Gulf of Thailand
Jade Dragon
BRUNEI
Celebes Sea
Longquan
Royal Nanhai
MALAYSIA
Borneo
Nanyang
Turiang
Strait of Malacca
Sumatra
SINGAPORE
Pulau Buaya
Banda Sea
Belitung
INDONESIA
Palembang
Java Sea
Intan
Cirebon
Jepara
Ocean
Java

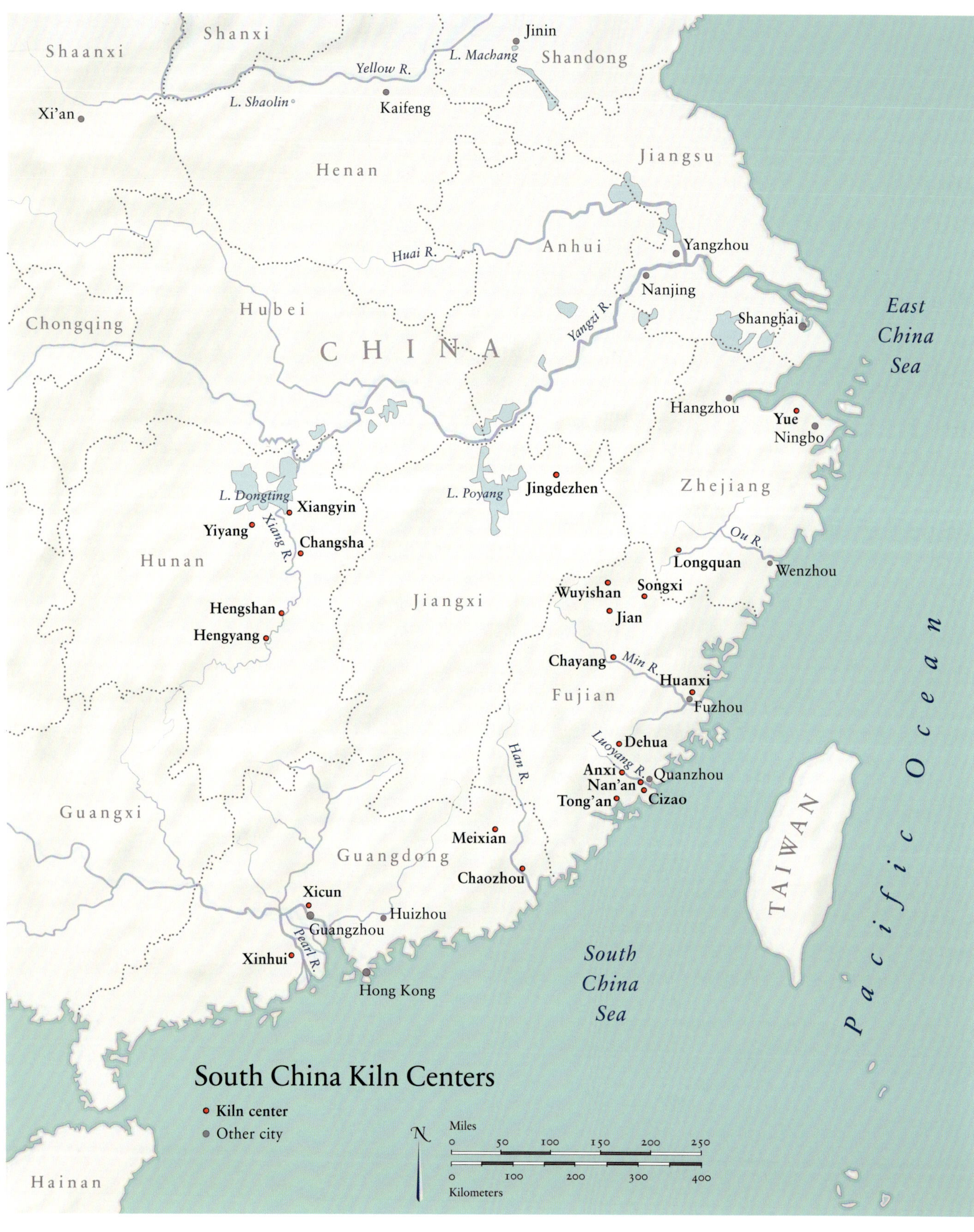

South China Kiln Centers
Kiln center
Other city
Miles
0 50 100 150 200 250
0 100 200 300 400
Kilometers
N
CHINA
Shaanxi
Shanxi
Shandong
Jiangsu
Henan
Anhui
Hubei
Chongqing
Hunan
Jiangxi
Zhejiang
Fujian
Guangxi
Guangdong
Hainan
TAIWAN
East China Sea
South China Sea
Pacific Ocean
Yellow R.
L. Machang
L. Shaolin
Huai R.
Yangzi R.
L. Dongting
L. Poyang
Xiang R.
Ou R.
Min R.
Han R.
Luoyang R.
Pearl R.
Jinin
Xi'an
Kaifeng
Yangzhou
Nanjing
Shanghai
Hangzhou
Yue
Ningbo
Jingdezhen
Xiangyin
Yiyang
Changsha
Hengshan
Hengyang
Longquan
Wenzhou
Wuyishan
Songxi
Jian
Chayang
Huanxi
Fuzhou
Dehua
Anxi
Quanzhou
Nan'an
Cizao
Tong'an
Meixian
Chaozhou
Xicun
Guangzhou
Huizhou
Xinhui
Hong Kong

# Note to the Reader

## Locations

Throughout the book, the current names of countries, provinces, and other locations are used.

## Medium

For objects in the collection of the Yale University Art Gallery, the medium does not include the colors or components of a glaze or pigment unless they are particularly noteworthy. Where possible, the ware type is noted in parentheses following the medium.

## Dimensions

For all objects, the maximum dimensions are provided, unless otherwise noted. The dimensions are given as height by width by depth, or as height (H.) by diameter (DIAM.). For vessels, width includes handles.

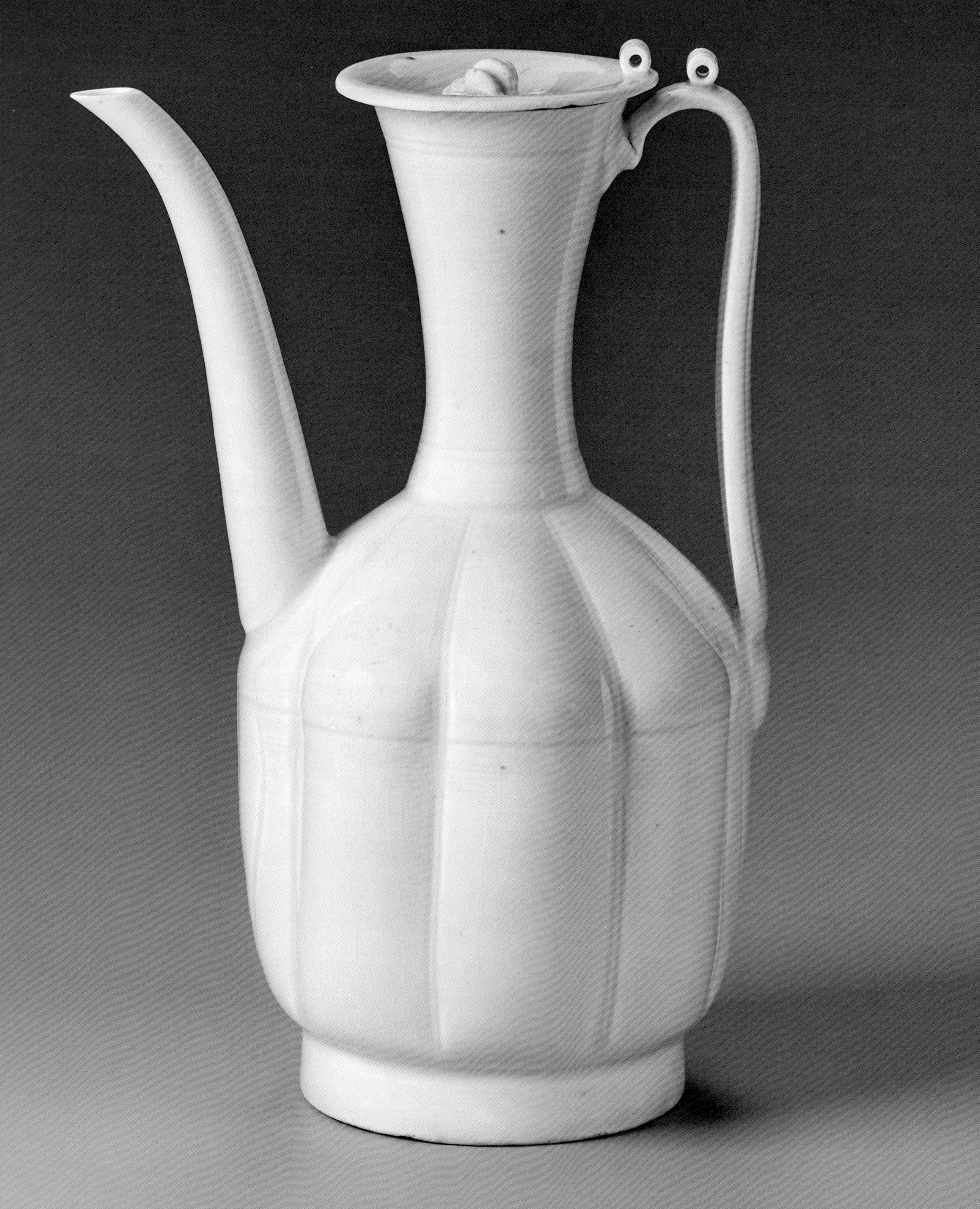

INTRODUCTION

# Chinese Ceramics and Maritime Trade

In the late eighth and ninth centuries C.E., as they began to be extensively traded throughout maritime Asia, Chinese ceramics were the most technically sophisticated, visually appealing, and durable in the world. They were crafted using refined clays, either stoneware or porcelain, and fired at high temperatures.[1] Stoneware pieces, which fire at a temperature of approximately 1,200 to 1,300 degrees Celsius, are buff or light or dark gray. Porcelains, which fire at 1,304 to 1,345 degrees Celsius and have a high percentage of a mineral known as kaolin, are white. After the body of a ceramic piece had been shaped and fired once, it was covered with a glaze—a combination of a clay, a colorant, and other substances that helped the glaze melt and adhere to the piece during a second or multiple firings, making it stronger, defining its shape, and enhancing its surface.[2] At this point in the history of Chinese ceramics, these glasslike glazes were usually white or delicate shades of green.

Ceramic objects had been crafted in China since the Neolithic period (ca. 10,000–2,000 B.C.E.), usually as low-fired granular earthenware that was sometimes painted or burnished. Until the late sixth century C.E., ceramics (some covered with lead-silicate glazes) were primarily used for display during funerals and as burial goods for the use of the deceased. By the Tang dynasty (618–907 C.E.), the ceramic industry had developed stronger clays and more stable glazes, and ceramics had become highly prized luxuries in China. They were extolled in poetry and other literature for their beauty and refinement and served as symbols of taste and wealth. The best examples from certain kilns were reserved for the use of the court, and some have markings on their bases indicating they were made to be sent there. Others served as much-desired gifts among regional or local officials. Ceramics were also used in religious rituals; in banquets and smaller, more intimate gatherings; and for the formal and informal drinking of wine or tea. During the Tang dynasty, the consumption of tea became very popular—an interesting parallel to the growing appreciation of the clay arts at that time.

A detail of a twelfth-century painting of a literary gathering (fig. 0.1) offers a tantalizing glimpse of the nature of these festivities, which were important as early as the eighth century C.E. The work has inscriptions at the top by Huizong (r. 1100–1126), the famed emperor-aesthete of the Northern Song dynasty (960–1127), whose pen name was Zhao Ji, and Cai Jing, one of his most influential ministers. It depicts a group of scholar-officials seated around a large black lacquer table filled with dishes, bowls, and trays heaped with delicacies. Each of the men has several items placed before him, including a cup on a stand. While the gray color of some dishes suggests that they were silver, the white and green colors of others indicate that they were made of clay. Some attendants accompany the gentlemen, and others prepare more food, wine, and tea in the foreground.

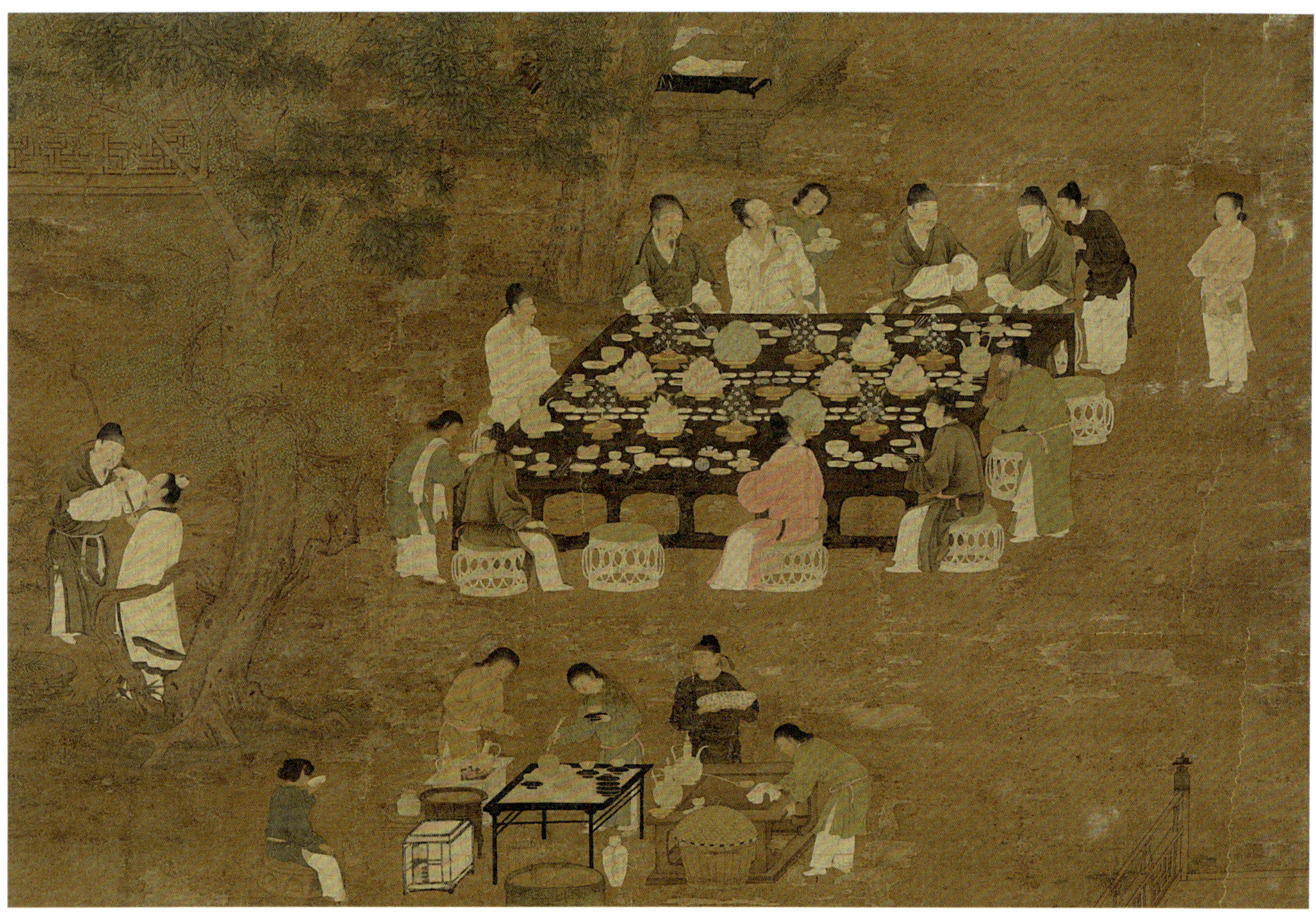

**Fig. 0.1**

Attributed to Emperor Huizong, *Elegant Gathering* (detail), China, Northern Song dynasty, 12th century. Hanging scroll; ink and color on silk, overall 50⅞ × 72½ in. (129.2 × 184.2 cm). National Palace Museum, Taipei, Taiwan, K2A000836N000000000PAA

A low table in the background holds a zither (*qin*), a musical instrument. In addition to playing music, painting and composing and reciting poetry were integral to such literati gatherings.

During the Tang dynasty, as the production of ceramics first flourished, China was the center of an international exchange system that linked the Mediterranean region, in the west, to Japan, in the east, by a series of overland routes collectively known as the Silk Road and, to a lesser extent, by sea. Communities of Arab, Persian, and Southeast Asian merchants who lived and worked in China or visited as part of commercial activities were based in the capital, Chang'an (present-day Xi'an), in the north, and in port cities such as Yangzhou, in Jiangsu Province, and Guangzhou (later known in Western writings as Canton), in Guangdong Province, in the south. In addition, Buddhist monks from India as well as from China, Korea, Japan, Indonesia, Sri Lanka, and Tibet traveled throughout Asia—by land and by sea—as part of an extensive Buddhist network that transcended national boundaries. They disseminated not only information regarding developments in Buddhist practices and imagery but also knowledge about the cultures, economics, and politics of different countries. As a result, Buddhist literature contains some of the earliest historical references to maritime travel and its inherent hazards;[3] indeed, the first known artistic representation of a seafaring vessel, dating to the fifth century C.E., appears in a Buddhist mural in the cave-temples in Ajanta, India.[4]

Chinese silk was one of the most desired luxuries in this international exchange system, as were Mediterranean and South Asian glass objects, gold and silver vessels from Iran and Central Asia, precious minerals, pearls, coral, spices such as pepper, dyes, tortoiseshell, ivory, and aromatic woods and resins. Interestingly, the first Chinese ceramics to gain interregional appreciation were the same types of wares that Lu Yu mentioned in his work *The Classic of Tea* (*Chajing*), a foundational guide to all aspects of growing, preparing, and drinking tea.[5] Lu specified the types of ceramics best suited to the presentation and enjoyment of the beverage, extolling white wares from the Xing kilns in the north, which he compared to silver, and green wares from the Yue kilns in the south, which he likened to jade.

It is impossible to imagine the effect that the appearance of these refined ceramics—unlike anything that had previously been seen anywhere in the world—must have had in the ninth and tenth centuries. Nonetheless, an intriguing glimpse of their impact is found in the records of a gift of such ceramics to the fifth Abbasid caliph, Harun al-Rashid (r. 786–809 C.E.). Harun is one of the protagonists of the *One Thousand and One Nights*, featuring the legendary Sinbad the Sailor and his adventures on the seas—a delightful reference to the rise in the intra-Asian maritime trade in the eighth and ninth centuries. In the late eighth century, a ruler in the northeastern part of Iran gave Harun two thousand ceramics, including twenty examples of Chinese white wares. Potters in Basra and other Iraqi ports and commercial centers immediately began to experiment to find ways to make comparable white ceramics, generally small bowls, which were described by a contemporary poet as having the shape of the moon and the luster of a pearl.[6]

Multiple factors, including government dysfunction, poor harvests, drought, famine, banditry, rebellions, and other woes, contributed to the downfall of the Tang dynasty in 907 C.E. In the tenth century, China was divided into competing polities, a time known as the Five Dynasties and Ten Kingdoms period. Control of northern China, and access to the overland trade routes, was later contested among the Northern Song dynasty, with its capital at Kaifeng, in Henan Province; the formerly nomadic-pastoralist Qidan Liao dynasty (916–1125), in the northeast; and the Tangut rulers of the Xixia dynasty (1038–1227), in the northwest. The Jurchen Jin dynasty (1115–1234), also originally a nomadic-pastoralist society, replaced the Liao and Xixia and eventually forced the Song court to move south, leading to the establishment of the Southern Song dynasty (1127–1279). Under the rule of the Mongol Yuan dynasty (1279–1368), Kublai Khan (r. 1264–94), the fifth Chinese khagan-emperor and grandson of Genghis Khan (r. 1206–27), reunited China, as well as parts of northern Vietnam, for the first time since the Tang dynasty.

Despite the chaos of the tenth to the thirteenth century, the Chinese ceramic industry expanded significantly during this period. Thousands of kilns flourished, some as part of large complexes and others as smaller entities. Kilns in northern and southern China—occasionally in competition with each other—continued to refine their products and to diversify their repertoires of shapes, glazes, and designs. The shapes and designs in ceramics produced during this period also reflect the endless and complex cross-media interactions between clay, glass, lacquer, metal, and other materials (some of which were imported) at the time. While the kilns in north China produced ceramics primarily for local, regional, or national use, those in the south made objects intended for both domestic use and trade. Initially, both white- and green-glazed Chinese wares were traded and sent abroad as diplomatic gifts; however, by the tenth century interregional trade was dominated by green-glazed wares produced in multiple centers in south China with access to ports on the South China Sea (see map on p. 10).

The Yue wares made in the ninth and tenth centuries in the southern province of Zhejiang, praised for their elegant "secret-color" gray-green glazes, were the first such wares to acquire both national and international fame. Over time, they were superseded by Longquan wares from the same province, which would be the first ceramics described as "celadon" in Western writing. The origin of the term "celadon" has traditionally been explained as a reference to Céladon, a character who wore green ribbons in the seventeenth-century pastoral romance *L'Astrée* by Honoré d'Urfé.[7] The word may alternatively derive from a corruption of the name of Salah al-Din (r. 1174–93), known as Saladin, the famous founder of the short-lived Ayyubid dynasty based in Egypt (ca. 1171–1260), who sent forty pieces of Longquan ware to the Syrian ruler Nur al-Din (r. 1146–74)—an example of the diplomatic gifting of these much-desired luxuries.[8] "Celadon" is also sometimes loosely used to refer to green-glazed ceramics produced in other parts of southern China, such as the Qingbai wares developed in Jiangxi Province, as well as to green wares produced in Japan, Korea, Thailand, and Vietnam. Green-glazed ceramics emulating the shapes and colors of Longquan and Qingbai wares were also made in Fujian, Guangdong, and Hunan Provinces for domestic use and trade.

The astonishing number of kilns active throughout China during this time gradually diminished after the middle of the fourteenth century, when a new type of ceramic—porcelain painted with cobalt blue under a clear glaze, known as blue-and-white ware—developed during the Yuan dynasty. These ceramics were produced primarily in the enormous kiln complex of Jingdezhen, in Jiangxi. By the sixteenth century, as Asian interregional maritime trade expanded

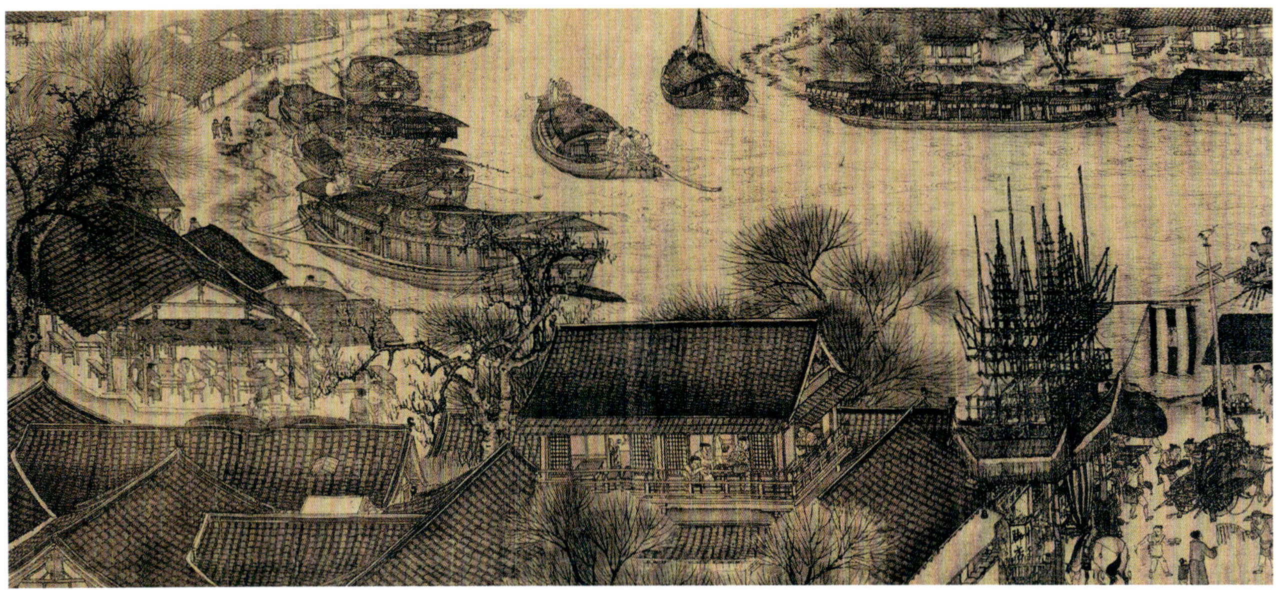

**Fig. 0.2**

Zhang Zeduan, *Along the River during the Qingming Festival* (detail), China, Northern Song dynasty, late 11th century. Handscroll; ink on silk, overall 9¾ × 20¹³⁄₁₆ in. (24.8 × 52.8 cm). Palace Museum, Beijing, K2A00090N000000000PA

to include trade with Europe and the Americas, blue-and-white wares had supplanted celadons as the most widely produced and traded Chinese ceramic.

Government control of maritime trade had begun as early as 714 C.E., when the court appointed a Commissioner for Trading with Foreign Ships to liaise with local prefects and to acquire foreign goods for the Tang rulers. In the tenth century, after the Northern Song had stabilized its relationship with different polities in the south, Superintendencies for Maritime Shipping were appointed in major port cities, such as Guangzhou (in 971); Hangzhou (in 989); Dinghai, near Minzhou (present-day Ningbo) (in 989); and Quanzhou (in 1087). Others were founded during the Southern Song dynasty. Officials in these bureaus were responsible for greeting and supervising foreign envoys, particularly those bringing diplomatic gifts, or tribute, to the court; establishing hotels for such visitors; managing foreign quarters; hosting banquets; assessing cargo; levying taxes; and supervising the distribution of goods, many of which were monopolized by the court.

Cargoes from ships arriving in these cities were often transported to the Northern and Southern Song capitals and throughout China by smaller ships that plied the major river systems. As early as the Sui dynasty (581–617 C.E.), the Grand Canal—the largest man-made waterway in the world, measuring over one thousand miles—linked the Yellow River and its tributaries in the north to the Yangzi riverine system farther south. The same extensive waterways also facilitated both the transport of the natural materials used to make ceramics to the kiln centers and the shipment of finished works from these complexes to major ports along the coast of China. A detail of a famous painting by Zhang Zeduan (fig. 0.2), which shows an idealized cityscape on the banks of a river (possibly the

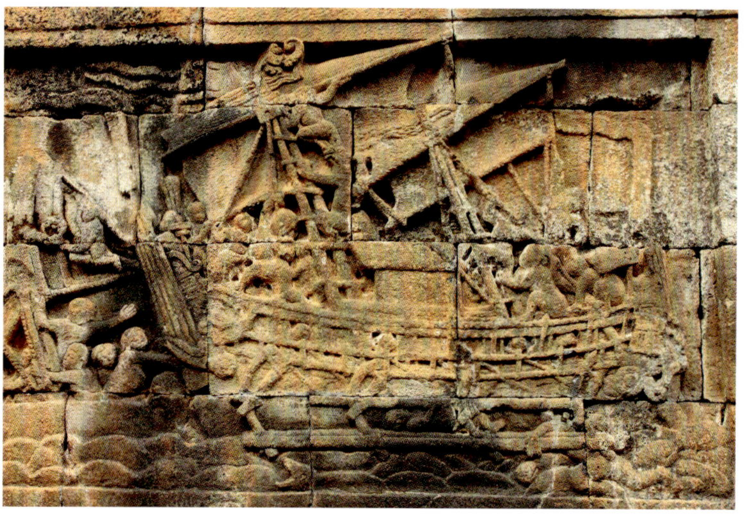

**Fig. 0.3**

*Narrative Scene with an Arab Dhow* (detail), Indonesia, Java, Borobudur, 9th century C.E. Andesite

Northern Song capital of Kaifeng[9]), attests to the range of watercraft found in China in the tenth century, including small barges for transporting grain and other goods, as well as enormous houseboats.

Despite the extensive use of boats internally and along the coastline, Chinese ships were not initially used for interregional maritime trade; rather, Arab dhows and Southeast Asian ships predominated trade from the ninth to the twelfth century. A dhow with the characteristic long hull, masts, and lateen sails is represented among the narrative scenes decorating the exterior of the ninth-century Borobudur (fig. 0.3), one of the most famous Buddhist monuments in Java, Indonesia. Shown with an outrigger, crew, and passengers, the boat moves through churning waters. The raised ridges on the hull illustrate the use of coir (a fiber derived from the husk of a coconut) for its construction, instead of nails or pegs, another characteristic of early dhows.

Because they are more durable than other luxuries, ceramics are the best-preserved items found in the cargoes of shipwrecks. Discovered in wrecks in quantities in the thousands—or, in some cases, hundreds of thousands—they provide important data regarding the breadth and extent of the southern Chinese industry and the critical role of Chinese ceramics in interregional trade from the ninth to the fourteenth century (see map on pp. 8–9). The early ninth-century Belitung shipwreck (fig. 0.4), discovered in 1998 and named after a city on the nearby island of Sumatra, is one of the oldest Arab dhows found in Indonesian waters. The shipwreck was not located near any of the stopping points of the ninth- and tenth-century maritime trade; it may have been blown off course and foundered during a storm. It was presumably sailing in the South China Sea down the coastline of Southeast Asia to Indonesia, stopping along the way to exchange goods and replenish food and water. By this time, ships

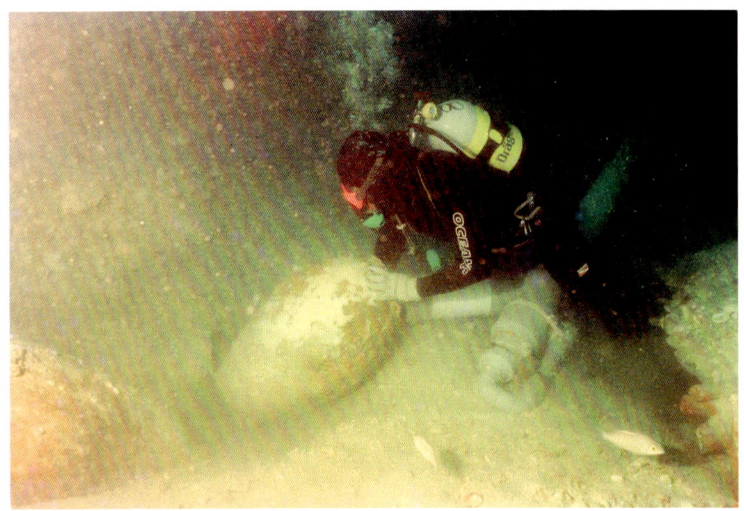

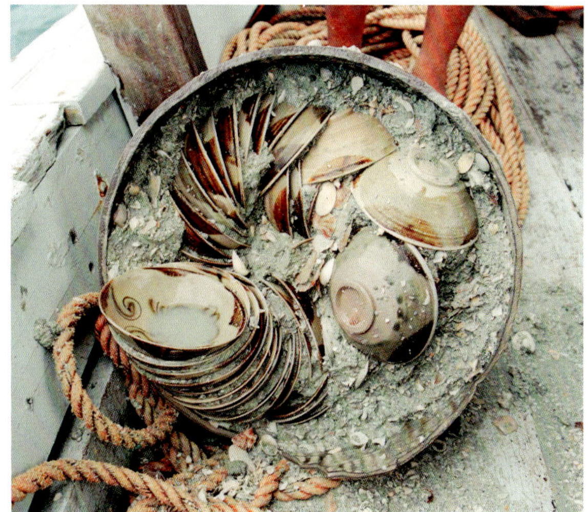

**Fig. 0.4**

View of the Belitung shipwreck, near Sumatra, Indonesia, 1999

**Fig. 0.5**

Changsha bowls in a transport jar excavated from the Belitung shipwreck, near Sumatra, Indonesia, 1999

traveling from Guangzhou, Quanzhou, and other Chinese ports sailed with the monsoon winds that moved from northeast to southwest between November and January, and from southwest to northeast between April and September. They could remain on the South China Sea or sail through the Strait of Malacca into the Indian Ocean, from which they could visit ports along the coasts of India and the Arabian Peninsula and could then potentially continue through the Gulf of Aden into the Red Sea.

The Belitung cargo—which most likely originally included silk and other fragile goods that have by now disappeared—yielded nearly sixty thousand Chinese ceramics, largely Changsha wares from Hunan; green-glazed Yue wares from Zhejiang; and white, blue-and-white, and splashed green wares from northern kilns. It also contained gold and silver from Yangzhou, spices such as star anise, and personal items of crew members and passengers. The ceramics had been layered into one another and packed in straw or placed inside larger ceramic transport jars (fig. 0.5), which were made in kilns near Guangzhou, the probable departure point for the Belitung ship. Green- and white-glazed ceramics similar to those preserved in the Belitung wreck have been found in Siraf (in present-day Iran)[10] and in other West Asian ports, as well as in Fustat, near Cairo.[11] Rather than making the journey this far west in a single ship, however, it seems likely that most of the Chinese ceramics found there would have been moved from one boat to another in ports along the way as part of the trade.

Chinese ceramics, primarily green-glazed Longquan wares from Zhejiang and Qingbai wares from Jiangxi, constituted 75 percent of the extraordinarily rich cargo found in the mid- to late tenth-century Cirebon wreck, discovered off the coast of Cirebon, Java, in 2003 and excavated in 2005. This was a Southeast Asian ship built with treenails, or wooden pegs, and dowels. The careful packing

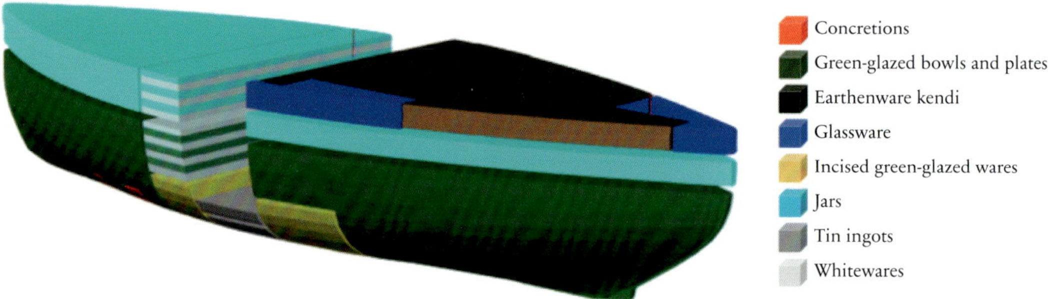


**Fig. 0.6**

Reconstruction of the cargo consignments of the Cirebon shipwreck, near Java, Indonesia

of this ship suggests that a large consortium, or perhaps even a single merchant, was responsible for the entire cargo. Almost every inch of space held goods, echoing a well-known passage in the *Matters Worth Discussing from Pingzhou* (*Pingzhou ketan*), a series of notes on aspects of maritime management, navigation, and shipping written by Zhu Yu around 1119. Zhu, whose father served as a Superintendent of Maritime Shipping in Quanzhou, observed that ships were filled with ceramics until there was not even a crevice left and that merchants sometimes slept on top of their cargo.[12] A reconstruction of the location of various goods in the cargo of the Cirebon ship (fig. 0.6) shows that ceramics were placed in the hull, while the more fragile West Asian glass was placed on the deck.[13] Like those on the Belitung, the ceramics on the Cirebon would have been packed in straw or within ceramic transport jars.

The large quantity of Chinese ceramics on the Cirebon ship suggests that it was moving south or west from China when it was shipwrecked. The cargo of the late thirteenth-century Quanzhou wreck (fig. 0.7), on the other hand, indicates that the ship had returned to China. Found near the Huzhou port in Fujian in 1973, this vessel was an example of Chinese shipbuilding, which used iron nails; it had three sails and was divided by twelve bulkheads into thirteen compartments. Although it contained Chinese coins, cowrie shells (also used as currency in Asia at the time), and a few ceramics, the primary cargo consisted of 5,300 pounds of incense woods from Southeast Asia, as well as tiny amounts of pepper from Java, ambergris from Somalia (used in perfumes), and frankincense from West Asia. The wide geographic range for these goods does not necessarily indicate that the ship had traveled as far west as Somalia. As was the case with ceramic cargoes, aromatics from Africa or West Asia and goods from Southeast Asia could have been brought by other ships to a port in Java or another trade center, collected or stored by merchants working there, and then sold to traders or other individuals traveling on ships to China, like the one in the Quanzhou wreck. While much of the cargo of this vessel had been lost prior to its excavation, archaeologists recovered ninety-five wooden tags that record the names or job titles of merchants, shops, and members of the imperial clan, all of whom

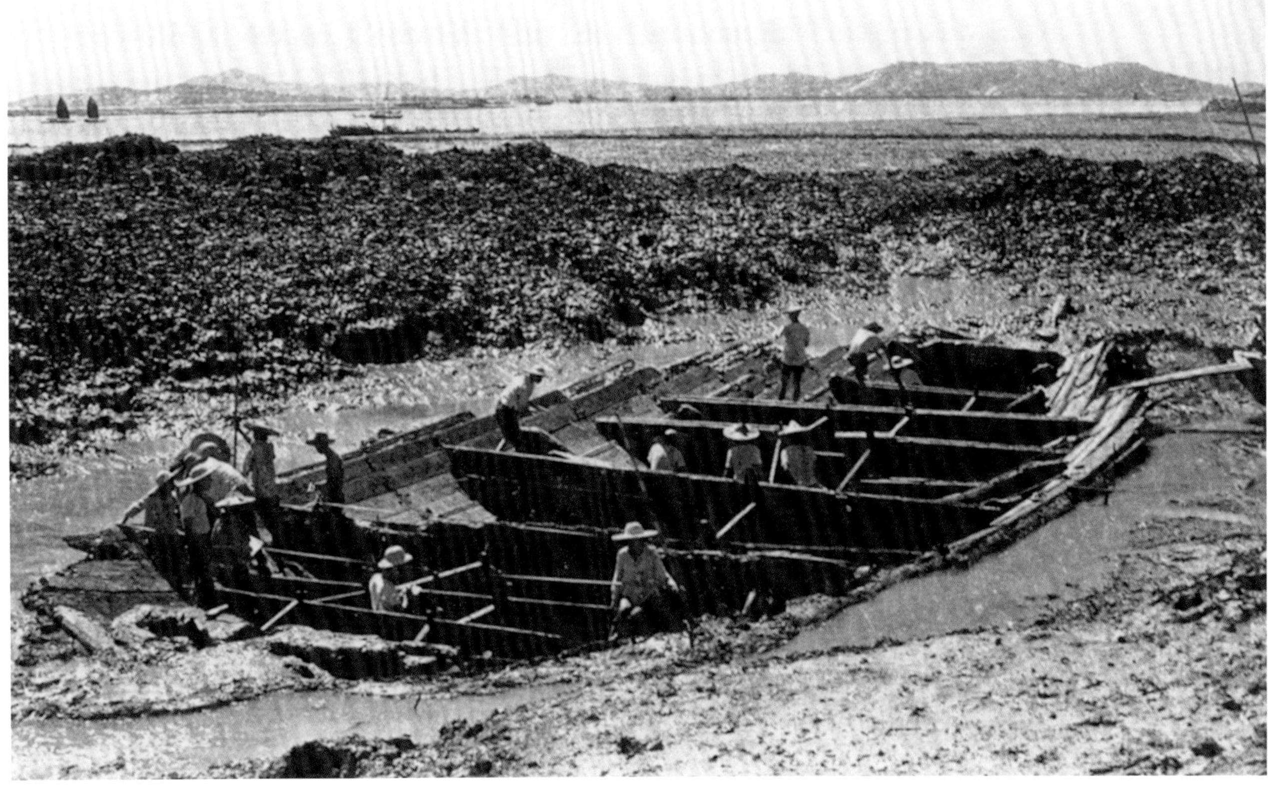

**Fig. 0.7**

Excavation of the Quanzhou shipwreck, near Huzhou, Fujian Province, China, 1970s

owned some part of the cargo. The name tags indicate that the Quanzhou wreck contained merchandise held by large and small groups as well as by individuals, including crew members.

By the eleventh century, multiethnic and multilingual communities similar to those established in China during the Tang dynasty could be found in major ports throughout the Asian maritime world. Some influential individuals among these groups were involved in local governments, in charitable ventures that supported people who were shipwrecked or stranded, or in the construction or restoration of religious establishments, such as Buddhist monasteries and Islamic mosques. These merchant communities, like the network of Buddhist monks, transcended national borders and were defined by the fostering and dissemination of specialized knowledge—in this case, the understanding and appreciation of the natural products and manufactured goods of Africa and West, Southeast, and East Asia. Because of their beauty and strength, Chinese ceramics played a significant role in this vast trade. Today, they provide delightful visual evidence of the sophisticated and cosmopolitan mercantile networks that united maritime Asia from the ninth to the fourteenth century—an endlessly fascinating period in global cultural history.

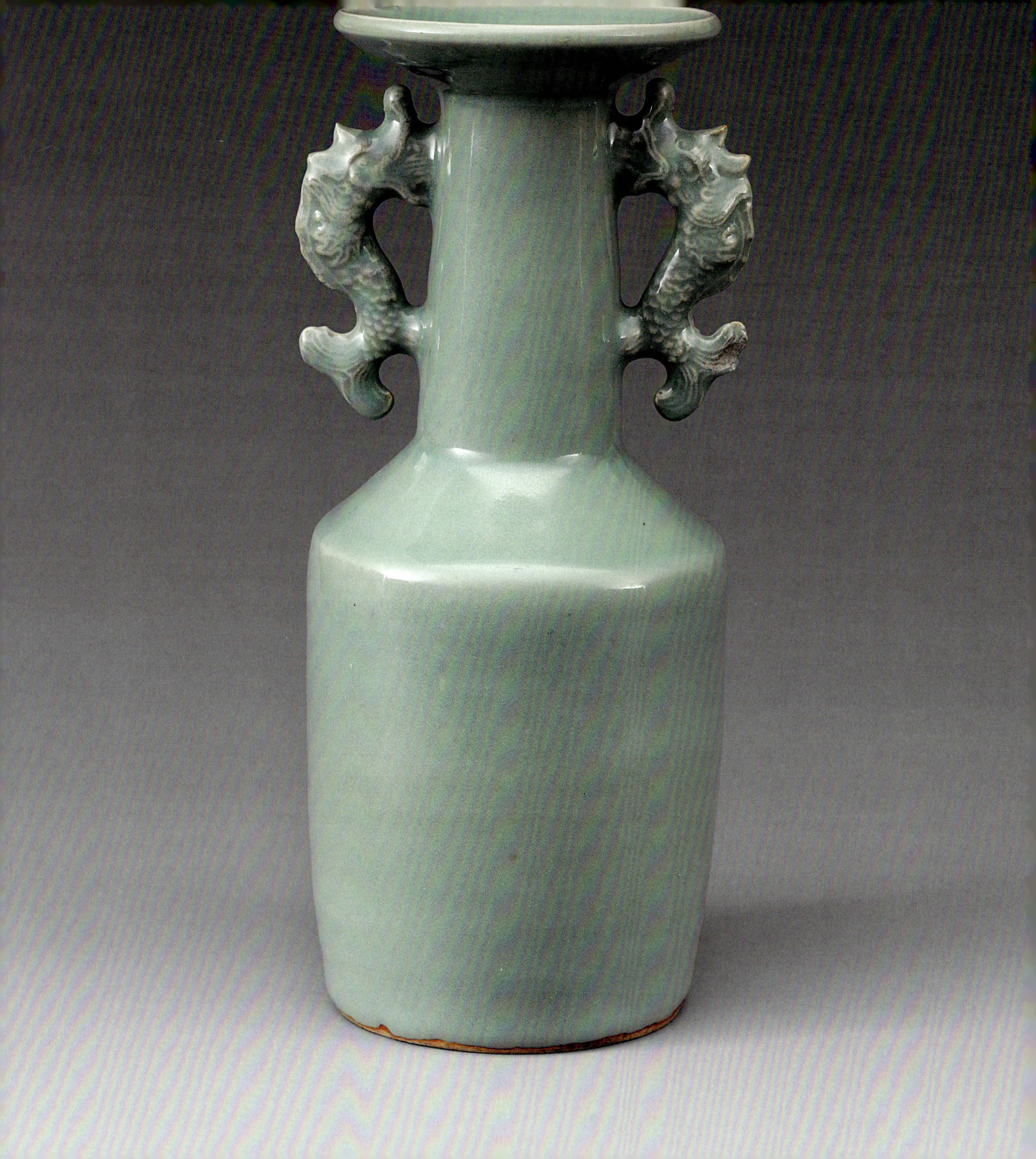

CHAPTER 1

# Zhejiang Province: The Innovative Green Glazes of Yue, Guan, and Longquan Wares

High-fired ceramics with glazes, particularly those in shades of green, have a long history in southern China, the first place in the world to create such wares.[1] Glazes produced accidentally, when ash interacted with clay vessels during firing, were being made there as early as the first millennium B.C.E. The somewhat uneven olive-green glaze covering the upper part of a large jar (fig. 1.1) produced in Zhejiang Province between the first century B.C.E. and the first century C.E., on the other hand, was created deliberately by mixing wood ash from the kiln with clay and water. This sturdy jar was potted using a buff- or ivory-colored stoneware that turned red during firing. Its shape and handles were based on an earlier bronze vessel, as were the three horizontal ridges on the upper half, which also prevented the glaze from running down the surface.

The creation of glazes, and the mastery of the chemical recipes required to produce them, is one aspect of the material knowledge and technical skill that characterize the making of ceramics in China. Another aspect is the development of kilns that could hold large quantities of clay pieces, fire them at high temperatures, and control oxygen (largely by reducing the amount flowing in the kiln) in order to create specific glaze colors.[2] The distinctive green glazes, or celadons, of southern China are derived from differing combinations of iron oxides, lime, and other chemicals, and from the combination of the glazes with the clay bodies. The type of clay varies depending on the geology of its source: clays from north China are mineral, whereas those from the south come from igneous rock materials, often magma, with high percentages of quartz and potassic mica. These clays require a higher firing temperature—a discovery that underlaid the initial development, in the first millennium B.C.E., of stoneware and glazes in southern China.

## Yue Ware

Chinese ceramics are generally (though not exclusively) catalogued using terms based on the historical or contemporary names for the geographic regions in which they were made. During part of the tumultuous time known as the Spring and Autumn period (770–476 B.C.E.), northern Zhejiang was under the control of the Wu Yue state (ca. 500–396 B.C.E.); as a result, the word "Yue" became a historical term for the region, and it was also used to define the ceramics produced there, particularly those made from the sixth to the tenth century. The gray-green glaze covering most of the body of a small jar (fig. 1.2) illustrates the development of green-glazed wares in southern China during the fourth and fifth centuries C.E. An incised line defines the shoulder of the jar, while iron spots—which were sometimes used to enhance later green wares—decorate the three trapezoidal lugs on the shoulder, possibly for attaching a cloth cover or carrying cords. This jar and contemporaneous pieces from the Zhejiang area are sometimes classified as proto-Yue wares.

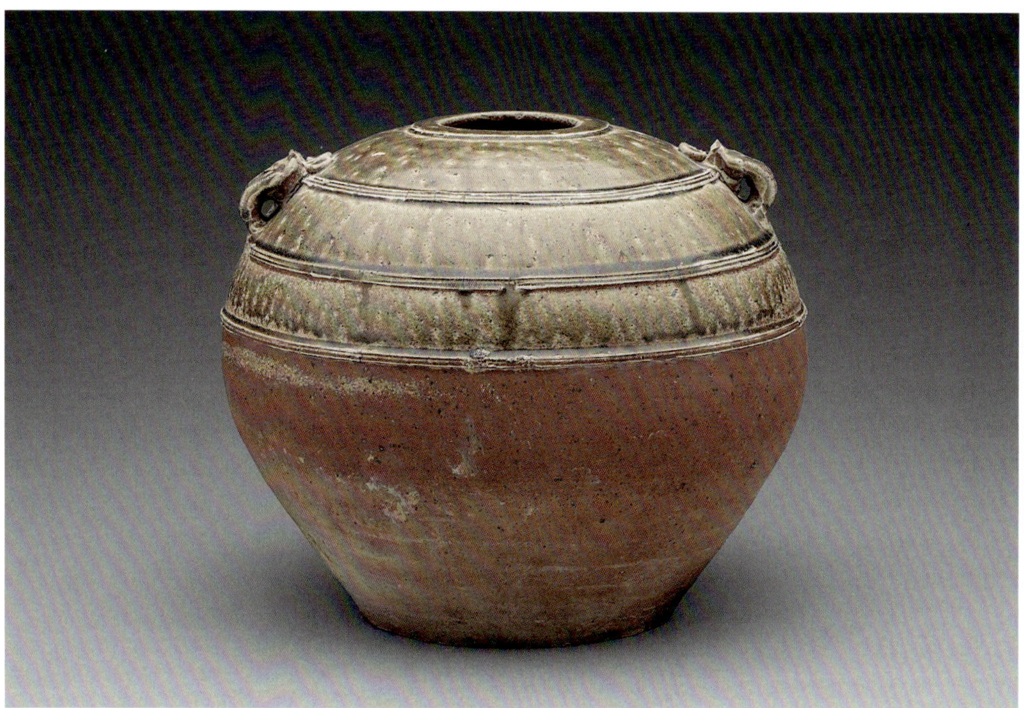

**Fig. 1.1**

*Jar*, China, Western Han dynasty, 1st century B.C.E.–1st century C.E. Stoneware with glaze, H. 12½ × DIAM. 14 in. (31.8 × 35.6 cm). Yale University Art Gallery, Gift of Molly and Walter Bareiss, B.S. 1940S, 2001.43.1

During the Tang dynasty, when a unified and wealthy China was the center of international trade, Yue wares were among the most treasured ceramics in the country. They were praised in poetry and other writings for their elegant shapes and the subtle gray-green color of their glazes. The ninth-century poet Lu Guimeng described this color as "robbing a thousand mountain peaks of their kingfisher blue."[3] In the late ninth century, the poet Xu Yin compared the color of Yue glazes to jade, water, and ice:

> Newly glazed in auspicious jade-like colors,
> The finished bowl was first offered to my lord.
> Skillfully molded like a full moon dyed with spring water,
> Deftly turned like a swirl of thin ice holding clouds,
> Like a moss-covered ancient bronze mirror present at this occasion,
> A tender, dew-soaked lotus parted from the river's edge,
> With Zhongshan bamboo-leaf wine freshly brewed.
> How can one weak as I withstand such intoxication?[4]

For a long time there was an academic debate regarding whether Yue wares were the "secret-color" (*mise*) wares discussed in historical Chinese writings.[5] In 1987 a discovery beneath the pagoda at the Famen Temple in Xi'an finally resolved this debate. The three underground chambers and a niche beneath the pagoda yielded an astonishing hoard of about three hundred items, including

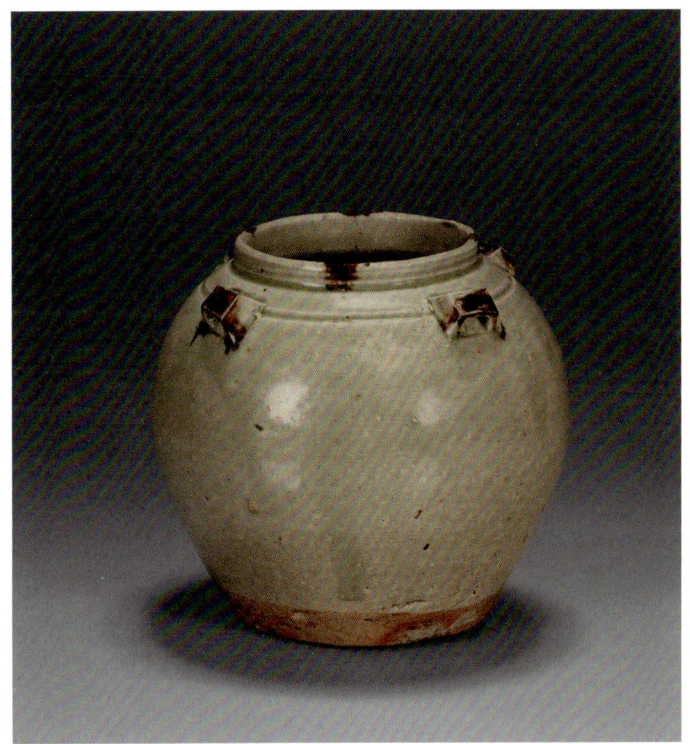

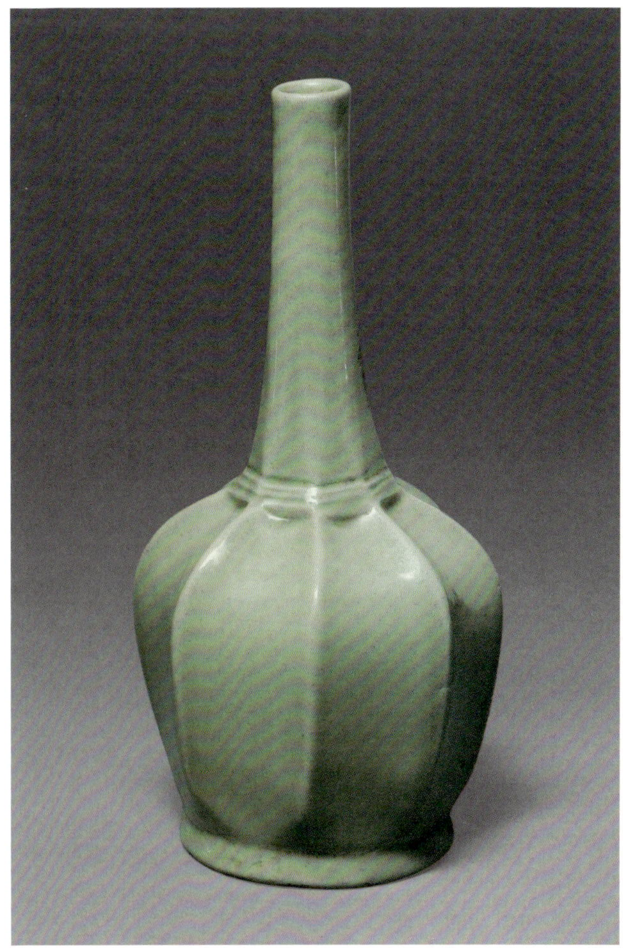

**Fig. 1.2**

*Jar*, China, Eastern Jin dynasty, 4th–5th century C.E. Stoneware with glaze and iron-brown spots, H. 4¼ × DIAM. 2 9/16 in. (10.8 × 6.5 cm). Yale University Art Gallery, Purchased with a gift from the B. D. G. Leviton Foundation, 1990.42.1

**Fig. 1.3**

*Sprinkler*, China, Tang dynasty, 9th century C.E., excavated from the pagoda at Famen Temple, Xi'an, China, in 1987–88. Stoneware with glaze (Yue ware), H. 8¼ in. (21 cm). Palace Museum, Beijing

gold and silver pieces, textiles, ceramics, Islamic glass vessels, and other goods that had been treasured luxuries in China in the ninth century. The items were buried in the crypt between 873 and 874, when the finger bone of the Historical Buddha Shakyamuni, the most important relic of the temple, was removed and taken to the court for display. In an inventory carved on a stone stele placed at the entrance to the crypt in 873, the fourteen ceramics in the deposit are specifically identified as "secret-color" wares. It seems likely that these pieces—examples of the most carefully crafted Yue wares—had been sent north to the Tang court as tribute and were then bestowed on the temple.

One of the ceramics found in the Famen Temple hoard is a vessel with an eight-sided body, a short foot, and a long, narrow neck (fig. 1.3). Although it could have been used for pouring, its elongated neck and small mouth suggest that it is a sprinkler. Sprinkling rosewater or another liquid on a practitioner as part of an initiation or purification rite was an important aspect of Tang Buddhist practice.[6] The shape of this sprinkler, particularly the lobes on the

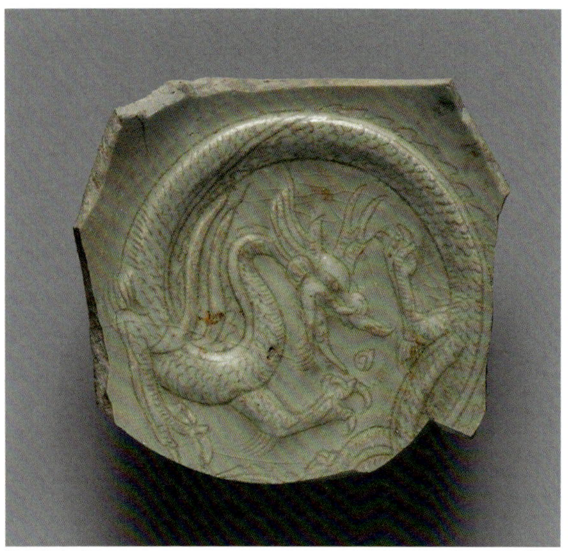

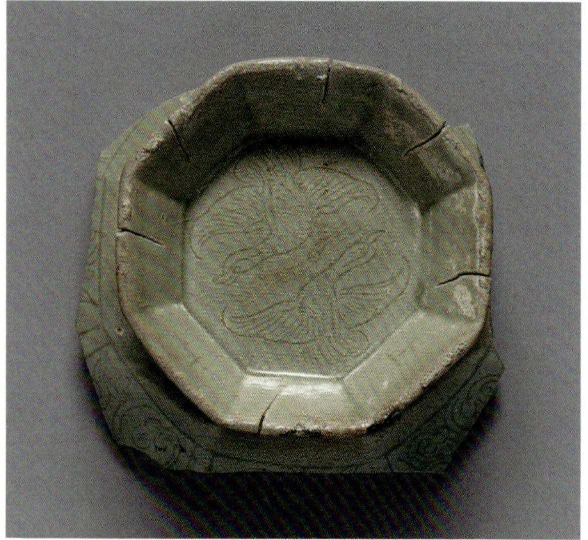

**Fig. 1.4**

*Fragment of a Cup or Bowl with a Dragon*, China, Five Dynasties period, 10th century. Stoneware with molded and incised decoration under glaze (Yue ware), ¾ × 2½ × 2½ in. (1.91 × 6.4 × 6.4 cm) (irreg.). Yale University Art Gallery, John Hadley Cox Collection, B.A. 1935, 1950.176

**Fig. 1.5**

Base of fig. 1.4

body, derives from a metal prototype that was probably imported from the greater Indian world. Notably, when the vessel was excavated, it contained nine minuscule glass beads. Such beads often serve as symbolic relics in Buddhism, suggesting that the vessel was repurposed as a reliquary when it was added to the Famen crypt. This sprinkler and another example excavated from the Housi'ao kiln near Lake Shanglin have the Chinese character *gong* (meaning "official tribute") carved on their bases, indicating that they were made under the supervision of a prefectural kiln office responsible for producing ceramics intended both for the ruling elite in Zhejiang and as tribute to the court in the north.[7]

The description of the subtle gray-green hue of Yue wares as a "secret color" reflects not only the addition of a new glaze color to the Chinese ceramic industry but also the advanced technology and skill underlying the production of these innovative works. Yue wares were made using a light gray clay that had been refined to eliminate other materials, and they were exquisitely shaped and decorated. The best examples, intended for the court and other elite venues, were fully covered with glazes showing no unevenness or dripping. This can be seen on a fragment of either a cup or small bowl with a raised and lobed foot (fig. 1.4). The lively dragon that twists around itself in the center of the fragment was created with a mold and then further enhanced with incisions defining its thin wings, horns, and scales and the small flaming pearl it is chasing. Incisions also render the clouds on the exterior and the two small geese circling each other on the foot (fig. 1.5).

Yue wares continued to be produced in the tenth century after the fall of the Tang dynasty, when China was once again subdivided into regional polities and northern Zhejiang was under the rule of the Wu Yue Kingdom (907–78 C.E.). The Qian kings controlled one of the more stable and prosperous polities at the

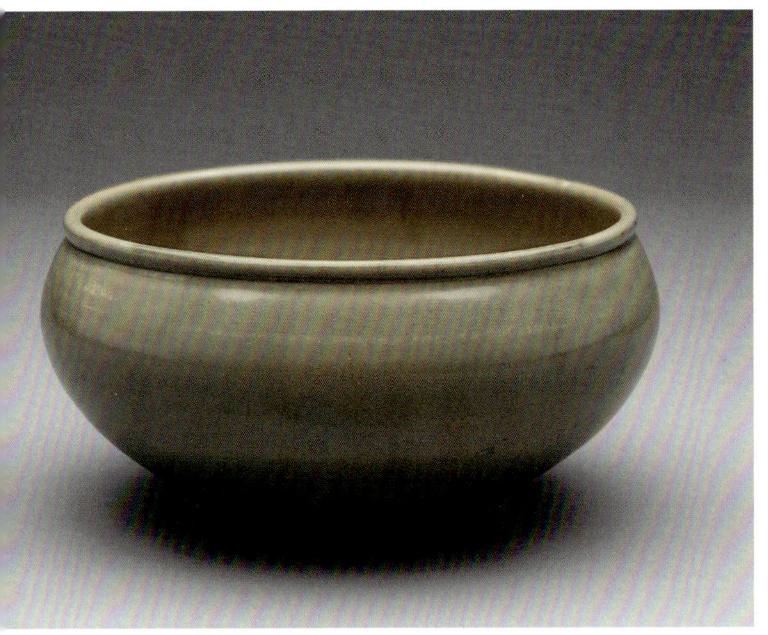

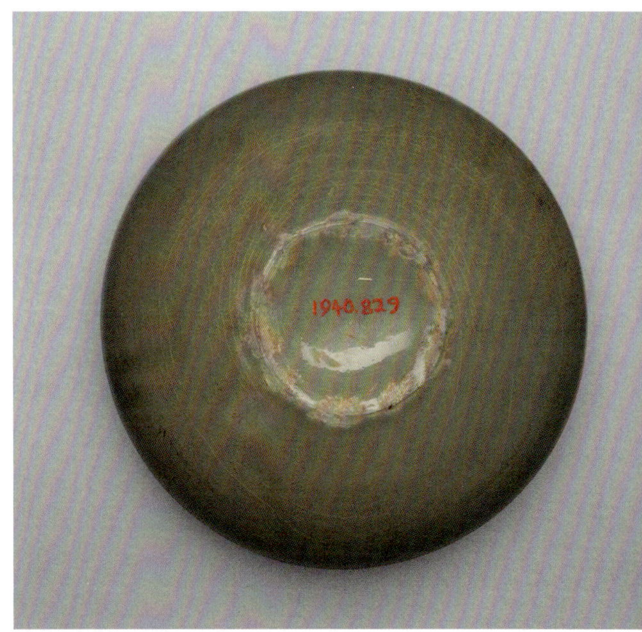


**Fig. 1.6**

*Alms Bowl*, China, Five Dynasties period, 10th century. Stoneware with glaze (Yue ware), H. 3⅞ × DIAM. 8 in. (9.8 × 20.3 cm). Yale University Art Gallery, Gift of Paul Mellon, B.A. 1929, L.H.D.H. 1967, 1940.829

**Fig. 1.7**

Base of fig. 1.6, showing remnants of the spurs used to support the vessel during firing

time and invested in hydraulic projects, sericulture, and ceramic production. Members of the Qian family were devout Buddhists, and some tenth-century ceramic pieces, such as a monk's alms bowl (fig. 1.6), likely were produced under court supervision or were commissioned by the court to be offered as gifts to temples or high-ranking clergy. The base of this alms bowl (fig. 1.7), used daily for the solicitation of food and other goods, retains the small ceramic spurs used to separate the piece from others during firing. The previously discussed fragment of the cup or bowl, on the other hand, has no spurs; this piece was fired individually in a saggar rather than in a stack of vessels—further indication of its production for an elite venue or individual. The shape of the fragment echoes a shape often found in silver, as does an elegant box (fig. 1.8), which could have been used to hold incense for Buddhist ceremonies, salt, spices for tea, or more personal goods, such as cosmetics or medicine.

Fragments of Yue wares have been excavated in significant numbers in Chinese port cities, such as Ningbo[8] and Yangzhou.[9] Of the nearly sixty thousand ceramics found in the early ninth-century Belitung shipwreck, only two hundred were Yue wares from Zhejiang or Yue-type wares made in Guangdong Province. Yet, over one thousand such wares were found among the ceramics in the early tenth-century Intan wreck that was excavated in the west of the Java Sea in 1997,[10] and over one hundred thousand were found in the mid- to late tenth-century Cirebon wreck, excavated in 2005.[11] Yue wares have also been recovered at port and inland sites in mainland and island Southeast Asia; at centers in the Persian Gulf region, such as Basra, Samarra, and Siraf; and as far west as the ancient city

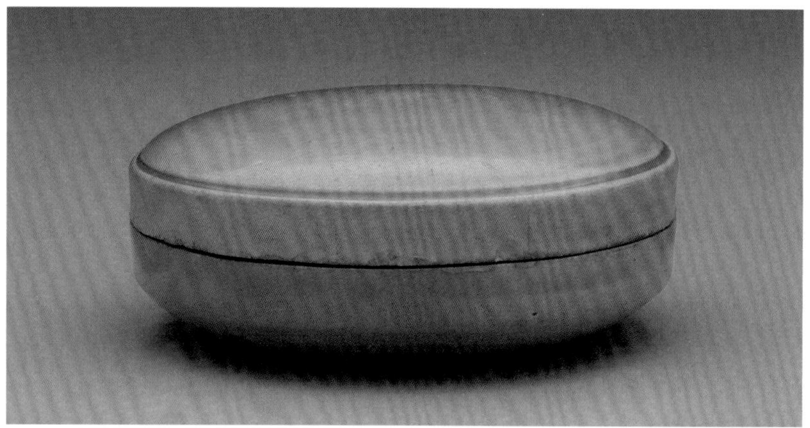

**Fig. 1.8**

*Box*, China, Five Dynasties period, 10th century. Stoneware with glaze (Yue ware), H. 1⅜ × DIAM. 3¼ in. (3.4 × 8.3 cm). Yale University Art Gallery, Wayland Wells Williams, B.A. 1910, Collection, Gift of Mrs. Frances Wayland Williams, 1948.47

of Fustat; as well as in Korea and Japan. The quality of Yue wares and the newly developed gray-green hue of their glazes were deeply appreciated in East Asia for centuries. A delightful echo of their initial impact is recorded in the fourteenth-century Japanese *Ocean River Commentary* (*Kakaisho*), which discusses the twelfth-century *Tale of Genji*, a famous novel that mentions the sophistication of the elegant "secret-color" wares, known as *hisoku* in Japanese. Yue wares were still treasured in Japan long after their initial creation in Zhejiang.[12]

## Longquan and Guan Wares

It remains unclear exactly why the production of green-glazed ceramics in Zhejiang gradually shifted from the Yue to the Longquan area, about two hundred miles south. It seems likely that there were several contributing factors, including uncertainty resulting from the fall of the Wu Yue Kingdom in the late tenth century and the need for access to new materials, such as wood and clay, possibly due to deforestation or the depletion of quarries. In addition, the Longquan area had greater accessibility, via the nearby Ou River, to the port city of Wenzhou, which became more important after a Superintendency for Maritime Shipping was established there in 1131.

Some of the kilns in this region that began to make Longquan wares in the mid-tenth century had initially produced Yue wares, and similarities between the two green-ware traditions are particularly evident in early Longquan works. A simple but elegant tenth-century Longquan jar (fig. 1.9), which has a short foot, an ovoid body with two lugs on the shoulder, a narrow neck, and a cover, is coated with a thin, delicate green glaze that shares the color of the characteristic gray-green Yue glaze. A late tenth- or eleventh-century jar (fig. 1.10), on the other hand, originally had a glaze (now visible in the incisions) that is more blue-green in hue—a characteristic Longquan glaze. The shape of this more elaborate jar is divided into five horizontal bands. The lower four are incised with lotus

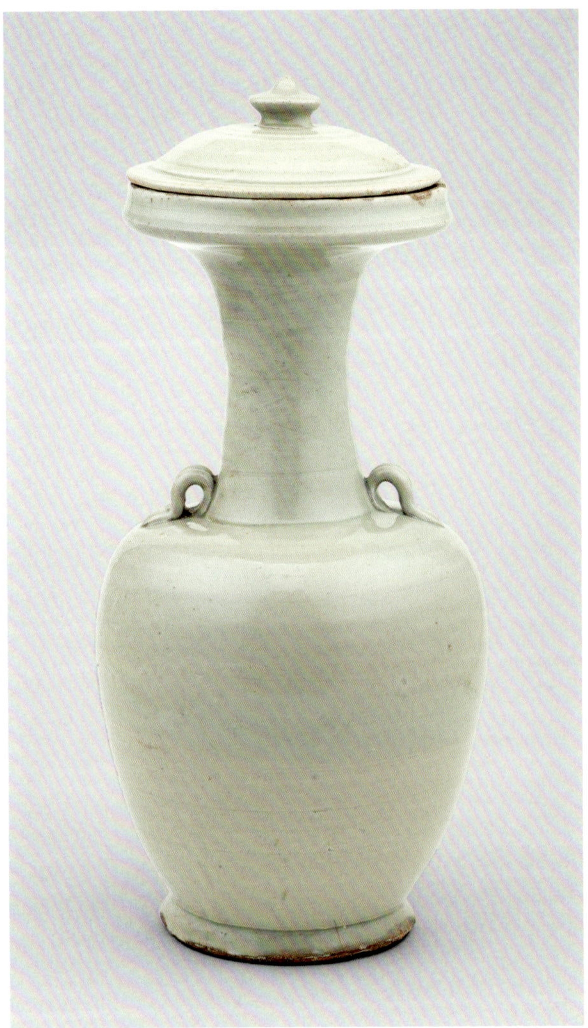

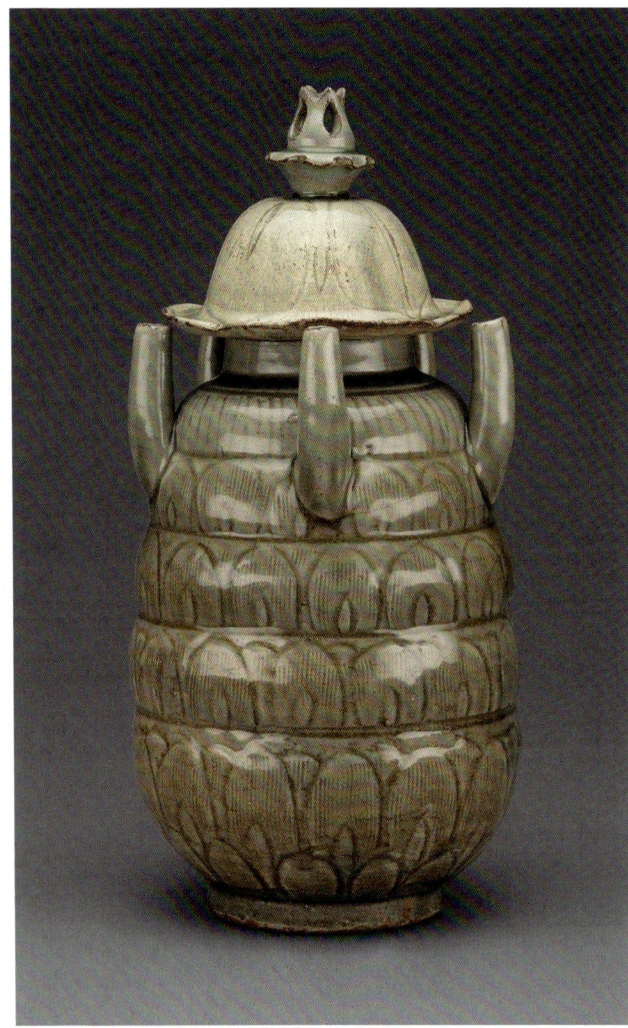

**Fig. 1.9**

*Funerary Jar*, China, Northern Song dynasty, late 10th century. Stoneware with glaze (Longquan ware), H. 12 13/16 × DIAM. 6 in. (32.6 × 15.2 cm). National Museum of Asian Art, Smithsonian Institution, Washington, D.C., Freer Collection, Purchase—Charles Lang Freer Endowment, F1961.27a–b

**Fig. 1.10**

*Funerary Jar with Five Spouts*, China, Northern Song dynasty, late 10th–11th century. Stoneware with carved and incised decoration under glaze (Longquan ware), H. 9½ × DIAM. 5¼ in. (24.1 × 13.3 cm). Yale University Art Gallery, Gift of Denise and George Hopper Fitch, B.A. 1932, 1959.64.3

petals, while the fifth has uneven vertical lines. In addition, the jar has five tubular spouts and a lotus-shaped cover, also decorated with incised petals, as well as a pomegranate-shaped knob.

Both jars would have been placed with the body of the deceased in the innermost chamber of a tomb, continuing the long-standing Chinese tradition of using ceramics as burial goods.[13] Sometimes a single jar was buried, and other times two vessels, one simple and the other more elaborate, formed a set. While the simpler jars held wine or another beverage, the elaborate ones with spouts—which can range in number from four to fifteen—stored rice or grains, essentials for the continuation (at least symbolically) of life in the tomb. Questions remain about the function and meaning of these undeniably striking, if peculiar, stalk-shaped spouts. They may symbolize wishes for bountiful harvests for future descendants of the deceased.

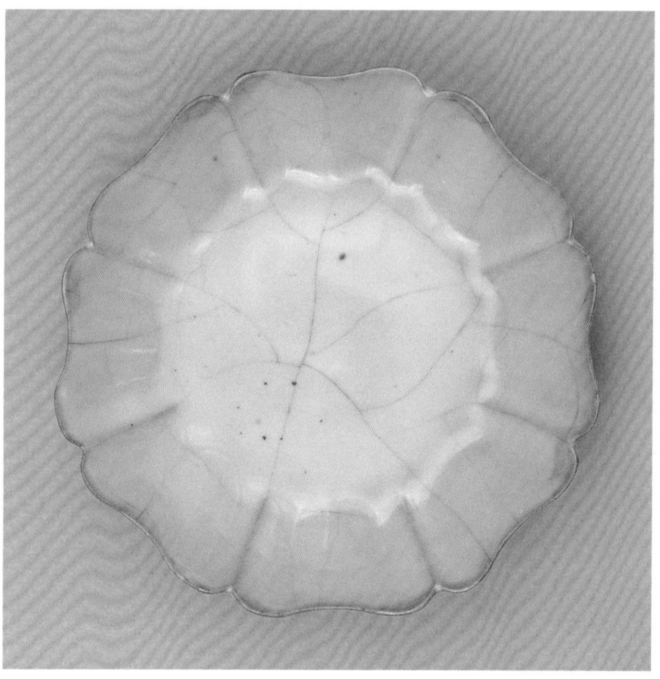

**Fig. 1.11**

*Eight-Petal Lobed Dish*, China, Southern Song dynasty, 12th–13th century. Stoneware with glaze (Guan ware), H. 1⁹⁄₁₆ × DIAM. 6⅝ in. (3.9 × 16.8 cm). British Museum, London, The Sir Percival David Collection, PDF,A.46

The move of the Northern Song–dynasty capital from Kaifeng, Henan Province, in the north, to Hangzhou, Zhejiang, in the south, and the subsequent founding of the Southern Song dynasty further spurred the expansion of the southern ceramic industry in the twelfth and thirteenth centuries. The needs of the court—combined with increasing demand created by growth of the southern population (a result of refugees from the north) and by the government sponsorship of maritime trade—led to the creation of new designs, glazes, and shapes, often inspired by those cherished in the north.

Following a precedent established in the Northern Song dynasty, the Southern Song set up two kilns in the Hangzhou region to make ceramics exclusively for the use of the court, which are known as Guan (official) wares. One was the Jiaotanxia kiln, discovered in the 1930s, and the other, excavated between 1999 and 2001, was the Laohudong kiln.[14] Both were under the supervision of the Department of Palace Supply, or Xiunesi. The extremely thick blue-green glaze covering a small dish potted with a dark gray clay (fig. 1.11) illustrates the style of the Guan wares made in these kilns. With eight large lobes, the dish is in the shape of a flower, probably a rose mallow, a popular form in metalwork and lacquer during the Southern Song dynasty. The large, wide cracks in the glaze, also known as "crackle" or "crazing," are deliberate. Both the crackle and the blue-green color of the glaze are visual references to Ru ware, the rarest and most revered of all Chinese ceramics. Produced at kilns in Ru Prefecture in Henan, not far from Kaifeng, Ru ware was made exclusively

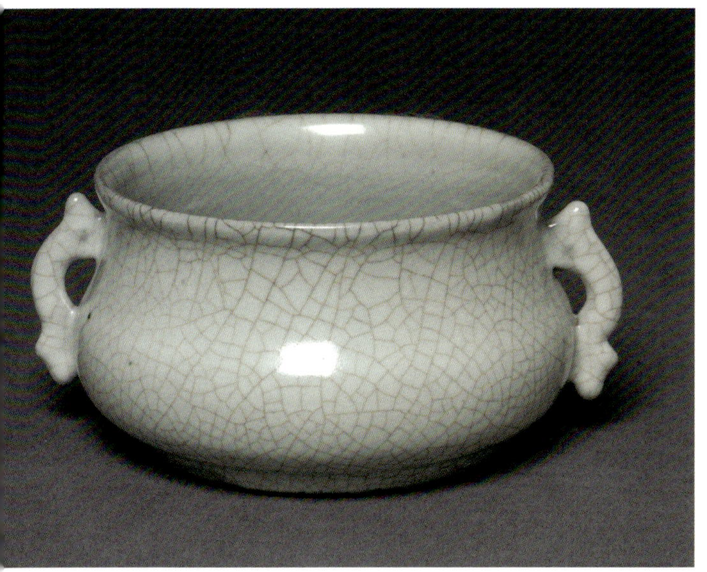

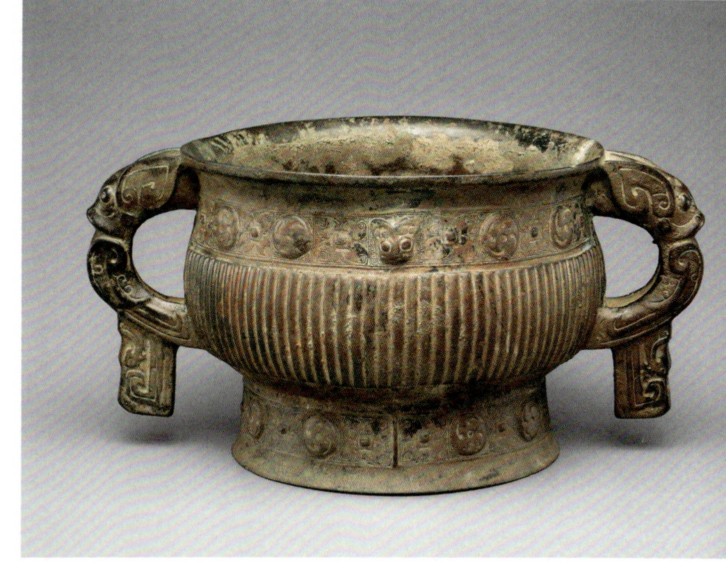

**Fig. 1.12**

*Incense Burner in the Shape of a Ritual Grain Server (Gui)*, China, Southern Song dynasty, 12th–13th century. Stoneware with glaze (Guan ware), H. 2⅞ × DIAM. 6⅛ in. (7.3 × 15.6 cm). Cleveland Museum of Art, Gift of Mr. and Mrs. Severance A. Millikin, 1957.63

**Fig. 1.13**

*Ritual Grain Server (Gui)*, China, Western Zhou dynasty, ca. 10th century B.C.E. Bronze, 6 × 12¼ in. (15.2 × 31.1 cm). Yale University Art Gallery, Hobart and Edward Small Moore Memorial Collection, Gift of Mrs. William H. Moore, 1954.49.4

for the Northern Song court, and for only a short period during the reign of Emperor Huizong. Ru wares were among the treasures brought south by the court after the defeat of the Northern Song, and they served as prototypes for the southern Guan wares. Zhang Jun, a powerful civil servant, presented sixteen Ru pieces (as well as jade, gold, glass, antique bronze vessels, paintings, and calligraphy) to Gaozong (r. 1127–62), the first emperor of the Southern Song, during a lavish banquet in 1151—an example of the many ways that northern taste moved south.[15] In addition to the officials, administrators, and others who followed the court to the south, potters and other skilled makers moved there, bringing a greater awareness of northern techniques, shapes, and designs to the southern ceramic industry.

Both the color of the glaze and the dense crackle on a Guan-ware incense burner (fig. 1.12) evoke the style of Ru wares. Moreover, the shape reflects the fascination with China's past that permeated the Northern Song court: the wide body and two vaguely zoomorphic handles of the vessel can be traced to a ritual grain server known as a *gui* (fig. 1.13) that was first produced in bronze during the Western Zhou dynasty (ca. 1046–771 B.C.E.). At least one example of a Western Zhou–period bronze *gui* was in the collection of the Northern Song court. It was recorded in the *Illustrated Catalogue of a Wide Range of Antiquities of the Xuanhe Period* (*Xuanhe bogu tu*), written in the twelfth century by the minister and scholar Wang Fu.[16] This shape was also introduced to some of the Longquan kilns in the twelfth century, when they began to produce works

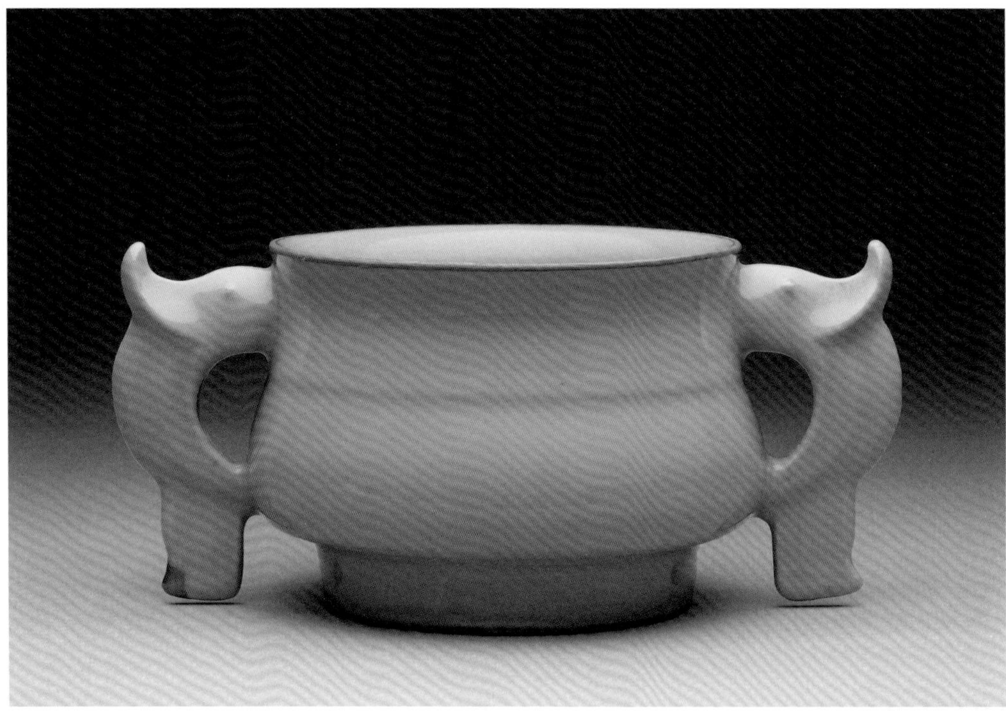

**Fig. 1.14**

*Incense Burner with Dragon-Shaped Handles*, China, Southern Song dynasty, 12th–13th century. Stoneware with glaze (Longquan ware), 3 11/16 × 8 in. (9.4 × 20.3 cm). British Museum, London, 1947,0712.114

in the style of contemporaneous Guan wares (fig. 1.14), either for the court or for other patrons seeking objects that resonated with imperial taste.

The production of incense burners at the Guan and Longquan kilns attests to the significance of aromatics and incense in Chinese culture. Imported from Southeast Asia or regions farther west, aromatic woods and resins not only perfumed homes and clothing but also were used in court ceremonies and religious rituals. Some aromatics were introduced to China with Buddhism as early as the fourth century C.E., and the expansion of maritime trade that began in the ninth century made them more accessible and more widely used.[17] The frankincense of medieval European lore, the resin from a tree found in southern Arabia and the Horn of Africa, is one example. In 1131 100,952 catties (a Chinese unit of weight equivalent to 500 grams) of frankincense were imported to China, delivered to the court, and dispersed throughout the country. Slightly later, in 1136, a merchant of Arab descent known by the Chinese name Pu Luxin imported 300,000 strings (a Chinese monetary unit) worth of frankincense, and in 1167 an envoy from the Champa Kingdom, in central and southern Vietnam, presented 100,730 catties to the Chinese court.[18]

In addition to incense burners in the shape of ancient bronze *gui* vessels, the Longquan kiln complex crafted other works reflecting existing forms or imported shapes, often in different media—further responding to the interest in early visual traditions. For example, the shape of a long, cylindrical Longquan vase (fig. 1.15)

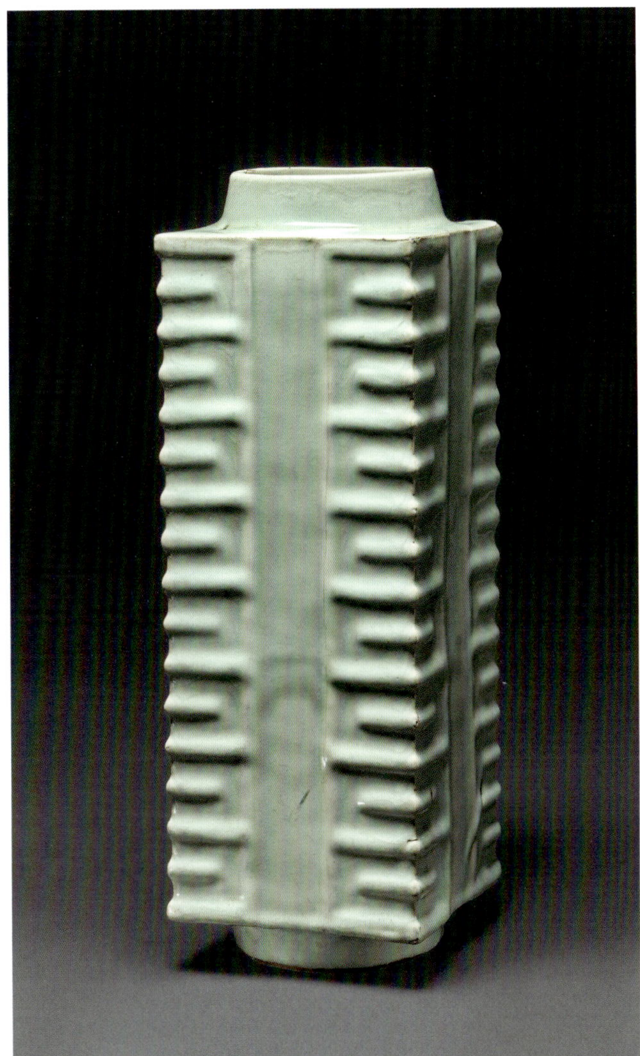

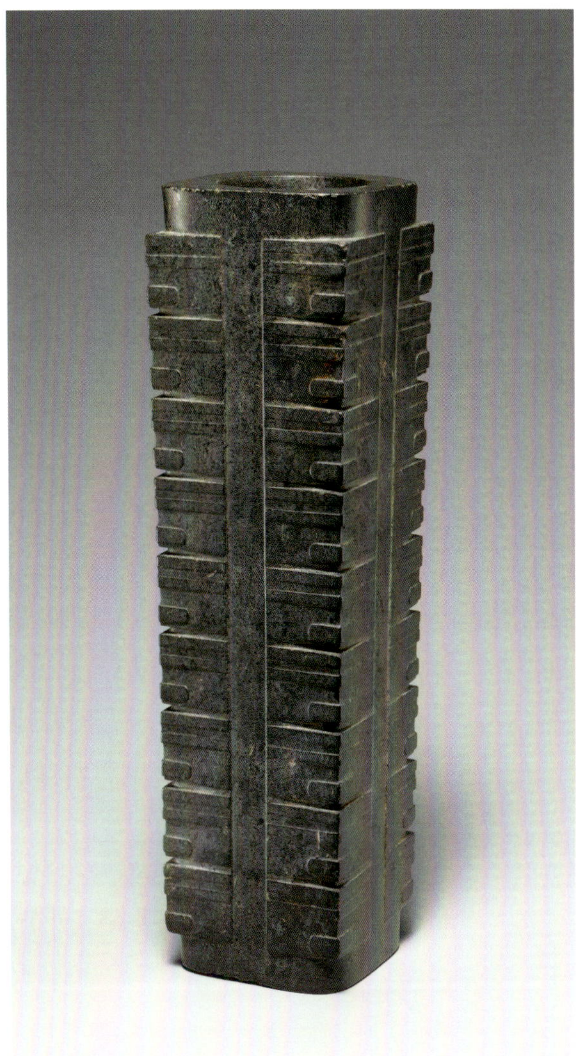

**Fig. 1.15**

*Vase in the Shape of a Ritual Object (Cong)*, China, Southern Song dynasty, 12th–13th century. Stoneware with glaze (Longquan ware), H. 16⅛ in. (41 cm). British Museum, London, The Sir Percival David Collection, PDF.233

**Fig. 1.16**

*Ritual Object (Cong)*, China, Neolithic period, Liangzhu culture, ca. 2400 B.C.E. Jade (nephrite), 10 × 2¾ in. (25.4 × 7 cm). Metropolitan Museum of Art, New York, Purchase, Sir Joseph Hotung Gift, 2004, 2004.52

and the horizontal ribs on its sides stem from an enigmatic Neolithic-period jade object known as a *cong* (fig. 1.16). *Cong* have been found in burials, placed in groups encircling the body of the deceased. They may have served a ritual or protective function or symbolized the union of earth and sky. The shape of the "dragon-fish" handles on another Longquan vase (fig. 1.17), on the other hand, parallels those found on the ancient bronze *gui* (see fig. 1.13). The dragon-fish—a combination of the dragon of Chinese mythology and the makara, an auspicious, mythical crocodile-like creature of India that was introduced to China with Buddhism—first appeared in southern ceramics in the twelfth and thirteenth centuries.

The shape of this vase, with an oblong body, flared neck, and disk-shaped mouth, was first found in Chinese ceramics in the eleventh century and derives from that of glass bottles made in Egypt and Iran from the ninth to the eleventh

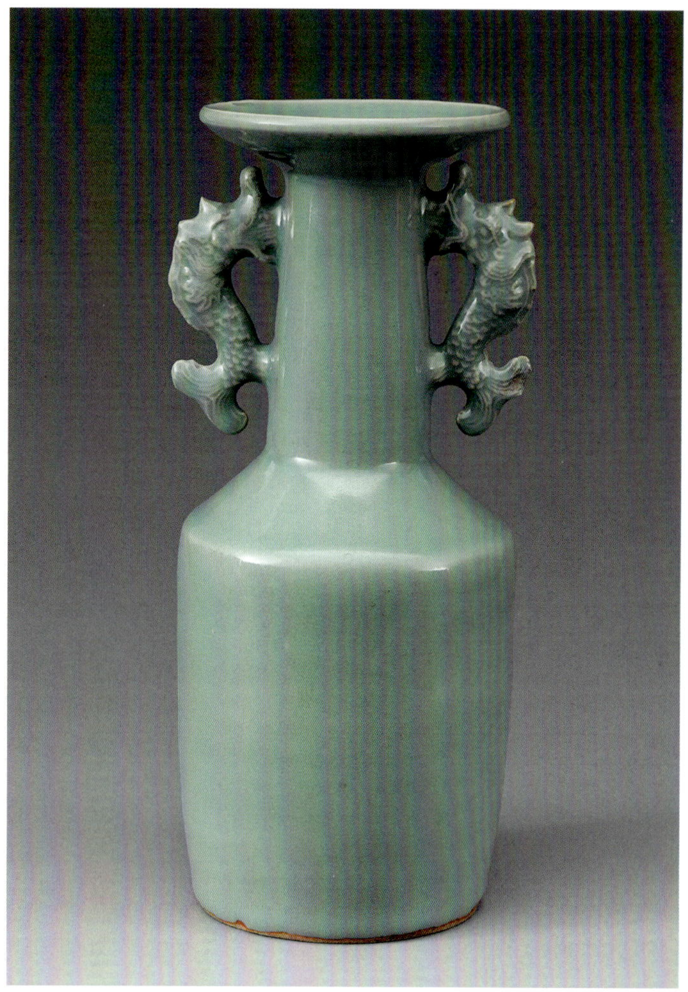

**Fig. 1.17**

*Vase with Dragon-Fish Handles*, China, Southern Song dynasty, 12th–13th century, excavated from the Sinan shipwreck, near Korea. Stoneware with molded and applied decoration under glaze (Longquan ware), H. 6¼ in. (15.8 cm). National Museum of Korea, Seoul, Sinan 6558

century (fig. 1.18).[19] Thirty-six such bottles or flasks, used to transport wines, perfumes, or other precious liquids, were found in the Cirebon shipwreck (fig. 1.19), in addition to glass fragments, beads, and ingots.[20] Though glass is often found in shipwrecks, the large quantity present in the Cirebon wreck is unusual.[21] The extremely luxurious cargo of the Cirebon also yielded pearls and other precious gems, including lapis lazuli from Afghanistan.

Imported glass was valued in China for its mysterious luminescence and transparency,[22] and it often served as a religious offering or held relics.[23] West Asian glass vessels, some undecorated and others carved, have been excavated in tenth- and eleventh-century sites throughout northern China. For example, a carved glass bottle with a broad rim is one of two imported bottles excavated in 1982 from the tomb of a princess of the Qidan Liao dynasty in Inner Mongolia.[24] She was buried with her husband, and their joint tomb also had gold jewelry and four beautiful examples of Yue ware, each marked with the

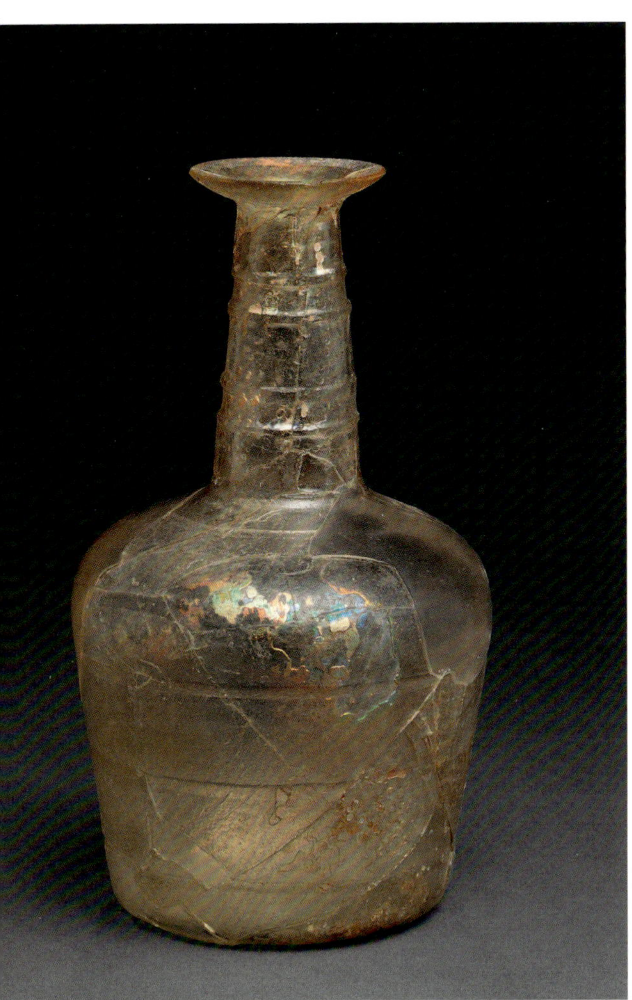

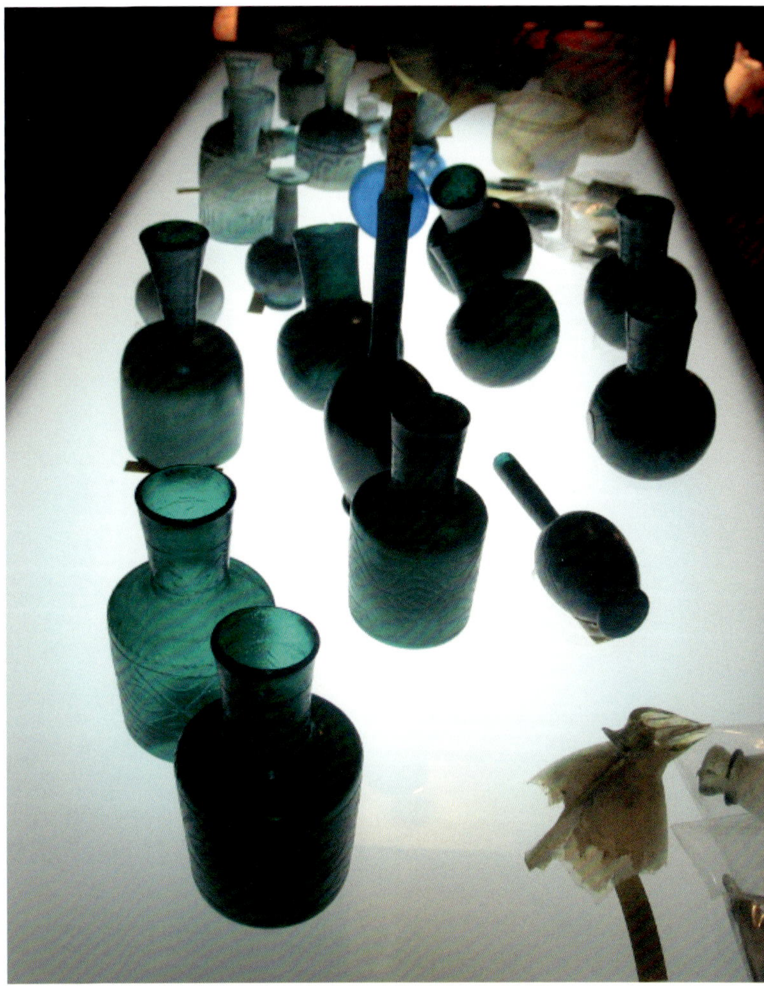

**Fig. 1.18**

*Flask*, Iran, Nishapur region, Abbasid period, 9th century C.E. Glass, free blown and cut, 9 1/16 × 5 1/8 in. (23 × 13 cm). Metropolitan Museum of Art, New York, Rogers Fund, 1940, 40.170.61

**Fig. 1.19**

Islamic glass vessels from the Cirebon shipwreck, near Java, Indonesia

character *guan* (official).[25] Another flask in the same shape was found among the eleventh-century offerings in a relic deposit inside the upper floors of a pagoda at the Dule Temple in the city of Tianjin, in Hebei Province. Ceramic variants of this Islamic glass shape, some of which have a broad rim, were made at the Ru kilns in the north[26] and the Guan kilns in the south,[27] as well as in Korea,[28] before the shape became popular in the Longquan repertoire and the dragon-fish handles were added.

The vase with dragon-fish handles (see fig. 1.17) is one of fourteen thousand Longquan pieces retrieved from the Sinan shipwreck near Jeungdo Island, off the west of coast of Korea. Discovered in 1975, this wreck was excavated in several campaigns between 1976 and 1984. It had a substantial cargo of over twenty thousand Chinese ceramics that had been loaded at Ningbo before the ship headed to Hakata (present-day Fukuoka), Japan.[29] Analysis of the cargo and a rare inscription on a wooden cargo tag indicate that the wreck dates to between

1323 and 1367. The glaze on the vase was applied in several layers, to enhance its depth and incandescence. This particular shade of blue-green—one of several for Longquan wares—is known as *fenqing*, or powdery blue-green, in Chinese, and as *kinuta seiji* in Japanese. The Japanese name derives from a term that a tea master used as an accolade for a similar vase known as *The Thousand Cries* (*Bansei*), a Japanese National Treasure now in the collection of the Bishamondo Temple in Kyoto.[30] He likened the shape of that vase to a *kinuta*, a mallet for pounding rice, and the term *kinuta seiji* was then applied to other Longquan wares with the same resonant blue-green glaze. The blue shade, which differs from the more gray-green or olive color of other Longquan glazes, likely illustrates awareness of the hues of the imperial Ru and Guan wares.

A lush glaze with a slightly lighter *fenqing* hue covers the surface of a tall vase (fig. 1.20) with a full, tapering, ovoid body; a long, ribbed neck; and a large mouth—a type that first appeared in the Longquan repertoire in the late thirteenth to early fourteenth century and was inspired by an earlier bronze shape. Vases of this type were used singly or in pairs with a matching incense burner, as part of a set known as the "three treasures" (*sangong*), and were placed on altars in religious institutions and family shrines. Both the shape of the vase and the lotus spray were created using a mold. In the thirteenth and fourteenth centuries, as the demand for Longquan wares intensified and the kilns needed to produce more pieces more quickly, they began to use molds extensively to form shapes and decorations.

By this time, kilns producing Longquan wares were the center of a massive industry. Over five hundred kilns—operating either as a single entity or as part of enormous complexes—were active in the greater Longquan area. Some kilns were over two hundred feet long and could fire up to twenty-five thousand pieces at a time. The industry was supported by a large and complicated infrastructure of craftsmen, laborers, and specialists. Some individuals sourced or transported materials such as fuel (primarily wood) and clays, and others refined and levigated the clays or produced kiln furniture, molds, wheels, and additional implements. Designers, potters, and workers made the pieces and applied glazes, while others packed the kilns, supervised the firings, and arranged for the sale and shipment of finished pieces. Examples of Longquan wares have been unearthed in sites throughout China.[31] They have also been recovered from shipwrecks: in addition to those in the Sinan shipwreck, significant numbers have been found in the twelfth- to thirteenth-century Nanhai I wreck, near the coast of China; the early fourteenth-century Jade Dragon wreck, near Borneo; and the late fourteenth-century Turiang wreck, not far from Singapore.[32] Like Yue wares, Longquan wares were traded throughout India, Japan, Korea, Southeast Asia, West Asia, and the east coast of Africa.

**Fig. 1.20**

*Vase with Lotuses*, China, Yuan dynasty, 13th–14th century. Stoneware with molded decoration under glaze (Longquan ware), H. 14¾ × DIAM. 6¼ in. (37.5 × 15.9 cm). Yale University Art Gallery, Hobart and Edward Small Moore Memorial Collection, Bequest of Mrs. William H. Moore, 1955.4.64

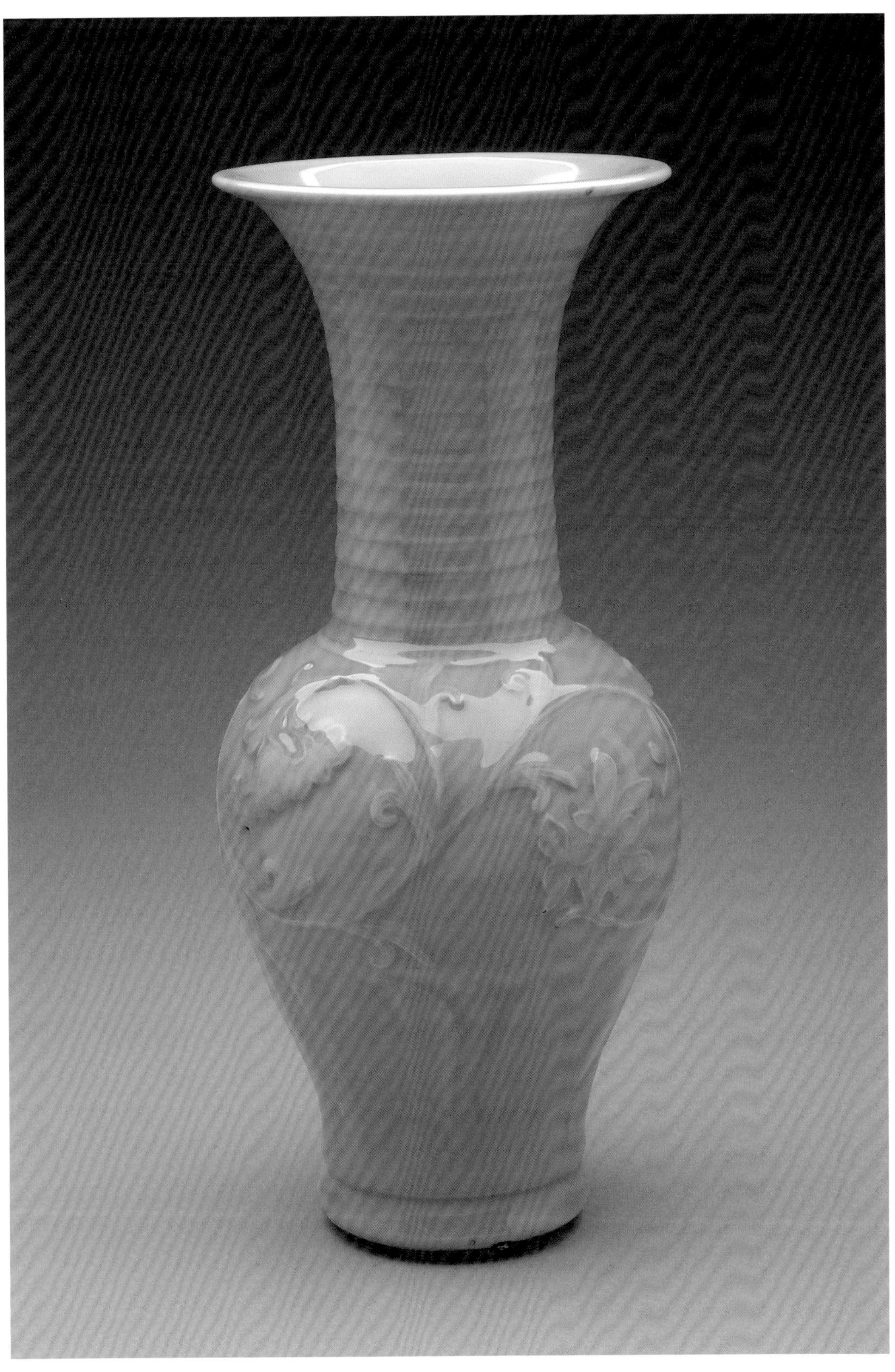

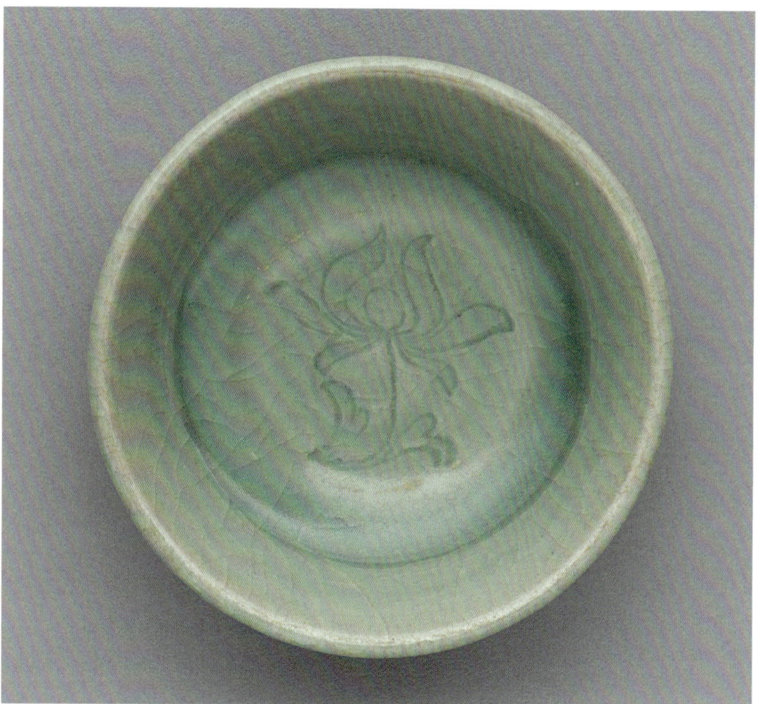

**Fig. 1.21**

*Brush Washer with a Lotus*, China, Southern Song dynasty, 12th–13th century. Stoneware with incised decoration under glaze (Longquan ware), H. 1½ × DIAM. 5 in. (3.8 × 12.7 cm). Yale University Art Gallery, Gift of Dr. Howard Balensweig, B.S. 1943, and Mrs. Carolyn Balensweig, 1972.123.11

The slightly sloping sides of a small round vessel (fig. 1.21) indicate that it served as a brush washer, an implement used in China, Korea, and Japan for holding water for refreshing an ink-filled brush while writing. The open blossom in the center, incised by hand, is the lotus, a flower long cultivated as food in southern China and featured in popular songs as a pun for love (the Chinese characters for "lotus" and "love" [*lian*] are homophonic). The lotus also plays a major role in Buddhist imagery as a symbol of purity and rebirth.

Large and small dishes with sloping sides and broad rims were widely produced at Longquan, used all over China, and traded throughout maritime Asia. These dishes were decorated with lotus petals on the exterior and either a single fish or two fish swimming around each other on the interior. The fish, a type of Chinese wild carp known as a goldfish (*jinyu*), symbolize wealth and prosperity. They are shown with pointed faces; open, staring eyes; and clearly rendered fins, scales, and forked tails. Representations of twin fish have a long history in China. They first appeared in the painted and carved decoration of tombs from the Han dynasty (206 B.C.E.–220 C.E.) and were considered auspicious omens (*xiangrui*).

Some Longquan pieces intended for elite clientele were more painstakingly produced. One dish shown here (fig. 1.22) is almost covered with glaze in the elegant blue-green *fenqing* hue, and it has a very unusual second fish added to the base (fig. 1.23). Two other dishes—one with two molded fish and a gray-green glaze (fig. 1.24) and the other with two impressed fish and an olive-green glaze (fig. 1.25)—

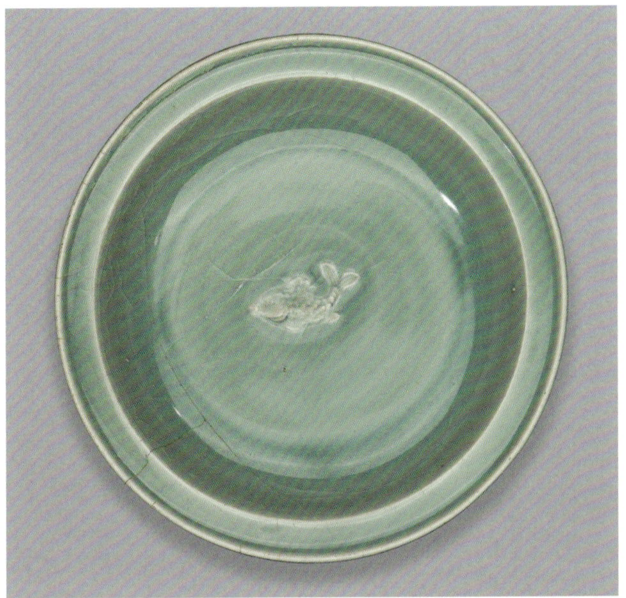

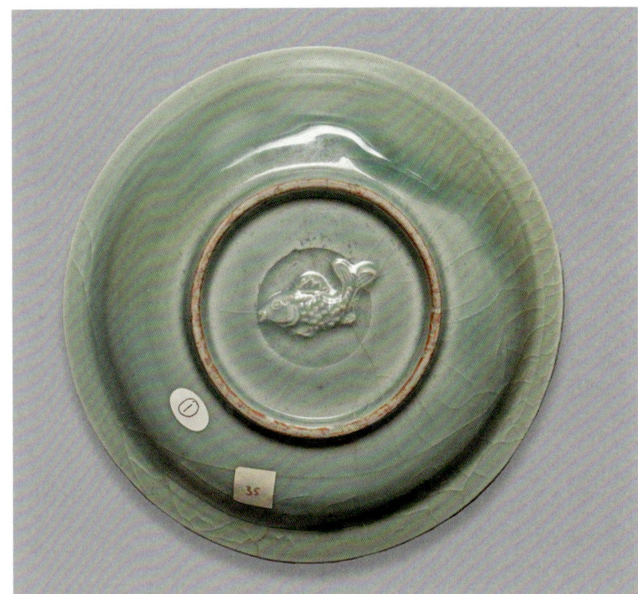

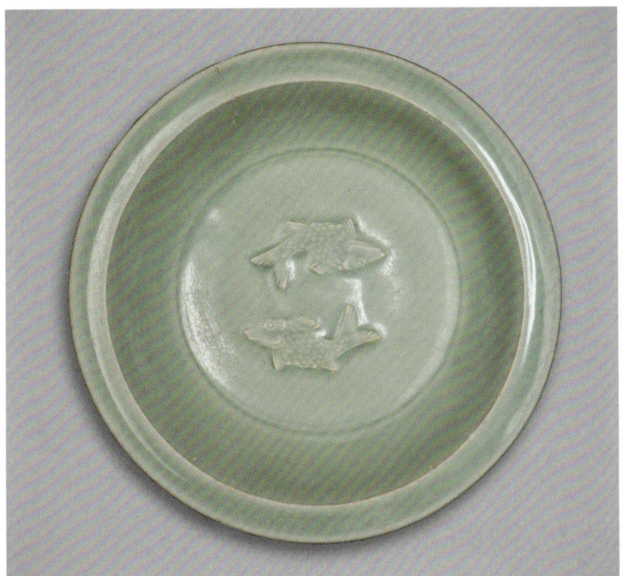

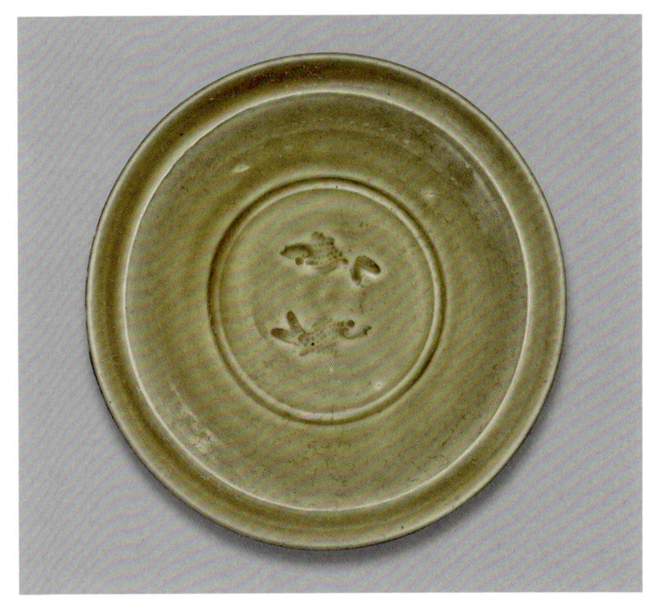

TOP ROW:

**Fig. 1.22**

*Dish with a Fish*, China, Southern Song dynasty, 12th–13th century. Stoneware with molded and applied decoration under glaze (Longquan ware), H. 1¾ × DIAM. 8½ in. (4.5 × 21.6 cm). Yale University Art Gallery, Gift of Ann and Gilbert H. Kinney, B.A. 1953, M.A. 1954, 1999.133.1

**Fig. 1.23**

Base of fig. 1.22

BOTTOM ROW:

**Fig. 1.24**

*Dish with Two Fish*, China, Southern Song dynasty, 12th–13th century. Stoneware with molded and applied decoration under glaze (Longquan ware), H. 1¹⁵⁄₁₆ × DIAM. 8½ in. (4.9 × 21.6 cm). Yale University Art Gallery, Gift of Ann and Gilbert H. Kinney, B.A. 1953, M.A. 1954, 1999.133.9

**Fig. 1.25**

*Dish with Two Fish*, China, Southern Song or Yuan dynasty, 13th–14th century. Stoneware with impressed decoration under glaze (Longquan ware), H. 1¾ × DIAM. 8⅞ in. (4.5 × 22.5 cm). Yale University Art Gallery, Gift of John Crockett, 2008.222.105

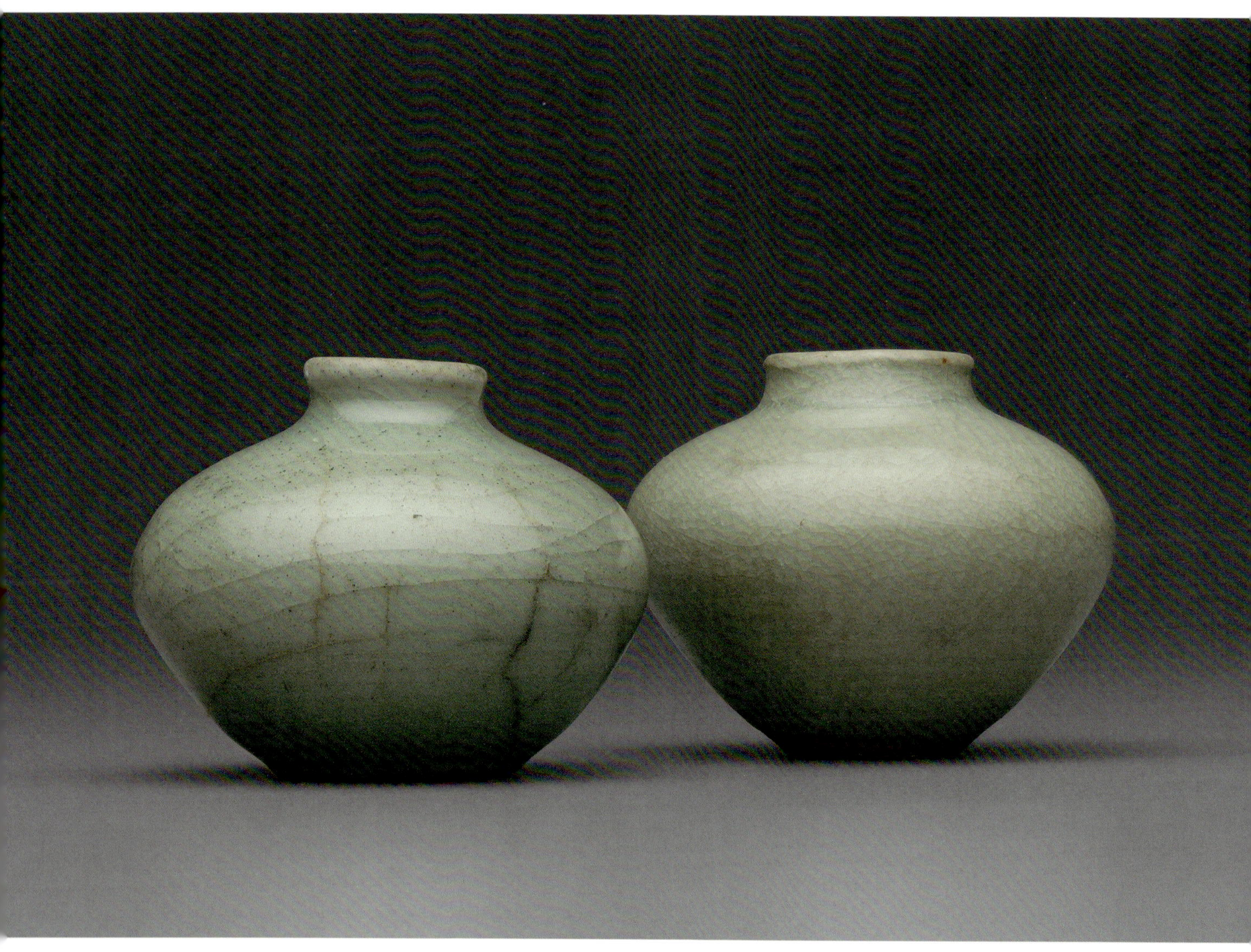

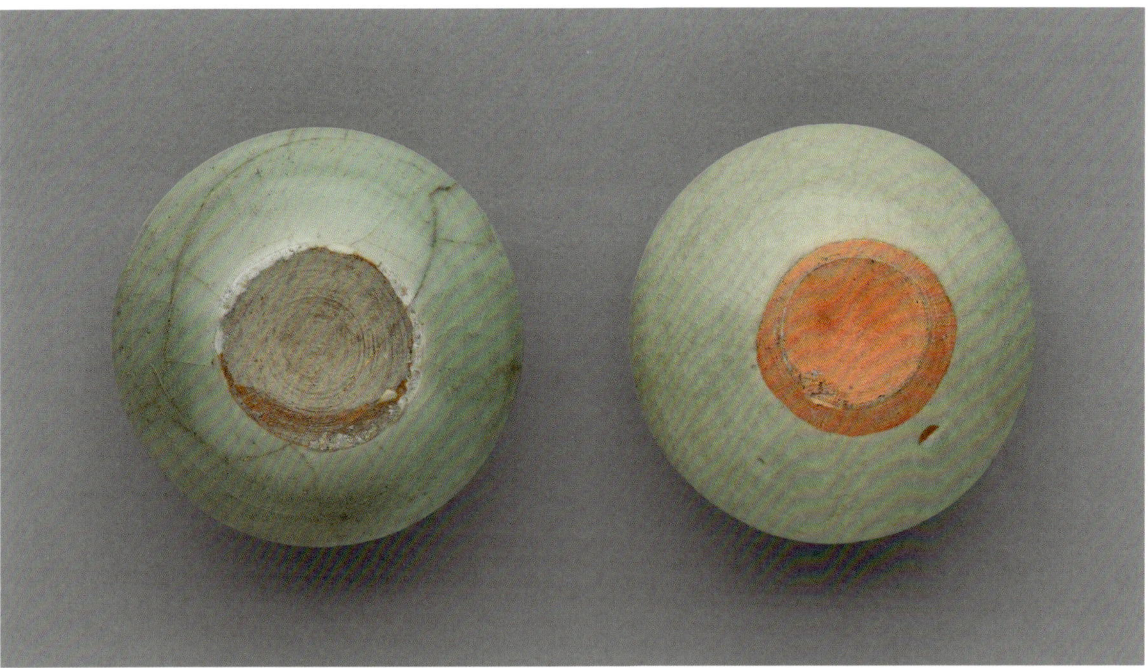

**Fig. 1.26**

(left) *Jar*, China, Southern Song dynasty, 12th–13th century. Stoneware with glaze (Longquan ware), H. 2 × DIAM. 8⅝ in. (5.1 × 22 cm). Yale University Art Gallery, Gift of John Crockett, 2008.222.77. (right) *Jar*, China, Southern Song dynasty, 12th–13th century. Stoneware with glaze (Longquan ware), H. 2⅛ × DIAM. 8⅝ in. (5.4 × 22 cm). Yale University Art Gallery, Gift of John Crockett, 2008.222.85

**Fig. 1.27**

Bases of the jars in fig. 1.26, showing the difference in the color of the clays

were unearthed in the Philippines.[33] Two small, bulbous jars (fig. 1.26)—another shape favored in the Longquan kilns that may also have been inspired by a glass vessel—were also found in the Philippines. Both jars are covered with the typical blue-green glaze and have crazing. While the clay body of one has fired gray, however, the body of the other is red (fig. 1.27). This indicates that the jars were made from clays that had been sourced from different areas and were fired in different kiln centers within the vast Longquan region.

Jars of this type most likely had a stopper or cover and were used to store or ship cosmetics, medicines, or other rare or precious substances, as well as more ordinary materials, such as fish brine. They were particularly valued in the Philippines, where they were placed in tombs as burial goods or were used to store potions and unguents. Some of these jars were buried for a period of time, unearthed, broken into small bits, and ground into a powder. This powder was then ingested, at times with other substances, as a type of medicine[34]—an intriguing paradigm of the awe engendered by alluring high-fired green-glazed Chinese ceramics as they moved throughout maritime Asia from the ninth to the fourteenth century.

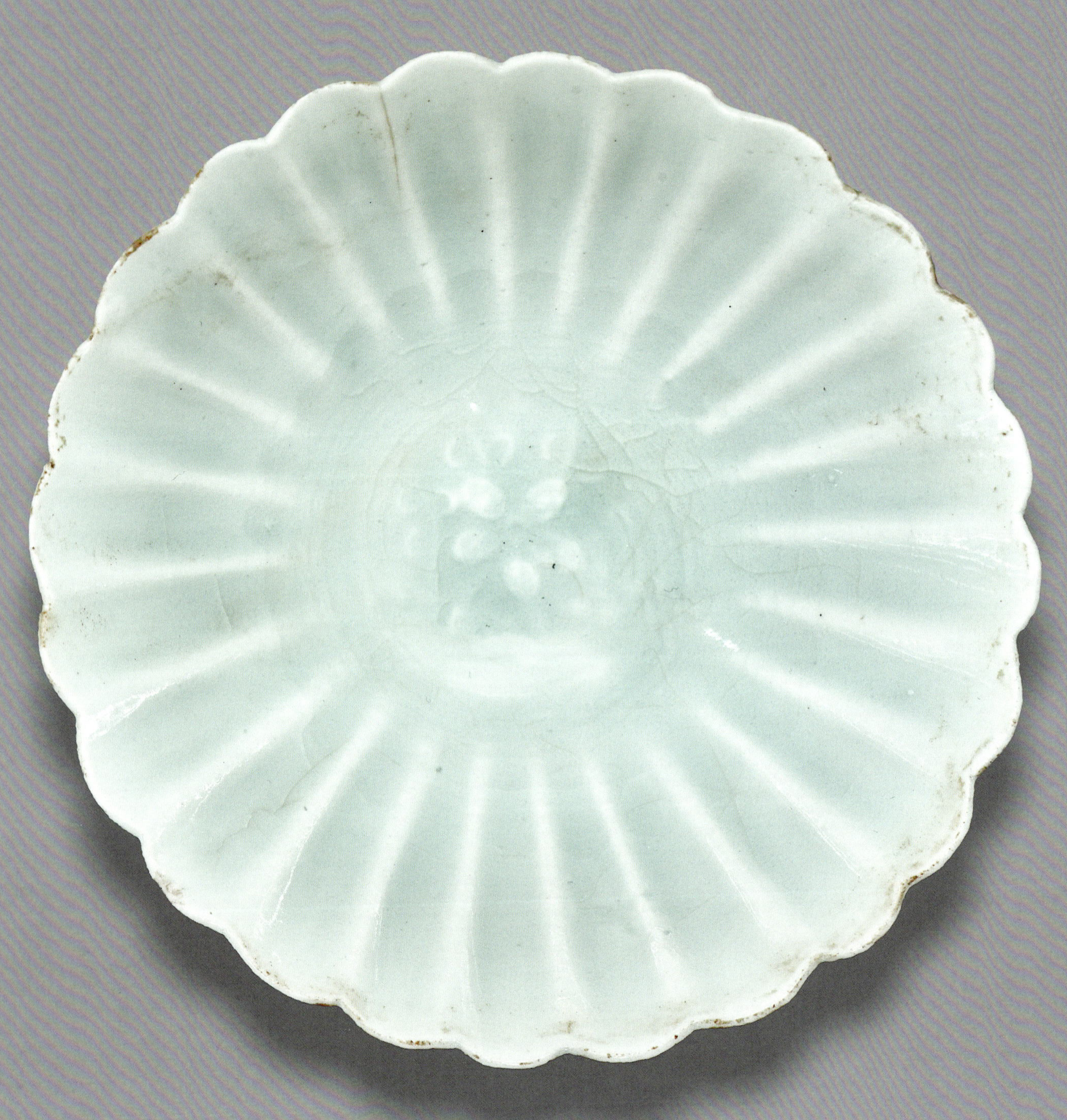

CHAPTER 2

# Jiangxi Province: Blue-Green and White, the Hues of Qingbai Ware

Most of the ceramics produced in the numerous kilns active throughout China from the ninth to the fourteenth century are classified by the location in which they were made. However, Qingbai wares, initially developed in Jiangxi and nearby Anhui Province[1] but later emulated throughout southern China, are classified by the color of their glazes. The term "Qingbai" translates as blue or green (the word *qing* is used for both colors in Chinese) and white (*bai*). The creation of Qingbai wares in the late tenth century is inextricably linked to both the rise of the great ceramic complex at Jingdezhen, in Jiangxi, and the Chinese development of the blue-and-white porcelain works that would ultimately surpass celadons in domestic and international trade.

Ceramics made with a white clay have a long history in China and can be traced to kilns active in the Henan Province area in the late sixth century C.E.[2] By the Tang dynasty, kilns in Hebei Province were producing white Xing and Ding wares, some of which bear marks indicating that they were more carefully crafted and were reserved for the court. Both Xing and Ding wares have been found at sites throughout China, in shipwrecks such as the Belitung, and at sites in West Asia.[3]

China stone (*ciqi*)—also known as Nangang stone or as *petuntse* (or *baidunzi*, in the more current romanization), meaning "little white bricks"—was first discovered or used in Jiangxi around the late tenth century, as part of the experimentation that had been spurred by the interest in white wares.[4] It inherently contains kaolin, the mineral needed for porcelain, and the choice of this type of clay represents a significant moment in the history of porcelain ceramics. In Jiangxi, kaolin was first employed to make Qingbai works. By the twelfth century, as the ceramic industry in Jiangxi expanded, a more kaolin-rich clay was developed for creating a more plastic porcelain that was less likely to shrink during firing. This type of clay makes Qingbai wares thinner and lighter than stoneware pieces from the Yue and Longquan kilns. Interestingly, kaolin is available throughout southern China, yet clays with this mineral were not widely used at kilns beyond Jiangxi until the Ming dynasty (1368–1644). While there is no obvious explanation for the decision to use kaolin in Jiangxi (at least in any extant source), it likely reflects an understanding and appreciation of earlier and contemporaneous northern white wares. It is worth noting that the shapes and designs of Qingbai wares often echo those of the northern Ding wares.[5]

The refined white clay visible in the foliate rim of an early Qingbai vessel with a lobed body (fig. 2.1) derives from China stone. Examples of ceramic and glass footed vessels with long, unarticulated bodies appeared in China as early as the Han dynasty and had parallels in contemporaneous Roman glass.[6] The lobed body of this tenth- to eleventh-century piece is comparable to those of eastern Mediterranean glass vessels from the first to the fourth century C.E.

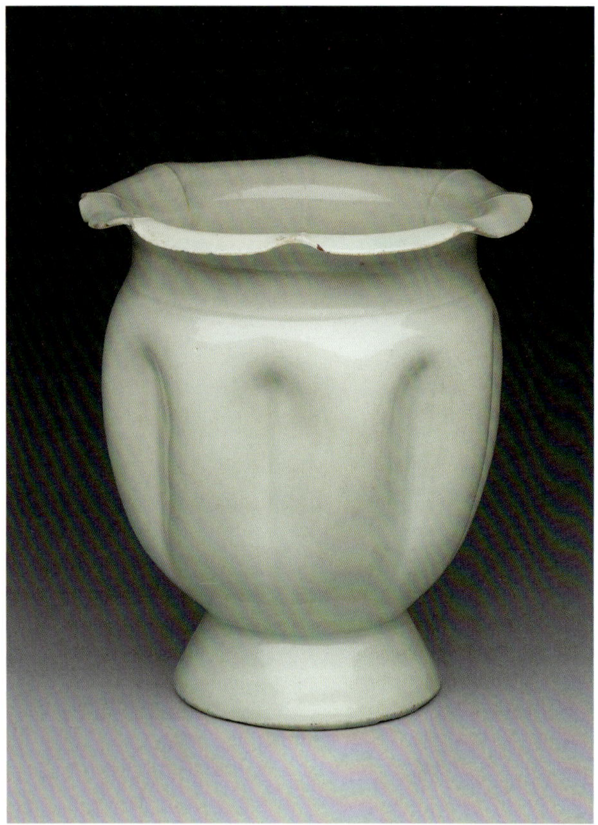

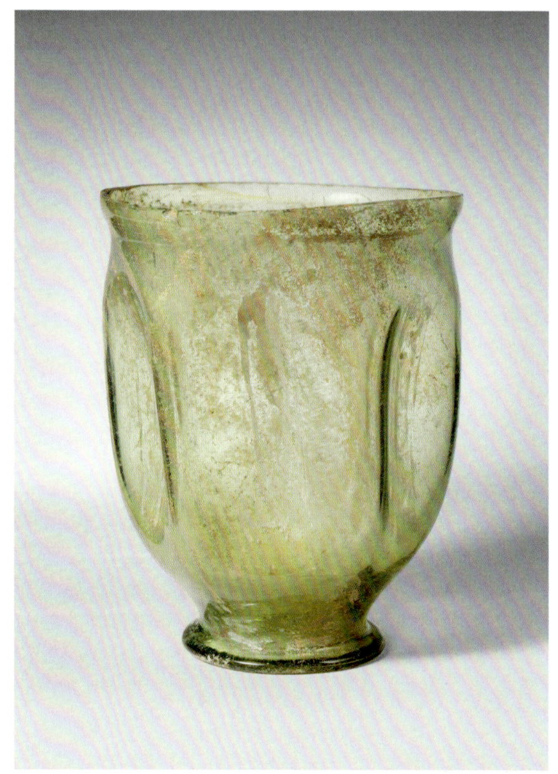

**Fig. 2.1**

*Flowerpot with a Foliate Lip*, China, Northern Song dynasty, 10th–11th century. Porcelain with glaze (Qingbai ware), H. 5¾ × DIAM. 5¼ in. (14.6 × 13.3 cm). Yale University Art Gallery, Hobart and Edward Small Moore Memorial Collection, Bequest of Mrs. William H. Moore, 1955.4.8

**Fig. 2.2**

*Beaker*, Roman, mid- to late 2nd century C.E. Glass, blown, cut, and tooled, H. 3 7/16 × DIAM. 2 13/16 in. (8.8 × 7.1 cm). Metropolitan Museum of Art, New York, The Cesnola Collection, Purchased by subscription, 1874–76, 74.51.230

(fig. 2.2), which suggests that trade in such glass vessels contributed to the appearance of lobed bodies in later Chinese ceramics. The dramatic rim, on the other hand, does not appear to have an imported or local prototype, and the function of this piece remains unclear. While glass objects of this shape served as beakers for drinking, the rim of this ceramic work would have made that use impossible. It seems likely that the vessel instead served as a pot to grow a bulb or flower, which would have been enhanced by the striking rim.

Like the kilns in Zhejiang Province, those in the Jingdezhen region produced a wide range of items, including bottles, bowls, dishes, and incense burners for both domestic use and trade. By the twelfth century, over one hundred kilns were producing such wares in the Jingdezhen area, and the light blue-white glaze on objects such as the flowerpot had been supplanted by a deeper blue-green glaze like that covering an enchanting duck-shaped incense burner (fig. 2.3). This hallmark color at Jingdezhen inspired the comparison of Qingbai ware to jade, a material long revered in Chinese culture. In his influential twelfth-century book *Ceramic Records* (*Taoji*), the scholar Jiang Qi defined Qingbai ceramics as "jades from Rao" (*Raoyu*).[7] *Rao* is an early historical name for the Jingdezhen region of Jiangxi; its current name was awarded in the early

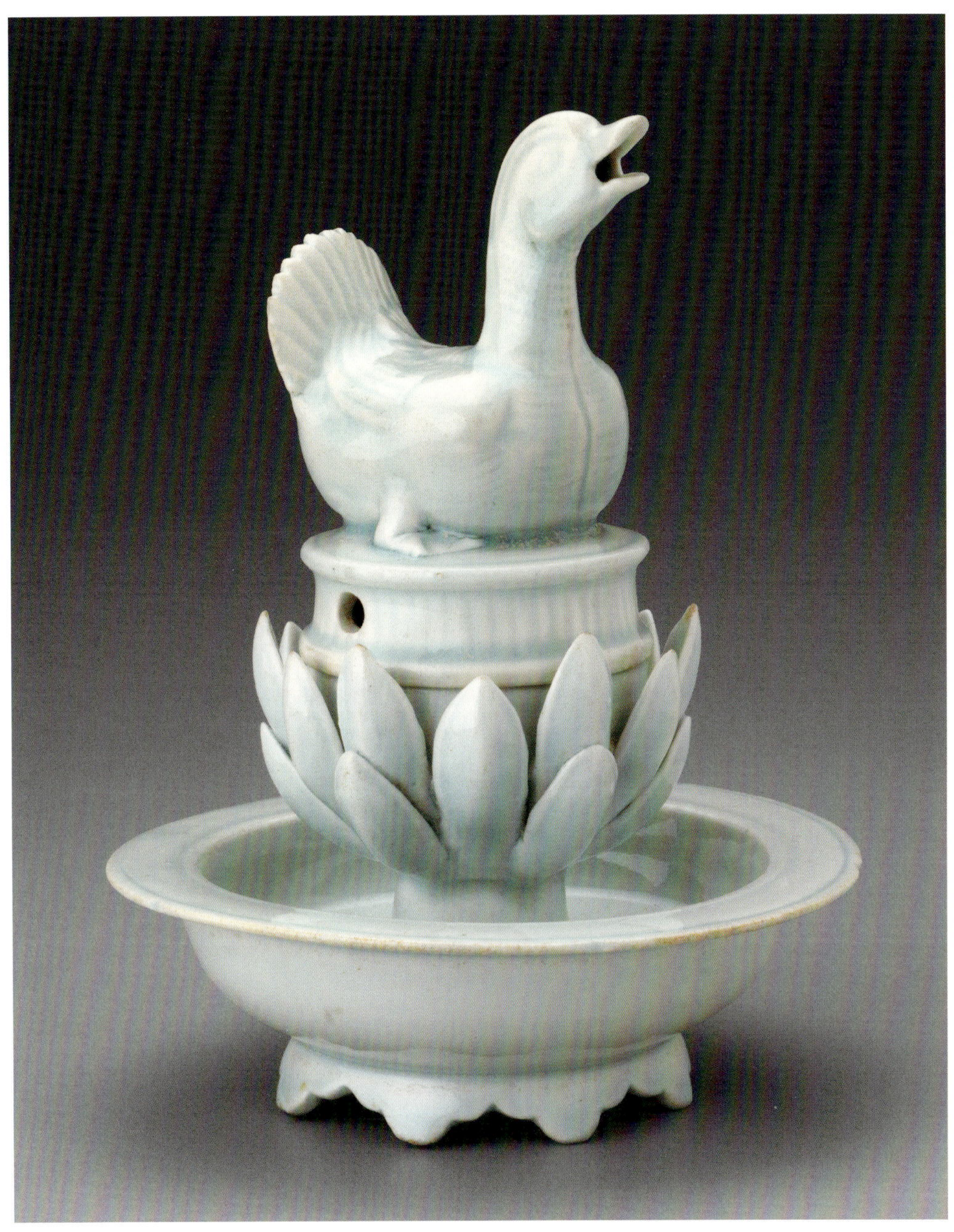

**Fig. 2.3**

*Incense Burner in the Shape of a Duck*, China, Southern Song dynasty, 12th century. Porcelain with molded and carved decoration under glaze (Qingbai ware), H. 7½ × DIAM. 6 in. (19.1 × 15.1 cm). Art Institute of Chicago, Gift of Russell Tyson, 1941.963

eleventh century by the emperor Zhenzong (r. 998–1027), who used the reign name Jingde between 1004 and 1007. He honored the growing commercial and cultural importance of this region by naming it after this reign period, probably in recognition of the elegant ceramics produced there. The blue-green color of Qingbai wares from the twelfth to the fourteenth century is comparable to the beloved blue-green, or "powdery blue," color of contemporaneous Longquan wares, attesting to the high value awarded to this recently developed hue. Like

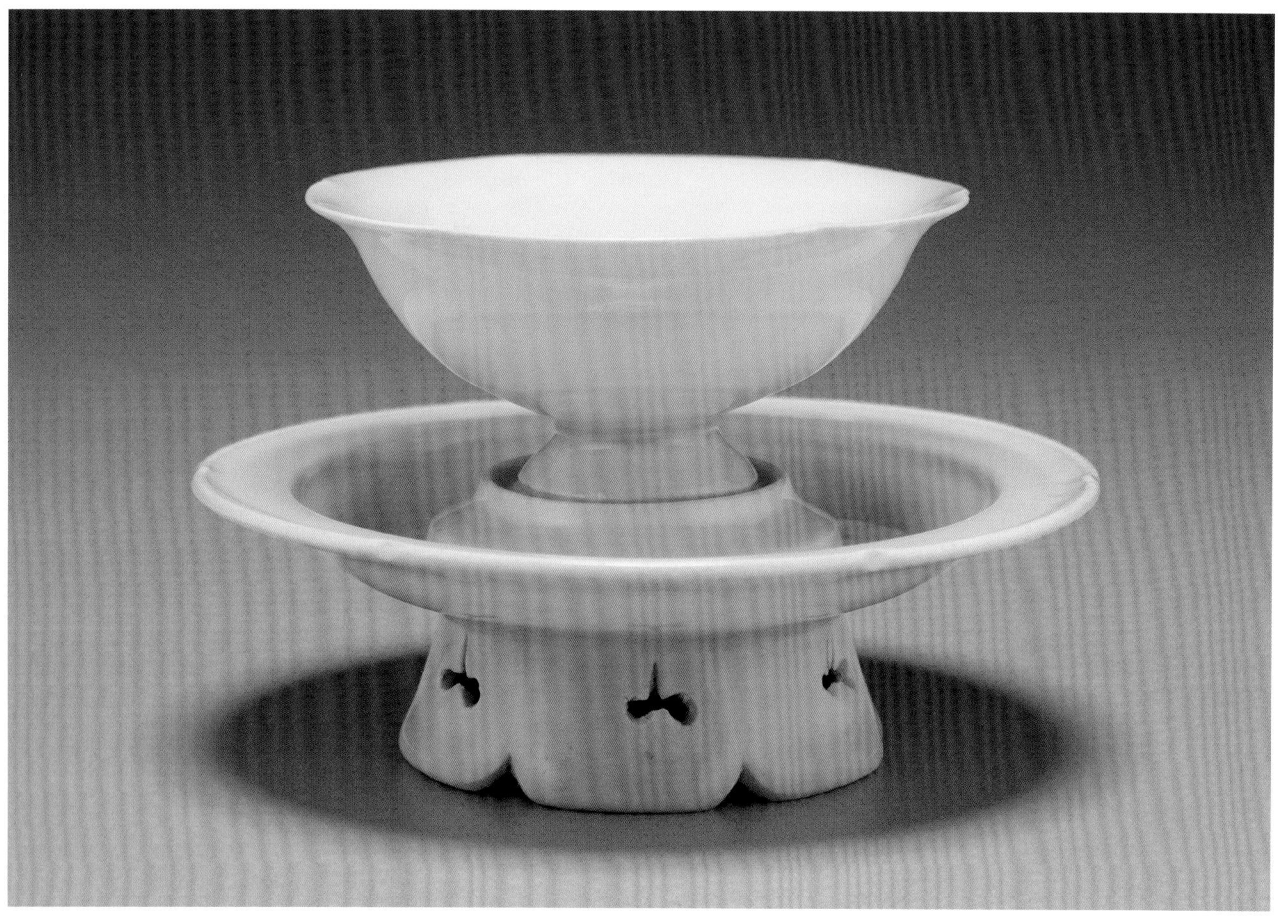

**Fig. 2.4**

*Cup and Stand*, China, Southern Song dynasty, 12th–13th century. Porcelain with incised decoration under glaze (Qingbai ware), H. 3½ × DIAM. 5½ in. (8.8 × 14 cm). Yale University Art Gallery, Gift of the Koo Liong Bing Collection, 2015.72.1a–b

the kilns in Zhejiang, the kilns producing Qingbai wares probably created this glaze at least partially in response to the color of imperial Ru and Guan wares.

The duck shape of this incense burner is one example of the many shapes and designs found in censers made in the Qingbai kilns, again reflecting the significance of imported aromatics in China.[8] Wafting from the mouth of the duck and from the two holes below it, fragrant smoke would have visually and olfactorily enhanced religious and courtly rituals, elegant gatherings, and personal spaces. The duck stands on the upper part of the burner; the lower part is nestled into a two-tiered lotus. The shape of the supporting stand, which was most likely based on metal prototypes, is similar to that of the stand paired with a delicately lobed floral-shaped cup (fig. 2.4) used for drinking either tea or wine. The darker color of the glaze on both the incense burner and the cup derives from the addition of lime to the glaze mixture, as well as from the application of multiple layers of glaze.

A lovely lobed ewer with reticulated decoration (fig. 2.5) is covered with the same characteristic blue-green Qingbai glaze. Standing on a high foot, the ewer

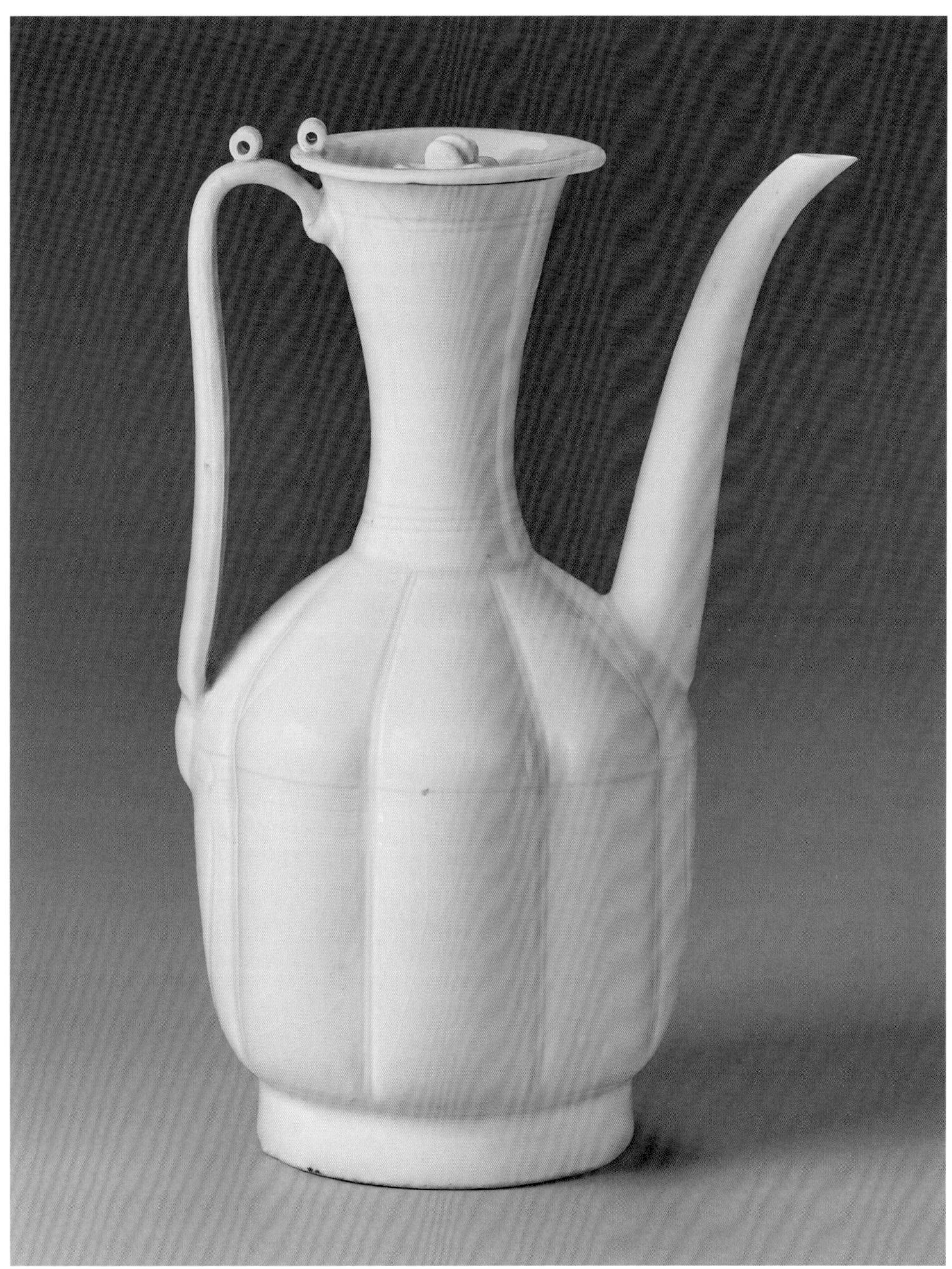

**Fig. 2.5**

*Ewer*, China, Southern Song dynasty, 11th–12th century. Porcelain with molded and incised decoration under glaze (Qingbai ware), 9¼ × 6¼ in. (23.5 × 15.9 cm). Yale University Art Gallery, Gift of Lily L. Chu, B.A. 1982, and Gerald W. Weaver II, B.A. 1977, 2016.53.1a–c

has a long, narrow spout; a handle; and a recessed cover with a stem-shaped knob. Images of leaves are incised below the handle and spout. A small round tab at the top of the handle matches that on the cover, and the two may have been joined with a cloth rope or metal chain that helped keep them together.

This alluring glaze also appears on a bottle with a carved abstract botanical design (fig. 2.6). Used for storing wine made of fermented grains or grapes, the vessel has a small mouth, a cover, and a body that tapers from the shoulder to

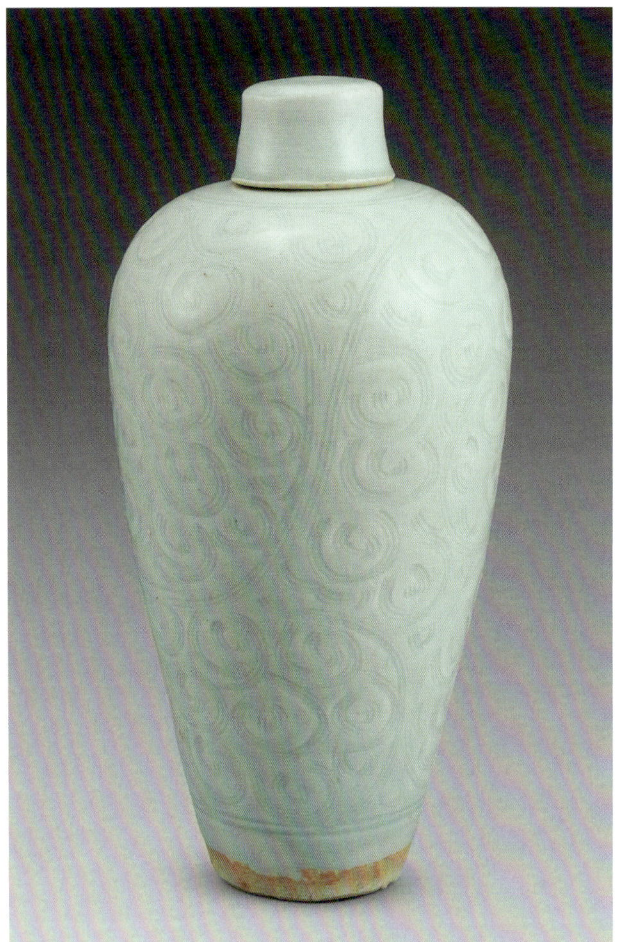

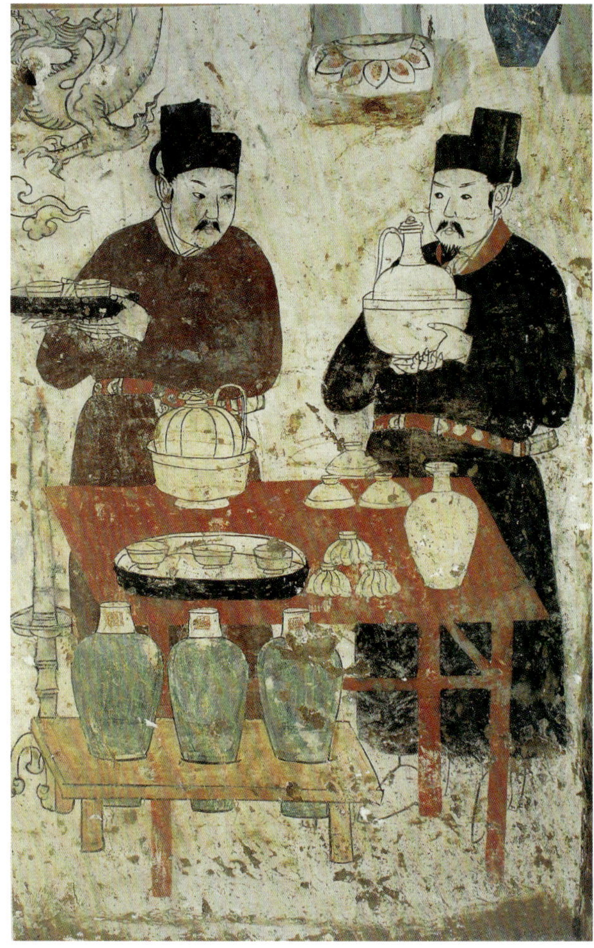

**Fig. 2.6**

*Wine Bottle (Meiping) with a Botanical Design*, China, Southern Song dynasty, 12th–13th century, excavated at Jinyuncun, Suining, China, in 1991. Porcelain with incised decoration under glaze (Qingbai ware), H. 8⅞ in. (22.5 cm). Sichuan Song Porcelain Museum, Suining, China

**Fig. 2.7**

*Banquet Preparation* (detail), from the tomb of Zhang Shiqing, China, Hebei Province, Liao dynasty, 1116. Water-based pigment over clay mixed with straw

the foot. Examples of this type of bottle first appeared in northern China around the eleventh century and were initially called *jingping*, or "vessel with straight sides." The name was changed to *meiping*, meaning "plum flower vase," around the eighteenth century, when bottles of this shape were also used to display branches of flowering blossoms.

Three ceramic *meiping*-shaped bottles—each covered with lead-green glaze—are depicted in a mural showing the preparations for a banquet (fig. 2.7) from the tomb of Zhang Shiqing, one of several tombs excavated from a cemetery near the city of Zhangjiakou, in Hebei, in 1971. Zhang, who died in 1116 at the age of seventy-four, was a Han Chinese who served in prominent positions, including chancellor of a university, under the Qidan Liao dynasty. In the foreground of the mural, the three bottles are set into a red lacquer stand placed before a table. Wine would have been stored in these larger bottles before it was decanted into smaller ones, such as that at the right on the table. Wine was also served in clay or metal ewers with matching basins that held hot water to keep the wine warm. In the mural, the attendant at the left holds a black lacquer tray with two upturned cups. Of the nine cups on the table, six have simple shapes and three are lobed. Three are upturned, suggesting that they are ready to be filled and offered to guests. Banquet scenes such as this one, and other scenes showing the preparation of tea, are depicted in both tomb paintings and religious murals from the tenth to the fourteenth century, reflecting the prevalence of these activities and illustrating the ways in which refined ceramics enhanced them.

The Qingbai *meiping*-shaped bottle with the botanical design (see fig. 2.6) was unearthed in 1991 in one of two hoards at Jinyuncun, in Suining, Sichuan Province, in the southwest—thousands of miles from the Jingdezhen area where it was produced. Hoards of ceramics dating from the ninth to the fourteenth century have been found throughout China. Typically placed in pits or in tombs that had been abandoned, the hoards were likely used to safeguard the possessions of prominent individuals—or, in this case, merchants' valuable stock—in response to the fighting and disruptions that characterized Chinese history at the time.[9] At Jinyuncun, Hoard 1 contained 774 Qingbai pieces, including this example and five other *meiping*-shaped bottles of varying size and decoration; 368 Longquan wares; a few ceramics from northern Chinese kilns; and several bronze vessels. The Qingbai wine bottles were placed in the top layer of the hoard with other large and unusual pieces, while smaller pieces, particularly bowls that were nestled into one another, made up the lower layers (fig. 2.8). This style of packing matches that used for ship cargo and was likely also used to transport ceramics by river and overland. The two hoards at Jinyuncun were unearthed near the Fujiang River, a tributary of the Yangzi River, and the Jingdezhen kiln complex was near Lake Poyang, which provided access to the Yangzi and its tributaries.

A small dish with two goldfish swimming in a lotus pond (fig. 2.9) represents another object type discovered in Jinyuncun Hoard 1, in which there were six such pieces.[10] The two fish swim in the same direction and are surrounded by large lotus flowers, an auspicious combination expressing wishes for wealth and progeny. Around the fish and flowers are small circles that are similar to the ring matting often found on silver vessels—another example of the sharing of shapes and designs in Chinese clay and metalwork. The dish has a flat bottom and an unglazed rim; the latter indicates that the dish was fired upside down, a technique practiced in Chinese kilns after the twelfth century. Like the use of molds to create the dish shape and fish, this method allowed for the firing of a greater number of pieces at one time. After the dish was fired, the unglazed rim would have been covered with a bronze, gold, or silver band. Small dishes such as this example and another in the shape of a chrysanthemum (fig. 2.10) (a type not found in Jinyuncun Hoard 1) were used to offer individual servings of

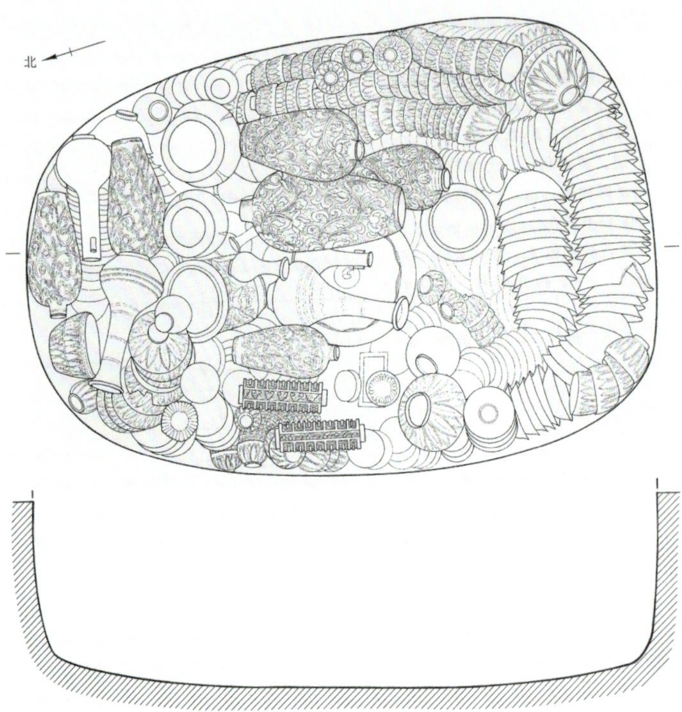


**Fig. 2.8**

Drawing showing the placement of Longquan, Qingbai, and other ceramics in Hoard 1, excavated at Jinyuncun, Suining, China, in 1991

**Fig. 2.9**

*Dish with Two Fish in a Lotus Pond*, China, Southern Song dynasty, mid-13th century. Porcelain with molded decoration under glaze (Qingbai ware), H. ¾ × DIAM. 4 in. (1.91 × 10.1 cm). Yale University Art Gallery, Wayland Wells Williams, B.A. 1910, Collection, Gift of Mrs. Frances Wayland Williams, 1948.46

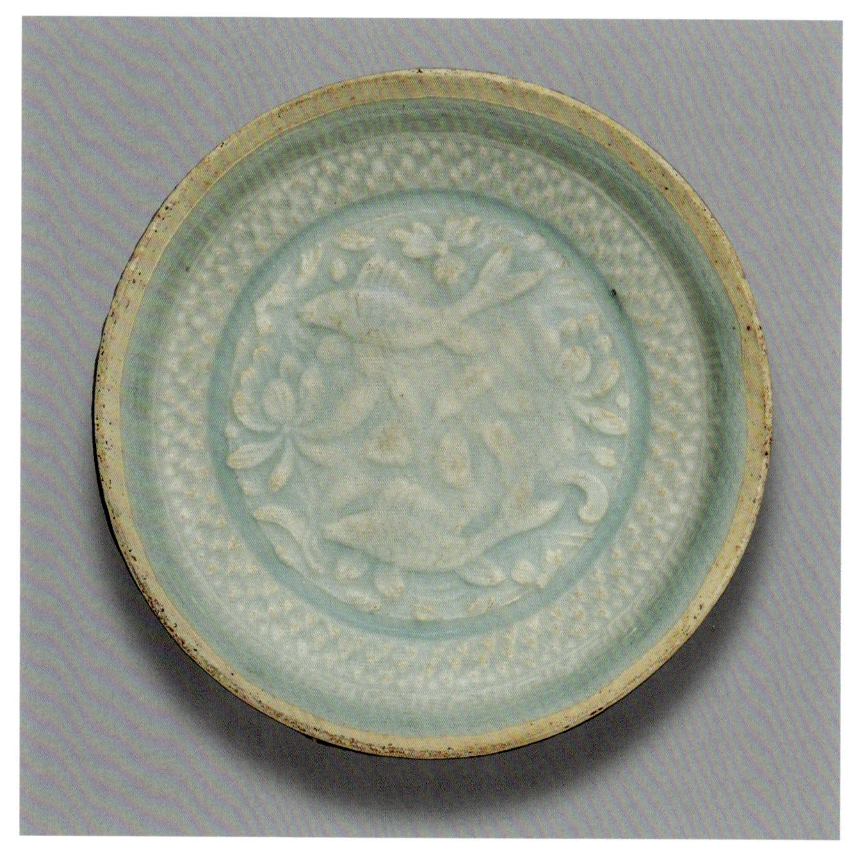

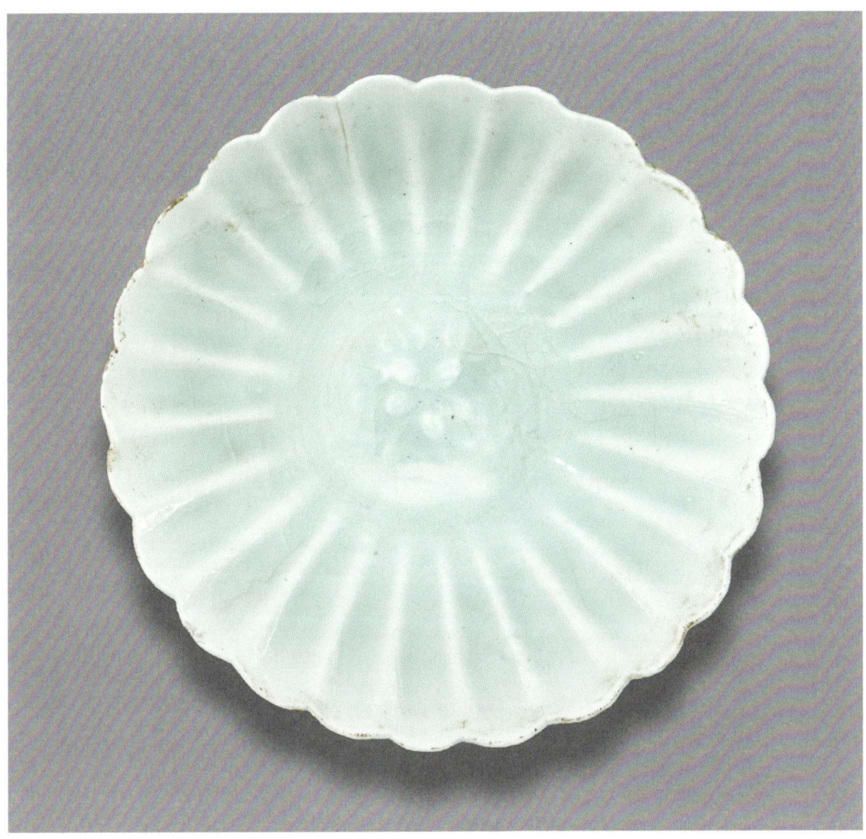

**Fig. 2.10**

*Dish in the Shape of a Chrysanthemum*, China, Southern Song dynasty, 12th–13th century. Porcelain, molded, with glaze (Qingbai ware), H. 1¾ × DIAM. 4½ in. (4.5 × 11.4 cm). Yale University Art Gallery, Hobart and Edward Small Moore Memorial Collection, Gift of Mrs. William H. Moore, 1954.49.46

candy or another delicacy. The chrysanthemum is multivalent in Chinese culture: it symbolizes longevity and other blessings and can be used in medicine or to make wine and tea.

Both the Longquan kilns in Zhejiang and the Qingbai kilns in Jiangxi also made clay sculptures, generally representations of religious figures; however, sculptures were a more significant aspect of production in Jiangxi, particularly in the thirteenth and fourteenth centuries. A representation of the Buddhist deity Bodhisattva Avalokiteshvara, known as Guanyin in Chinese (fig. 2.11), illustrates the style of sculptures produced in the Qingbai kilns during the Mongol Yuan dynasty. Guanyin—the embodiment of the virtue of compassion—was the most popular Buddhist deity in Asia from the tenth to the fourteenth century. The figure sits with its right leg upright and bent at the knee and its left leg folded in front. Known as the "posture of royal ease," this position indicates that Guanyin is shown in the Water-Moon (Shuiyue) manifestation, one of its thirty-three principal avatars. Images of Guanyin in this posture represent the bodhisattva in a personal pure land, or paradise, known as Mount Potalaka, a perfect realm practitioners could visit to help achieve enlightenment, the ultimate goal of practice. Although Potalaka was initially understood to be located somewhere in the Indian Ocean, by the twelfth century it had mysteriously been translocated to Mount Putuo, an island off the coast of Zhejiang that was renamed after the mythical Indian mountain and remains a popular pilgrimage site. Guanyin wears clothing derived from Indian monastic garb, including a long, saronglike lower garment and a short cape with ribbons or ties. In addition to a diadem with long ribbons, the bodhisattva wears a spectacular necklace and a girdle, earrings, and bracelets. This jewelry, which can also be seen in contemporaneous Tibetan sculptures and paintings, illustrates the importance of Tibetan Buddhist traditions at the Yuan court and the spread of these practices and related imagery to southern China.[11]

Qingbai sculptures were not important as trade goods (though a few small, and not particularly elegant, examples have been found in the Philippines). Qingbai vases and dishes, on the other hand, were traded throughout China, as exemplified by the objects in the Jinyuncun hoard, and abroad. Like the Yue and Longquan wares from Zhejiang, Qingbai wares were traded to Korea and Japan as well as to West Asia and the east coast of Africa.[12] Examples were discovered in the tenth-century Intan and Cirebon shipwrecks and in the twelfth- to thirteenth-century Jepara wreck, near Java, and the Nanhai I wreck, both of which contained ceramics from various kilns.[13] They were also found in the fourteenth-century Sinan wreck.

The delicate beading in the adornments on the sculpture of Guanyin also appears on the famed fourteenth-century Gaignières-Fonthill Vase (fig. 2.12), one of the first Chinese Qingbai pieces—and one of the first examples of porcelain—to reach Europe. On this vase, the beading articulates the abstract curls on the neck and outlines the four cartouches on the body. Peonies and chrysanthemums, respectively signifying summer and autumn, and wealth and longevity, fill the cartouches, while Indo-Tibetan-style lotus petals decorate the lower part of the vase. The three-dimensionality of the surface—a result of the extensive use of raised beads and the deep relief carving of the flowers and leaves in the cartouches (which are not found in Southern Song ceramics)—illustrates the taste of the ruling Yuan dynasty in the late thirteenth and fourteenth centuries.

Defined by a globular body, narrowing neck, and flared mouth, vessels of this type are known as *yuhuchun* (usually translated as "spring jade vase [or jar]"), a term that derives from a line in a poem by the Tang-dynasty author Sikong Shu that describes wine as "spring in a jar."[14] Vessels in this shape, made in clay or metal, first appeared in China around the eleventh century and most likely also had an imported glass prototype. One example is depicted in the mural in the tomb of Zhang Shiqing.

The Gaignières-Fonthill Vase is renowned not only for its beauty and elegance, and for the technical sophistication underlying its shape and decoration,

**Fig. 2.11**

*Bodhisattva Avalokiteshvara in Water-Moon Manifestation (Shuiyue Guanyin)*, China, Yuan dynasty, 14th century. Porcelain with molded and applied decoration under glaze (Qingbai ware), H. 10½ in. (26.7 cm). Victoria and Albert Museum, London, C.30-1968

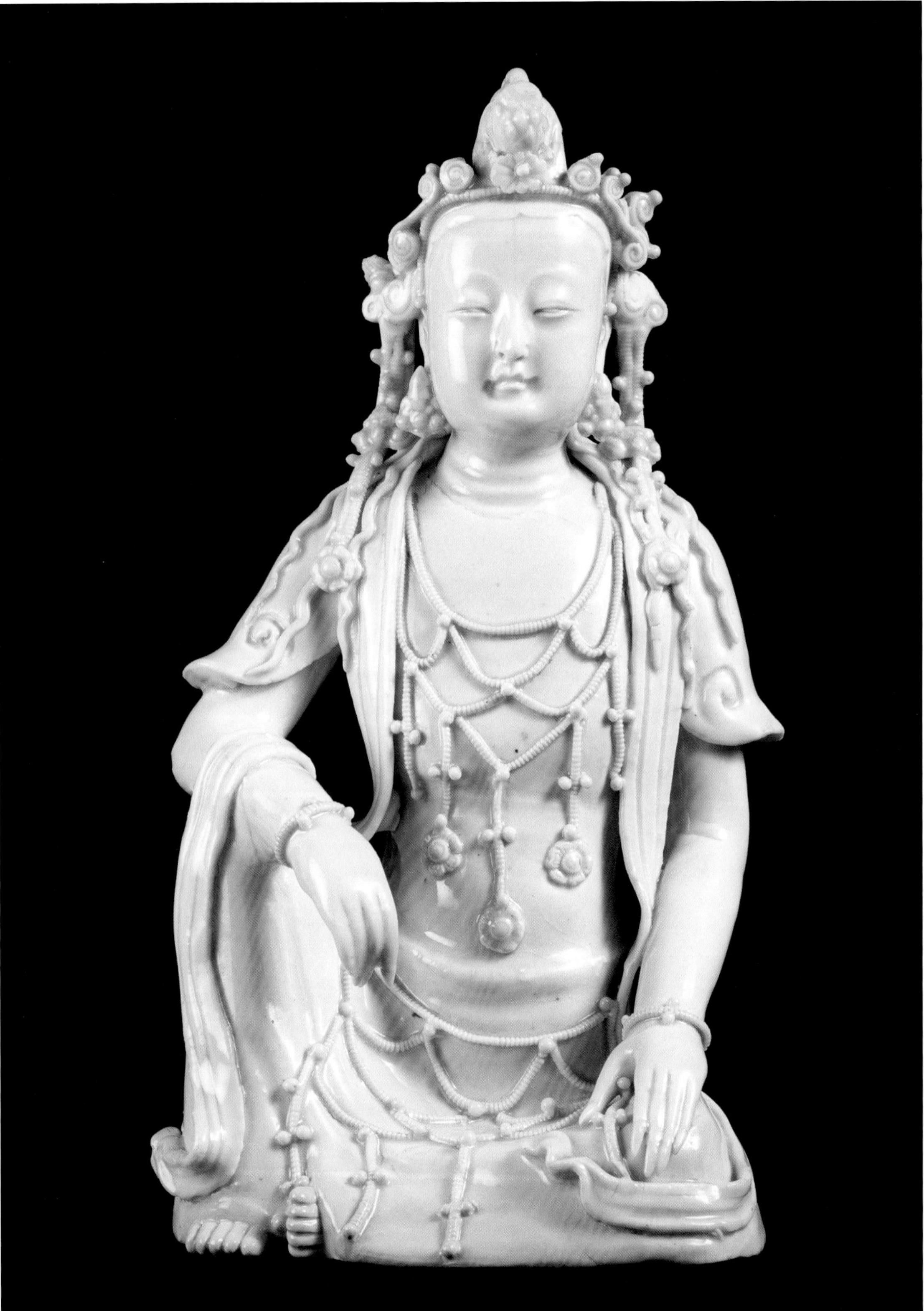

but also for its unusually well-documented history. The vase is thought to have been a gift to Louis the Great of Hungary (r. 1342–82) from the Yuan delegation to Pope Benedict XII in 1338. Not long after its arrival in Hungary, the vase was fitted with gilt silver and enamel mounts on the cover, handle, spout, and foot (now removed). Embellishing Chinese and Japanese porcelain objects with gold and silver mounts was a standard practice in Europe for centuries.[15] The mounts, which bear the coat of arms of Louis the Great, help prove that the Gaignières-Fonthill Vase was in Europe in the fourteenth century.[16] Louis presented the mounted vase to his relative Charles III of Naples (r. 1382–86) in 1381. The vase was later owned by Louis, the Grand Dauphin, the eldest son of Louis XIV (r. 1643–1715), the famous Sun King of France. In the eighteenth century, it was in the collection of François Lefèvre de Caumartin, who allowed it to be depicted in a work in 1713 by Barthélemy Remy (fig. 2.13), valet to Roger de Gaignières, thereby providing the only record of the appearance of the vase with its elaborate mounts. It was later in the possession of William Beckford of Fonthill Abbey, near Salisbury, England, as well as that of John Farquhar, another owner of Fonthill Abbey, before it was sold at auction in 1882. The vase is now in the National Museum of Ireland, in Dublin.

Chinese ceramics had a transformative impact in Europe when they first arrived there in the fourteenth century and as they became widely available in the late sixteenth and early seventeenth centuries. As had been the case in West Asia in the ninth and tenth centuries, when Chinese ceramics first appeared there in significant numbers, nothing as beautiful, strong, and hygienic as ceramic objects like the Gaignières-Fonthill Vase had ever been made or used in Europe up to that time. Before the introduction of Chinese porcelain in large quantities, people had been eating and drinking from wood, silver, or pewter vessels or, in some cases, earthenware covered with a white glaze derived from tin (maiolica). It is therefore not surprising that, rather than using this extraordinary example of Qingbai ware as a bottle, as originally intended, or as a vase, its early European owners fitted it with decorative mounts, had it prominently displayed, and ultimately repurposed it as a much-desired diplomatic gift.

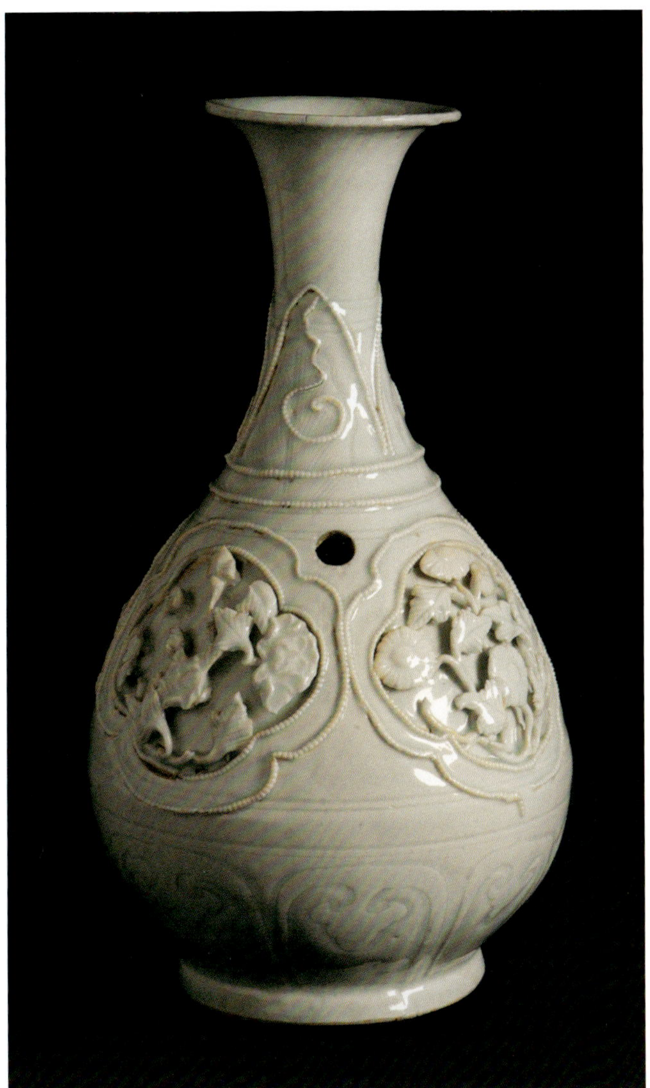

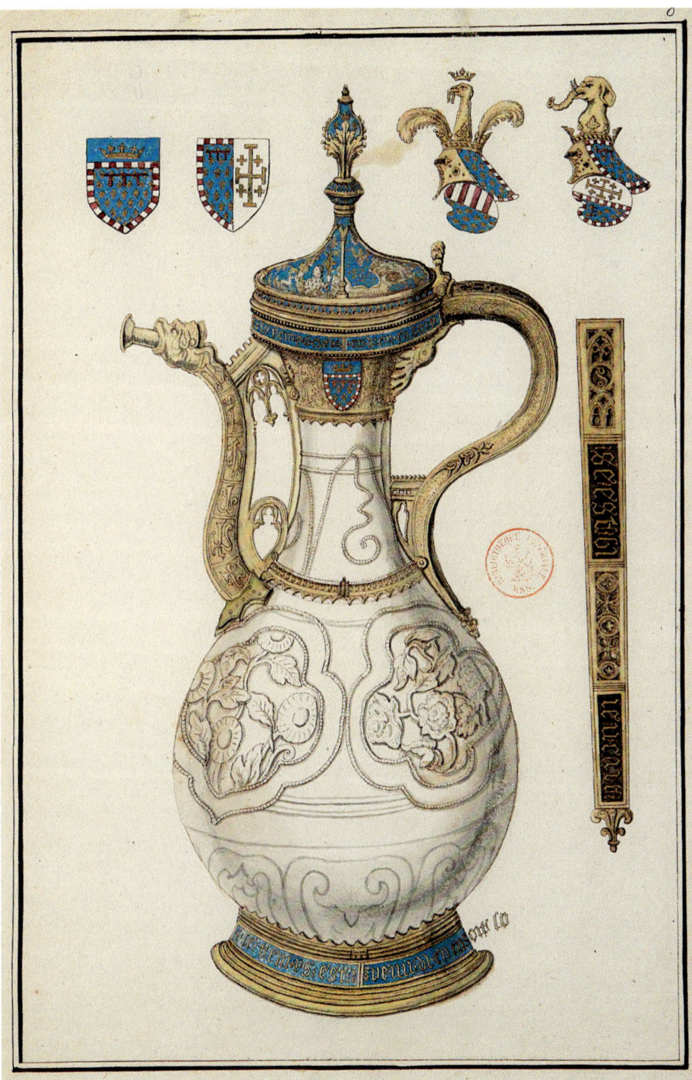

**Fig. 2.12**

*Vase with Floral Cartouches, known as the Gaignières-Fonthill Vase*, China, Yuan dynasty, early 14th century. Porcelain with molded, carved, incised, and applied decoration under glaze (Qingbai ware), H. 11⅛ in. (28.3 cm). National Museum of Ireland, Dublin

**Fig. 2.13**

Barthélemy Remy, *Gaignières-Fonthill Vase with Gilt Silver Mounts*, 1713. Ink wash on paper, 20⅞ × 15 in. (53 × 38 cm). Bibliothèque Nationale de France, Paris, Département des Manuscrits, Français 20070, fol. 8

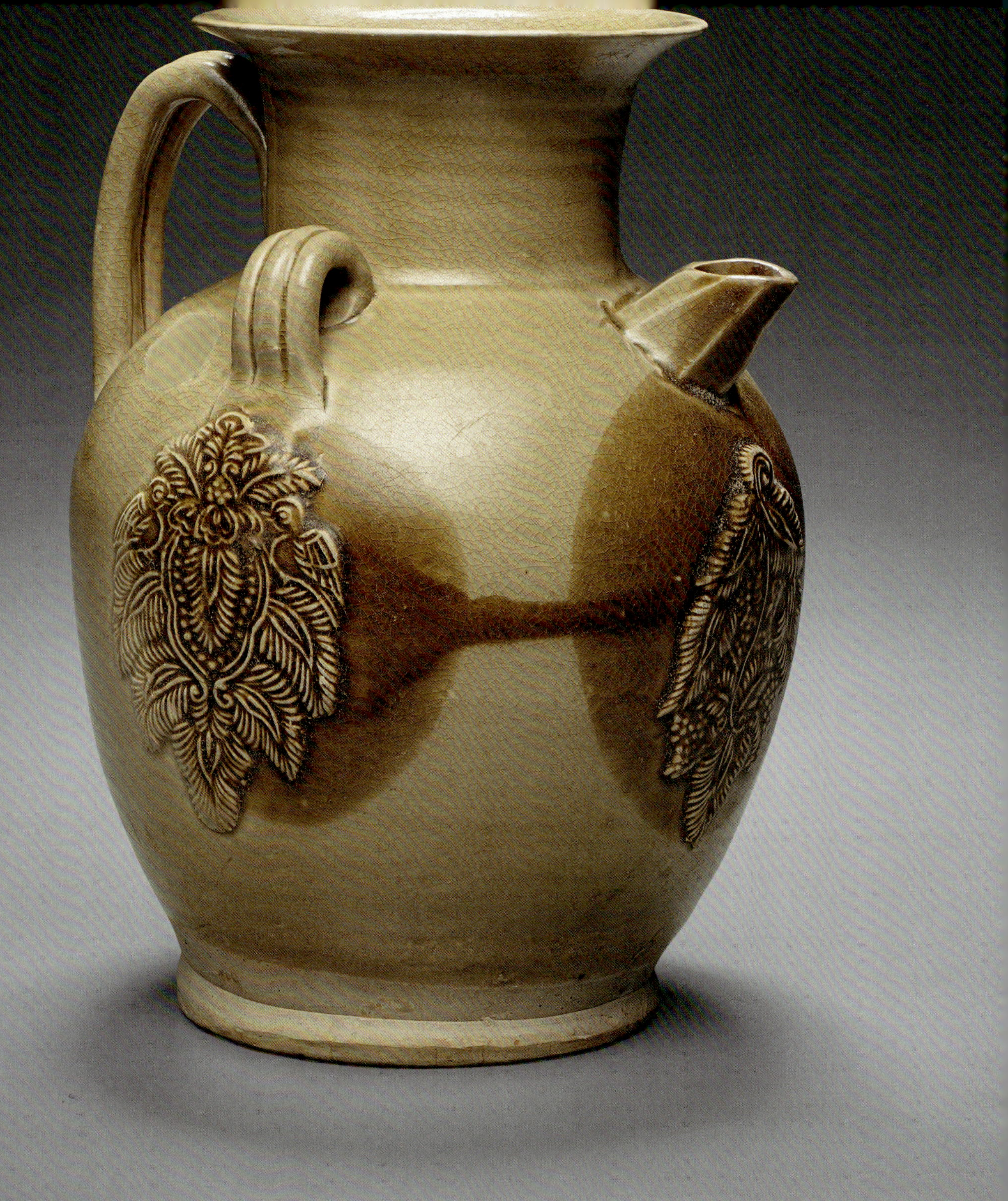

CHAPTER 3

# Hunan Province: Xiangyin, Changsha, and Hengyang Wares

In the ninth and tenth centuries, while kilns in the Yue and Longquan areas of Zhejiang Province and those making Qingbai wares in the Jingdezhen region of Jiangxi Province developed the green-glazed wares that would come to be known as "celadons," kilns in landlocked Hunan Province, in the southwest, were producing imaginative and distinctive local wares, some with shapes and designs similar to those produced in complexes on the eastern seaboard. The Xiangyin kilns, in the eponymous prefecture on the southeastern shore of Lake Dongting, in northeast Hunan, were active from the fourth to the ninth century C.E. The Changsha kilns, farther south, were active from the eighth to the tenth century. Both the Xiangyin and Changsha kilns were located near the Xiang River, the largest in Hunan, which runs from north to south. While Xiangyin wares were traded domestically, Changsha wares were traded throughout China and overseas. Ceramics that were transported north on the Xiang River were connected to the Yangzi River and ports such as that at Yangzhou; those moving south were connected via tributaries to the city of Guangzhou, another important port from the eighth to the tenth century. Neither Xiangyin nor Changsha wares were made after the tenth century, when production in Hunan shifted to the area around the city of Hengyang, also near the Xiang River. Kilns there began to make ceramics with green glazes that echoed the shapes and colors of the contemporaneous, popular, and highly coveted Longquan and Qingbai wares.

### Xiangyin Ware, 4th to 10th Century C.E.

Active from the Eastern Jin dynasty (317–420 C.E.) to the early Tang dynasty, the Xiangyin kilns crafted vessels for drinking, eating, writing, and other daily activities. The ceramics produced there are characterized by their iron-rich red clay and crackled yellow-green glazes, both of which can be seen in a chicken-headed ewer (fig. 3.1). Chickens are a sign of fertility and therefore signify the growth of families and populations, and chicken-headed ewers were understood to be auspicious. Produced in kilns throughout southern China from the fourth to the sixth century C.E., they often show slight regional differences in their shapes or glazes. The broad, squat body and short neck of this example and of a comparable piece made in the Yue kilns in Zhejiang (fig. 3.2) date them to the late fourth or early fifth century. Both ewers have a wide rim at the mouth, a tapering handle, and two small, square lugs. Details such as the eyes and cockscomb were shaped separately and applied to the surface prior to glazing. The handle of the Xiangyin piece has three incised lines at the top, suggestive of feet or claws, and the Yue piece has greater detail in the face of the chicken. Moreover, the Yue work has gray clay and a gray-green glaze, which further distinguish it from the Xiangyin ewer, with its buff clay and crazing. The crazing in the Xiangyin glaze may have been either a deliberate surface

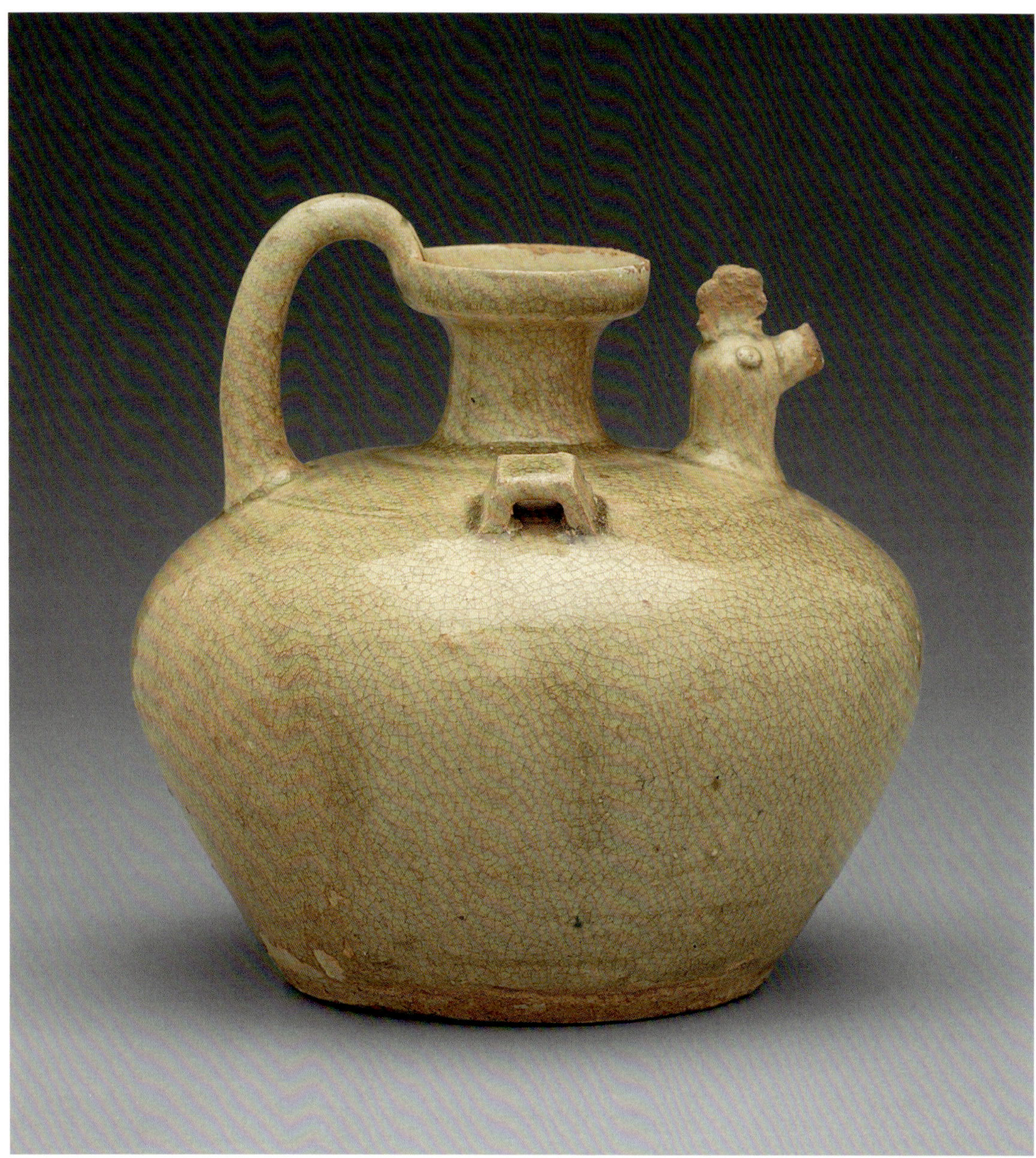

**Fig. 3.1**

*Chicken-Headed Ewer*, China, Northern and Southern Dynasties period, 4th–5th century C.E. Stoneware with glaze (Xiangyin ware), H. 5½ × DIAM. 3¼ in. (14 × 8.3 cm). Yale University Art Gallery, Gift of John Hadley Cox, B.A. 1935, 1941.18

effect or a flaw resulting from a less well-developed glaze formula or a lack of control during firing.

An inkstone with five water wells (fig. 3.3) represents a unique Xiangyin product. The user would have ground a stick composed of soot, glue, and another material, such as incense, on the center of the inkstone and added water from the wells to make ink for writing and painting. Like the Xiangyin chicken-headed ewer, this implement was potted with an iron-rich red clay and covered with the characteristic crackled yellow-green glaze.

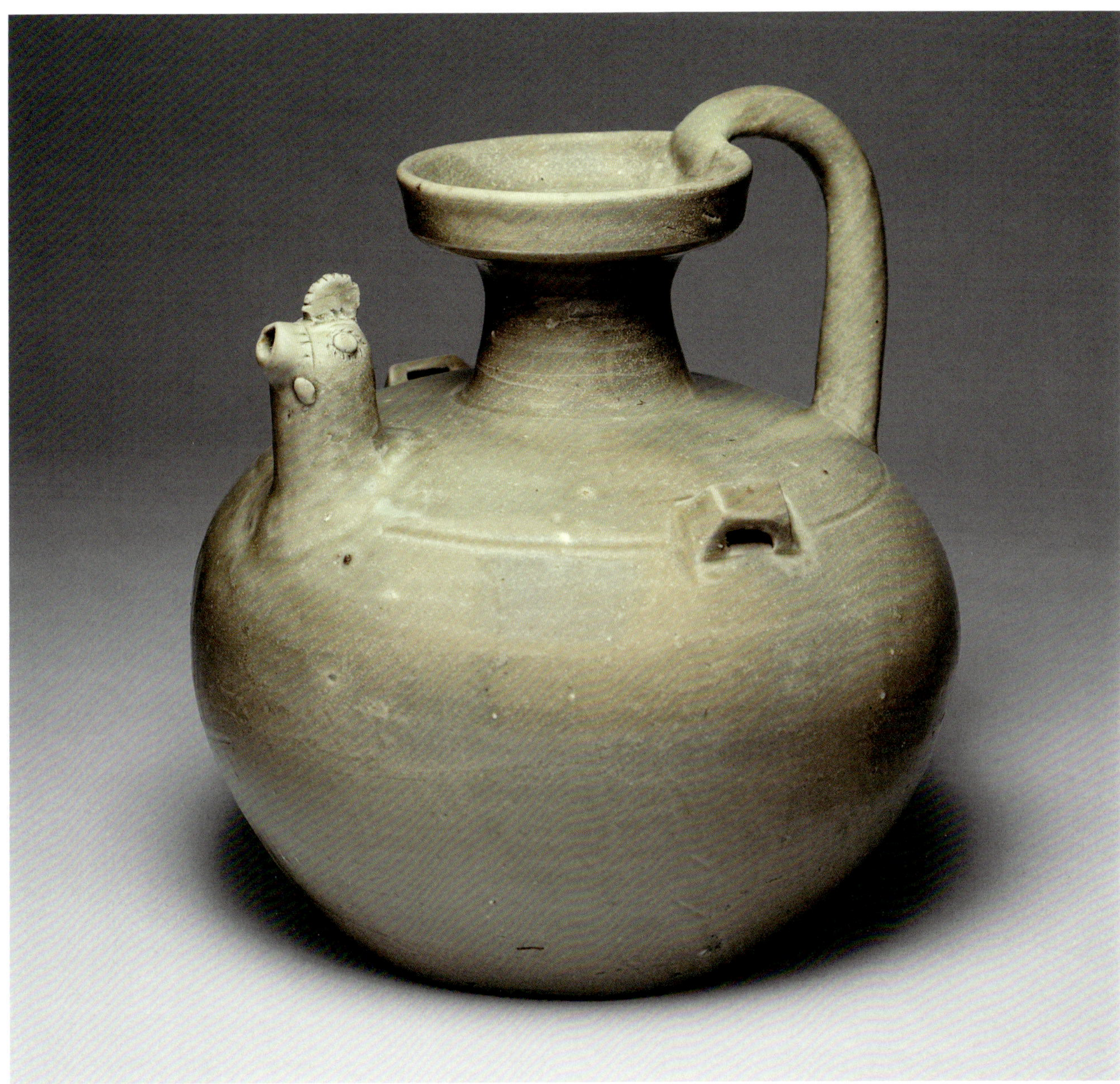

**Fig. 3.2**

*Chicken-Headed Ewer*, China, Eastern Jin dynasty, 4th–5th century C.E. Stoneware with glaze (Yue ware), H. 7 5/16 × DIAM. 7 1/16 in. (18.5 × 18 cm). Princeton University Art Museum, N.J., Gift of Richard and Ruth Dickes, 2004-448

Although they have not been found in excavations in other parts of China, Xiangyin wares are mentioned by Lu Yu in his foundational eighth-century book *The Classic of Tea*, indicating that they had gained recognition beyond Hunan. Lu listed them as "Yuezhou" wares, after an ancient name for the region in which they were produced, and rated them just below the gray-green Yue wares from Zhejiang and the white Xing wares from Hebei Province as suitable for drinking tea.[1] Two small cups (fig. 3.4), in slightly different sizes, were made with the typical iron-rich clay and covered with a crackled yellowish-green glaze,

**Fig. 3.3**

*Inkstone with Five Water Wells*, China, Sui or Tang dynasty, 6th–7th century C.E. Stoneware with glaze (Xiangyin ware), H. 1 × DIAM. 3⅞ in. (2.5 × 9.8 cm). Yale University Art Gallery, Gift of John Hadley Cox, B.A. 1935, 1950.189

**Fig. 3.4**

(left) *Cup*, China, Northern and Southern Dynasties period, 5th–6th century C.E. Stoneware with glaze (Xiangyin ware), H. 2 × DIAM. 3 in. (5.1 × 7.6 cm). Yale University Art Gallery, Gift of John Hadley Cox, B.A. 1935, 1950.187. (right) *Cup*, China, Southern Dynasties period, 5th–6th century C.E. Stoneware with glaze (Xiangyin ware), H. 1⅝ × DIAM. 2⅝ in. (4.1 × 6.7 cm). Yale University Art Gallery, Gift of John Hadley Cox, B.A. 1935, 1941.20.b

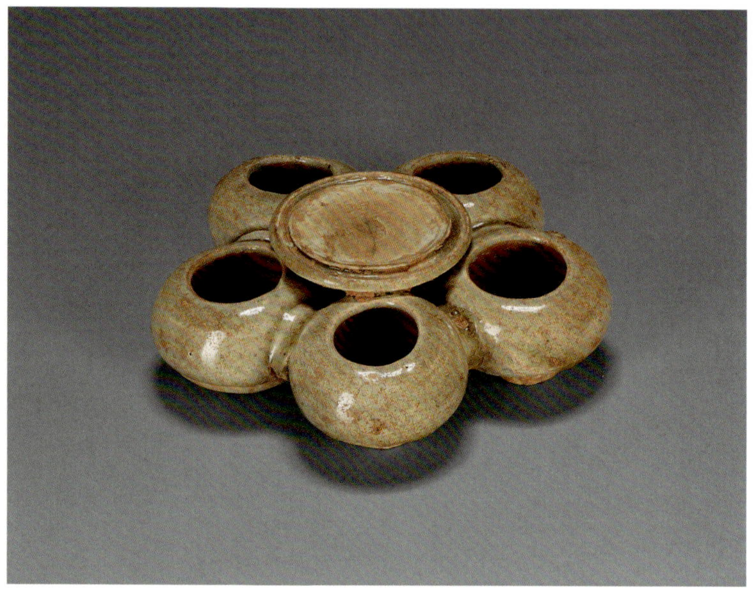

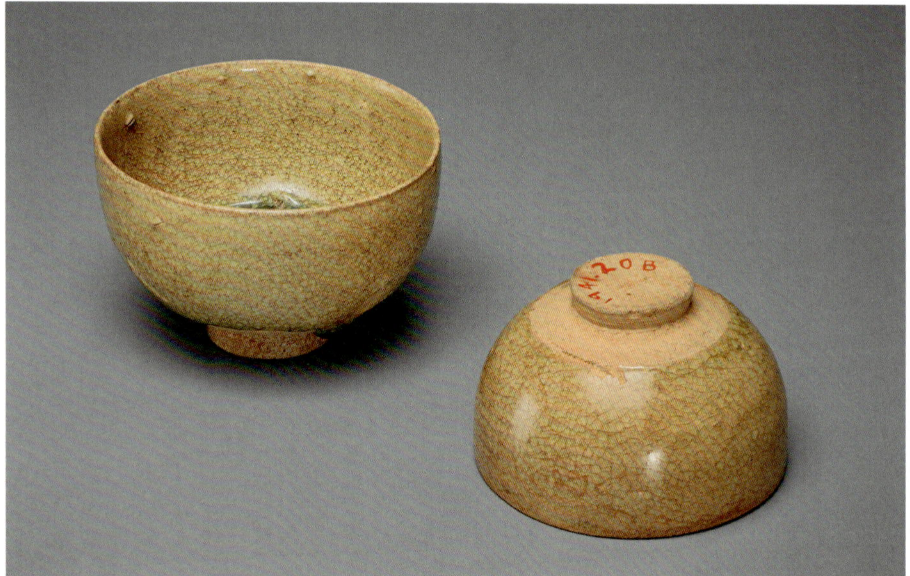

which pooled into a darker green in the interior and on the edges of the exterior. Like all works produced in the Xiangyin kilns, these cups are not glazed toward the base or on the foot. On a few excavated examples of this type of cup, the phrase *da guan*, or "great official," is impressed into the base,[2] indicating that the pieces were considered among the best products of the Xiangyin kilns and that they were reserved for the use of local and regional governments or possibly sent north to the courts of the Sui and Tang dynasties—further attesting to the value awarded to certain Hunanese ceramics at the time.

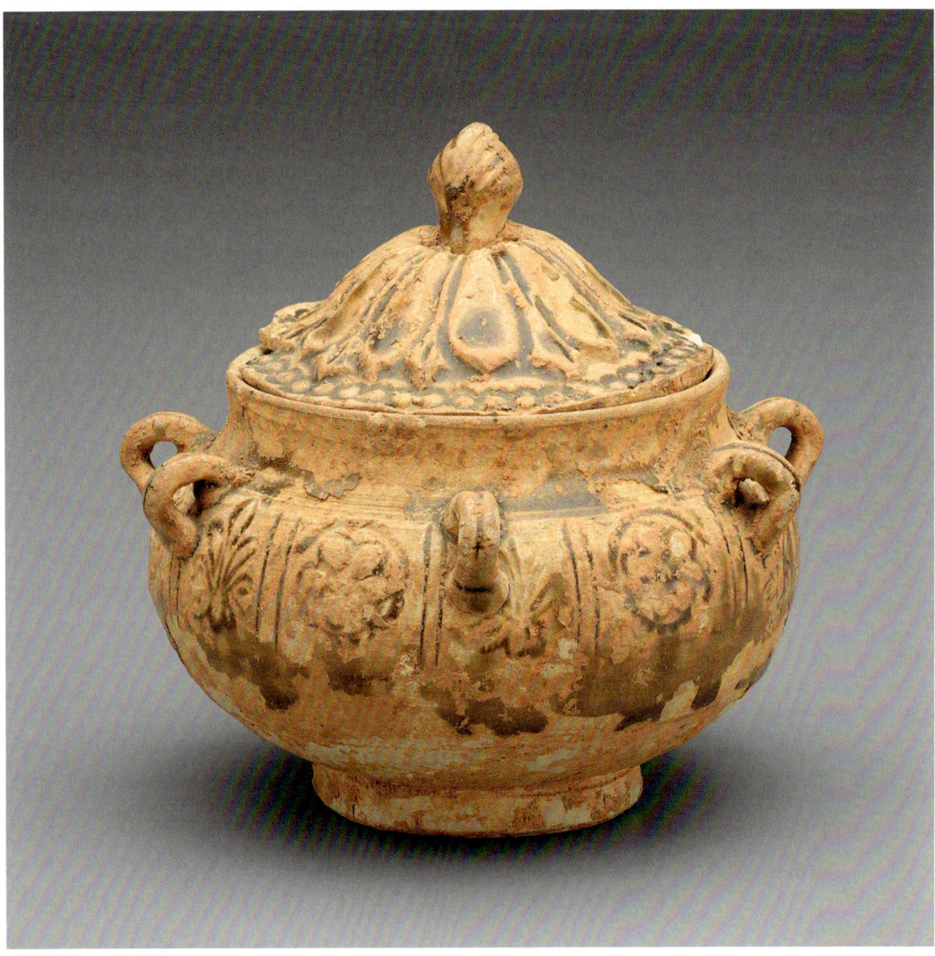

**Fig. 3.5**

*Jar with Flowers and Palmettes*, China, Sui or Tang dynasty, 6th–7th century C.E. Stoneware with carved, stamped, and applied decoration under glaze (Xiangyin ware), H. 4¼ × DIAM. 4½ in. (10.8 × 11.4 cm). Yale University Art Gallery, Gift of John Hadley Cox, B.A. 1935, 1940.379

A charming jar with carved and stamped designs of flowers and palmettes subdivided by incised vertical lines (fig. 3.5) represents another unusual Xiangyin object that was made in the sixth and seventh centuries. The jar has a cover shaped like an open lotus flower and five lugs on one side yet none on the other—a perplexing configuration that may have been used for attaching cords to the cover, though it would not have been particularly stable. The color of the glaze, which has abraded, is similar to the dark green in the interior of the two Xiangyin cups.

## Changsha Ware, 8th to 10th Century

By the late eighth century, the Changsha kilns, centered in the area of Lakes Machang and Shizu, were the most prominent in Hunan Province, making bowls, dishes, writing implements, and small figures of people and animals (probably toys[3]) for domestic consumption and overseas trade. A pronounced nose, bulging eyes, and heavy eyebrows define the face of the tiger supporting

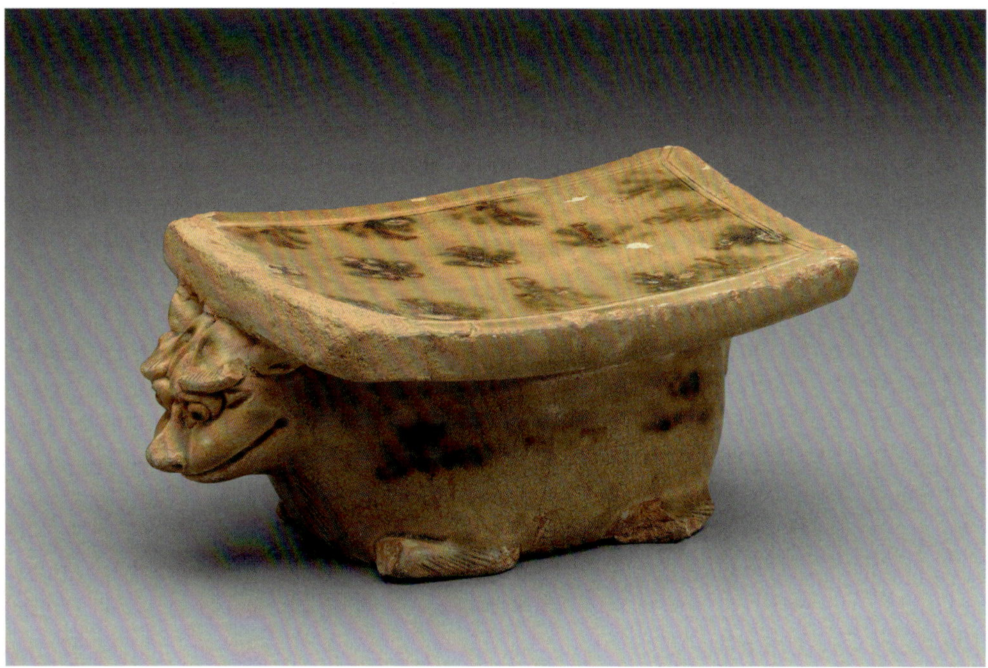

**Fig. 3.6**

*Head or Wrist Rest in the Shape of a Tiger*, China, Tang dynasty, 9th century C.E. Stoneware with slip and iron-brown and copper-green pigment under glaze (Changsha ware), 2⅞ × 6¼ × 4 in. (7.3 × 15.9 × 10.2 cm). Yale University Art Gallery, Gift of John Hadley Cox, B.A. 1935, 1940.363

**Fig. 3.7**

Changsha bowls from the Belitung shipwreck, near Sumatra, Indonesia. Asian Civilisations Museum, Singapore, Tang Shipwreck Collection

a small ceramic rest made in the Changsha kilns (fig. 3.6). The creature's paws are visible at the bottom, and its stubby tail protrudes at the back. At the top are painted designs of ferns similar to the stamped decoration on the covered jar from the Xiangyin kilns (see fig. 3.5). Rests like this had various functions: some supported a person's neck (typically a woman with an elaborate hair style) and are therefore defined as pillows, while others—particularly smaller ones such as this—were used to brace a person's wrist while they were writing or having their pulse taken during a medical examination.

The Changsha kilns were the first in China to extensively use pigment in the decoration of ceramics. The works were crafted using red, light gray, or buff clay, brushed with a white slip, and then painted with a brown pigment derived from iron or a green pigment derived from copper, before being covered with a thin yellowish-green or straw-colored glaze. Painted freehand in a lively, spontaneous manner, the whimsical and engaging designs on Changsha wares generally represent abstracted botanical motifs, though landscapes, birds and other animals, people, and buildings were depicted as well. Changsha wares were also the first Chinese ceramics to be sent overseas in large quantities. As previously mentioned, they made up the bulk of the cargo recovered from the Belitung shipwreck. Painted bowls, each measuring about five inches in diameter, comprised the majority of the Changsha wares in this wreck (fig. 3.7).

Changsha wares were the first Chinese ceramics to have inscriptions written on them, some of which state that the items were used for drinking tea and

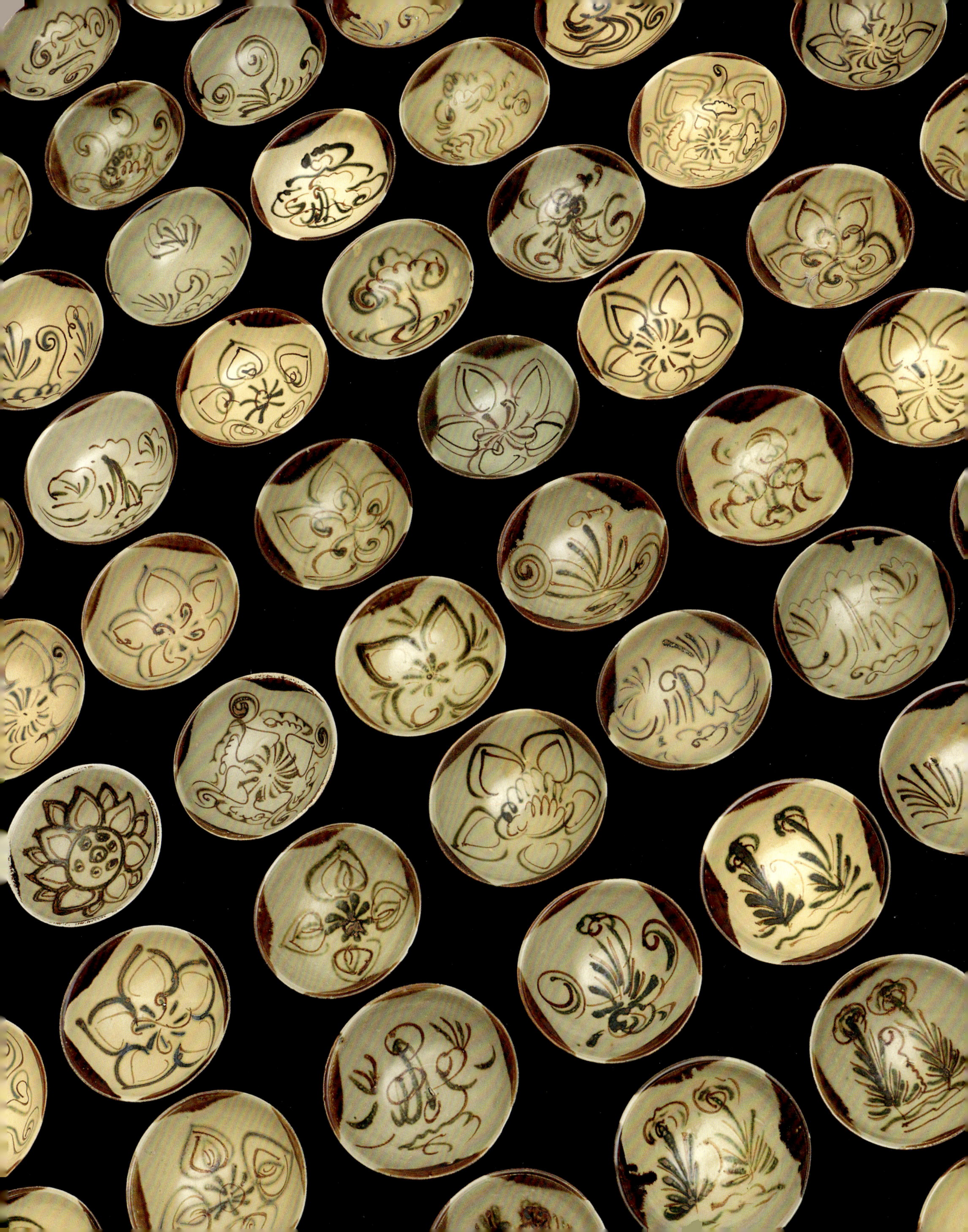

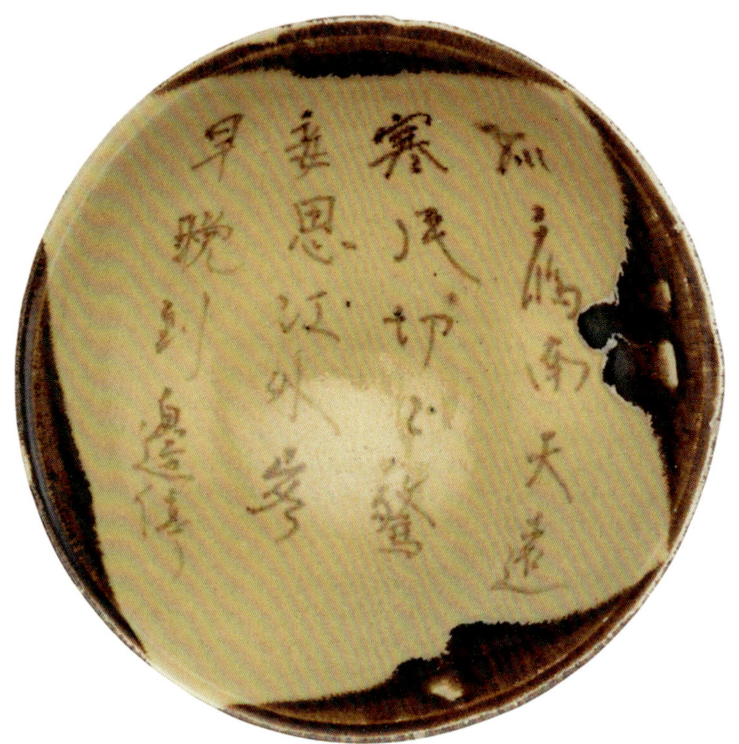

**Fig. 3.8**

*Bowl with a Poem*, China, Tang dynasty, 9th century C.E., excavated from the Belitung shipwreck, near Sumatra, Indonesia, in 1998. Stoneware with slip and iron-brown pigment under glaze (Changsha ware), DIAM. 5 15/16 in. (15.1 cm). Asian Civilisations Museum, Singapore, 2005.1.00578

wine.[4] Other inscriptions are excerpts from poems.[5] Some of the poems are identifiable, but others are unknown, possibly local verses, such as that on a bowl discovered in the Belitung shipwreck (fig. 3.8) that was probably used for drinking:

> The lonely goose has flown to the far southern skies,
> and the cold wind startles one with mournful whispers.
> The maiden pines for that guest flown by on the rivers,
> who sooner or later will come back to cross the frontier.[6]

The discovery of such inscriptions on ceramics in the cargo of a ship that had sailed so far from China raises interesting questions regarding the taste and knowledge of merchants and consumers of Changsha wares in the ninth century. Although many of the merchants and their affiliates throughout maritime Asia were multilingual, not everyone could read Chinese. It is possible that the inscriptions on pieces like those found in the Belitung were understood throughout Asia as symbols of a Chinese culture that consumers perceived as intriguing and exotic.

The expansion of production at the Changsha kilns sometime around 780 C.E. may have reflected the need for new products among foreign merchants living in China at the time. Foreign merchants in Jiangsu Province had been attacked in 760 as part of the looting of Yangzhou, one of many disruptions in the eighth and ninth centuries that ultimately led to the dissolution of the Tang

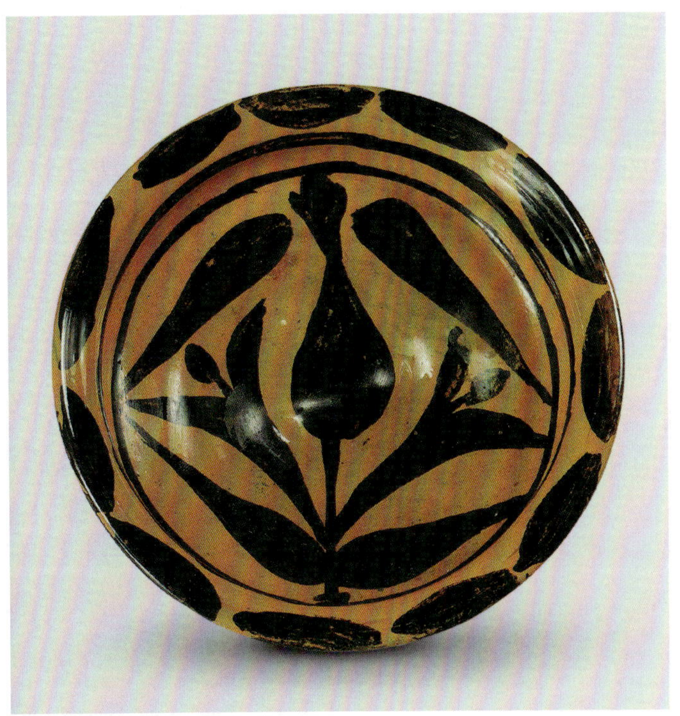

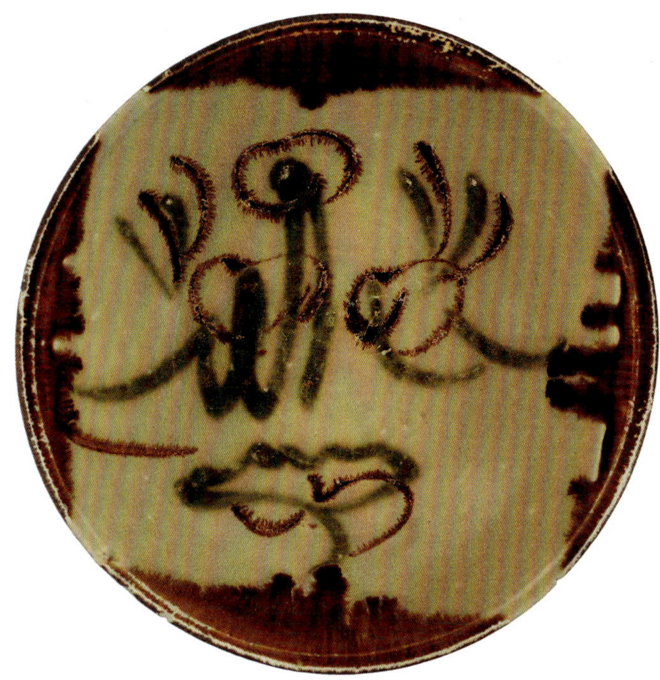

**Fig. 3.9**

*Dish with a Floral Design*, Iraq, Abbasid period, 9th century C.E., excavated from Famen Temple, Xi'an, China, in 1987–88. Glass with enamel, DIAM. 5½ in. (14 cm). Famen Temple Museum, Xi'an, China

**Fig. 3.10**

*Bowl with a Floral Design*, China, Tang dynasty, early 9th century C.E. Stoneware with slip under glaze (Changsha ware), H. 2⅛ × DIAM. 6⅛ in. (5.3 × 15.5 cm). Art Gallery of New South Wales, Sydney, Gift of Steven Zador 2003, 353.2003

dynasty in the early tenth century. It seems likely that at least some of those individuals fled to a more hospitable location that already had goods they could buy and sell to maintain their businesses. References to designs in West Asian visual traditions play an interesting role in the decoration of Changsha wares; it is possible that the merchants who were trading them during this period collaborated with the potters to develop motifs that could appeal to a range of consumers.

Although no comparable piece has been found in Hunan, a rare early Iraqi glass dish (fig. 3.9), excavated from the crypt of the pagoda at the Famen Temple between 1987 and 1988, has a painted enamel design that is strikingly similar to the oval, brown borders on the edges of bowls produced in the Changsha kilns. Moreover, the semiabstract depiction of a bud, two blossoms, and leaves at the center of the Iraqi dish is comparable to the rendering of buds and leaves at the center of one of the Changsha bowls recovered from the Belitung (fig. 3.10). On both the Iraqi glass dish and the Chinese ceramic bowl, the leaves of the flowers are depicted as broad, flat forms with little articulation—a style of painting also found in contemporaneous Iraqi and Iranian ceramics.[7]

Tang-period China was linked to the Sasanian Empire (224–651 C.E.) and, later, the Umayyad caliphate (661–750 C.E.) overland via the Silk Road, which enabled artistic and cultural exchanges. These expanded and developed in the late eighth and ninth centuries, as maritime trade allowed for the transfer of a much greater quantity and range of goods (more goods could be transported

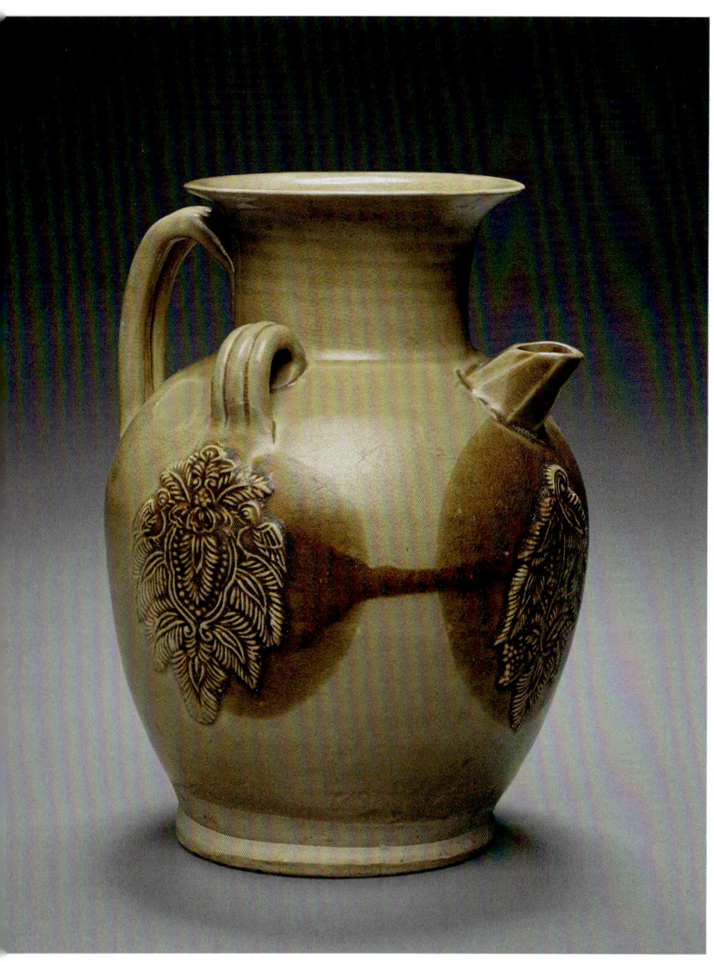

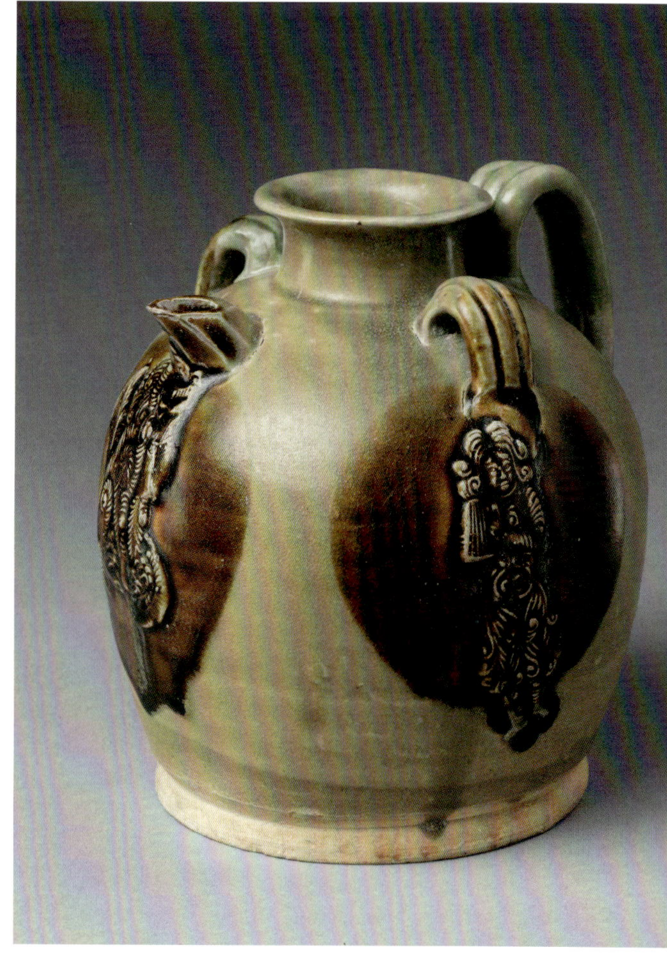

**Fig. 3.11**

*Ewer with Date Palms and Birds*, China, Tang dynasty, 9th century C.E. Stoneware with slip, applied decoration, and iron-brown splashes under glaze (Changsha ware), H. 8⅛ × DIAM. 4⅛ in. (20.6 × 10.5 cm). Yale University Art Gallery, Archer M. Huntington, HON. 1897, Fund, 1986.63.2

**Fig. 3.12**

*Ewer with Date Palms, a Lion, and a Dancer*, China, Tang dynasty, 9th century C.E. Stoneware with slip, applied decoration, and iron-brown splashes under glaze (Changsha ware), H. 6 in. (15.2 cm). Metropolitan Museum of Art, New York, Purchase, Friends of Asian Art Gift, 1986, 1986.113

by a ship than on the back of a person or camel) and intensified the interactions among China, the Abbasid caliphate (750–1258), and the many port cities in between.[8] On a Changsha ewer (fig. 3.11), three molded and applied elements, covered with splashed brown glazes, illustrate a date palm—a plant believed to have originated in Iraq and cherished for its sweet fruit, which was made into wine and used medicinally in China for centuries. Additional applied pieces show two birds facing each other, a West Asian motif frequently depicted on textiles that was transmitted to China via overland and maritime trade during the Tang dynasty.[9] While the date palm is the most commonly found motif in the appliqués on Changsha wares, some pieces depict lions, a motif that also derives from the imagery of the greater Persian and Indic regions and was imported to China with Buddhism. Others show dancers with curly hair wearing long robes and boots (fig. 3.12), a reference to the foreign entertainers, particularly those from Sogdia (a region in present-day Uzbekistan), who performed in venues throughout China.[10]

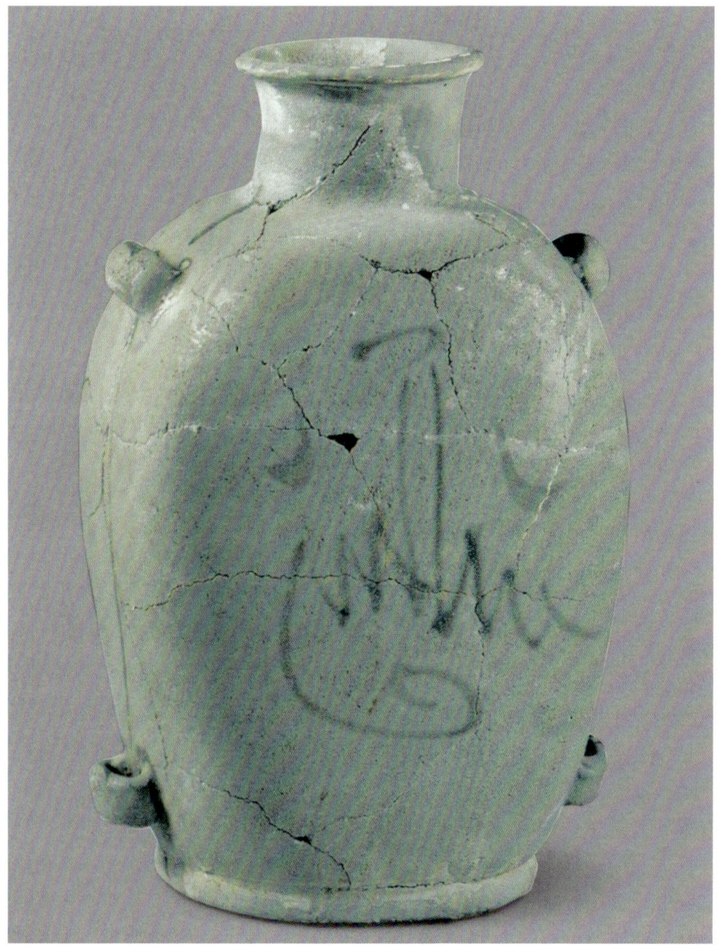

**Fig. 3.13**

*Flask with an Inscription*, China, Tang dynasty, 9th century C.E. Stoneware with pigment under glaze (Changsha ware), H. 6¹³⁄₁₆ in. (17.3 cm). Yangzhou Museum, China

The shape of the Changsha ewers with applied decoration has parallels in earlier Chinese ceramics. The shape of a Changsha flask (fig. 3.13) found in Yangzhou, on the other hand, derives from a West Asian prototype made of leather or metal. This flask has four lugs, two at the top and two at the bottom. One side has an inscription, and the other has a sketchy rendering of a cloud or vapor. Although the writing appears similar to the Kufic script used at the Abbasid court and elsewhere in West Asia, it is actually an illegible pseudoscript intended to reference the prevalence of writing in the decoration of Abbasid ceramics and textiles. Arabic, the language of the Qur'an, became one of the more important languages for international trade during the ninth and tenth centuries, and allusions to West Asian calligraphy—often rendered as thin rising and falling lines on Changsha wares—are another reflection of the international taste shared throughout Asia at the time.[11]

The impact of West Asian goods on Changsha ware is further illustrated by the use of a turquoise color, both as a glaze and as a pigment. A turquoise glaze

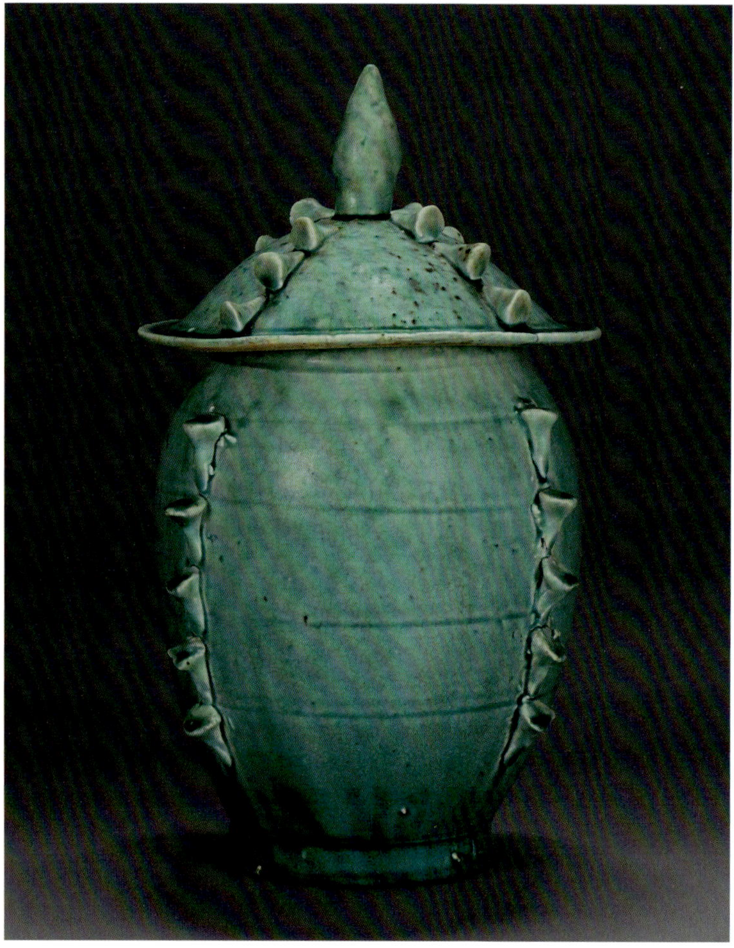

**Fig. 3.14**

*Funerary Jar*, China, Tang or Northern Song dynasty, 9th–10th century. Stoneware with applied decoration under glaze (Changsha ware), H. 10¼ × DIAM. 6¼ in. (26 × 15.9 cm). Yale University Art Gallery, Hobart and Edward Small Moore Memorial Collection, Bequest of Mrs. William H. Moore, 1955.4.90

covers the surface (but not the base) of an intriguing, rare jar with distinctive nail-shaped appliqués along its body and cover (fig. 3.14). Currently, no other examples of this type of jar are known; however, the combination of a turquoise glaze and a buff clay that turned red during firing suggests that it was produced in the Changsha region. Other jars with applied decoration that have been unearthed in tombs in Hunan were found placed near the head of the deceased, sometimes in specially designated niches.[12] Like the jars made in Zhejiang, these pieces were intended to hold beverages or grains for the afterlife.

The use of turquoise glazes on Changsha wares was most likely inspired by similar glazes on ceramics produced in Iran, Iraq, and elsewhere in West Asia. A flask with a turquoise glaze made during the Parthian Empire (247 B.C.E.–224 C.E.)[13] was excavated in 1985 from one of over a thousand Han-dynasty tombs in a cemetery in Hepu, in Guangxi Province.[14] Turquoise glazes usually covered large West Asian jars that stored goods during overland or overseas transport, examples of which have been preserved as far west as Africa and as far east as Japan.[15] Three

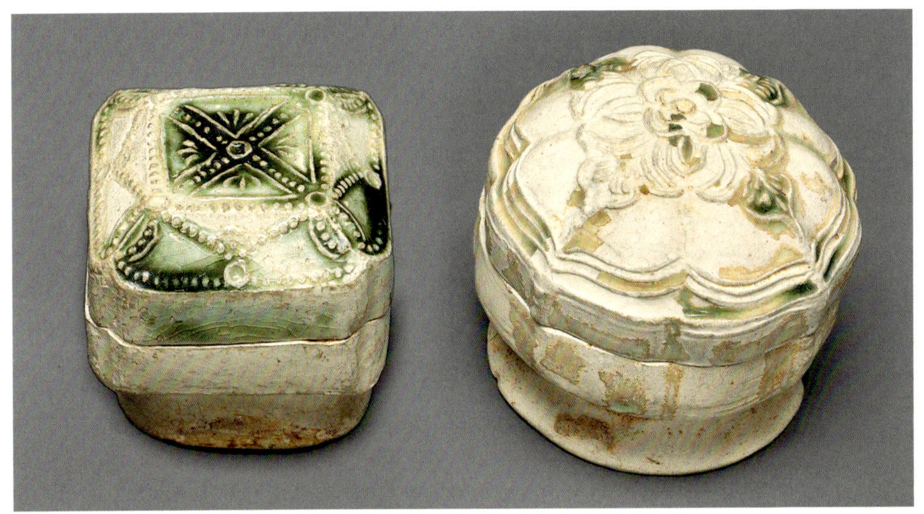

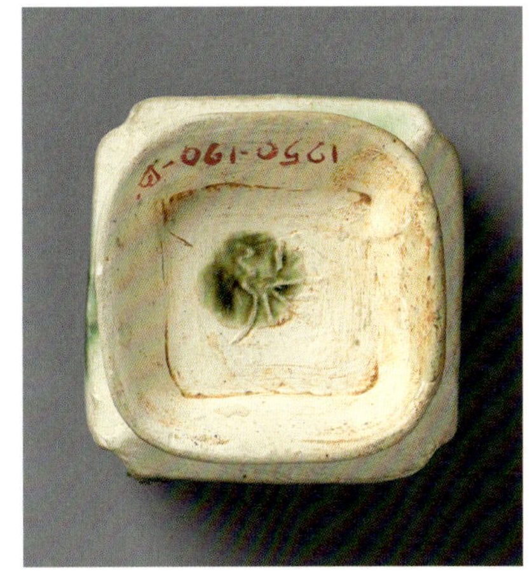


**Fig. 3.15**

(left) *Box with a Lozenge*, China, Tang dynasty, 9th–10th century. Porcelain with molded decoration and green splashes under glaze (Changsha ware), 2 × 2¼ in. (5.1 × 5.7 cm). Yale University Art Gallery, Gift of John Hadley Cox, B.A. 1935, 1950.190. (right) *Box with a Lotus*, China, Tang dynasty, 9th–10th century. Porcelain with molded decoration and green splashes under glaze (Changsha ware), H. 2¼ × DIAM. 2¾ in. (5.7 × 7 cm). Yale University Art Gallery, Gift of John Hadley Cox, B.A. 1935, 1940.382a–b

**Fig. 3.16**

Base of the square box with a lozenge in fig. 3.15, showing a merchant mark reading "Zhang"

large turquoise-glazed West Asian transport jars were found in 1975 in the tomb of Liu Han in Fuzhou, a port city in Fujian Province. Liu, who died in 930 C.E., was the daughter of the king of the independent kingdom of the Southern Han (917–71 C.E.), which controlled most of Guangdong and Guangxi Provinces during the tumultuous tenth century.[16] She was married to the king of Min (910–45 C.E.), another independent state based in Fujian. Placed on stone pedestals in the front chamber of Liu's tomb (she was interred in the larger back chamber), the repurposed jars were filled with oil and functioned as everlasting lamps—a common feature in Chinese Buddhist burials at the time.

Two small boxes with raised feet and molded decoration, one square and the other octagonal (fig. 3.15), further demonstrate the dialogue among Changsha wares, other Chinese ceramics, and imported goods. Both boxes were presumably made to hold, or perhaps to offer as gifts, precious substances, such as cosmetics, incense, or medicine. While the square box is decorated with a West Asian lozenge, the octagonal box bears the ubiquitous Buddhist lotus. The small beads that help define the lozenge share the appearance of ring matting, a design of tightly packed small circles that derives from the decoration often found in metalwork (this design is also found in Qingbai and other ceramic wares).[17] Both boxes were made with a white clay that darkened during firing. White clay was used in the Changsha kilns for the first time in the tenth century and presumably was inspired by the prevalence of white clay in the north, in Hebei, during the Tang dynasty, and in the south, in Jiangxi, in the tenth century. The boxes have splashes of green glaze, a reference to a type of ceramic made in the Gongxian kilns in Hebei, examples of which were found in the Belitung shipwreck.[18] On the square box, the Chinese surname Zhang, probably that of a merchant, is molded into the base (fig. 3.16).[19] Inscriptions of merchants' names on the bases of ceramics, first recorded in Changsha wares, are also found on later southern trade ceramics.

Changsha pieces have been excavated at sites throughout southern China, as well as in mainland Southeast Asia, South and West Asia, and Japan. In addition to the astonishing hoard recovered from the Belitung wreck, Changsha wares have been found in other shipwrecks, such as that discovered near Chau Tan, Vietnam.[20]

## Green Wares from the Hengyang and Related Kilns, Late 10th to 12th Century

In the tenth century, several factors contributed to the faltering of the Changsha kilns, including the development of Qingbai and Longquan celadons in conjunction with the flourishing of ports on China's southeastern seaboard and the intense international desire for green-glazed ceramics. While production diminished and then ceased at Changsha, other kilns located on the Xiang River continued to make ceramics that were often inspired by the widely popular and extensively traded Qingbai and Longquan wares, examples of which have been excavated in Hunan.[21]

Qingbai wares were made at several smaller kiln centers in Hunan, including those near the city of Yiyang, in the northwest, and others near the city of Hengyang, to the south. The large lotus petals defining the lower part of the body of an engaging ewer with a twisted handle and a spout with a dragon's head (fig. 3.17) help date the work to the tenth century, when such large petals were in vogue.[22] The vessel was potted with an iron-rich tan clay and covered with a thin bluish-white glaze that replicates the color of the influential early Qingbai wares from Jiangxi.

Kilns in the Hengyang area also produced green-glazed wares comparable to those made in the Longquan kilns, such as a ewer with a carefully formed spout and a looped handle (fig. 3.18).[23] The wide rim of the ewer dates the piece to the tenth century. The ewer has a dark gray clay body and is covered with a green glaze that echoes the olive-green color popular in Longquan wares. Yet the crackled glaze is thinner than that on pieces from Longquan, and it has abraded over time. A dark gray clay was also used for a large jar (fig. 3.19) produced in the Hengshan kilns, one of the more prominent centers in the Hengyang area. This jar has a powdery white slip and is covered with a dark green glaze at the top and a brown glaze at the bottom. In a central band, it is painted with a freehand rendering of bamboo—a continuation of the imaginative use of clay surfaces as canvases that was first developed in the Changsha kilns. The green bamboo leaves and brown stems are covered with a transparent glaze.

Like other ceramic-producing centers throughout China, the Hengshan kilns used molds to shape and decorate bowls and other ceramics pieces during

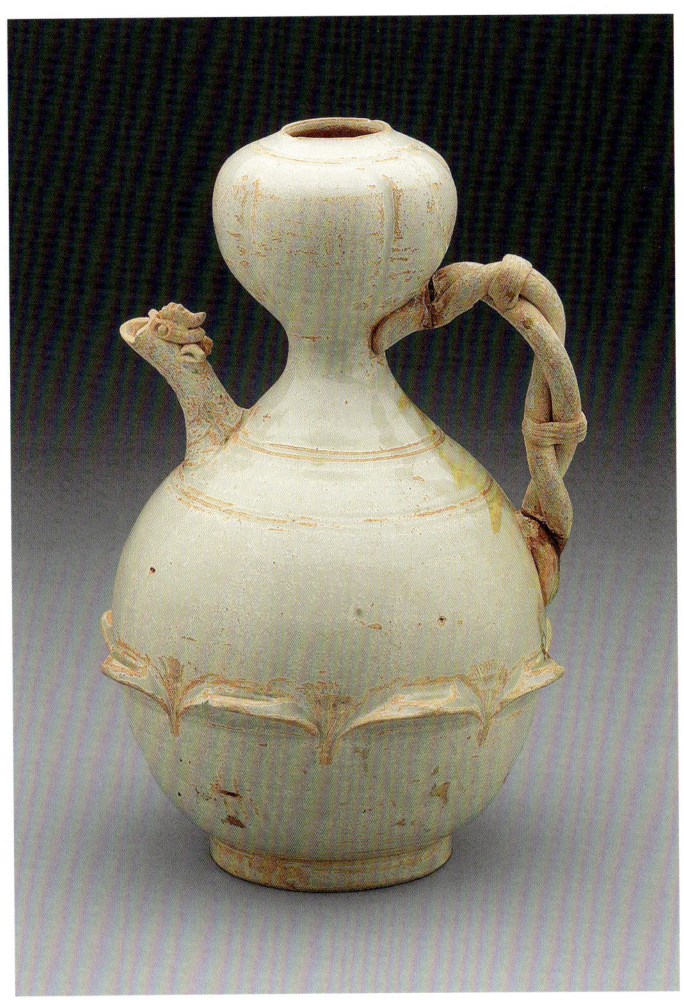

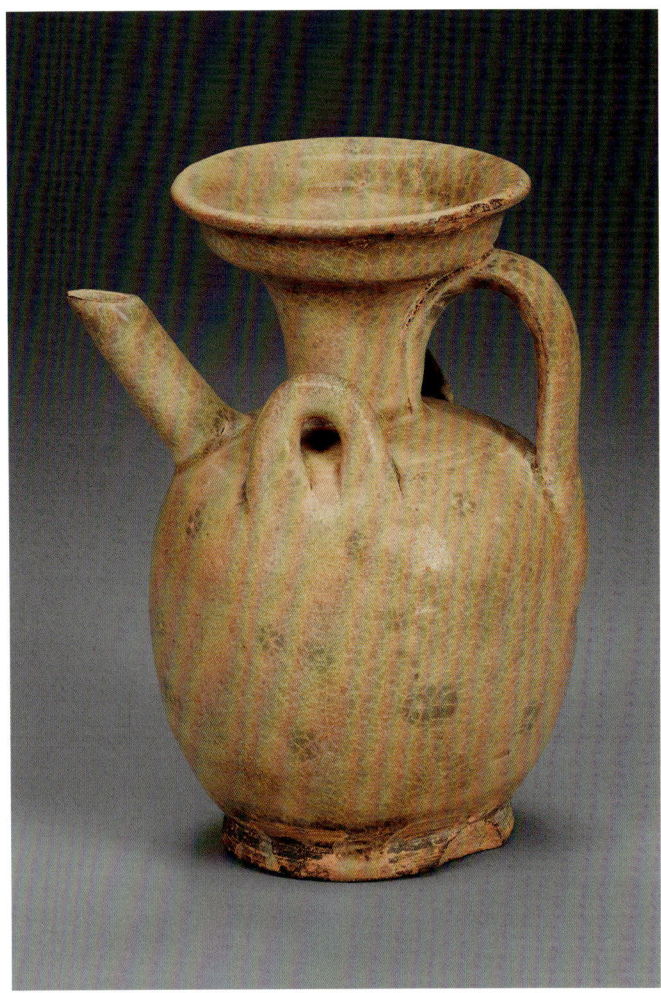

**Fig. 3.17**

*Ewer with Lotus Petals and a Spout in the Shape of a Dragon Head*, China, Five Dynasties period, 10th century. Stoneware with molded and applied decoration under glaze (Hunan Qingbai ware), H. 14 9/16 × DIAM. 7⅞ in. (37 × 20 cm). Yale University Art Gallery, Gift of John Hadley Cox, B.A. 1935, 1950.183

**Fig. 3.18**

*Ewer*, China, Five Dynasties period, 10th century. Stoneware with glaze (Hengyang ware), 4½ × 2⅞ in. (11.4 × 7.3 cm). Yale University Art Gallery, Gift of John Hadley Cox, B.A. 1935, 1940.366

the Southern Song dynasty. A bowl decorated with a scrolling lotus vine and covered with an olive-green glaze (fig. 3.20) has an unglazed space at the bottom of its interior, left that way for the stacking of bowls in the kiln. Mass-production techniques such as this, used at kilns throughout China, facilitated the output needed to manage the wide-ranging demand for Chinese ceramics. Though dense patterns like the one in this bowl typify Chinese ceramic decoration at this time, Hengshan wares are distinguished by a linearity and precision in their patterns, as well as by their mottled glazes.

Ceramics made in the Hengshan or other kilns in the Hengyang region are not known to have been traded domestically or internationally. It is notable, however, that bowls with strikingly comparable molded decoration were made in some numbers in Vietnam during the twelfth and thirteenth centuries, as the ceramic industry there expanded, partly in competition with the kiln complexes in China.[24] Many of the bowls made in Vietnam also have a blank space

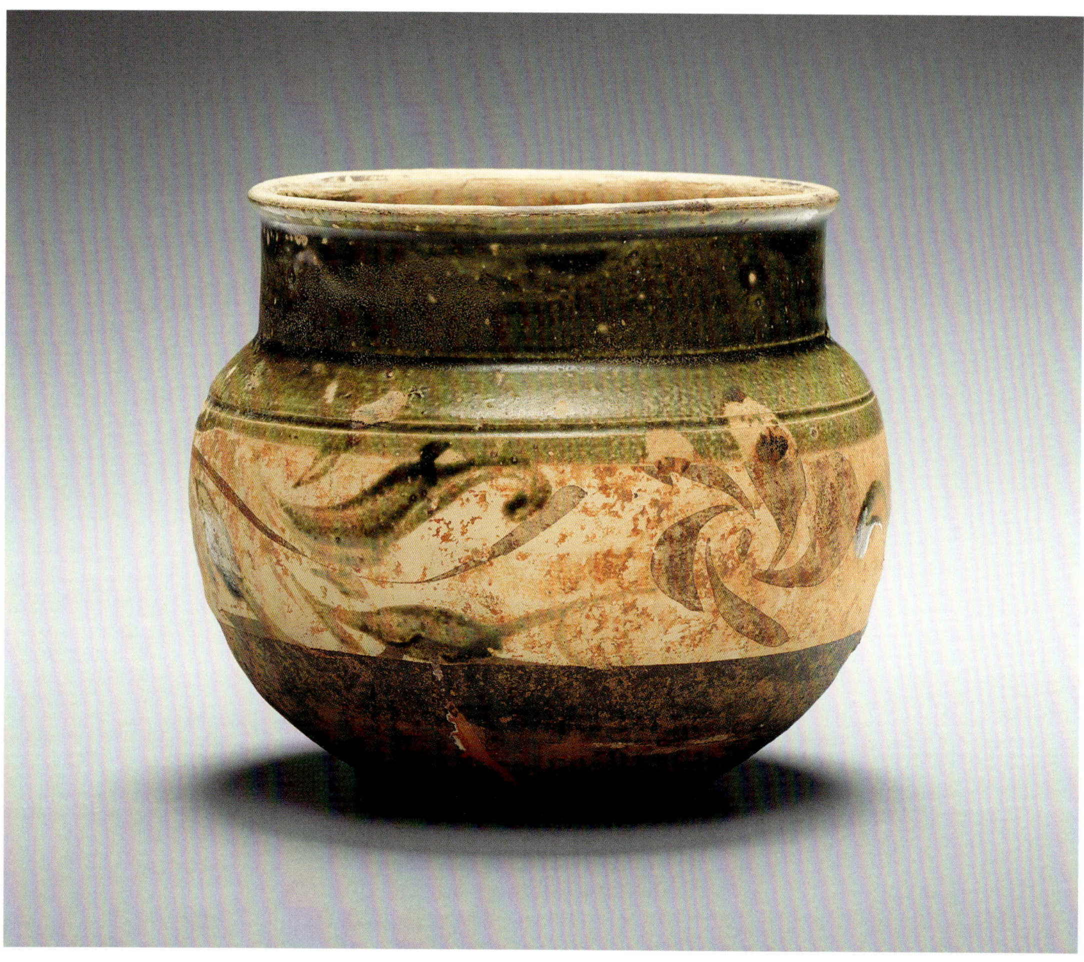

**Fig. 3.19**

*Jar with Bamboo*, China, Northern Song dynasty, 11th–12th century. Stoneware with white slip and iron-brown and copper-green pigment under glaze (Hengshan ware), H. 4⅜ × DIAM. 4⅞ in. (11.1 × 12.4 cm). Yale University Art Gallery, Gift of John Hadley Cox, B.A. 1935, 1940.828

in the bottom of the interior. On one example (fig. 3.21), both the shape of the bowl and the design of the flowers of the four seasons—lotus, peony, chrysanthemum, and plum—are shared with Chinese ceramics. The similarity in the appearance and production method of these two bowls suggests that the potters in Vietnam had knowledge of ceramics from the Hengshan and other Hunan kilns. While there is no evidence for trade between Hunan and Vietnam at the time, it is worth noting that southwest China and mainland Southeast Asia were linked by waterways as early as the late first millennium B.C.E. and have traditionally maintained cultural and economic ties that were not necessarily part of larger government-sponsored activities. Presumably, a small number of Hunanese ceramics were traded to Vietnam and other regions on the peninsula as part of an unrecorded regional (as opposed to intra-Asian) market system that connected makers in southwestern China with consumers in mainland Southeast Asia who preferred ceramics with lively, somewhat abstract decoration and quickly applied glazes.

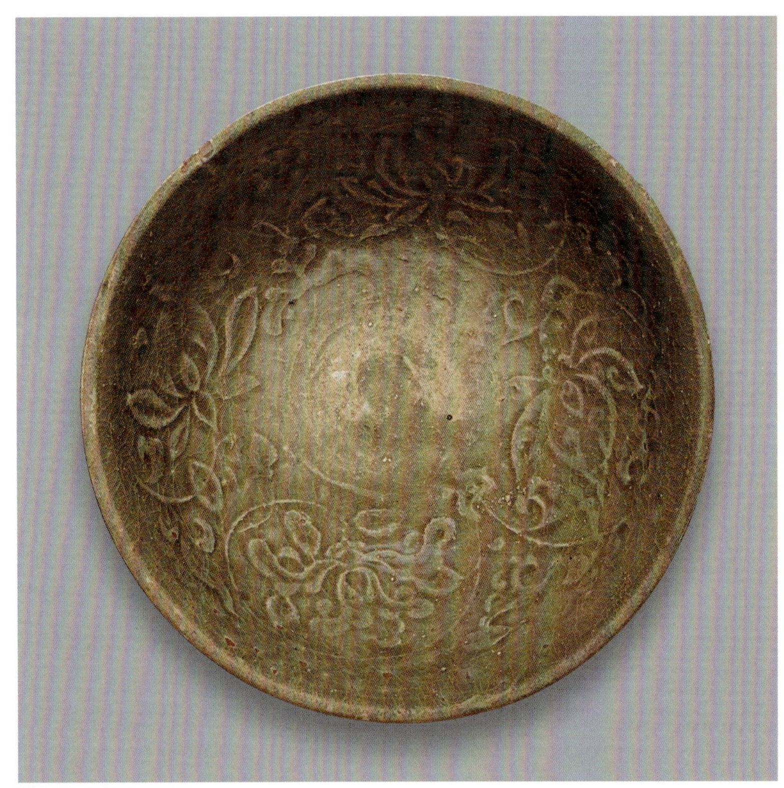

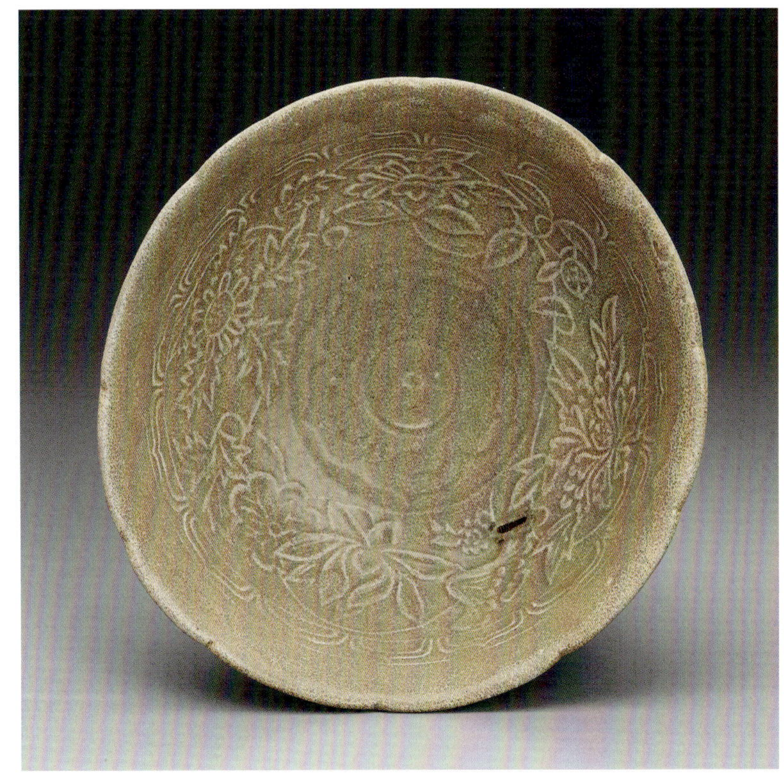

**Fig. 3.20**

*Bowl with Lotuses*, China, Southern Song dynasty, 12th–13th century. Stoneware with molded decoration under glaze (Hengshan ware), H. 2⅝ × DIAM. 6⅜ in. (6.7 × 16.2 cm). Yale University Art Gallery, Gift of John Hadley Cox, B.A. 1935, 1941.40

**Fig. 3.21**

*Bowl with Flowers of the Four Seasons*, Vietnam, Ly dynasty, 14th–15th century. Stoneware with carved and incised decoration under glaze, H. 3 1/16 × DIAM. 6 15/16 in. (7.7 × 17.6 cm). Museum of Fine Arts, Boston, Gift of John D. Constable, 1989.790

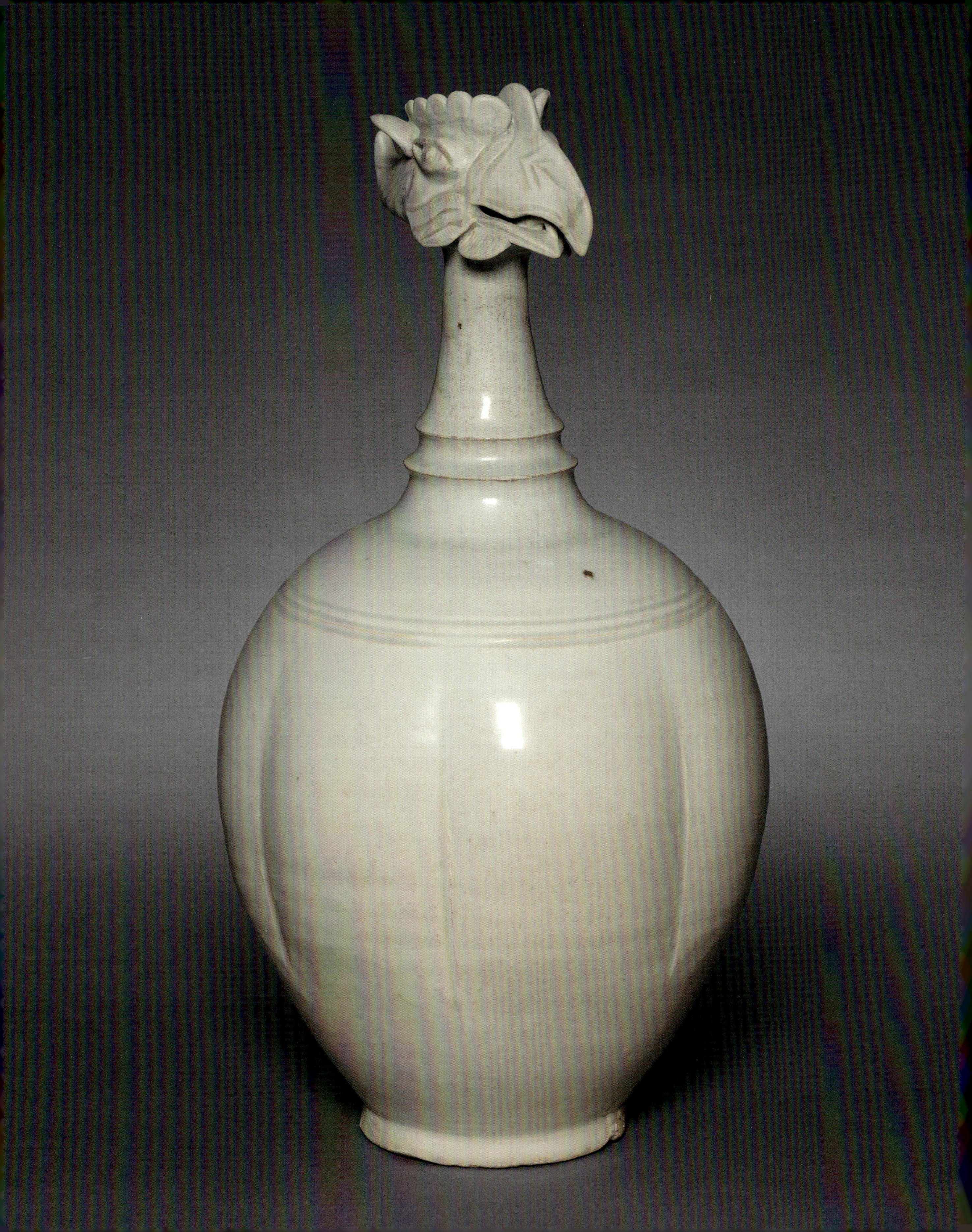

CHAPTER 4

# Guangdong Province: Responding to Regional and International Tastes

Guangdong Province, on the southeast coast of China, straddles cultures that blend traditions from the local area with those from north and east China as well as Southeast Asia. Coastal trade has long been a critical factor in these exchanges: over 1,300 rivers in Guangdong feed directly or indirectly into the Zhujiang River (also known as the Pearl River)—the third largest river in China—and ultimately into the Pearl River delta, historically an entrepôt for southern China, islands such as Hong Kong, and polities throughout mainland Southeast Asia. By the first century B.C.E., goods from South and West Asia and the Mediterranean region could be found in southern Chinese sites. For example, imported cymbals, glass, garnet, rock crystal, gold beads, and other goods, many dating from the first century B.C.E. to the third century C.E. (including the flask with a turquoise glaze mentioned in the previous chapter), have been excavated at the extensive cemetery at the port city of Hepu, located on the Pearl River in nearby Guangxi Province.[1] The *History of the Later Han Dynasty* (*Hou Han shu*), written by Fan Ye and others in the late fifth century C.E., records the arrival in 166 C.E. of a Roman ship (probably from Egypt) at Rinan, a Chinese military outpost in Vietnam.[2] The arrival in China and Southeast Asia of ships, people, and goods from the Mediterranean reflects the first-century discovery of the shifting monsoon winds in the Indian Ocean and their importance in the expansion and development of maritime trade. Merchants and others on this Roman ship, whom the commander at Rinan sent to the court in Luoyang, identified themselves as emissaries from the emperor whose name is rendered as *Andun* in Chinese—most likely Marcus Aurelius (r. 161–80 C.E.).

By the Tang dynasty, Guangdong was a major center of maritime trade, and Guangzhou—its capital, most prominent city, and premier port—was home to a self-governing multiethnic community that included merchants and their families. Some were living there permanently, while others were visiting for commercial reasons or sojourning as they waited for the direction of the winds to change. Individuals within this community supported the construction of Hindu temples and Islamic mosques and cemeteries as well as other charitable activities. The prominence and wealth of some individuals complicated their relationships with local officials and other residents, occasionally with tragic consequences. In 684 C.E., for example, a ship captain, who was possibly Malay, is said to have killed the governor of the province in response to the governor's excessive demands for goods and bribes.[3] In 758 to 759 C.E., the city was sacked by foreign merchants, purportedly infuriated by a loss of income due to increasing taxation and widespread corruption. This resulted in a drastic reduction of trade in Guangzhou and centers throughout Guangdong, which lasted for around fifty years; after these events, merchants relocated their activities to sites in Vietnam and other parts of Southeast Asia.

Guangdong was also affected by the broader disruptions that marked the dissolution of the Tang dynasty in the ninth and early tenth centuries. The province was captured in 869 C.E. during the Huang Chao rebellion, when, according to the ninth-century Arab geographer Abū Zayd of Siraf, over 120,000 Persians, Arabs, and other foreigners were killed during battles in Guangzhou.[4] Like other provinces in southern China at the time, Guangdong was then briefly under the control of an independent kingdom, the Southern Han, before it was gradually incorporated into the Northern Song dynasty in the eleventh and twelfth centuries.[5]

Unlike the kiln complexes in the provinces discussed earlier in this volume, which specialized in a single ware, those in Guangdong produced a range of ceramic types. From the ninth to the fourteenth century, there were approximately three hundred kilns active in the province and, as was the case throughout southern China, the ceramic industry there expanded in the twelfth and thirteenth centuries due to both the population growth following the Song court's move to the south and the increasing importance of maritime trade. Guangdong complexes had between four and twelve kilns each and were smaller than the complexes making Longquan or Qingbai wares. Those near Guangzhou, concentrated on the east and west banks of the Pearl River, and those centered around the city of Chaozhou, on the Han River, were the most active from the tenth to the fourteenth century. Guangdong kilns are less studied than those in Zhejiang and Jiangxi Provinces, and it remains difficult to attribute any ceramic object to a specific kiln rather than to a region.

## Kilns in South and Central Guangdong Province

The straight sides and mottled yellow-green glaze of a jar (fig. 4.1) characterize the green wares made in the Xinhui region to the southwest of Guangzhou. Potted with a gray clay, the jar has a round rim and two lugs where the body meets the shoulder; these were used to attach a cloth cover or cords for lifting or moving the jar. Hundreds of similar thick, green-glazed jars, made at kilns near Guangzhou and used to store and transport trade goods as well as water, food, and other necessities, were found in the Belitung shipwreck. Larger jars could hold up to 140 Changsha dishes stacked into one another (fig. 4.2) and arranged in a spherical cluster (see fig. 0.5). Smaller jars held precious metalwork and spices such as star anise (fig. 4.3), native to southern China and Vietnam and used in cooking and medicine. Jars of this type were also used domestically, and examples have been unearthed in the excavation of the Southern Han palace complex, in Guangzhou,[6] as well as in local tombs.[7]

**Fig. 4.1**

*Transport Jar*, China, Tang dynasty, 9th century C.E. Stoneware with applied decoration under glaze (possibly Xinhui ware), H. 7¾ × DIAM. 7½ in. (19.7 × 19.1 cm). Yale University Art Gallery, Gift of John Hadley Cox, B.A. 1935, 1940.346

**Fig. 4.2**

Items recovered from the Belitung shipwreck, near Sumatra, Indonesia, 1999, showing a Guangdong transport jar filled with Changsha ceramics

**Fig. 4.3**

A Guangdong transport jar with star anise from the Belitung shipwreck, near Sumatra, Indonesia, 1999

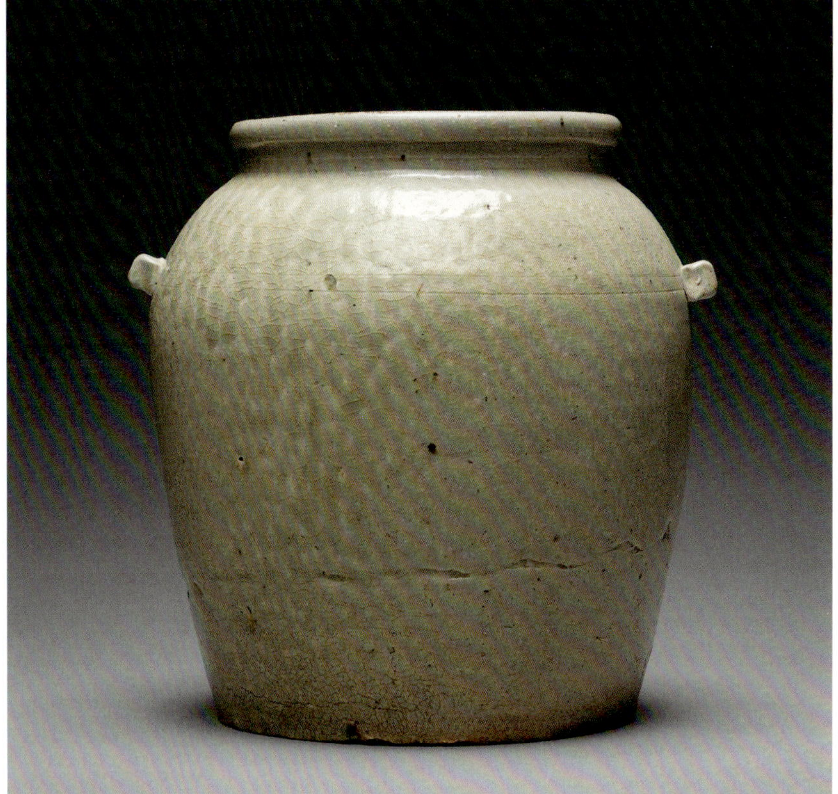

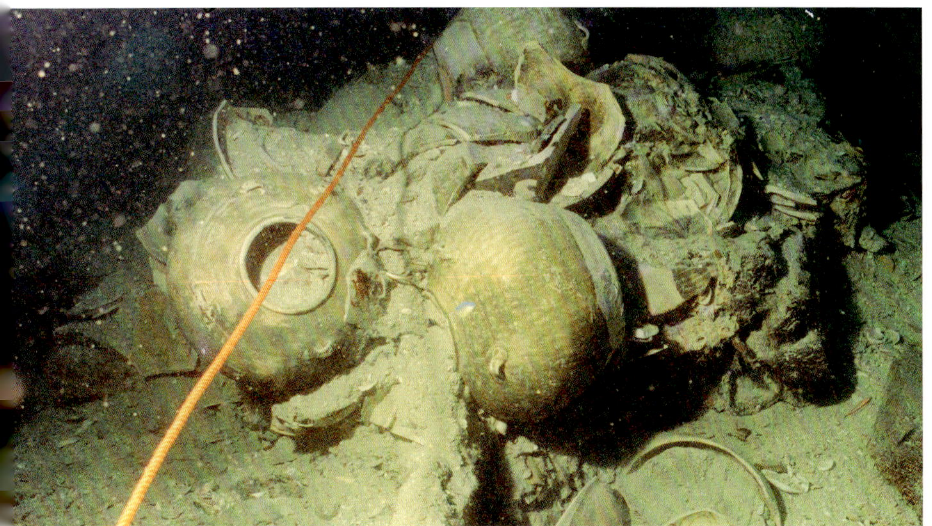

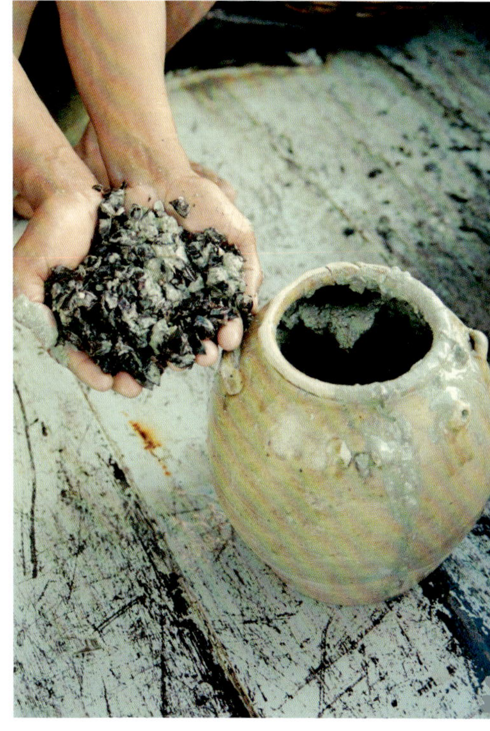

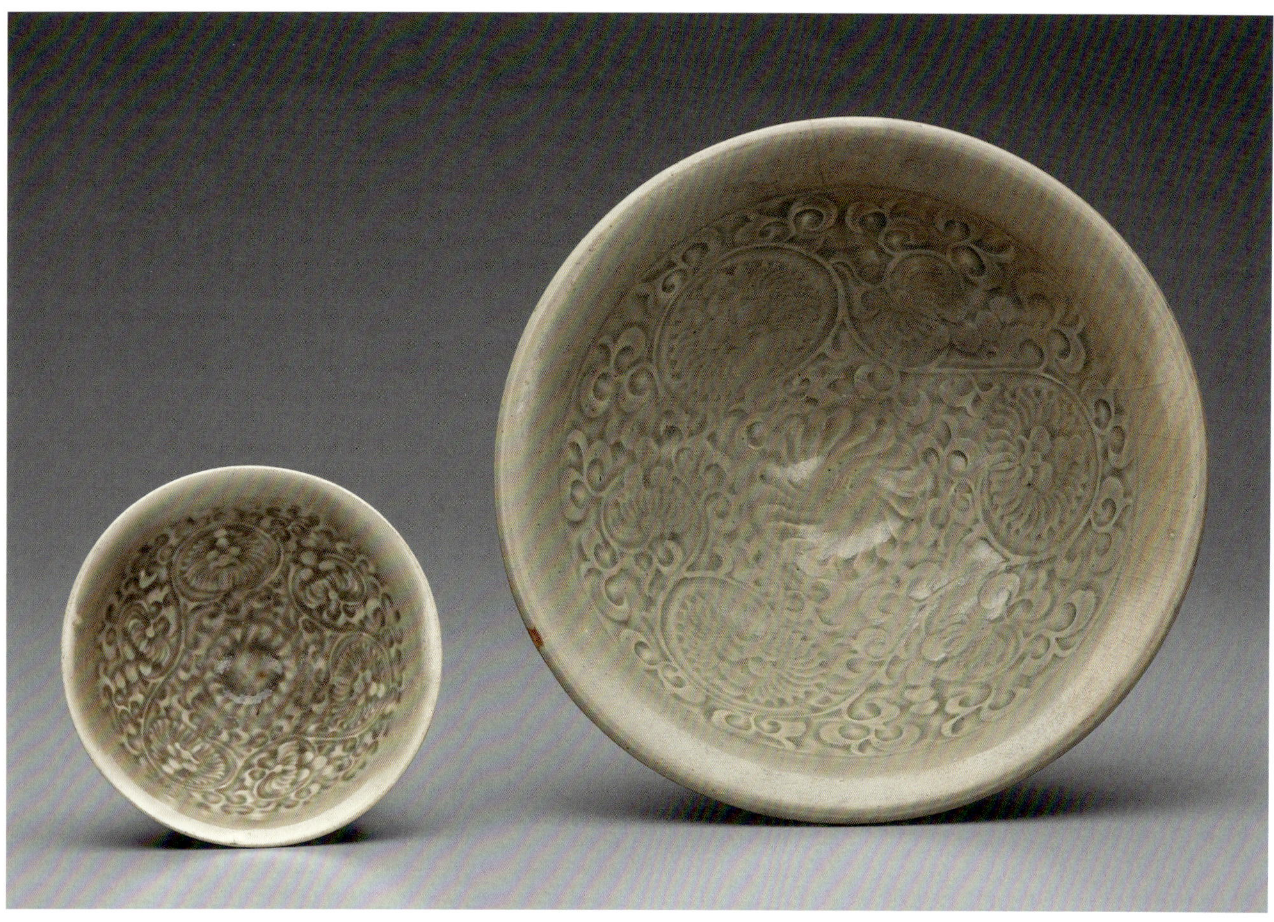

**Fig. 4.4**

(left) *Bowl with a Peony Scroll*, China, Northern Song dynasty, 11th–12th century. Stoneware with molded and incised decoration under glaze (Yaozhou ware), H. 2 × DIAM. 4⅜ in. (5.1 × 11.1 cm). Yale University Art Gallery, Gift of Dr. Howard Balensweig, B.S. 1943, and Mrs. Carolyn Balensweig, 1970.17.1. (right) *Bowl with a Peony Scroll*, China, Southern Song dynasty, 12th–13th century. Stoneware with molded and incised decoration under glaze (Xicun ware), H. 3 × DIAM. 8¼ in. (7.6 × 21 cm). Yale University Art Gallery, Gift of John Hadley Cox, B.A. 1935, 1950.192

The olive-tinged glaze on the jar from the Xinhui region (see fig. 4.1) is also found on ceramics produced at kilns in south and central China, particularly at Xicun, a complex north of Guangzhou that is named for a nearby village. A similar glaze covers a large twelfth- or thirteenth-century bowl from Xicun (fig. 4.4, right) with a molded design of a lush peony scroll on the interior. This design is identical to those found on bowls produced in the Yaozhou region of Shaanxi Province, in north China (fig. 4.4, left), further illustrating the continual interactions and competition between kilns in the north and south. Active from the Tang dynasty until the fourteenth century, the Yaozhou kilns first made green wares in the tenth century, most likely in response to the growing prominence of ceramics from Zhejiang Province. The classic olive-green glaze of Yaozhou wares was created during the Northern Song dynasty, when the wood used for fueling the kilns was replaced by coal as a result of deforestation or in response to the different temperatures achieved by coal firing. Although Yaozhou ceramics, like most northern wares, are not well documented as trade goods, the striking similarities between the Xicun and Yaozhou bowls suggest the existence of some

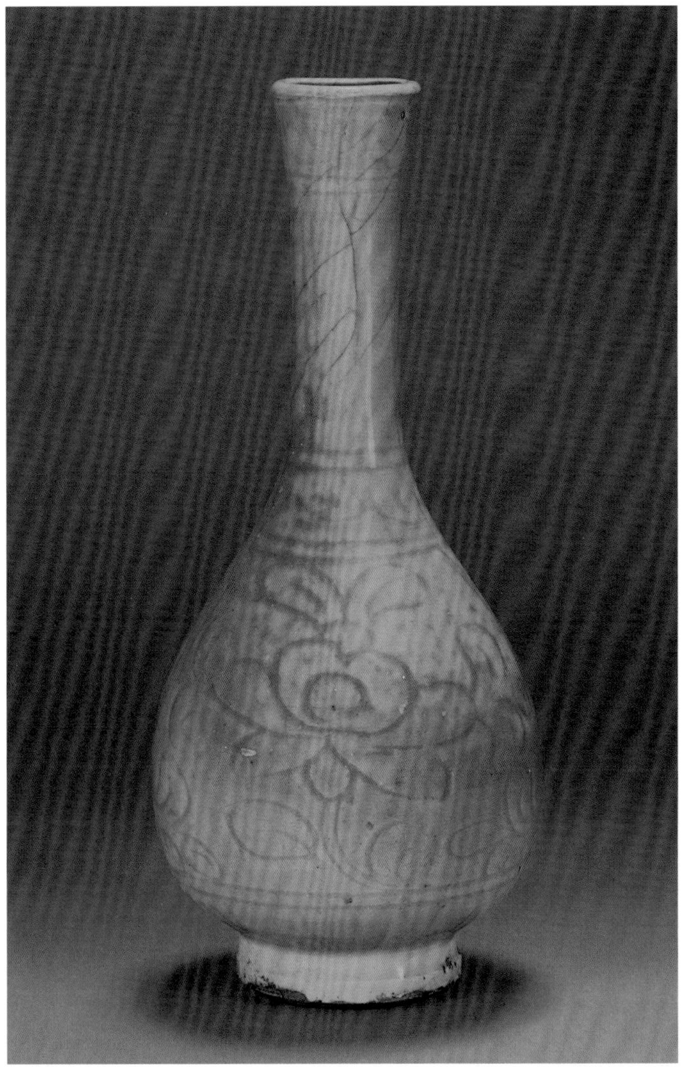

**Fig. 4.5**

*Bottle with a Lotus*, China, Yuan dynasty, 13th–14th century. Stoneware with incised decoration under glaze (Xicun ware), H. 11¾ × DIAM. 5 in. (29.8 × 12.7 cm). Yale University Art Gallery, Bequest of Edith Malvina K. Wetmore, 1966.81.166

type of market for them. The bowl from Xicun is noticeably larger and heavier than that from Yaozhou, and it is less carefully glazed.

The same olive-green glaze covers a bottle with an incised lotus flower and petals (fig. 4.5). The use of a clay that has fired red suggests that the piece was also produced in the Xicun kilns. The sketchy rendering of the lotus, however, points to a later date, in the thirteenth or fourteenth century. While the kilns in the north produced many bottles in this *yuhuchun* shape, it is rare within the Yaozhou repertoire. Its use in the far south in a piece that shares the appearance of Yaozhou ware attests to the Guangdong industry's ongoing reinterpretation of shapes and designs from other parts of China.

Xicun wares not only were used domestically, including at the Southern Han court, but also were traded in Southeast Asia. Substantial numbers have

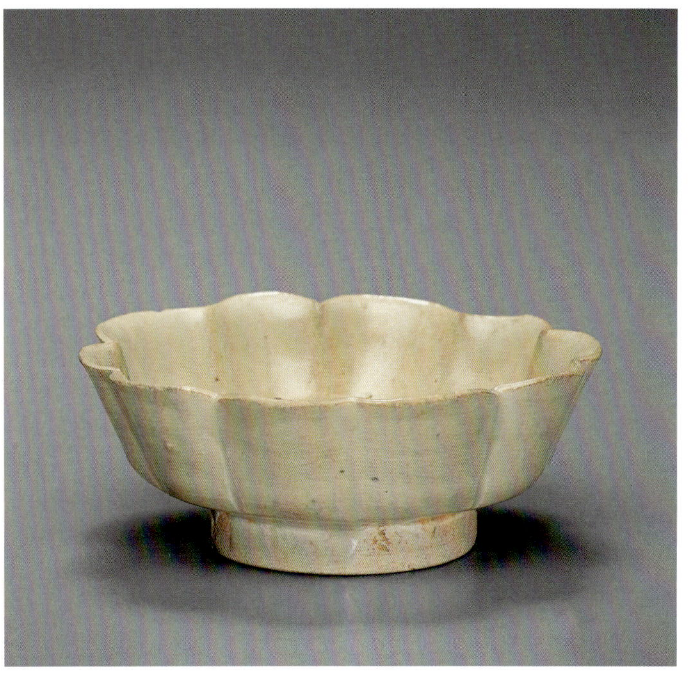

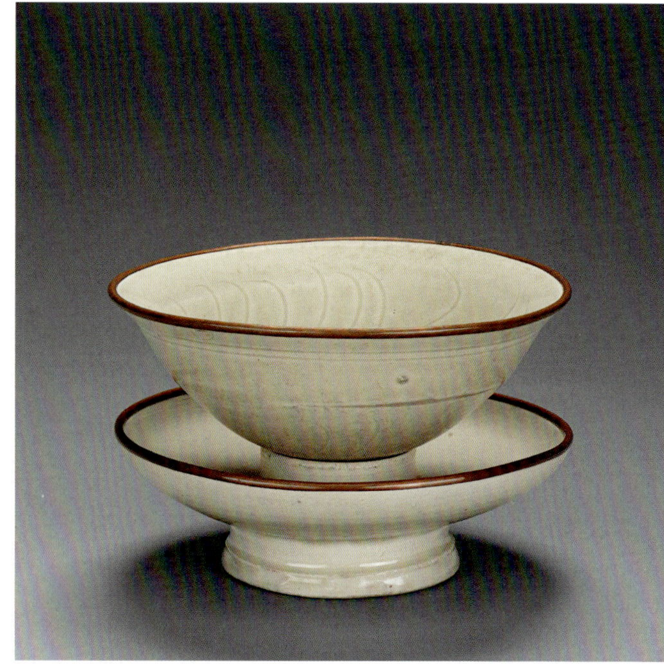

**Fig. 4.6**

*Dish in the Shape of a Lotus*, China, Five Dynasties period or Northern Song dynasty, 10th–11th century. Stoneware with glaze (Xicun ware), H. 1⅝ × DIAM. 4¼ in. (4.1 × 10.8 cm). Yale University Art Gallery, Gift of John Hadley Cox, B.A. 1935, 1940.351

**Fig. 4.7**

*Cup and Stand*, China, Five Dynasties period or Northern Song dynasty, 10th–11th century. Stoneware with incised decoration under glaze with metal rim (Xicun ware), H. 3½ × DIAM. 5 in. (8.9 × 12.7 cm). Yale University Art Gallery, Hobart and Edward Small Moore Memorial Collection, Gift of Mrs. William H. Moore, 1954.49.40, .62

been unearthed in the Philippines[8] and Malaysia, and Xicun wares comprised the bulk of the Pulau Buaya shipwreck, found in Indonesian waters in 1998.[9] The grayish-white hue of the crackled glaze covering a small dish in the shape of a ten-petaled flower (fig. 4.6) represents another glaze color on ceramics produced at the Xicun kilns.[10] The lotus shape suggests that dishes of this type, which could have been used as brush washers or to offer a delicacy during drinking or dining, might also have been used for offerings during Buddhist or ancestral ceremonies. Interestingly, similar dishes with slightly different profiles were made in other kilns in Guangdong, as well as in Anhui[11] and Fujian Provinces, and were also traded throughout Southeast Asia.[12]

A cup with a matching stand (fig. 4.7) is likewise coated with the distinctive grayish-white Xicun glaze. This cup was used for drinking tea and wine. Its interior is incised with sickle-shaped leaves typical of Xicun wares; the exterior and stand, however, have no incised decoration. The metal rims of both the cup and stand enhance their appearance and indicate, once again, that the pieces were fired upside down.

Like the Changsha and Hengshan wares from Hunan Province, the Xicun kilns sometimes used ceramic surfaces as canvases for painting. The lively rendering of a chrysanthemum blossom and leaves on a painted Xicun dish (fig. 4.8) echoes the botanical imagery on earlier Changsha wares. Yet the naturalistic representation of the flower and the sure, quick, calligraphic brushstrokes depicting its petals and leaves are distinctive to Xicun ware. This dish has a two-character

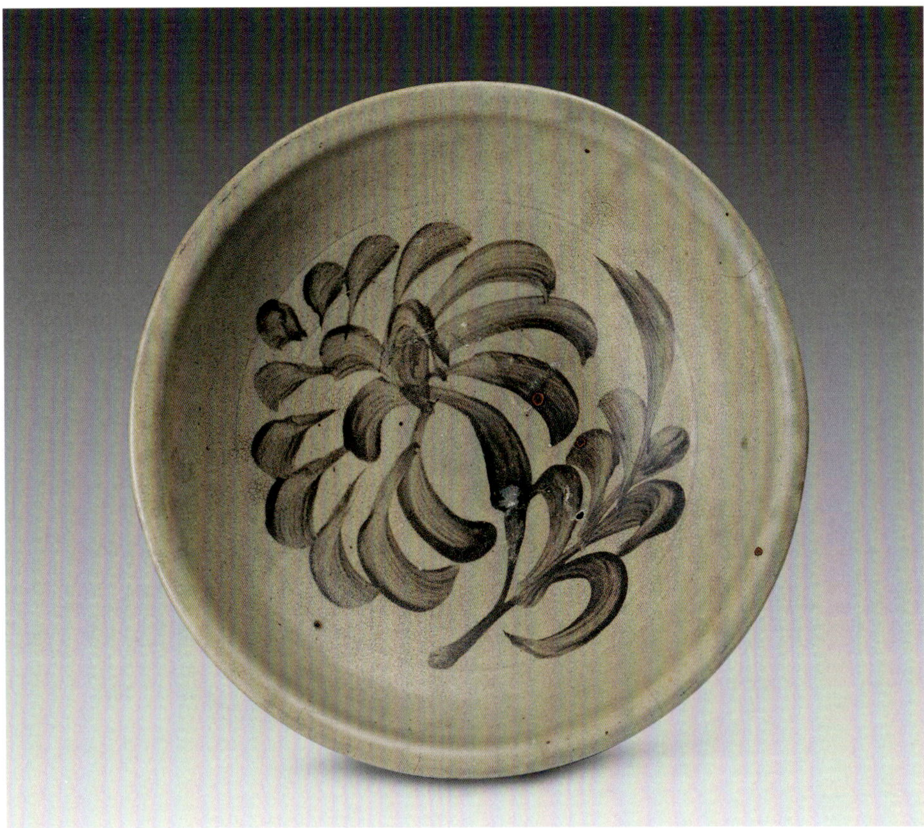

**Fig. 4.8**

*Dish with a Chrysanthemum*, China, Northern Song or Southern Song dynasty, 11th–12th century. Stoneware with iron-brown pigment under glaze (Xicun ware), DIAM. 13⅜ in. (34 cm). Fondation Baur, Geneva, Donation of Ambassador and Mrs. Charles Müller, FB.CM.2004.QC41

inscription painted on the base. Though somewhat abraded, it appears to read "huaya," possibly a reference to the individual who commissioned or owned the piece.

## Kilns in Northeast Guangdong Province

It is not surprising that the kilns in the northeastern area of Guangdong, which abuts Fujian and Jiangxi, had a greater awareness of the types of wares and the technical innovations developed in nearby provinces. Kilns in northeast Guangdong produced Yue-type wares both in competition with and as substitutes for the acclaimed Yue wares from Zhejiang, and they were widely traded in the tenth century. The gray-green glaze and the simple but strong shape of a Tang-period dish made at the Meixian kilns in far northeast Guangdong (fig. 4.9) echo the style of Yue wares. In addition, the round foot of the dish (fig. 4.10)—a type scholars refer to as a "bi-shaped foot," because it resembles the form of a Neolithic jade implement called a "bi"—parallels the shape of the feet on tenth-century Yue pieces. However, the dish is more thickly potted than the thin Yue wares, and the glaze is thinner and slightly more olive in hue than Yue glazes, indicating that it was made in Guangdong.

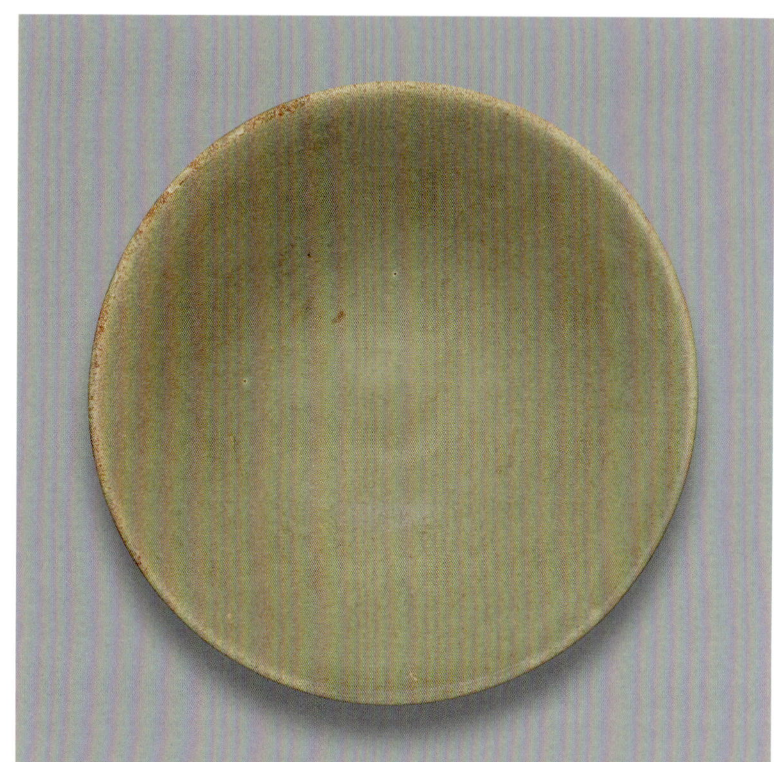

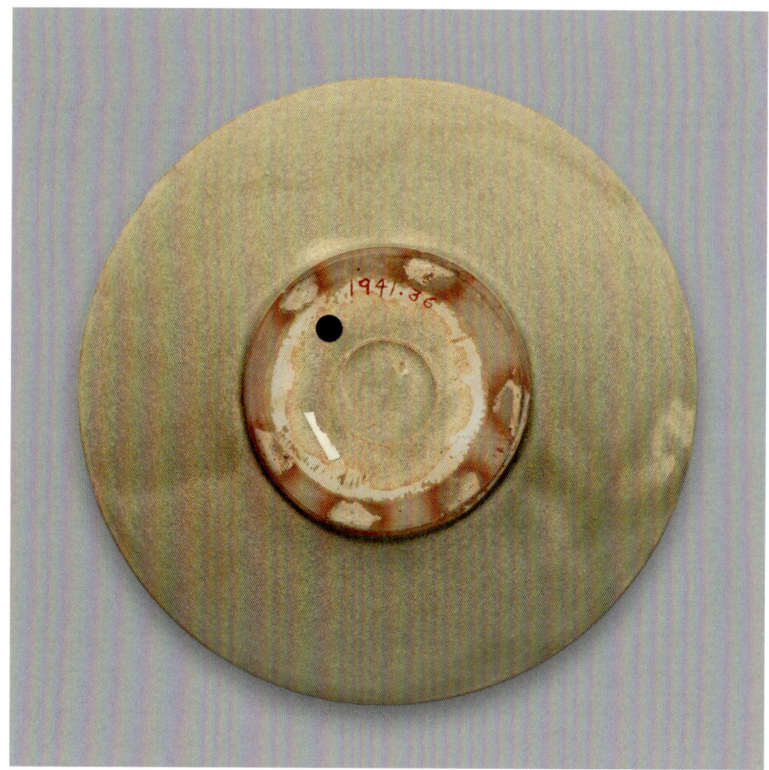


**Fig. 4.9**

*Dish*, China, Tang dynasty, 9th–10th century. Stoneware with glaze (possibly Meixian ware), H. 1½ × DIAM. 6 in. (3.8 × 15.2 cm). Yale University Art Gallery, Gift of John Hadley Cox, B.A. 1935, 1941.36

**Fig. 4.10**

Base of fig. 4.9

OPPOSITE:

**Fig. 4.11**

*Jar*, China, Five Dynasties period or Northern Song dynasty, 10th–11th century. Porcelain with applied decoration under glaze (Chaozhou Qingbai ware) H. 6½ × DIAM. 5 in. (16.5 × 12.7 cm). Yale University Art Gallery, Gift of Dr. Howard Balensweig, B.S. 1943, and Mrs. Carolyn Balensweig, 1973.162.20

**Fig. 4.12**

*Phoenix-Headed Ewer*, China, Five Dynasties period or Northern Song dynasty, 10th–11th century. Porcelain with incised and applied decoration under glaze (Chaozhou Qingbai ware), H. 15¼ in. (38.7 cm). Cleveland Museum of Art, Gift of Mr. and Mrs. Severance A. Millikin, 1965.468

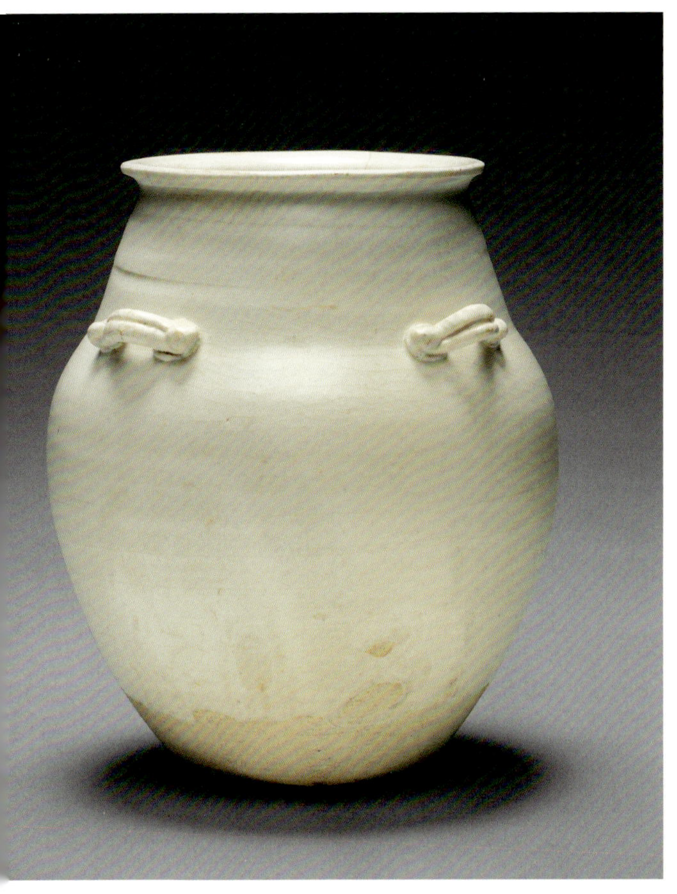

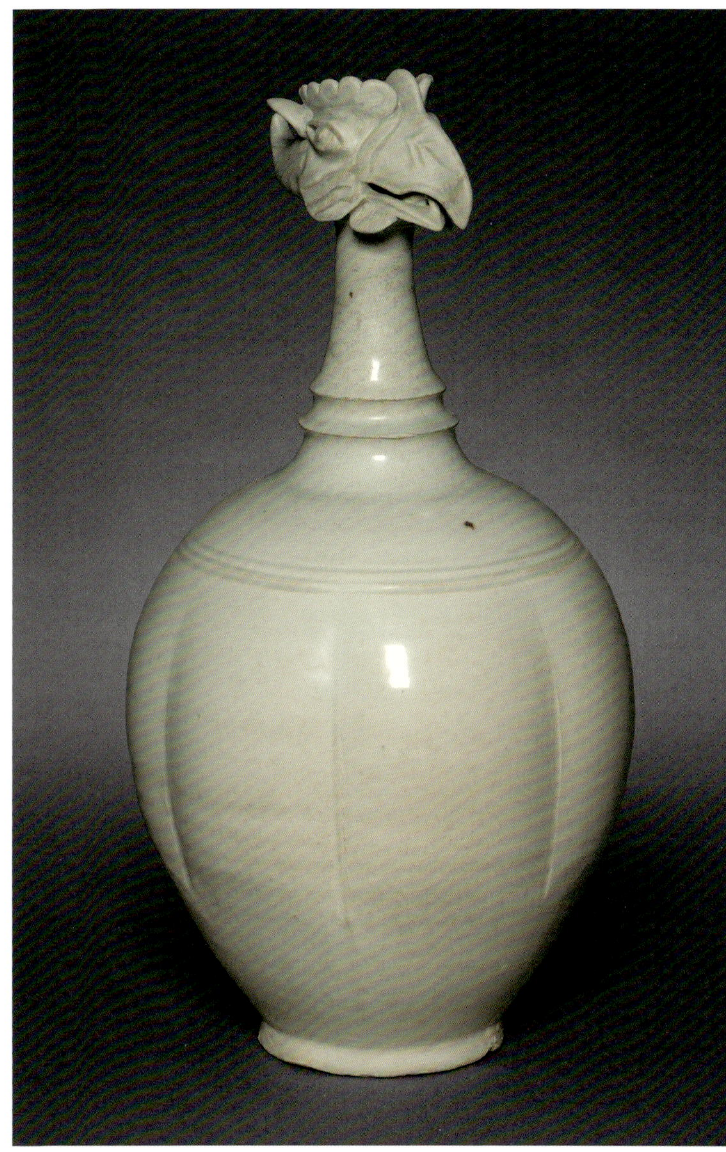

Kilns in the vicinity of Chaozhou, to the south of Meixian, also produced ceramics in tandem with, and in response to, the wares of other provinces such as Jiangxi and Zhejiang. A lovely jar (fig. 4.11), which could have been used for storage and transport, is attributed to the Chaozhou kiln complex because of the similarity of its body and glaze to those of a ewer with a phoenix head (fig. 4.12), one of the more distinctive products of this complex.[13] Phoenix-headed ewers first appeared in Tang-period ceramics in north China. Their shape was derived in part from glass and metal ewers with pinched lips made throughout West Asia, some of which most likely reached China as luxurious gifts or trade goods.[14] While the phoenix-headed ewers made in north China

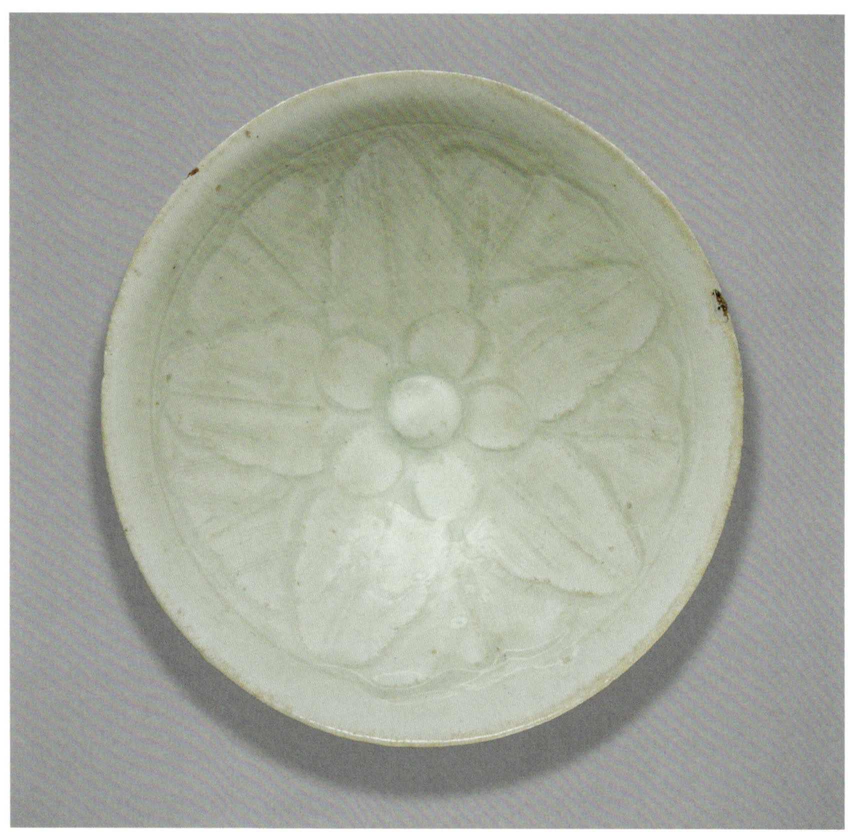

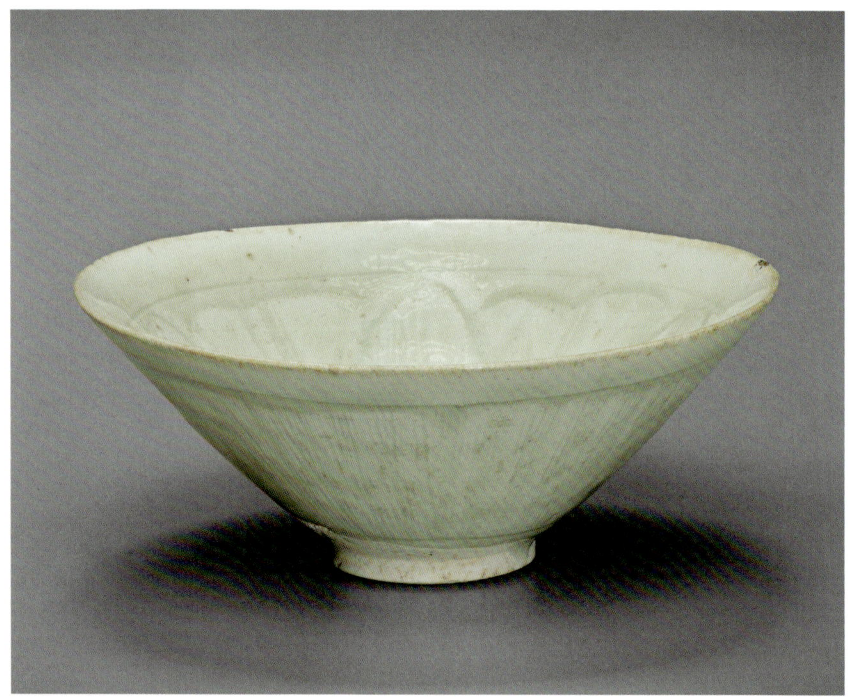

**Fig. 4.13**

*Bowl with Plantain Leaves*, China, Southern Song dynasty, 12th–13th century. Porcelain with incised decoration under glaze (Chaozhou Qingbai ware), H. 2⅛ × DIAM. 5¼ in. (5.4 × 13.3 cm). Yale University Art Gallery, Hobart and Edward Small Moore Memorial Collection, Gift of Mrs. William H. Moore, 1954.49.48

**Fig. 4.14**

Side of fig. 4.13

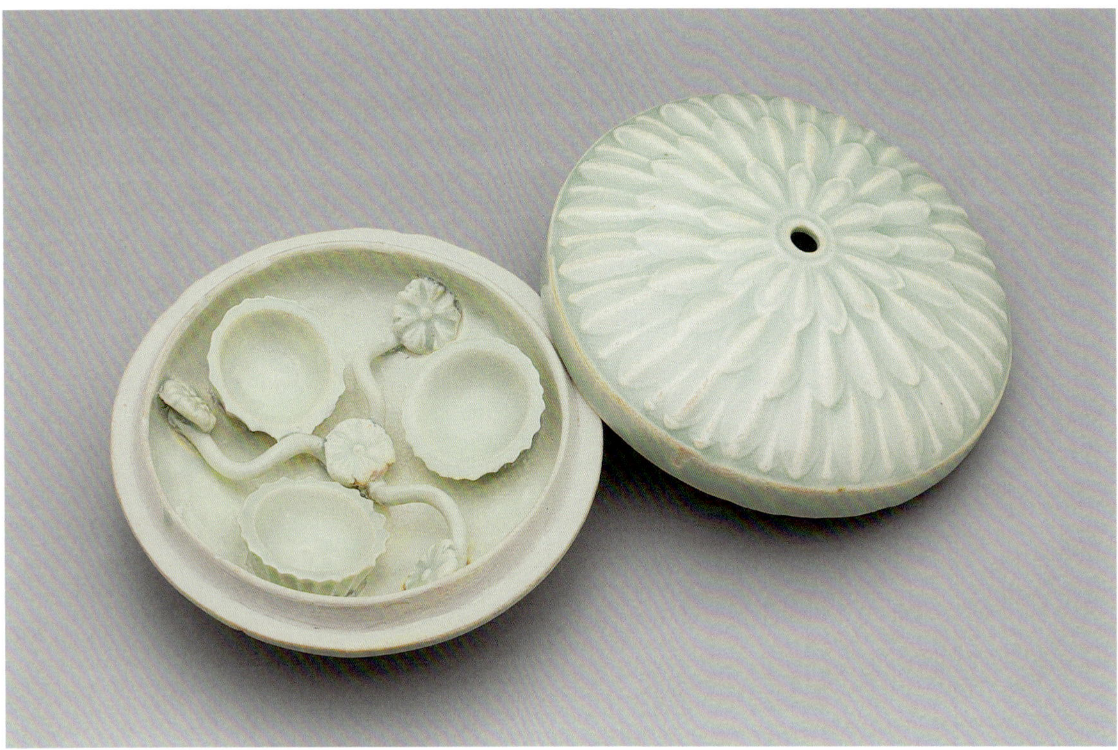

**Fig. 4.15**

*Cosmetic Box in the Shape of a Chrysanthemum*, China, Southern Song dynasty, 12th–13th century. Porcelain with molded, incised, and carved decoration under glaze (Chaozhou Qingbai ware), H. 2$\frac{7}{16}$ × DIAM. 4¼ in. (6.2 × 10.8 cm). Yale University Art Gallery, Archer M. Huntington, HON. 1897, Fund, 1990.44.2a–c

have primarily been found in burials, Guangdong phoenix-headed ewers were used domestically and traded overseas.[15] This example shares the round shape of the body of the jar, but it is articulated with subtle lobes and has two raised rings along the neck. Both pieces are made of refined clay and have a whitish-green glaze.

The darker blue-green glaze on a small bowl with incised overlapping plantain leaves in the interior (fig. 4.13), on the other hand, reflects contemporaneous developments in the glazes on the Qingbai wares of Jiangxi. Unlike the glazes used in Jiangxi, however, the one on this bowl is thin and does not cover the object's foot; it has also abraded along the rim. The shallowly carved, unequal parallel lines on the exterior (fig. 4.14) are characteristic of Guangdong wares.

The bowl was potted with a granular, bright white porcelain, which was also used to make a small cosmetic box in the shape of a chrysanthemum (fig. 4.15). The long, narrow petals on the cover of this box are characteristic of ceramics from northeast Guangdong.[16] The floral imagery continues on the interior, where there are four small blossoms and three larger open flowers that would have stored cosmetics, including a white powder for the face, brown paint for the eyebrows, and rouge for the cheeks. Produced throughout southern China, small cosmetic boxes with Qingbai glazes were a significant item in the Chinese

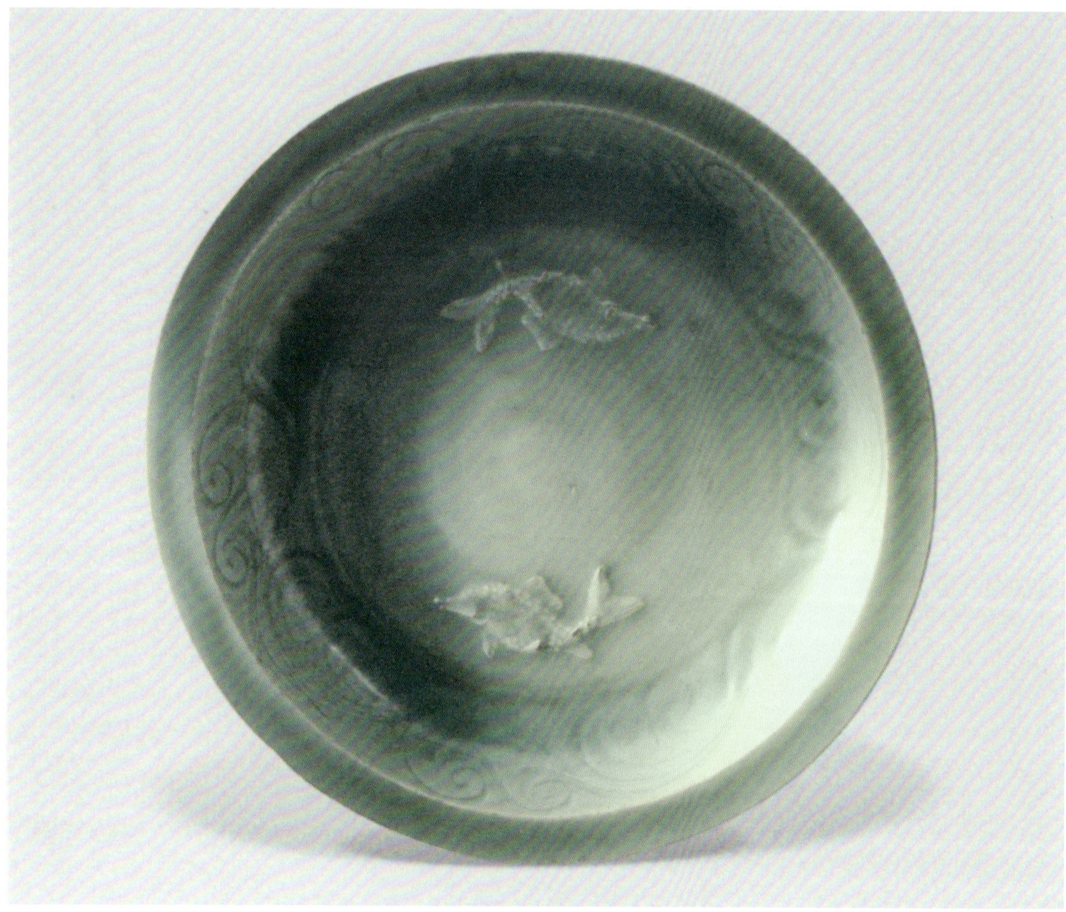

**Fig. 4.16**

*Dish with Two Fish*, China, Yuan dynasty, 13th–14th century, excavated in Chaozhou, China. Stoneware with molded and incised decoration under glaze (Chaozhou ware), DIAM. 14⅞ in. (37.8 cm). Guangdong Provincial Museum, Guangzhou, China

ceramic industry; they were produced for both domestic use and export to places throughout Asia. Interestingly, some examples were repurposed in Japan, where they were buried as reliquaries after being filled with glass beads, which, as previously mentioned, function as symbolic relics in Buddhism.[17]

As can be seen in a large dish with two fish that was unearthed in Chaozhou (fig. 4.16), kilns active in the Chaozhou area also responded to the popularity of products from the Longquan kilns in Zhejiang. The fish swimming around one another on this piece are strikingly similar to those on Longquan dishes, although they have more space between them and do not occupy the center of the dish. Unlike the Longquan dishes, this piece has a wavy scroll carved in the cavetto (the curved area between the outer rim of the dish and the interior).

Like those in Zhejiang and Jiangxi, kilns in the Chaozhou region also produced funerary and religious sculptures during the eleventh and twelfth centuries. In 1922 four sculptures of seated Buddhas with inscribed dates ranging from 1067 to 1069 were discovered in a trench in the eastern Chao'an district of Chaozhou. An incense burner, presumably for use in Buddhist ceremonies, was found with

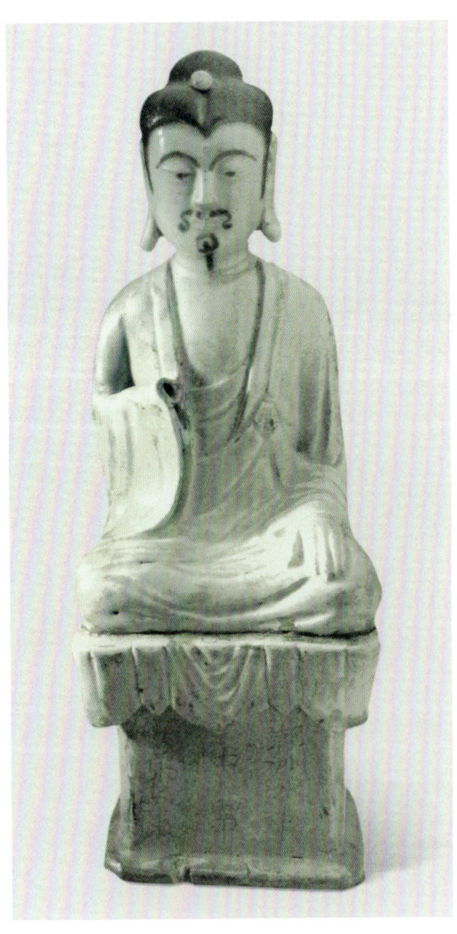

**Fig. 4.17**

*Buddha*, China, Northern Song dynasty, dated 1069. Stoneware with molded, carved, incised, and painted decoration over glaze (Chaozhou ware), H. 12 7/16 in. (31.5 cm). Guangdong Provincial Museum, Guangzhou, China

the sculptures, yet it remains unclear whether the sculptures were part of a set and would have been used and displayed together or whether they were separate commissions for individuals or a temple. One of the Buddhas (fig. 4.17), dated 1069, is seated in meditation on a square pedestal (a reference to Mount Meru, the center of the Indic cosmos) covered with a cloth. He wears traditional monastic clothing, including a long, saronglike garment and a large rectangular shawl tied with a clasp. He is further identified as a Buddha by physical indicators, such as the tuft of hair in the center of his forehead (known as an *urna* in Sanskrit and as a *baihao* in Chinese) and the bump at the top of his head (called an *ushnisha* or *foding*)—both of which symbolize supernal wisdom—as well as the elongated earlobes. The Buddha's left hand rests on his knee, and his right hand (now missing) was most likely held up with the palm facing out to express reassurance, one of the common ritual gestures, or mudras, depicted in Buddhist sculpture. The hair, eyebrows, eyes, mustache, and goatee were painted black over the glaze.

In addition to providing a date, the inscription—written on the front, back, and sides of the sculpture—identifies the Buddha as Shakyamuni (Shijiamouni, in Chinese), the founder of the religion, who is also known as the Historical Buddha. It also indicates that the sculpture was commissioned by a woman and seven couples, in the hope of having children and to pray for favorable rebirths for seven generations of ancestors.[18] The inscription names both the Shuidong kiln where the sculpture was produced and, very unusually, the potter, Zhou Ming. Shuidong is located in the Bijiashan area, one of the most prominent kiln centers in Chaozhou at the time.

The relocation of the Song court to Hangzhou in Zhejiang and the establishment of the Southern Song dynasty in 1127, both of which contributed significantly to the extraordinary expansion of the Longquan kilns from the twelfth to the fourteenth century, also spurred the development of ceramic production in Guangdong and Fujian. Although the works produced in these provinces have received less attention from scholars and collectors, they made up a substantial portion of the ceramics distributed in maritime trade during this period. By the twelfth century, the Fujianese city of Quanzhou had replaced Guangzhou as the premier port in south China and the southern ceramic industry.

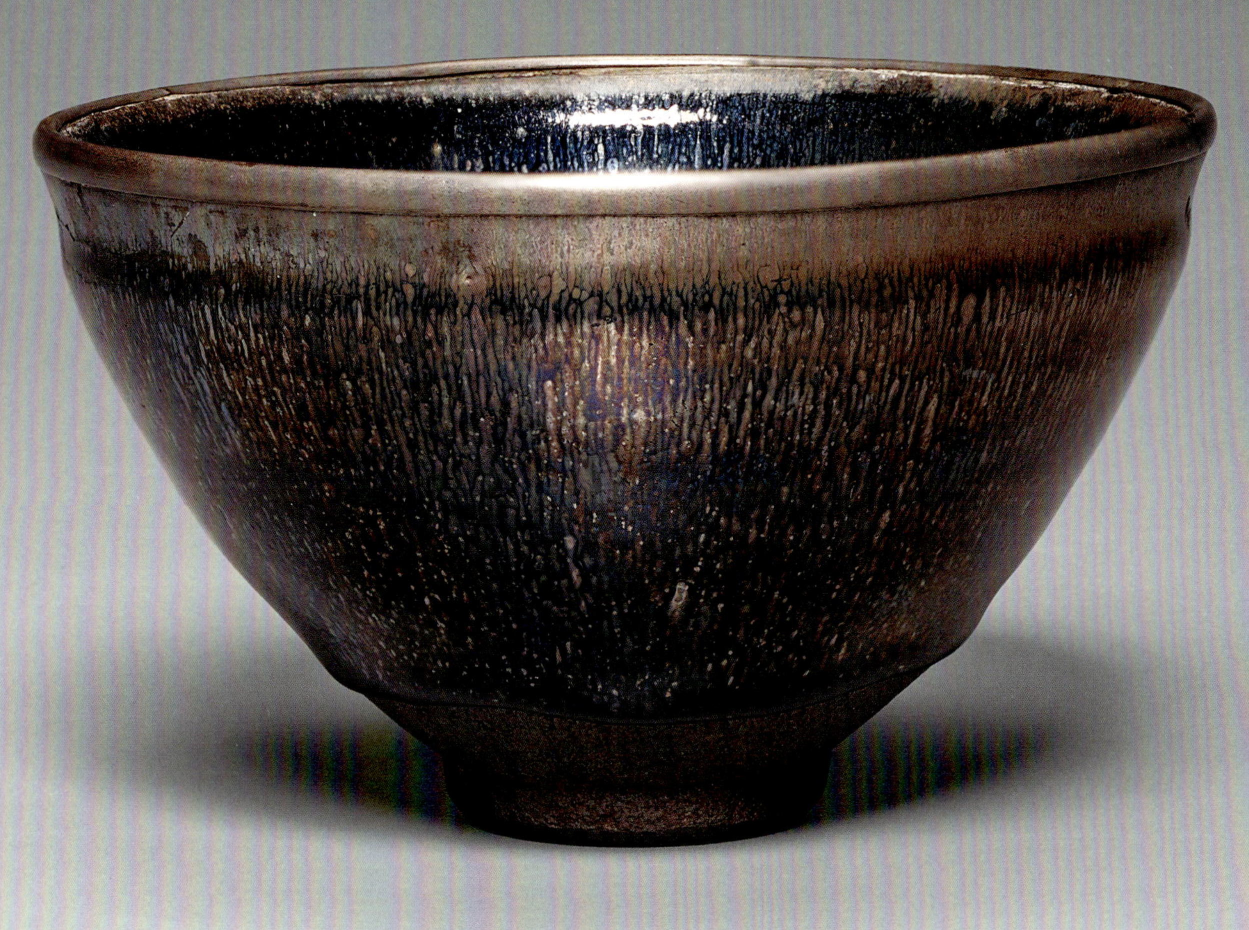

CHAPTER 5

# Fujian Province: Ceramic Diversity and Tea Culture in East Asia

The establishment of a Superintendency of Maritime Shipping in the port city of Quanzhou in 1087—nearly a century after such bureaus were established in Guangzhou and Yangzhou—reflects the growing importance of Quanzhou at that time. The city was one of the primary ports in China from the twelfth to the fourteenth century. Located in southern Fujian, the southeasternmost province, it was perfectly positioned as an entrepôt for China's extensive maritime trade. According to Zhao Rugua, who served as a Superintendent of Maritime Shipping in Quanzhou, there were forty-six countries—ranging from Japan and Indonesia to Somalia, Tanzania, and even Spain—that were active in trading at the time.[1] Zhao's two-volume book *Descriptions of Barbarian Nations: Records of Foreign Peoples* (*Zhufan zhi*) discusses the peoples in Quanzhou in the early thirteenth century, including their politics and customs, as well as the origins and uses of luxuries and goods, such as animals, jewels, precious stones, textiles, and aromatic woods and resins.

Like the cities of Hangzhou, Guangzhou, and Yangzhou, Quanzhou was home to a large population of resident merchants, many of whom had deep personal connections to the region and to local and national governments.[2] For example, Pu Shougeng, who was a member of the influential Pu clan and had strong ties to the Mongol Yuan government, served as a Superintendent of Maritime Shipping and as a naval officer during the late thirteenth century; one of his sons was the Supervisor of Maritime Affairs, and a nephew supported the restoration of the Qingjing Mosque (also known as the Ashab Mosque).[3] First constructed in 1009, Qingjing is the oldest mosque still standing in China, and it is one of several sites in Quanzhou on the UNESCO World Heritage list because of their importance to the history of maritime trade. Other Quanzhou residents of foreign or mixed ethnicity supported Buddhist monasteries, Hindu temples,[4] or Manichean or Nestorian Christian establishments.[5]

The ceramic industry in Fujian has a long history and expanded in the tenth century under the control of the independent Min Kingdom. As was the case throughout southern China, the industry in Fujian further developed after the Southern Song–dynasty court was established in Hangzhou, and in response to the growing demand for ceramics both domestically and throughout the Asian maritime world. By the twelfth and thirteenth centuries, hundreds of kilns producing hundreds of thousands of ceramics were active in Fujian. While at first the kiln complexes there were based along the coast, such as in the port cities of Quanzhou and Fuzhou (the Min capital), over time others were established inland, often in mountainous regions, possibly to meet growing demand or to be closer to the natural materials required to support such an extensive industry, including clay and firewood. The complexes were frequently located near important rivers, such as the Min River, in the north, and the Luoyang River, in the south.

Unlike kiln centers in Zhejiang and Jiangxi Provinces, which produced only one type of ceramic ware, complexes throughout Fujian—like those in Guangdong Province—were noted for their diversified production, making ceramics with green, brown, black, and white glazes for regional, national, and international markets. The cargoes of the twelfth- to thirteenth-century Nanhai I shipwreck and the mid- to late thirteenth-century Java Sea wreck,[6] each of which contained ceramic pieces from different kilns, had substantial quantities of Fujian ceramics. Though Longquan wares comprised the bulk of the Chinese ceramics in the fourteenth-century Sinan wreck, the ship also carried 1,500 pieces from Fujian, as well as a small number of wares from Guangdong and even fewer pieces from kilns in northern China, further attesting to the role Fujian ceramics played in overseas trade at the time.

## Green-Glazed Wares

Fujian borders both Zhejiang and Jiangxi, and its ceramic industry shares glazes, shapes, and designs found in Longquan and Qingbai wares. A pretty dish (fig. 5.1) has been attributed to the Songxi kilns in the eponymous county, located near the Min River.[7] The dish is potted with a dark buff clay similar to one of the clays used in some Longquan kilns, and it is covered with a green glaze that is slightly more yellow than the glazes on Longquan pieces. While the exterior is undecorated, the interior is filled with a carved and incised blossoming lotus flower and leaves, surrounded by an abstract scroll. This type of scroll, sometimes described as a cloud pattern or as floral decoration, is often found in ceramic pieces made in northern and southern Fujian.

The similar, sketchy scroll that fills the interior of a thick bowl (fig. 5.2) typifies the taste for quickly rendered, lively designs in the southern ceramic industry at this time. This bowl is covered with a thin, slightly mottled, light green glaze that has pooled into darker green droplets along the sides (fig. 5.3). Unlike the glaze on the dish from Songxi, this glaze does not completely cover the bowl but ends just short of the foot on the exterior, which is enhanced by groups of parallel lines that resemble those on some contemporaneous Guangdong pieces. Although ceramics like this bowl were not exclusively made in the kilns in Tong'an County on the coast, Chinese and Western scholars have at times catalogued them as Tong'an wares.[8] In Japan, Tong'an wares are classified as *Jukō seiji*, or Jukō-style green wares—a reference to Murata Jukō, an influential tea-ceremony master partially credited with the development of the *wabi*, or rustic, style of tea that flourished in the sixteenth century.[9] Whereas earlier tea ceremonies in Japan were more elaborate and emphasized the use of exotic or luxurious objects, wabi-style tea typically features objects that are less than perfect and, therefore, are assumed to be more approachable or intimate. The development of the

**Fig. 5.1**

*Dish with a Lotus and Scroll*, China, Southern Song dynasty, 12th–13th century. Stoneware with carved and incised decoration under glaze (Songxi ware), DIAM. 11 13/16 in. (30 cm). Edwin R. Bautista and Maria Angelica L. Bautista Collection

**Fig. 5.2**

*Bowl with a Botanical Scroll*, China, Yuan dynasty, 14th century. Stoneware with incised decoration under glaze (possibly Minzhou ware), H. 3 × DIAM. 7 in. (7.6 × 17.8 cm). Yale University Art Gallery, Gift of John Crockett, 2008.222.98

**Fig. 5.3**

Side of fig. 5.2

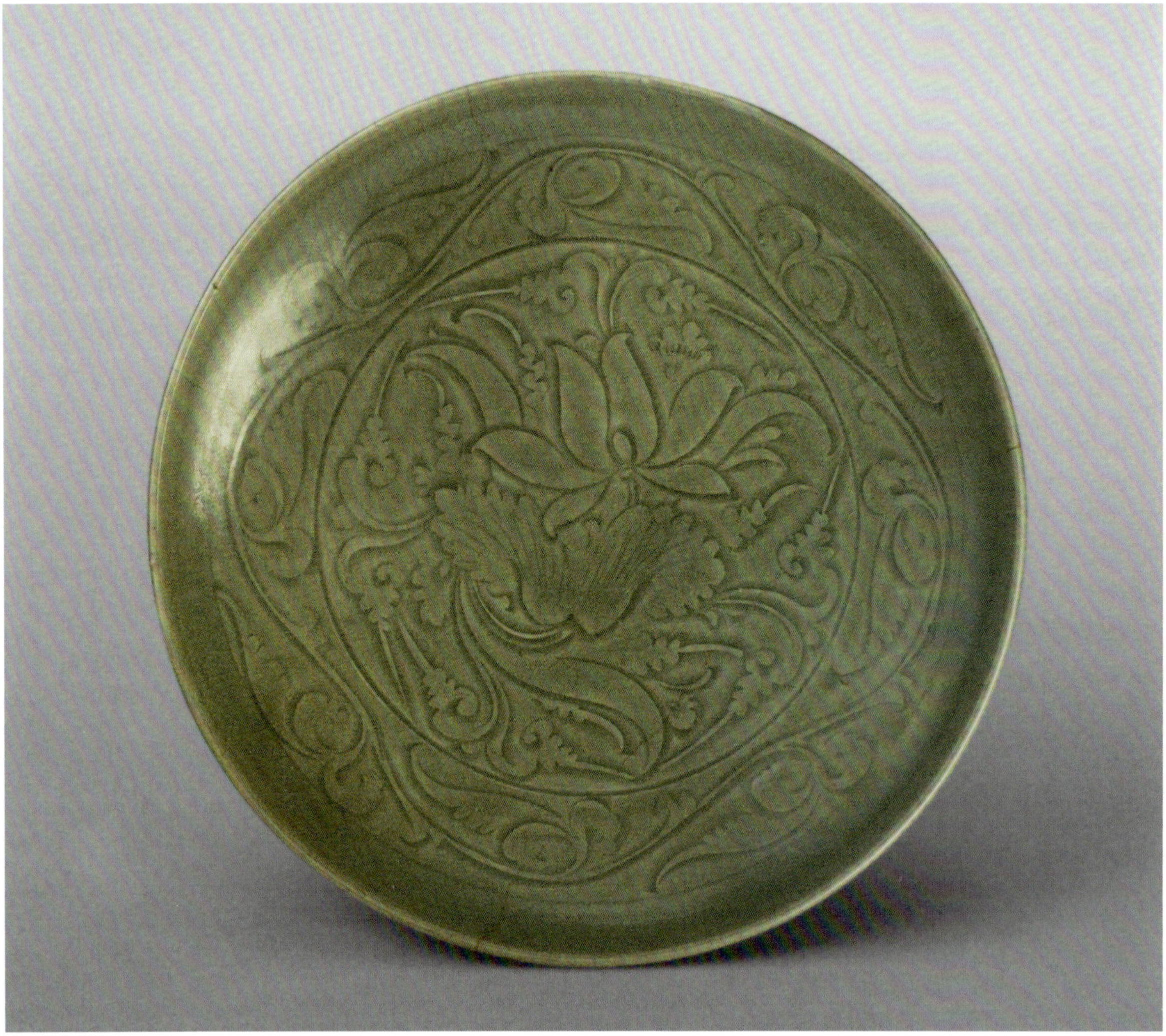

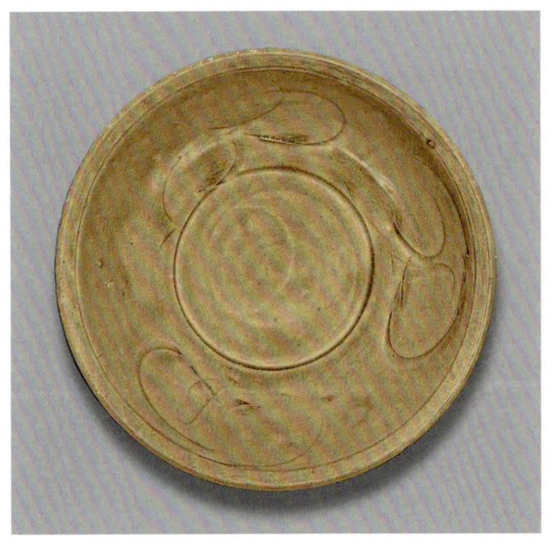

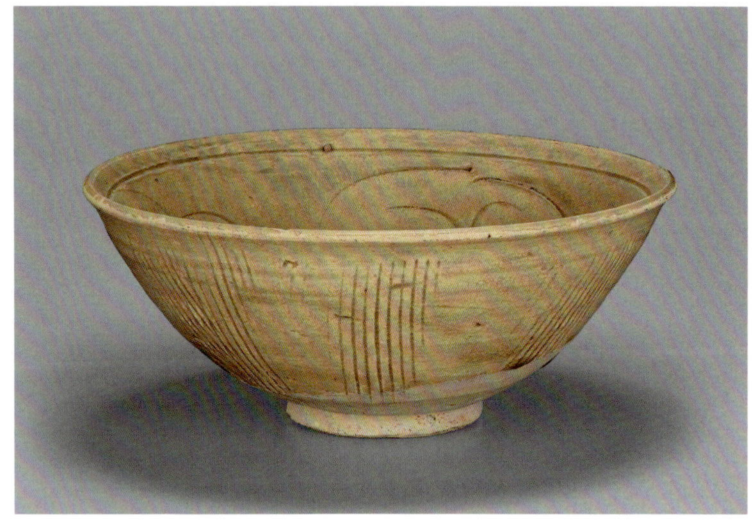

wabi-style tea ceremony fostered greater Japanese interest in different types of Chinese ceramics and in Japanese wares made for everyday use.[10] Although this bowl was found in the Philippines, comparable pieces traded to Japan would have been valued for their unpretentious charm and for the sense of quickness and immediacy in the creation of their shapes and decoration.

A jar with a round body, a long neck, and an elaborate cover (fig. 5.4) continues the Chinese tradition of producing distinctive funerary jars to hold offerings of food and drink. At the top of the cover, a bird with outstretched wings perches. Around the body of the jar, a dragon prowls near a small reclining figure of a child (fig. 5.5) and a coiled snake. The bird and the recumbent child symbolize the continuation of the soul (or an aspect of the soul) in the afterlife, while the snake and dragon have transformative powers, presumably a reference to the passage between life and death. The dragon is chasing a flaming pearl (*cintamani*), a Buddhist symbol for the granting of wishes. In Chinese imagery, dragons also symbolize the east, one of the four cardinal directions. Such funerary jars were often made in pairs—one decorated with a dragon and the other with a tiger, another powerful and protective creature, which signifies the west. Potted with a light gray clay, this jar is covered with the thin Qingbai glaze used in many kilns in Fujian, particularly in Huanxi, in the north near Fuzhou, and in Minqing and Jiangle, in the central region of the province. The gray tinge of the glaze suggests that it was made in one of the kilns in central Fujian.[11]

The same grayish-green hue is found on the glaze covering a dish with an ingenious design of chrysanthemums in the interior (fig. 5.6): a large open blossom impressed at the center is encircled by a molded scroll of four smaller flowers with buds and leaves in the cavetto. Surrounding the chrysanthemums is an additional border with a geometric pattern often described as a key-fret design. The rim of the dish was left unglazed, suggesting that it was once fitted with a metal band. As mentioned, such metal embellishments were used by kilns in the north and south to cover the rims of clay pieces that had been fired upside down.

Both this dish and a vase with curvilinear handles in the Yale University Art Gallery's collection (fig. 5.7) display the thick potting, buff clay, and thin grayish Qingbai glaze that are characteristic of certain Fujian wares. The vase is enhanced with a delicate plum sprig, a perennial motif in poetry and a symbol of spring, morality, and integrity. Vases of this type were popular and have been found in archaeological sites throughout southern China as well as in shipwrecks.[12] Though they could have been used individually, they were often part of a ritual "three-treasures" set that included two such vases and an incense burner in the *gui* shape. The buds and branches on the front of an incense burner excavated from a tomb at Shangqing Temple in the city of Chongqing (fig. 5.8), now in the National Museum of Three Gorges, were designed to match the plum

**Fig. 5.4**

*Funerary Jar with a Dragon and Bird*, China, Southern Song dynasty, 13th century. Stoneware with molded, carved, and incised decoration under glaze (Fujian Qingbai ware, possibly from the Minqing region), H. 16⅝ × DIAM. 9 in. (42.2 × 22.9 cm). Yale University Art Gallery, Stephen Carlton Clark, B.A. 1903, Fund, 1991.92.2a–c

**Fig. 5.5**

Detail of fig. 5.4

**Fig. 5.6**

*Dish with Chrysanthemums*, China, Yuan dynasty, late 13th–14th century. Stoneware with molded decoration under glaze (Fujian Qingbai ware), H. 1½ × DIAM. 6 in. (3.8 × 15.2 cm). Yale University Art Gallery, Gift of John Hadley Cox, B.A. 1935, 1940.832

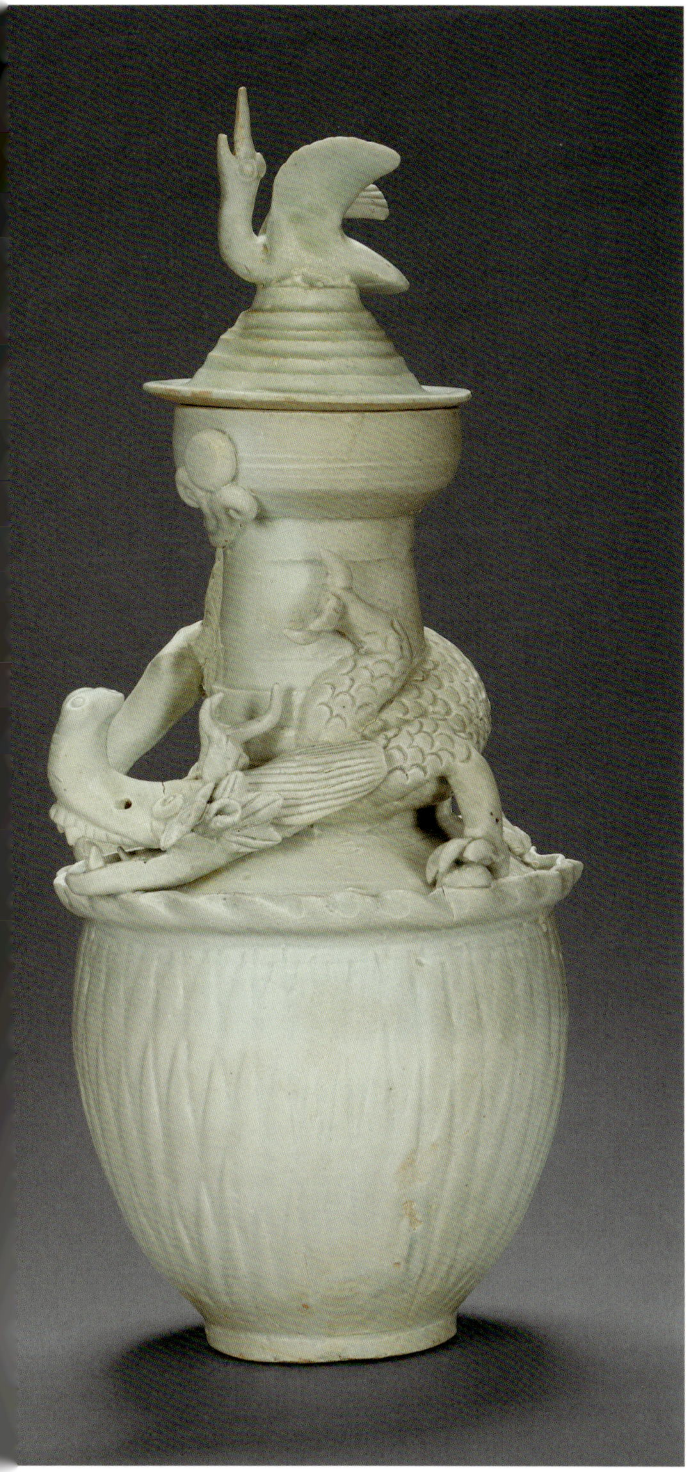

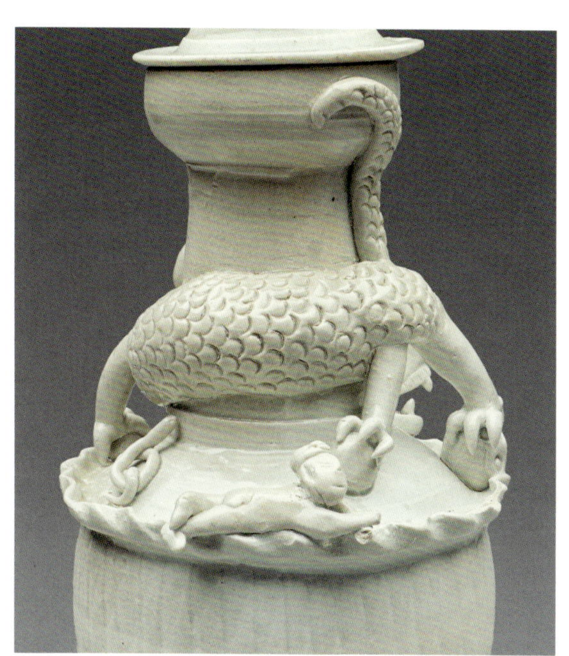

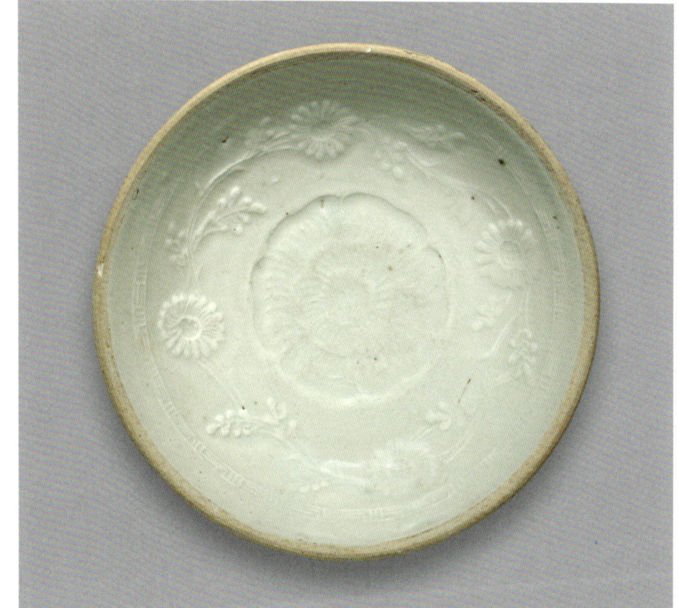

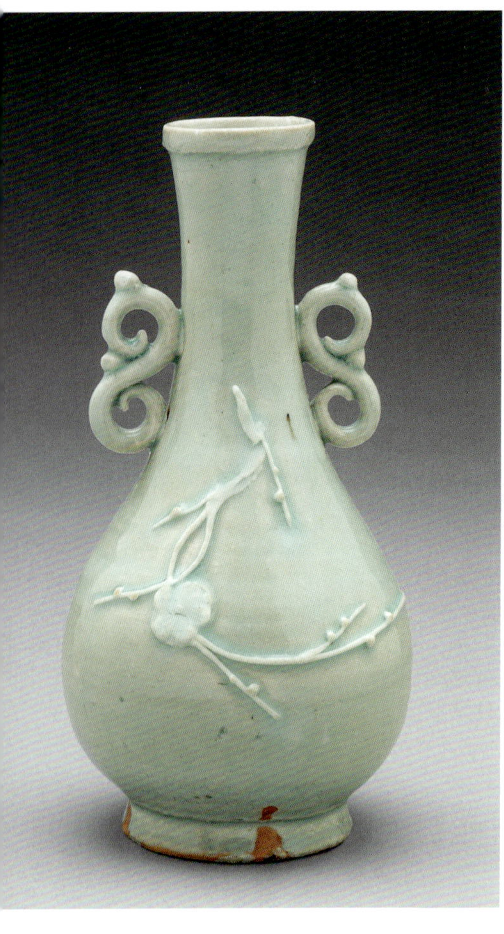

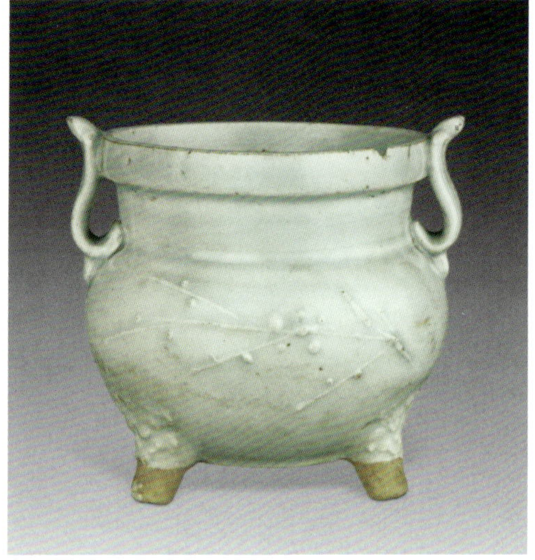

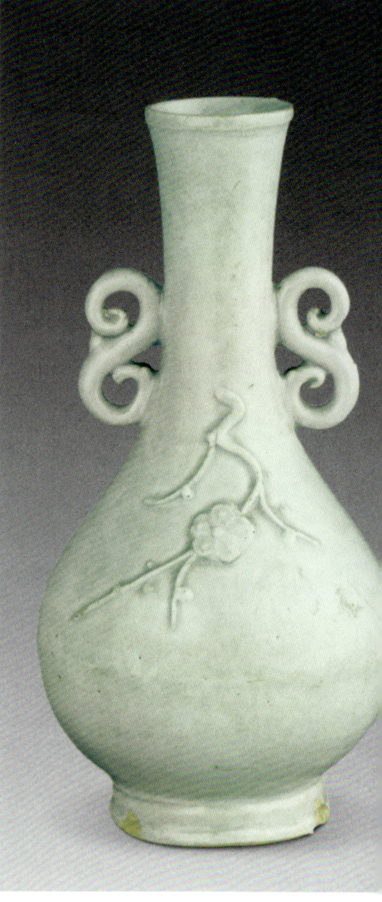

**Fig. 5.7**

*Vase with a Plum Spray*, China, Yuan dynasty, late 13th–14th century. Stoneware with molded and applied decoration under glaze (Fujian Qingbai ware), H. 7¾ × DIAM. 3¹³⁄₁₆ in. (19.7 × 9.7 cm). Yale University Art Gallery, Leonard C. Hanna, Jr., Class of 1913, Fund, 1989.15.1

**Fig. 5.8**

*Incense Burner with a Plum Spray*, China, Yuan dynasty, late 13th–14th century. Stoneware with molded and applied decoration under glaze (Fujian Qingbai ware), H. 4 × DIAM. (base) 2 in. (10 × 5 cm). National Museum of Three Gorges, Chongqing, China

**Fig. 5.9**

*Vase with a Plum Spray*, China, Yuan dynasty, late 13th–14th century. Stoneware with molded and applied decoration under glaze (Fujian Qingbai ware), H. 7¾ in. (20 cm). National Museum of Three Gorges, Chongqing, China

spray on a nearly identical vase excavated at the same site (fig. 5.9). The stem, leaves, and plum blossom on the excavated vase veer to the left, suggesting that it would have been placed to the right of the incense burner. Another vase with a floral spray leaning to the right—similar to the vase in the Gallery's collection—would have completed the set.

Some ceramics with Qingbai glazes produced in Fujian were enhanced with iron-brown spots splashed along the surface. These pieces were made primarily for export and have been found in large quantities in the Philippines and throughout Southeast Asia. Some are intriguingly tiny versions of well-known shapes (fig. 5.10) and would have been placed on family shrines to hold symbolic offerings of grains or seeds. It seems likely that such miniature pieces, some of which were made with attached stands (fig. 5.11), were produced for a specific segment of the vast Chinese and Southeast Asian markets, presumably individuals who wanted the larger full-size versions of the vessels, probably for ceremonial use, but were content, possibly for financial reasons, with smaller iterations of these expensive luxuries.

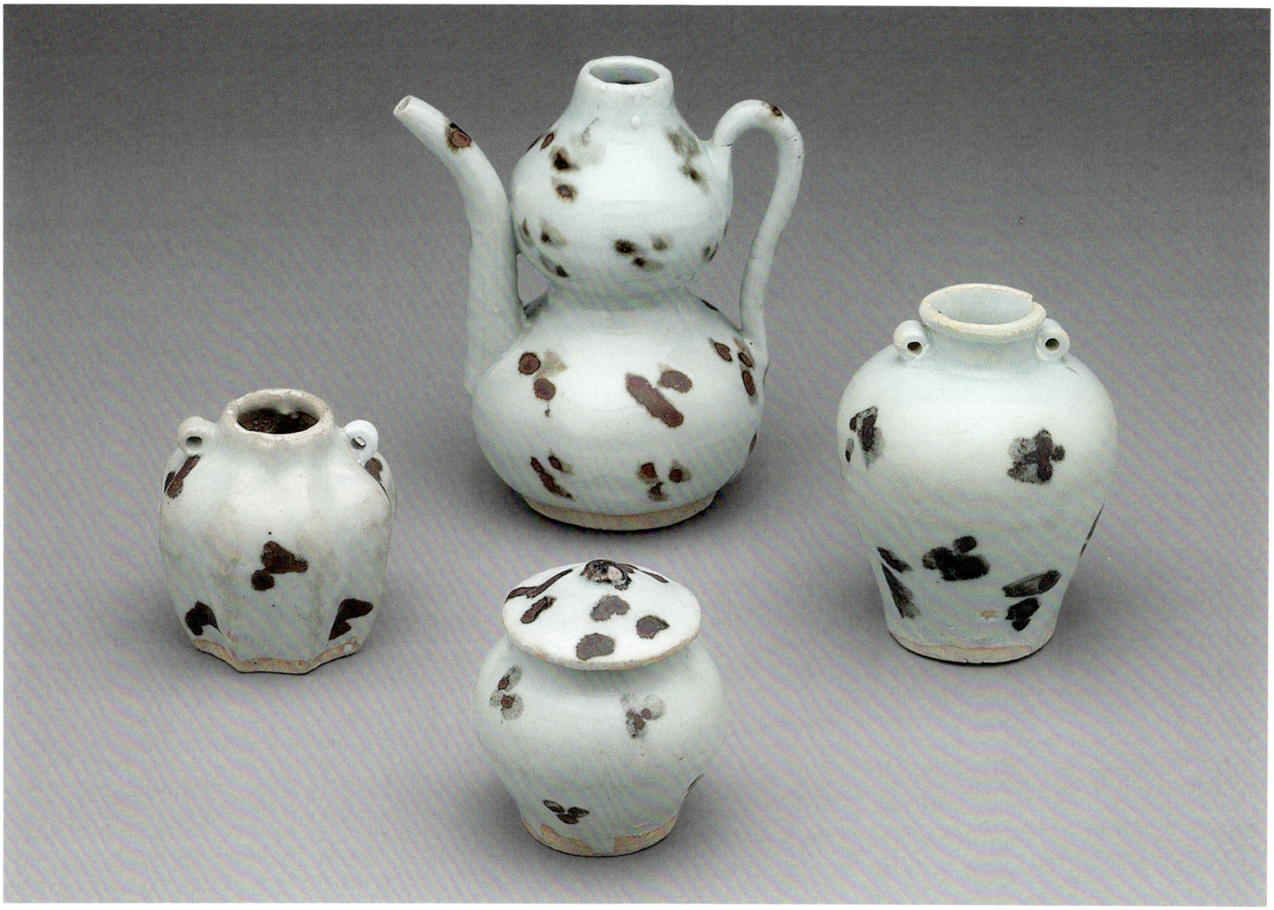

**Fig. 5.10**

*Four Vessels*, China, Southern Song or Yuan dynasty, 13th–14th century. Stoneware with iron-brown splashes and glaze (Fujian Qingbai ware), (clockwise from left) jar with eight lobes: H. 2¼ × DIAM. 2½ in. (5.7 × 6.4 cm); double-gourd-shaped ewer: 4⅜ × 4⅛ in. (11.1 × 10.5 cm); jar: H. 3⅛ × DIAM. 3 in. (7.9 × 7.6 cm); jar with cover: H. 2½ × DIAM. 2¼ in. (6.4 × 5.7 cm). Yale University Art Gallery, Gift of Ann and Gilbert H. Kinney, B.A. 1953, M.A. 1954, 1999.133.11–.12, .14–.15

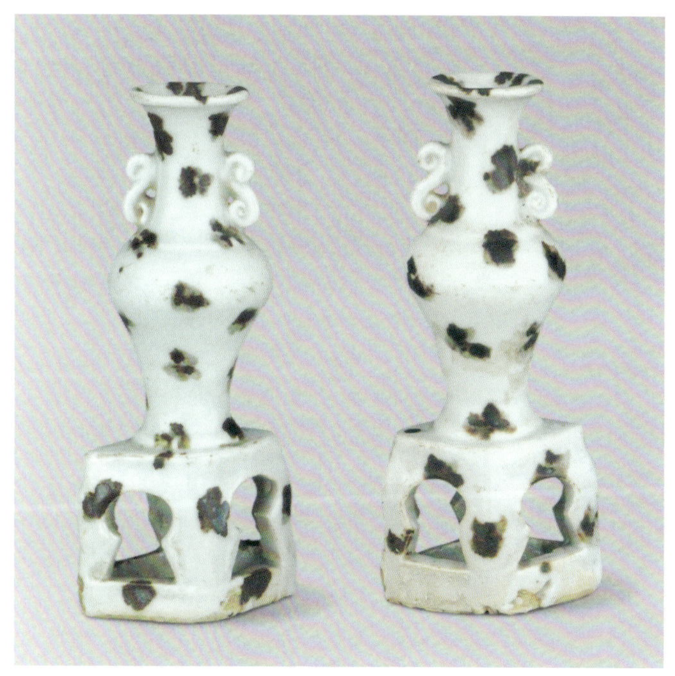

**Fig. 5.11**

*Pair of Vases*, China, Yuan dynasty, late 13th–14th century, excavated at Huaiyi village, Chongqing, China. Stoneware with iron-brown splashes and glaze (Fujian Qingbai ware), each H. 5¾ in. (14.5 cm). National Museum of Three Gorges, Chongqing, China

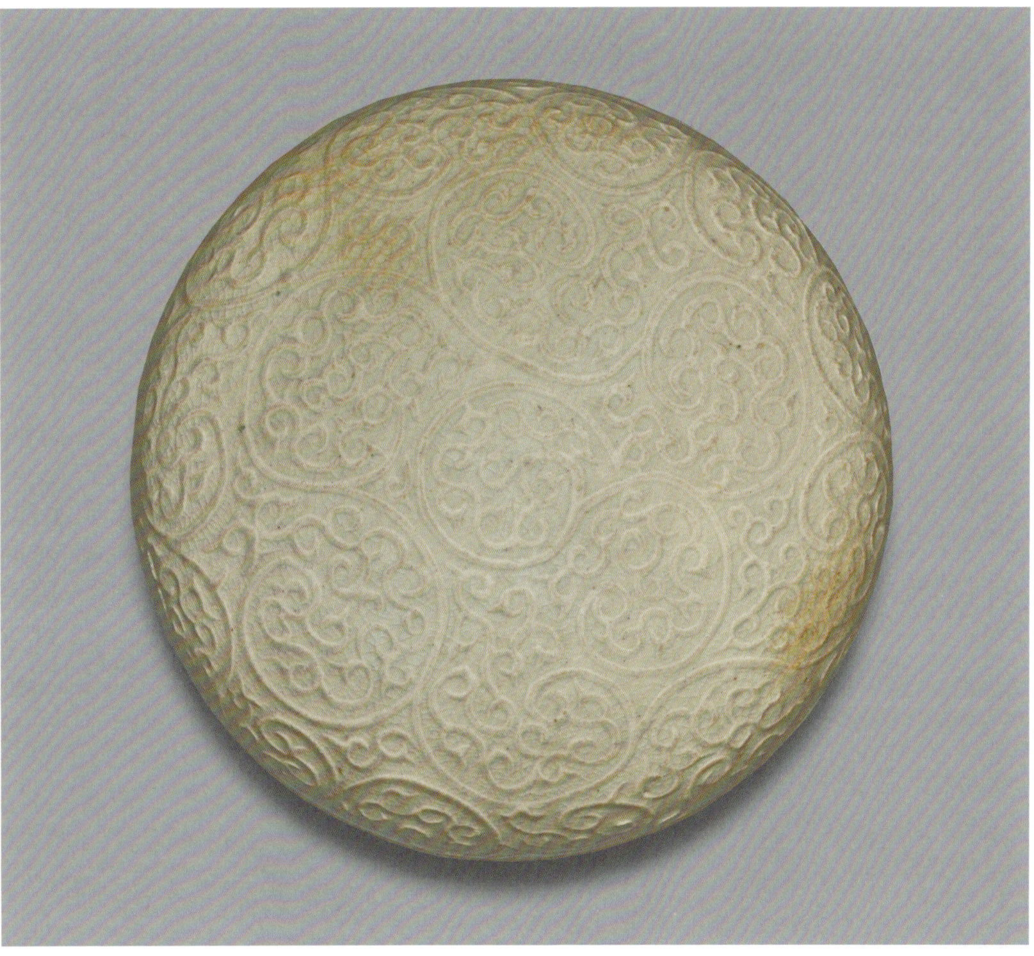

**Fig. 5.12**

*Box with a Botanical Scroll*, China, Yuan dynasty, 14th century. Porcelain with molded decoration under glaze (Dehua ware), H. 5⅞ × DIAM. 3 in. (14.9 × 7.6 cm). Yale University Art Gallery, Gift of Ann and Gilbert H. Kinney, B.A. 1953, M.A. 1954, 1999.133.10

## Shades of White: Dehua Wares

The interest in white ceramics with pale glazes that drove the development of Qingbai wares in Jiangxi in the tenth century also spurred the production of Dehua wares in Fujian. Named for the complex near the city of Dehua, these ceramics were made in kilns throughout southern Fujian and were crafted using a local porcelain clay. They were first produced in the late tenth century, around the same time that porcelain stone was used in the Jiangxi kilns. A wonderful box decorated with a flowing botanical scroll at the top and sides (fig. 5.12) demonstrates the characteristic thin, somewhat brittle white body and light ivory glaze of early Dehua wares.

The word "porcelain," used to describe white, high-fired, glazed ceramics, is attributed to the famous Venetian explorer Marco Polo. In the late thirteenth century, on his return to Italy after traveling throughout China, Polo reached Quanzhou (which he referred to as "Zaitun," its Arabic name). He thought that the color and consistency of the white ceramics he saw around Quanzhou

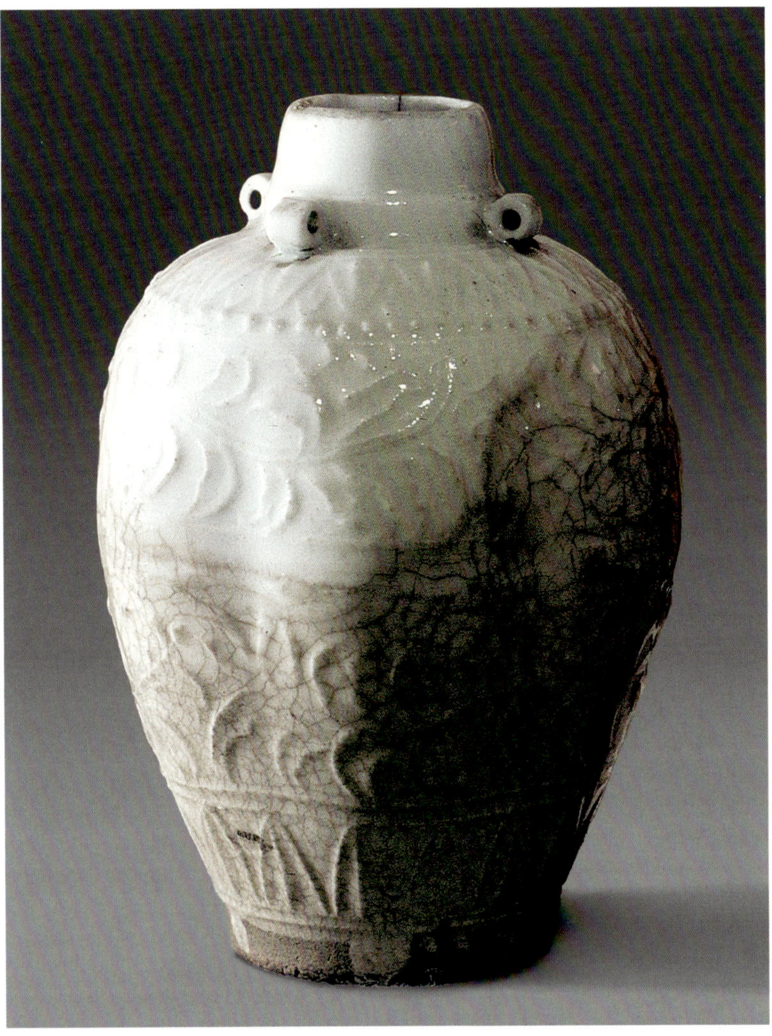

**Fig. 5.13**

*Vase, known as the Marco Polo Vase*, China, Yuan dynasty, 13th century. Porcelain with molded decoration under glaze (Dehua ware), H. 4¾ in. (12 cm). Treasury of San Marco, Venice

resembled the interior of a type of cowrie shell known in Italian as *porcellana*, and his description eventually led to the widespread use of the word "porcelain" to describe this type of ceramic. Polo has traditionally been associated with a small Dehua jar he purportedly brought back to Italy (fig. 5.13).[13] Used to store and transport items such as spices and unguents, the jar was made with a thin white clay and covered with a light ivory glaze. It is decorated with two bands of molded floral scrolls at the center and a band of lotus petals at the top and bottom. While the jar was perceived as extraordinary and rare in Europe at the time, it was, in fact, a standard product of the Dehua kilns and was made in significant quantities. Examples of this type of jar have been excavated at sites throughout mainland Southeast Asia and in the broader Indian Ocean world.

Dehua wares—which are still produced today—would become an important global trade good beginning in the late sixteenth century. From the seventeenth

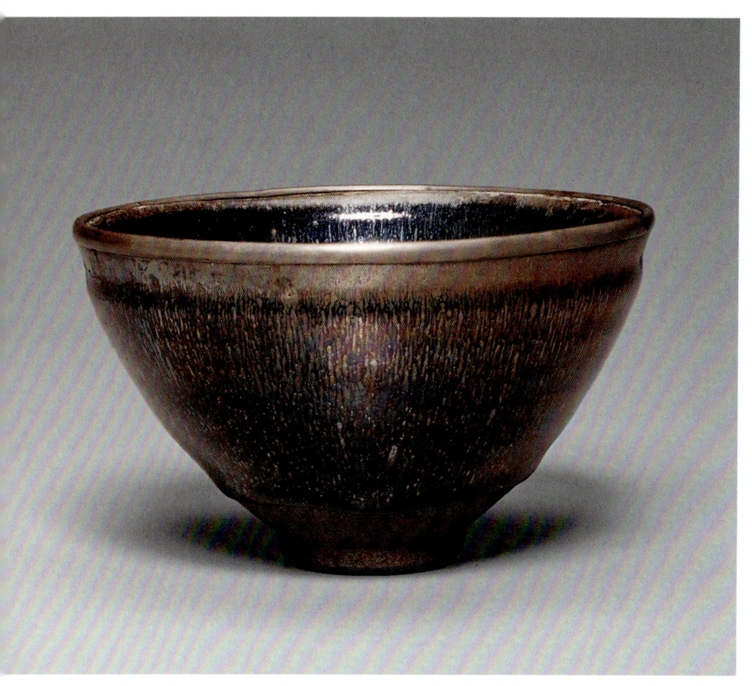

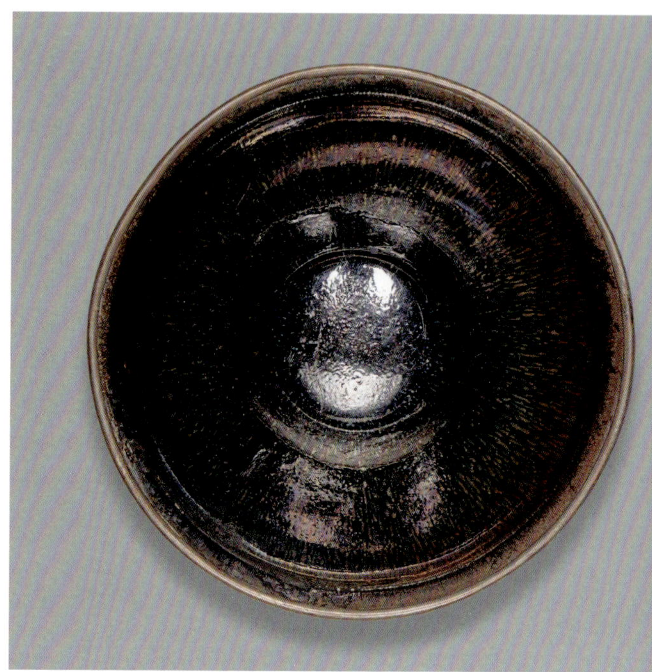

**Fig. 5.14**

*Tea Bowl with "Hare's-Fur" Glaze*, China, Southern Song dynasty, 12th–13th century. Stoneware with iron-oxide glaze (Jian ware), H. 2⅞ × DIAM. 4¾ in. (7.3 × 12.1 cm). Yale University Art Gallery, Wayland Wells Williams, B.A. 1910, Collection, Gift of Mrs. Frances Wayland Williams, 1947.78

**Fig. 5.15**

Interior of fig. 5.14

to the nineteenth century, thousands of Dehua pieces were shipped to Europe. These later wares are known in the West by the French term *blanc de chine*, or "white from China."

## Brown- and Black-Glazed Wares

Fujian kilns, particularly the Jian kilns in the area around the market town of Shuiji, in Jianyang County, expanded their production to respond to the changes in tea drinking that began around the tenth century. During the Tang dynasty, when the drinking of tea was first formalized in China—and, not coincidentally, when ceramics became treasured goods—brick tea was preferred. A piece of a brick composed of tea leaves, stalks, and dust was broken off and boiled in water, and the liquid was then enhanced with additives, such as ginger, jujubes, or peppermint. It was thought that the reddish hue of brick tea looked best in green-glazed bowls, such as the Yue wares of Zhejiang, which contributed to their popularity during the ninth and tenth centuries. Over time, white tea—especially that from Fujian, the most valued and treasured during the Song period—became preferred at the court and among connoisseurs. Made from leaves that were dried, powdered, and then whipped to a white froth in the tea bowl, white tea looked best in black- or brown-glazed bowls.

The Jian kilns were first active during the Han dynasty. During the Tang dynasty, they made green-glazed wares that echoed Yue wares, before focusing on black and brown tea bowls in the late tenth century. Like green glazes, black

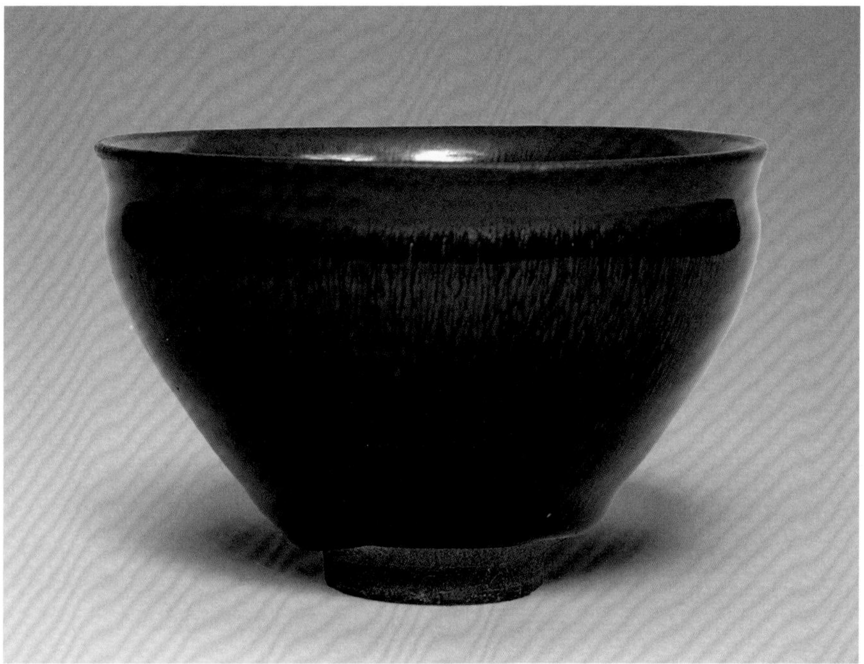

**Fig. 5.16**

*Tea Bowl with Indented Lip and Russet "Hare's-Fur" Markings*, China, Southern Song dynasty, 12th–13th century. Stoneware with iron-oxide glaze (Jian ware), H. 3 3/16 × DIAM. 4 13/16 in. (8.1 × 12.2 cm). Harvard Art Museums/Arthur M. Sackler Museum, Cambridge, Mass., Shumei Culture Foundation Fund, 1995.7

and brown glazes use iron oxides as the primary coloring agent. Changes in the percentages of the ingredients in these compounds create the colors and unique glaze patterns of Jian wares. Known as "hare's fur" in Chinese writings, the silvery streaks seen in the glaze covering the exterior and interior of a tea bowl (figs. 5.14–.15) derive from an excess of iron, which segregates itself during firing. This bowl was carefully designed to enhance the drinking of tea: it has a somewhat conical shape that fits snugly into cupped hands, a subtle indentation under the lip to encourage drinking in tiny sips, and a thick glaze that simultaneously keeps the tea warm and protects the hands. The rim of the bowl, which was fired upright, is covered with a metal band that served to accentuate the extraordinary hare's-fur pattern in the glaze and to protect the piece during transport.[14]

Minor changes in the amount of iron oxide in the glaze produced the russet, as opposed to silver, hare's-fur pattern on an elegant, beautifully balanced Jian tea bowl (fig. 5.16). This bowl was also covered with a thick glaze that pools just above the foot; it was then glazed a second time at the top with a slurry (a thick mixture of water and clay), to hide the areas along the rim that had been revealed as the first application of glaze dripped along the body. A two-character inscription incised into the foot reads "gongwu" (tribute object), suggesting that the bowl was made for the use of the Northern Song court at Kaifeng or the Southern Song court at Hangzhou. As early as the tenth century, the Northern Song court supervised and operated the Beiyuan Garden in Fujian, the source of the most cherished tea at the time. By the late tenth to the early eleventh century,

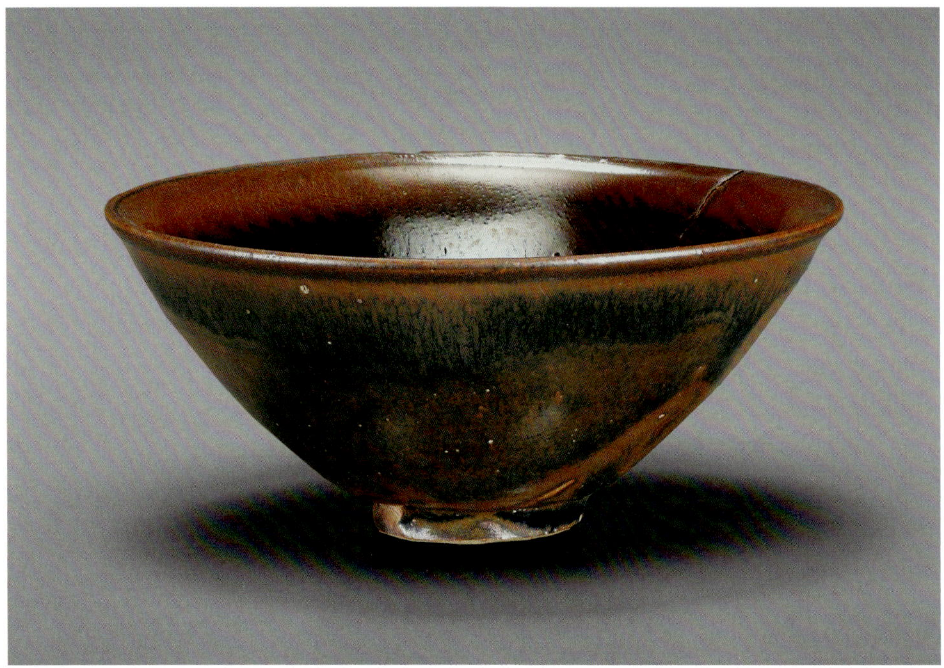

**Fig. 5.17**

*Tea Bowl with "Hare's-Fur" Glaze*, China, Southern Song dynasty, 12th–13th century. Stoneware with iron-oxide glaze (Chayang ware), H. 2⅛ × DIAM. 4⅞ in. (5.4 × 12.4 cm). Yale University Art Gallery, Wayland Wells Williams, B.A. 1910, Collection, Gift of Mrs. Frances Wayland Williams, 1947.58

OPPOSITE:

**Fig. 5.18**

*Tea Bowl*, China, Southern Song or Yuan dynasty, 13th–14th century. Stoneware with slip and glaze (Wuyishan ware), H. 2³⁄₁₆ × DIAM. 4⁷⁄₁₆ in. (5.5 × 11.2 cm). Yale University Art Gallery, Gift of Pia Christina Ossorio in memory of Frederic E. Ossorio, B.A. 1942, 2024.23.1

**Fig. 5.19**

Images of the contents of case C3, recovered from the Sinan shipwreck, near Korea

tea from this garden, tea bowls from the Jian kilns, and spring water from the city of Wuxi, in Jiangxi, were collectively known as the "three excellences" by courtiers and other intelligentsia. At times, such individuals participated in formal tea ceremonies and in contests in which teas and bowls from Fujian were judged.

The intensity of demand for Jian brown-glazed tea bowls during the late Northern and Southern Song periods is reflected in the production of comparable bowls in other kiln centers in Fujian and elsewhere in China; however, those from the Jian kilns in Fujian and the Jizhou kilns in Jiangxi are, justifiably, the most renowned in global ceramic history.[15] A tea bowl (fig. 5.17) that was most likely produced in the Chayang kilns in northwest Fujian, not far from the city of Nanjing on the Min River, illustrates another Fujianese variant of the popular hare's-fur pattern. Potted with a light buff clay that differs from the darker clay used for Jian works, this bowl has an interesting, if somewhat haphazard, combination of a hare's-fur design and a russet glaze. The alternating brown and blue-black glazes partially covering another bowl (fig. 5.18), which was potted with light gray clay and does not have any patterning in the glaze, indicate that it was made in the Wuyishan kilns in northwest Fujian, another region famous for its tea.[16]

Evidence from the Sinan shipwreck suggests that Fujian tea bowls were occasionally sold as part of a set of items needed for the formal preparation and drinking of tea. For example, case C3 (fig. 5.19), one of many Japanese wood containers on this boat, held an interesting assemblage of goods, including a

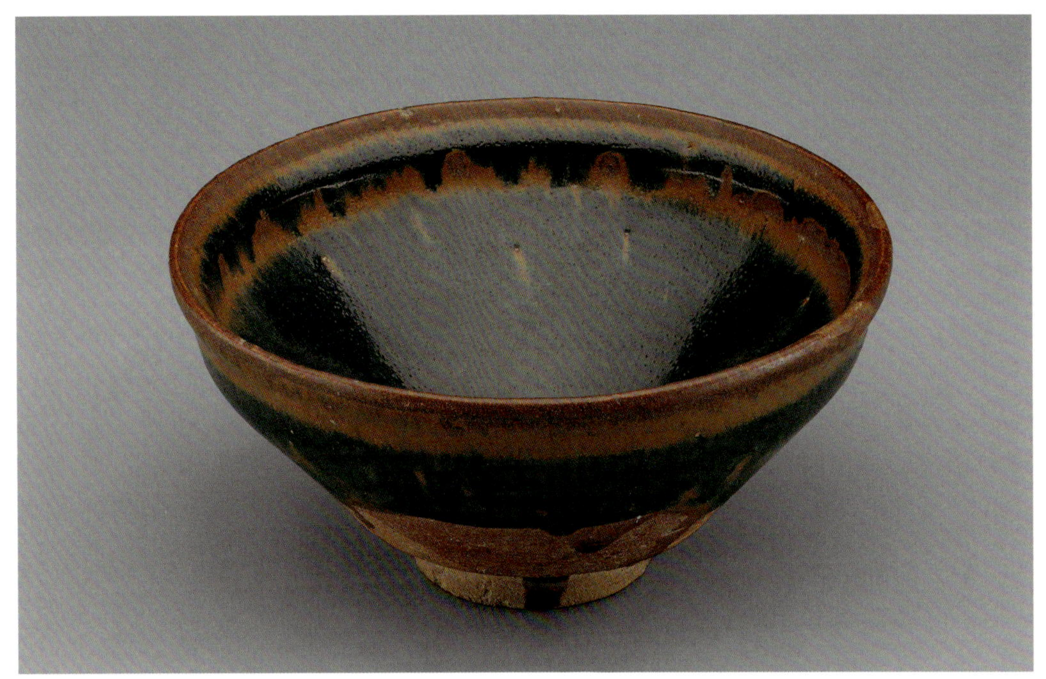

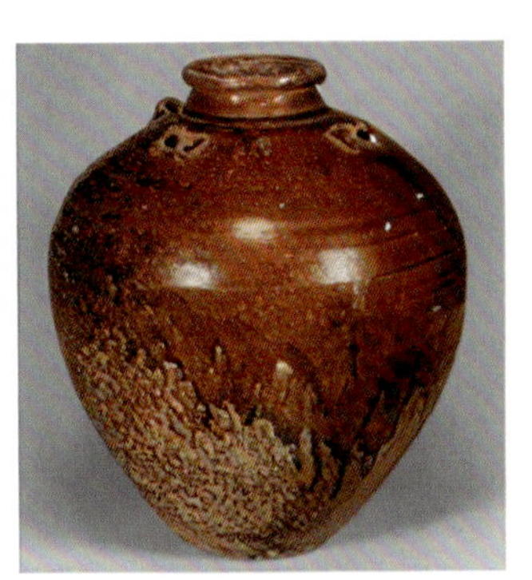

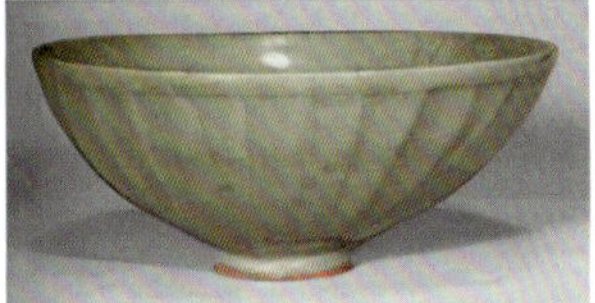

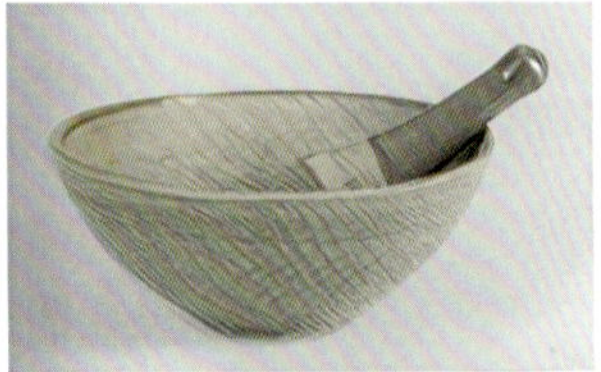

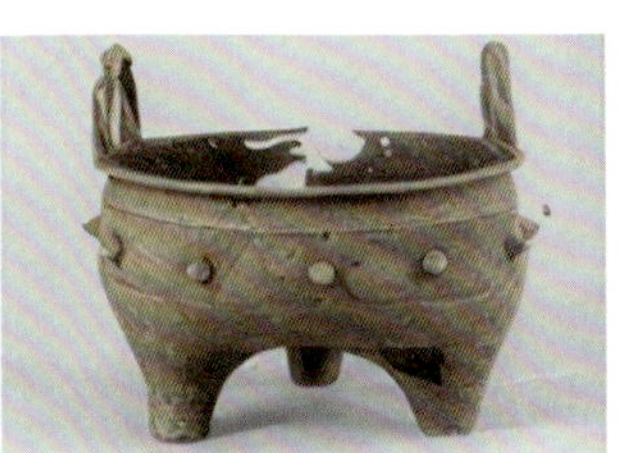

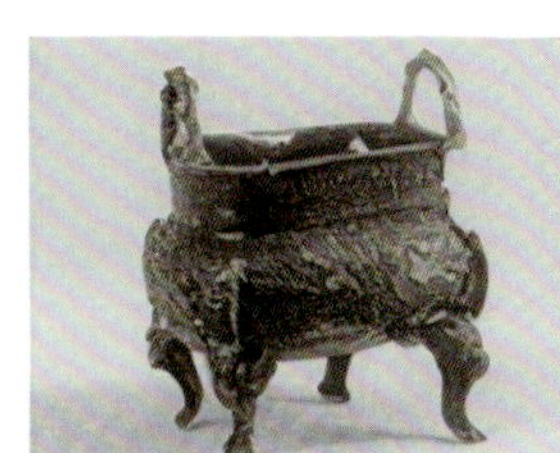

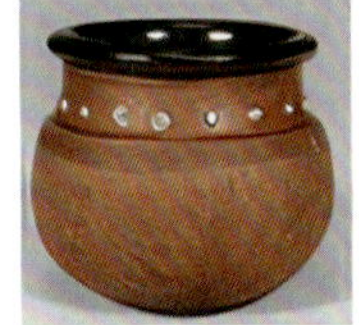

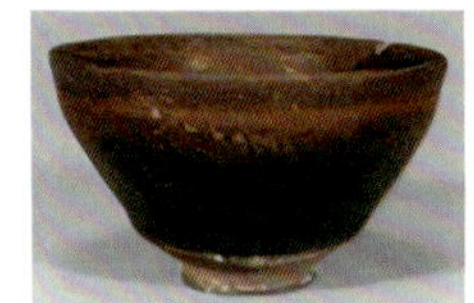

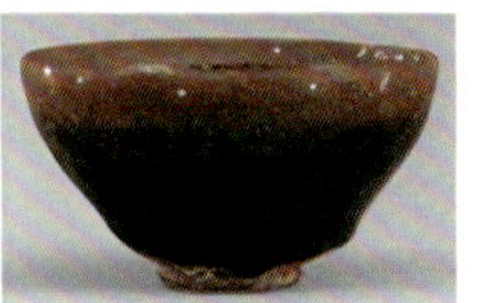

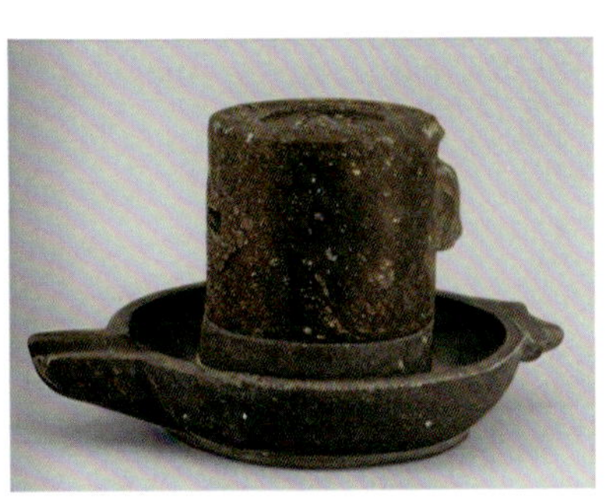

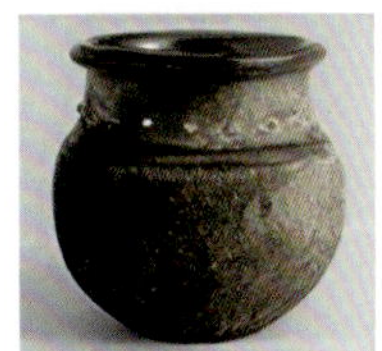

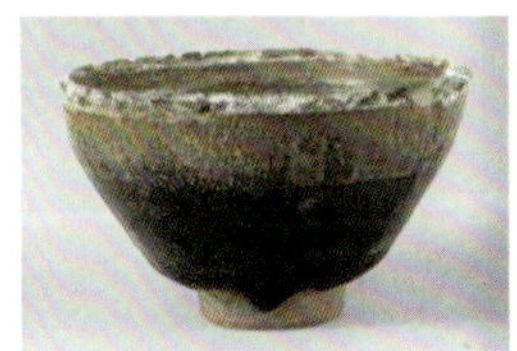

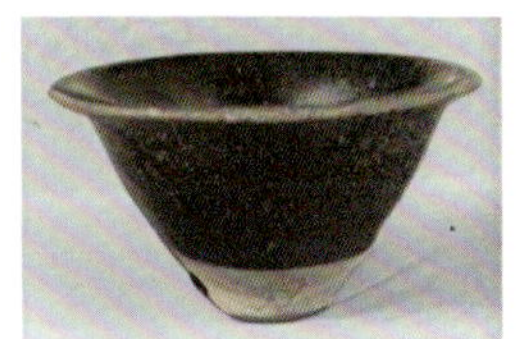

mortar, two bronze incense burners, and multiple ceramic pieces: two green-glazed bowls, four brown-glazed tea bowls, a large jar for storing tea leaves, and two smaller jars, possibly for storing spices or other additives.[17] While an individual may not necessarily have used all of the items in this set in every ceremony, the number of items in the group—particularly the combination of green and brown bowls—would have enabled them to choose the appropriate items for a certain season or theme.

In addition to being shipped in significant quantities to Japan, some tea bowls were brought there individually by travelers, often Buddhist monks who had journeyed throughout China studying and practicing at prominent monasteries, including those on Mount Tianmu (its name meaning "heavenly eyes"), near Hangzhou. The Japanese pronunciation of the Chinese characters that read *tianmu* is *tenmoku*. As a result, Jian and other brown- and black-glazed bowls are often called *tenmoku* wares in Japanese sources. Bowls made in Seto and other kilns in Japan, which began operation in the thirteenth century, sometimes re-created the appearance of Chinese wares; by the sixteenth century, Japanese kilns were producing their own tea bowls intended for such ceremonies.[18] Chinese and Japanese brown- and black-glazed ceramics were introduced to Europe and North America in the late nineteenth and early twentieth centuries as part of the Arts and Crafts movement. Today, the Japanese word *tenmoku* is widely used in Western languages to describe brown and black glazes, particularly those covering tea bowls and other ceramics in East Asian shapes.[19]

Brown-glazed ceramic wares were also produced in the Cizao kilns in southern Fujian, a major center for trade wares that also made pieces with glazes in dark green and other colors, as well as large transport vessels.[20] Three small jars from Cizao (fig. 5.20), all of which were found in the Philippines and were most likely used to transport precious luxuries, such as cosmetics, incense, or spices, attest to the wide range of Cizao production. While the glaze on the squat jar (fig. 5.20, left) is deep brown, that on the thinner, rounder jar (center) is green, and the one covering the jar with a wide mouth (right) is more amber in hue. The dragons applied to the jar with the green glaze are a type of decoration often found on Cizao wares.

A similar dragon appears on a brown-glazed spouted vessel (fig. 5.21) known as a *kendi*, a type of object made in multiple kiln complexes, including Dehua and Cizao, and specifically intended for markets in Southeast Asia. *Kendi* is a Malay word stemming from *kundika*, the Sanskrit term for an Indian pouring vessel introduced throughout Asia with Buddhism. In Southeast Asia, *kendi* hold water collected from sacred rivers and sites, as well as medicines and spirits, and are used in religious rituals, ceremonies such as investitures, and important moments in daily life. They are used for both pouring and drinking—a person

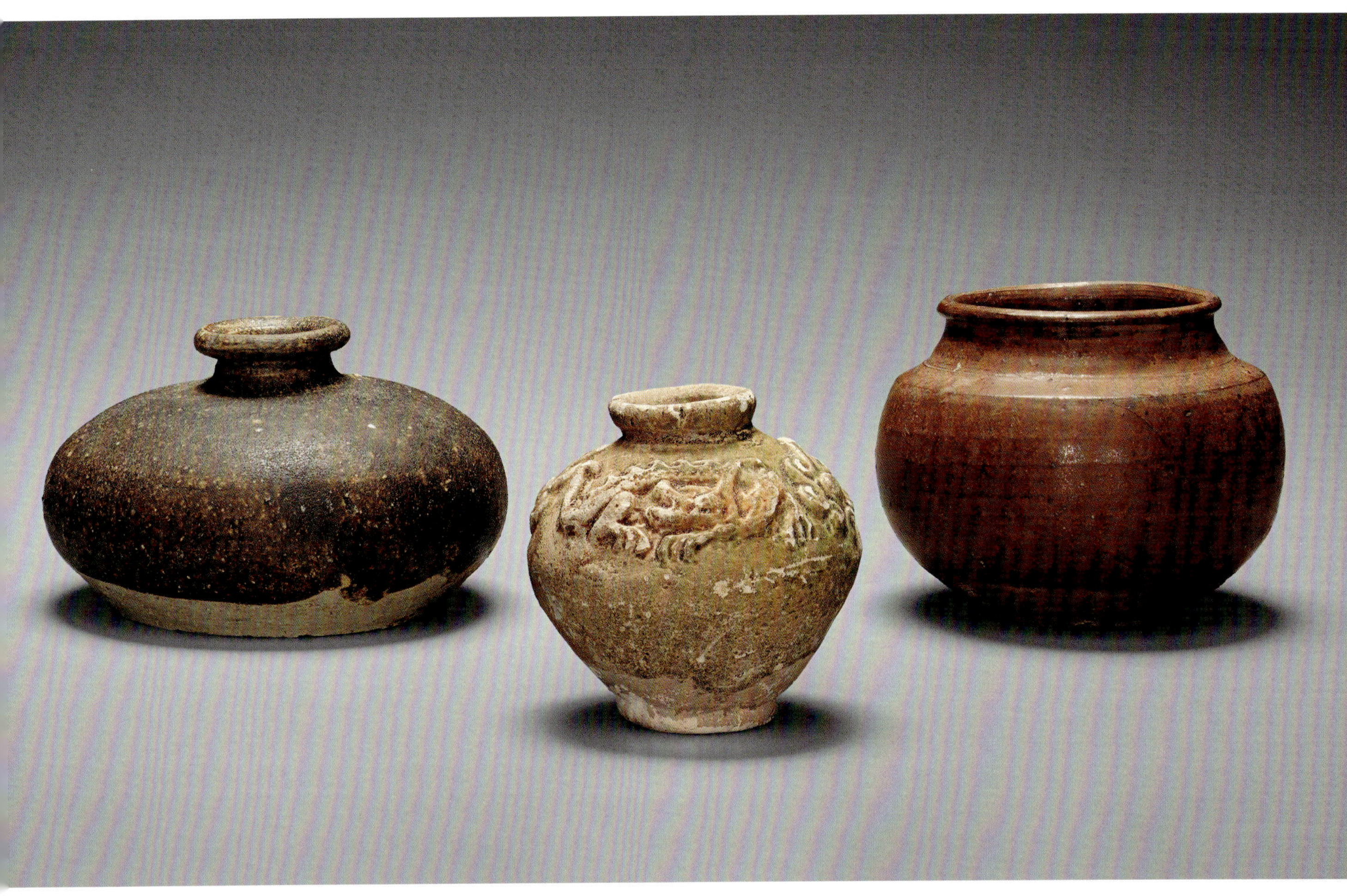

**Fig. 5.20**

(left) *Jar*, China, Yuan dynasty, late 13th–14th century. Stoneware with glaze (Cizao ware), H. 2¼ × DIAM. 13 in. (5.7 × 33 cm). Yale University Art Gallery, Gift of John Crockett, 2008.222.9. (center) *Jar with Two Dragons*, China, Yuan dynasty, late 13th–14th century. Stoneware with molded and applied decoration under glaze (Cizao ware), H. 2¹¹⁄₁₆ × DIAM. 8⅝ in. (6.8 × 22 cm). Yale University Art Gallery, Gift of John Crockett, 2008.222.103. (right) *Jar*, China, Yuan dynasty, 13th–14th century. Stoneware with glaze (Cizao ware), H. 2¾ × DIAM. 11¹³⁄₁₆ in. (7 × 30 cm). Yale University Art Gallery, Gift of John Crockett, 2008.222.30

drinking from such a vessel would raise it above their head and pour liquid from the spout into their mouth. *Kendi* are often depicted in the hands of Buddhist and Hindu deities in sculptures.

A bottle with a deep brown glaze but an unglazed shoulder (fig. 5.22) represents a distinctive Cizao variant of the *meiping* bottle produced throughout north and south China beginning in the tenth and eleventh centuries. This variant, with a broad shoulder and a long, tapering body, is classified as a "chicken-leg" (*jitui*) shape in Chinese sources. Produced at Cizao from the late eleventh to the fourteenth century, bottles of this type have sometimes been catalogued as "mercury jars," suggesting that they were used primarily for the sale and transport of this desirable liquid, which is plentiful in China.[21] Mercury is toxic, and the shape of these bottles, specifically the wide shoulder and small mouth, would have made spills less likely. However, the excavation of a bottle of this type with the label "grape wine jar" in 1958 at the Wulanchabu city site in Inner Mongolia[22] indicates that such vessels (undoubtedly repurposed over time)

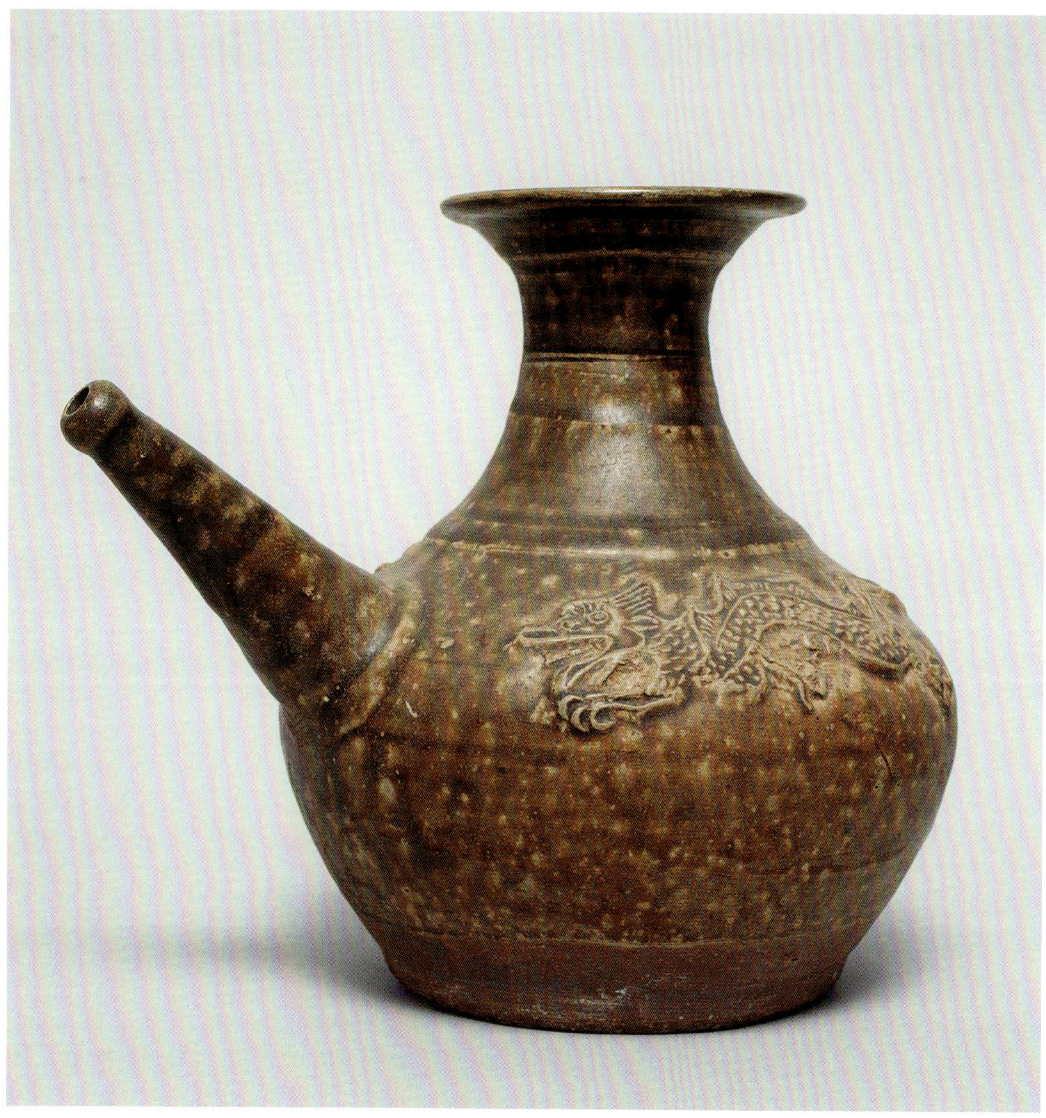

**Fig. 5.21**

*Pouring Vessel (Kendi) with a Dragon*, China, Yuan dynasty, 13th–14th century. Stoneware with molded decoration under glaze (Cizao ware), 6⅞ × 6 in. (17.5 × 15.2 cm). Detroit Institute of Arts, Gift of the Honorable and Mrs. G. Mennen Williams, 72.673

**Fig. 5.22**

*Bottle*, China, Yuan dynasty, late 13th–14th century. Stoneware with molded decoration under glaze (Cizao ware), H. 13¹³⁄₁₆ × DIAM. 6⁵⁄₁₆ in. (35 × 16 cm). Yale University Art Gallery, Gift of Joann and Gifford Phillips, Class of 1942, 2008.115.4

were also used for wine, another important product of southern Fujian that was traded domestically and abroad.

As was true throughout China, most of the kilns in Fujian declined after the fourteenth century, due in part to the growing importance of blue-and-white wares, made of porcelain with cobalt blue under the glaze. These works were first produced in significant numbers at Jingdezhen, in Jiangxi, and later were produced in much smaller quantities at Zhangzhou, in Fujian. They were also made in Korea and Vietnam beginning in the fifteenth century and in Japan in the early seventeenth. By the sixteenth century, blue-and-white wares had replaced celadons as the most desired ceramics in international trade, beginning another rich and fascinating chapter in the story of Chinese ceramics.

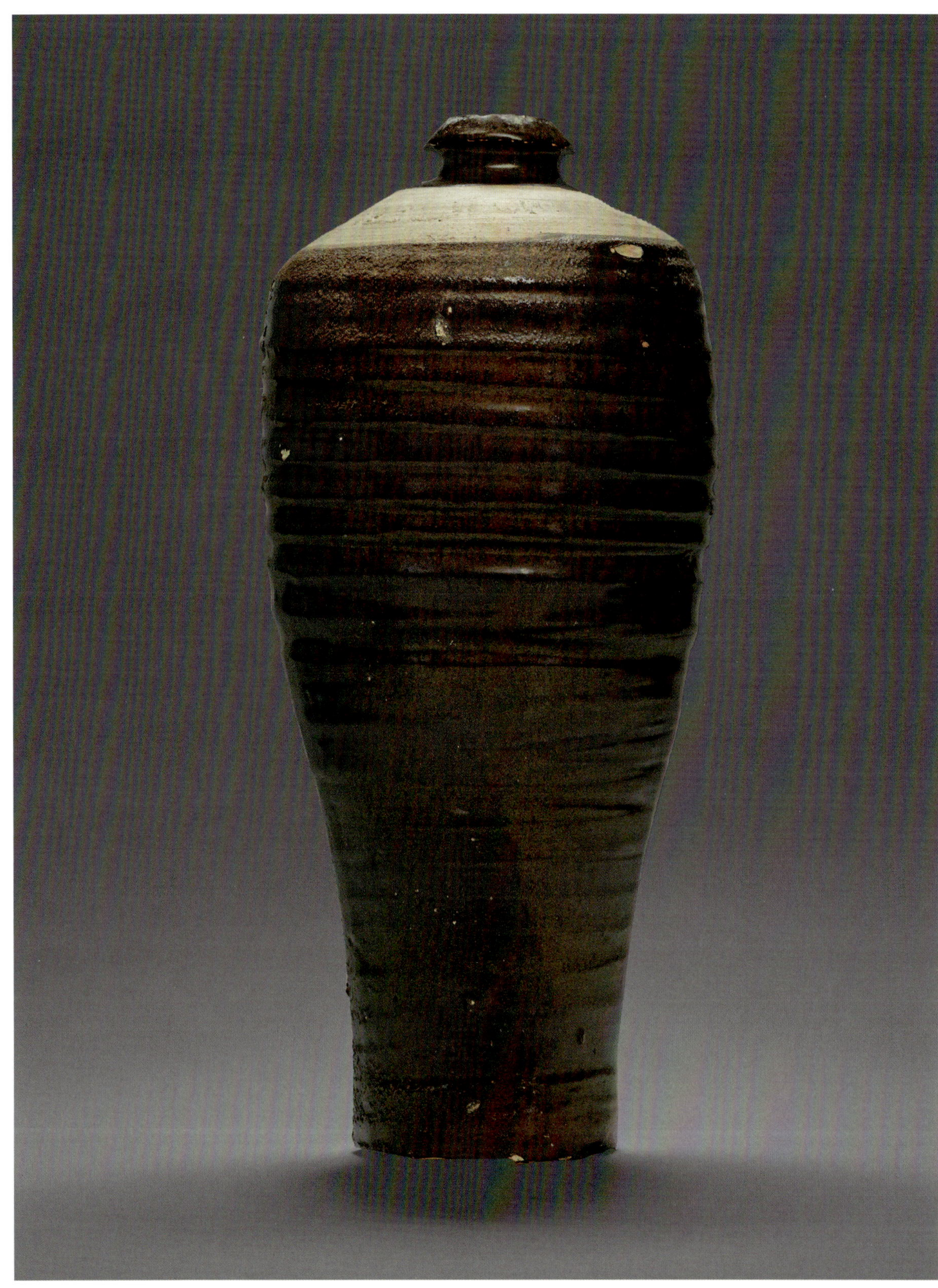

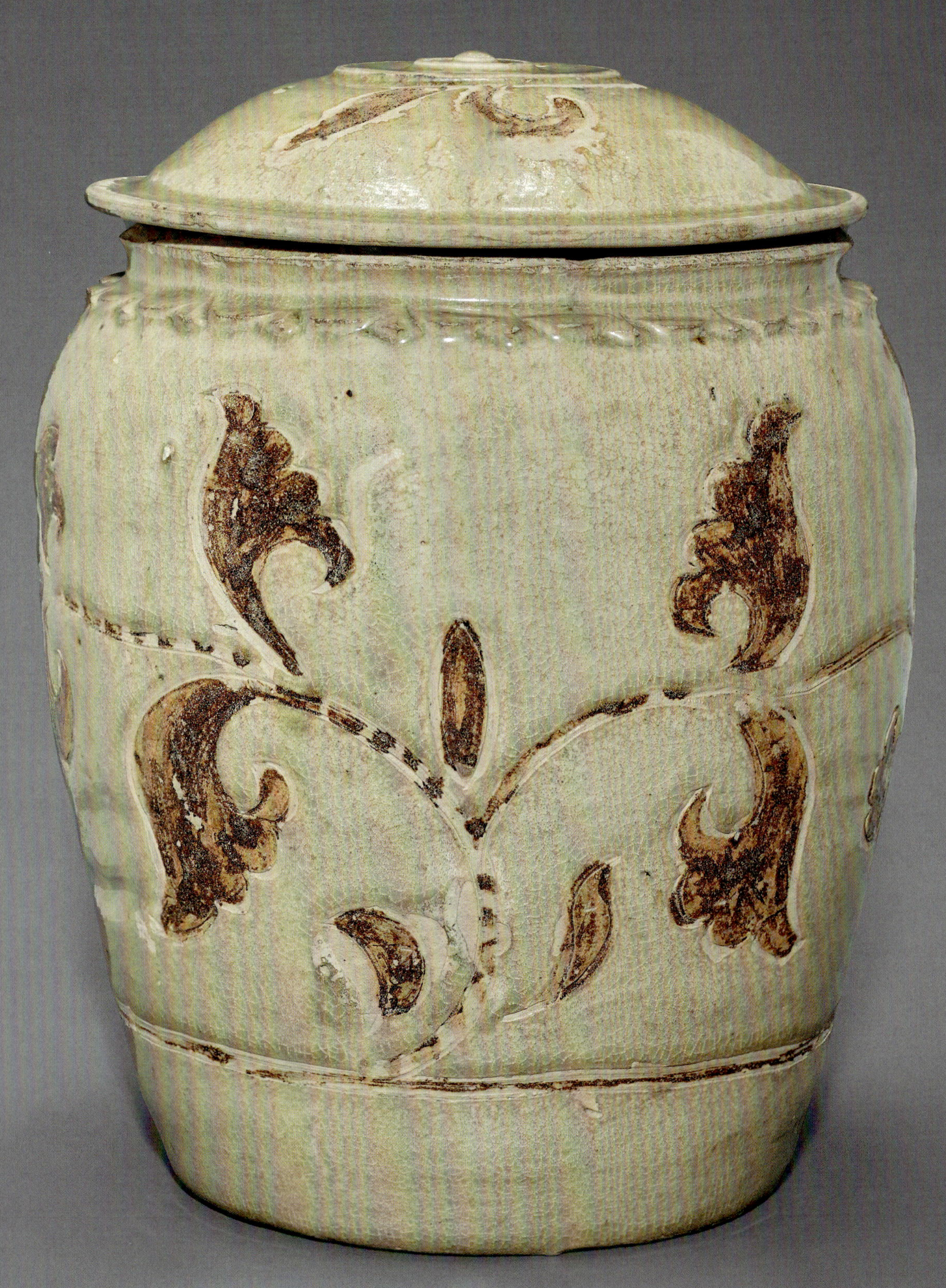

CHAPTER 6

# Mainland Southeast Asia and the Southern Chinese Industry

Waterways and coastal trade have long linked regions in Southeast Asia to each other, to southern China, and to the east coast of India. The South China Sea, Gulf of Thailand, and Bay of Bengal, which surround the Southeast Asian peninsula, are connected to the hinterland by five major river systems, three of which begin on the Tibetan plateau. Two of these rivers—the Mekong, the twelfth-longest river in the world (known as the Lancang in Chinese), and the Salween (Nujiang)—pass through Yunnan Province, in southwest China, where they intersect with the Yangzi, thereby connecting Southeast Asian and Chinese centers. As a result, as early as the fourth or third century B.C.E., cultures based in southwest China and mainland Southeast Asia—such as the Dian in Yunnan; the Nan Yue in Guangxi, Guangdong, and southern Fujian Provinces and in northern Vietnam; and the Dongson in mainland and island Southeast Asia—all shared a material culture defined by ceremonial bronze drums, cowrie containers, and the style of quotidian implements such as axes, daggers, and spearheads.[1] By the first century B.C.E., the southern and coastal areas of this region were involved in the expanding maritime trade with China, West Asia, and the Indian Ocean world.

Evidence for an early trading polity called Oc'Eo (known as Funan in Chinese) is found in Chinese sources beginning in the third century C.E. Located near Ba Phnum (in present-day Cambodia) and linked to the interior by canals, Oc'Eo (ca. 68–627 C.E.) was either a single entity or a confederation of several small states centered on a capital also known as Oc'Eo, a port city in the Mekong delta, in what is now southern Vietnam. According to sixth-century records, the Chinese envoys Kang Tai and Zhu Yi visited in the third century and reported that Oc'Eo benefited from an agricultural productivity that enabled the housing and feeding of sailors from many foreign lands, who were often forced to wait up to five months for the monsoon winds to shift before they could continue their journeys. Oc'Eo had palaces and stone houses as well as repositories for books and other treasures. Excavations there have revealed Chinese mirrors, Roman coins, and early stone and wood sculptures. It is possible, albeit fanciful, to imagine that the Roman ship recorded in Vietnam in 166 C.E. (as discussed in chapter 4) also stopped in Oc'Eo during its travels.

In the mid-seventh century, as Oc'Eo faltered, mainland Southeast Asia split into several smaller polities. The southernmost lands became part of Srivijaya (active from the seventh to the thirteenth century), a fascinating thalassocracy, or maritime empire, based around Palembang, on the island of Sumatra. Srivijaya was a major center for Buddhist practice and study and was often visited by monks from China and other countries. The empire benefited from the increasing use of the Strait of Malacca to sail between the South China Sea and the Indian Ocean, and it grew wealthy and influential due to its pivotal role in maritime trade. In the early eleventh century, Srivijaya began to decline as a result of incursions from the rival Chola Kingdom (ca. 880–1279), a significant maritime empire based in southern India, and it was ultimately incorporated into the Singhasari Kingdom (1222–92), based in the eastern part of Java.

Most of mainland Southeast Asia, on the other hand, became part of the Khmer Empire in the early ninth century. Like many early cultures around the world, those in mainland Southeast Asia had produced ceramics as early as the Neolithic period, pieces that were usually low-fired and were sometimes stamped or painted. Such wares continued to be made for local consumption and use for centuries. By the Khmer period, however, high-fired glazed wares in shades of green and brown were also being produced.

## Ceramics in the Khmer Empire, 9th to 15th Century

The Khmer Empire (802–1431) covered an area that included present-day Cambodia, Laos, Thailand, and parts of southern Vietnam. Today it is known for its complicated hydraulic systems and monuments such as Angkor Wat, an early twelfth-century Buddhist establishment that is one of the largest religious complexes in the world. Although Khmer ceramics are covered with green and brown glazes comparable to those made in China from the tenth to the fourteenth century, they often have unique shapes with no parallels in the Chinese industry. A charming eleventh- or twelfth-century pot in the shape of a cat (fig. 6.1) illustrates the prevalence of zoomorphic forms—including birds, boars, fish, horses, and lions—in the Khmer repertoire. In addition to vessels in the shape of animals, some objects have animal or human faces as lids or sides.[2] The cat-shaped pot is covered with a light green glaze with a delicate crackle. Incised lines articulate the paws of the crouching feline as well as its facial features, and a combination of applied decoration and incisions define its form.

The lime stored in this pot would have been used for the consumption of betel nuts (the seeds of the betel palm), a social practice with a long tradition in India and Southeast Asia that is comparable to the drinking of coffee or tea in other parts of the world. Ground lime and a nut were wrapped together in a palm leaf and consumed during personal events and political or religious ceremonies. Spices, particularly luxuries such as cardamon, clove, or turmeric—some regional and others imported—were occasionally added to the lime-nut mixture in the same way that such goods were used to flavor tea in China. Like coffee and tea, the betel nut is thought to have medicinal properties: it purportedly can alleviate headaches and skin problems and improve relationships between men and women.

The shape of the flared mouth and foot of a large ovoid jar (fig. 6.2) indicates that it derives from a metal prototype—as do many Khmer ceramic forms. Covered with a dark brown glaze, the vessel was potted with a light gray

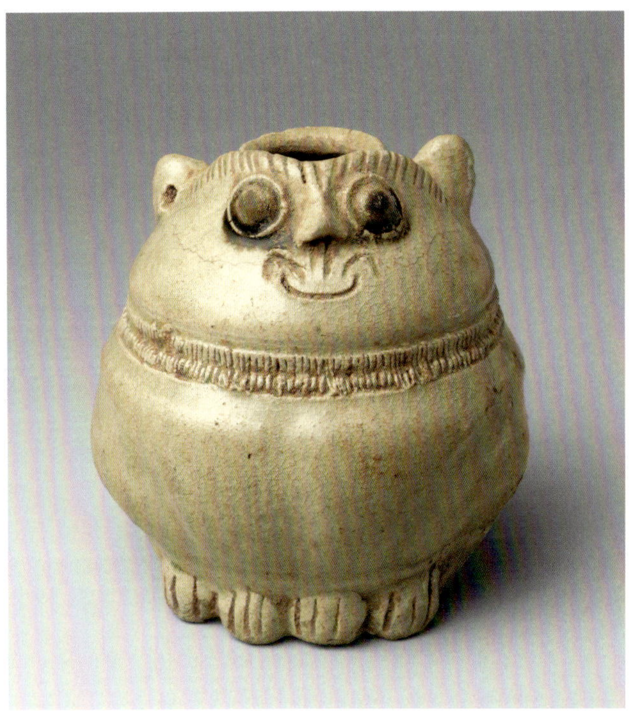

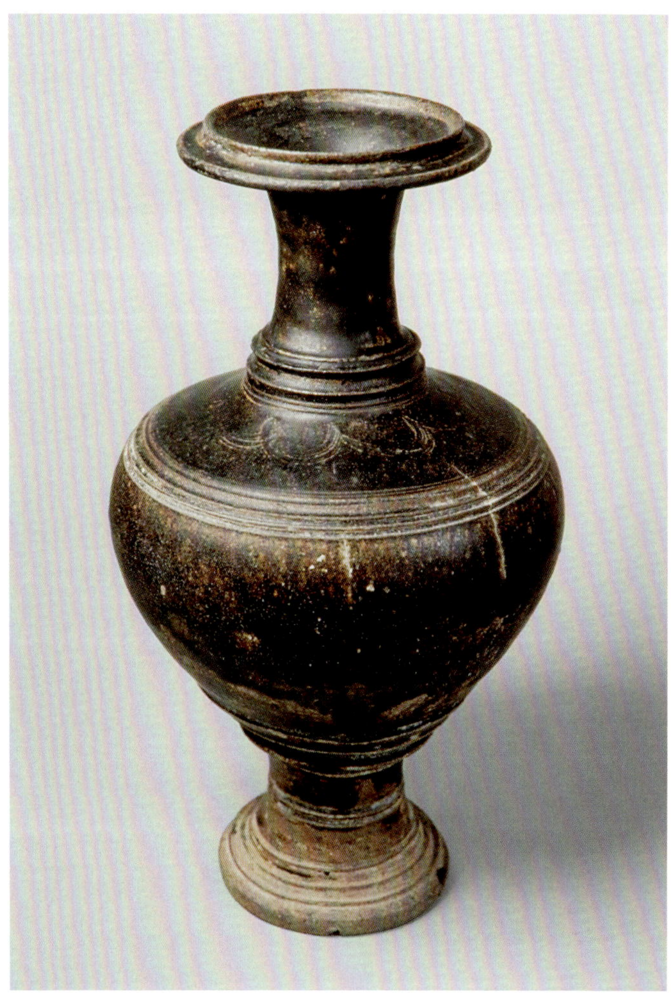

**Fig. 6.1**

*Lime Pot in the Shape of a Cat*, Cambodia or Thailand, Khmer Empire, 11th–12th century. Stoneware with incised and applied decoration under glaze, 3½ × 3¼ in. (8.9 × 8.3 cm). Metropolitan Museum of Art, New York, Purchase, The Vincent Astor Foundation Gift, 2007, 2007.260

**Fig. 6.2**

*Jar*, Cambodia or Thailand, Khmer Empire, 11th–12th century. Stoneware with molded decoration under glaze, H. 15⅛ × DIAM. 8½ in. (38.4 × 21.6 cm). Asian Art Museum of San Francisco, The Avery Brundage Collection, B72P9

clay. Incised rings enhance the mouth, shoulder, and foot. Similar jars have been recovered from temple sites, such as that of Prasat Ban Phluang, in Surin Province, Thailand, suggesting that one of their functions was to hold water or other liquid offerings in a sacred precinct or possibly during ceremonies.[3] The shape of this jar is not found in Southeast Asian ceramics made after the dissolution of the Khmer Empire in the late fourteenth to early fifteenth century. Yet, the references to earlier metalworking traditions and the zoomorphic forms that characterize Khmer ceramics are found in other Southeast Asian ceramics, first in Vietnam, from the tenth to the fourteenth century, and then in Thailand, after the mid-fourteenth century.

## Ceramics in Vietnam, 10th to 14th Century

The northern part of Vietnam and the southernmost region of China have historically had a complicated cultural, economic, and political relationship.

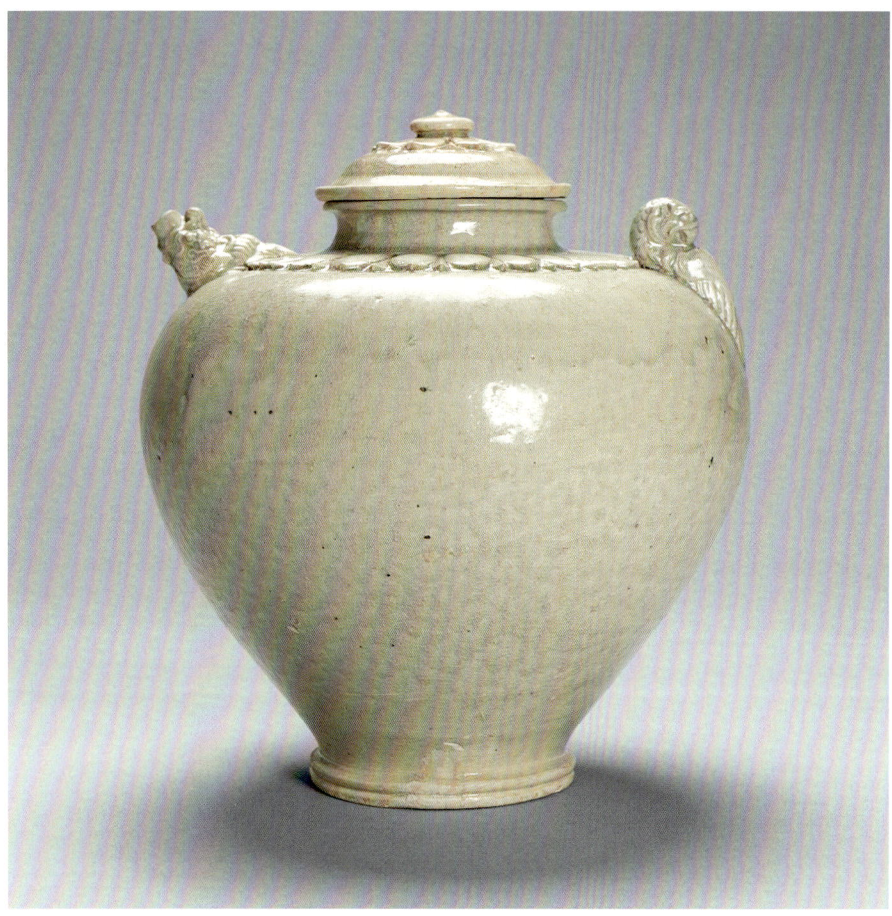

**Fig. 6.3**

*Ewer with a Makara and Parrot*, Vietnam, Ly dynasty, 11th–13th century. Stoneware with molded, carved, and incised decoration under glaze, H. 9 13/16 × DIAM. 9 1/16 in. (24.9 × 23 cm). Herbert F. Johnson Museum of Art, Cornell University, Ithaca, N.Y., Acquired through the George and Mary Rockwell Fund, 2006.029

Vietnam was once part of the independent Nan Yue (Nam Viet) Kingdom (204–111 B.C.E.), which also included Guangdong and Guangxi, parts of southern Fujian, Hong Kong, and Macau. Indeed, *Viet* is the Vietnamese reading of the Chinese word *Yue*, which is often used to define the regions and peoples of southern China. Nan Yue was one of the kingdoms incorporated into the territories of the powerful Han dynasty in about 111 B.C.E. Chinese authority in the region waned from the second to the sixth century C.E., but it was reasserted from the seventh to the ninth century under the Tang dynasty.

After the collapse of the Tang, Vietnam—like Guangdong, Fujian, and other southern provinces in China—returned to local control. The Ly dynasty (1009–1225), established in the early eleventh century, and the subsequent Tran dynasty (1225–1400) marked a period of vibrancy and innovation in the arts, including ceramics. A lively Ly-dynasty ewer (fig. 6.3) with lotus petals on the shoulder and cover, a spout in the shape of a makara, and a delightful parrot turning its head to groom its feathers exemplifies the imaginative creation of new shapes at the time. The wide shoulder and tapering body are comparable to those of the large

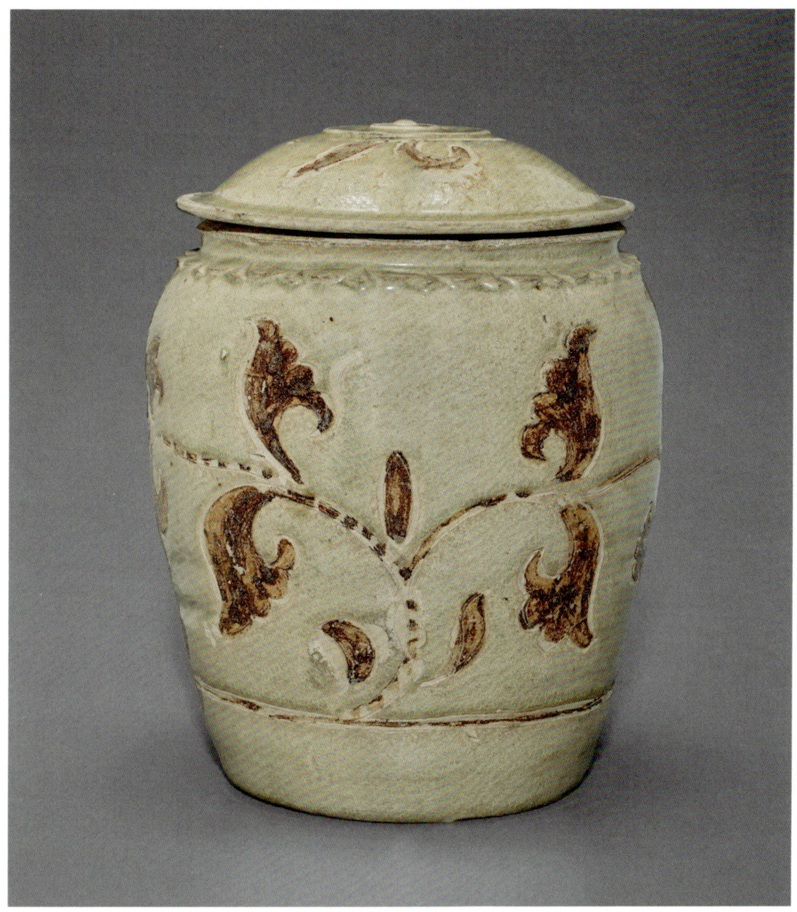

**Fig. 6.4**

*Jar with a Lotus Scroll*, Vietnam, Ly or Tran dynasty, 12th–14th century. Stoneware with carved decoration and inlaid iron-brown glaze under glaze, H. 9¾ × DIAM. 7⅜ in. (24.8 × 18.7 cm). Yale University Art Gallery, Gift of Steven M. Kossak, B.A. 1972, 2021.37.1

Khmer jar previously discussed (see fig. 6.2). Lotus flowers and petals are prominent in Ly-dynasty ceramics, reflecting the importance of Buddhism in Vietnam in the tenth and eleventh centuries. As mentioned, lotuses, which rise from muddy waters to bloom, serve as symbols of purity in Buddhism.

The thin, light greenish-white glaze on the ewer is similar to that found in the tenth century in Jiangxi, Hunan, and Fujian—evidence of the perennial dialogue between Chinese and Vietnamese ceramics. Works with white glazes were not produced in mainland Southeast Asia before this time. It seems likely that Vietnamese potters became interested in the color because of their awareness of contemporaneous trends in China, and as part of the ceramic experimentation undertaken during the the Ly and Tran dynasties.

Crafted with a light gray clay and covered with a thin ivory glaze, a barrel-shaped jar with a convex cover (fig. 6.4) has lotus petals at the shoulder and an animated lotus scroll around the body that almost appears to be dancing. The scroll was carved into the jar after the piece was glazed; it was then inlaid with a brown glaze before the jar was fired a second time. This technique, which adds an interesting depth to the design, has no parallels in China. Intriguingly, it is found in Korean ceramics produced around the same time. There is no written or visual evidence providing a link between Vietnamese and Korean ceramics—but it is worth noting that the coastlines of both nations are linked by the South and East China Seas.

The bold, slightly tapered shape of the jar echoes Khmer forms and alludes to certain types of Bronze Age vessels produced by the Dongson culture (ca. 700 B.C.E.–100 C.E.) of mainland and island Southeast Asia, some of which were decorated with images of warriors in astonishing feathered headdresses sailing on waters filled with fish and aquatic birds (figs. 6.5–.6). Comparable bronze vessels were produced in the Nan Yue Kingdom and in the Dian culture (279–109 B.C.E.), centered in Yunnan.[4] Ceramic jars in this shape are often referred to as "Thanh Hoa jars," after the name of a series of kilns located in Thanh Hoa Province, south of Hanoi, where examples were made, but they were also produced elsewhere in Vietnam.

These ceramic jars appear to have served many functions. A few have been preserved with matching stands, which suggests that they were displayed in temples or palaces and had a ritual function, presumably to present offerings.[5] One excavated example has the Chinese phrase for "wine container" (*pan jiu*) brushed on the underside of the lid, indicating that the jars were intended to hold or serve liquids.[6] Another, excavated in 1985 in a tomb in the region of former Hai Hung Province, Vietnam, contained fourteenth-century Chinese ceramics, including celadons with Qingbai-type glazes and other pieces painted with cobalt blue.[7] Although the shape of Thanh Hoa jars evokes that of urns, and they have therefore sometimes been identified as funerary vessels, no example containing any remains has been found.

The spontaneous and suggestive, rather than representational, rendering of lotuses and other botanical forms on Vietnamese ceramics typifies a southern aesthetic or taste shared by potters and consumers in Vietnam as well as in Fujian, Guangdong, and Hunan Provinces. This can ultimately be traced back to the lively and abstract style of the flowers and other designs painted on Changsha wares, which were among the first Chinese ceramics to have been widely traded overseas. As mentioned earlier, examples of Changsha wares have been found on the Southeast Asian peninsula. The blossoming lotus painted in iron brown on the body of a ewer (fig. 6.7) used for serving wine, tea, or other liquids was rendered with quick, thin brushstrokes. Covered with a light gray-green glaze, this piece has a wide, bulbous body, a small spout, and a curvilinear handle. The articulation of the handle and the makara-like shape of the spout—an echo of the zoomorphic imagery of Khmer ceramics—are distinguishing features of Vietnamese ewers. The same features appear on a ewer with a taller,

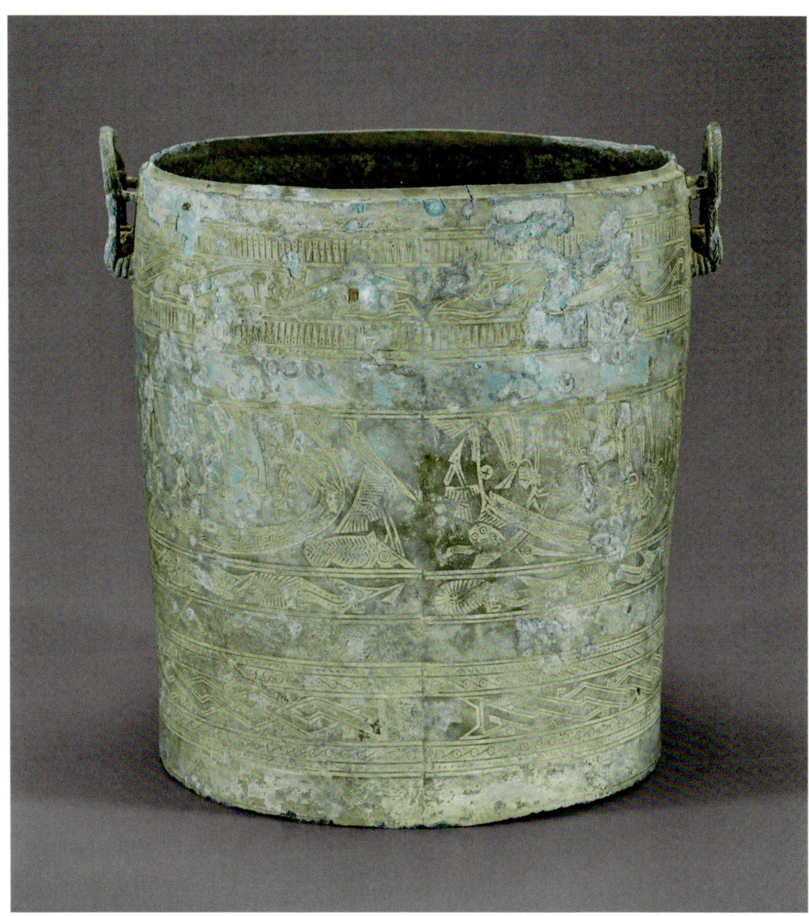

**Fig. 6.5**

*Vessel with Warriors on Boats*, Vietnam, Dongson culture, 300 B.C.E.–100 C.E. Bronze, H. 12⅝ × DIAM. 13 in. (32 × 33 cm). Collection of Thomas Jaffe, B.A. 1971

**Fig. 6.6**

Detail of fig. 6.5

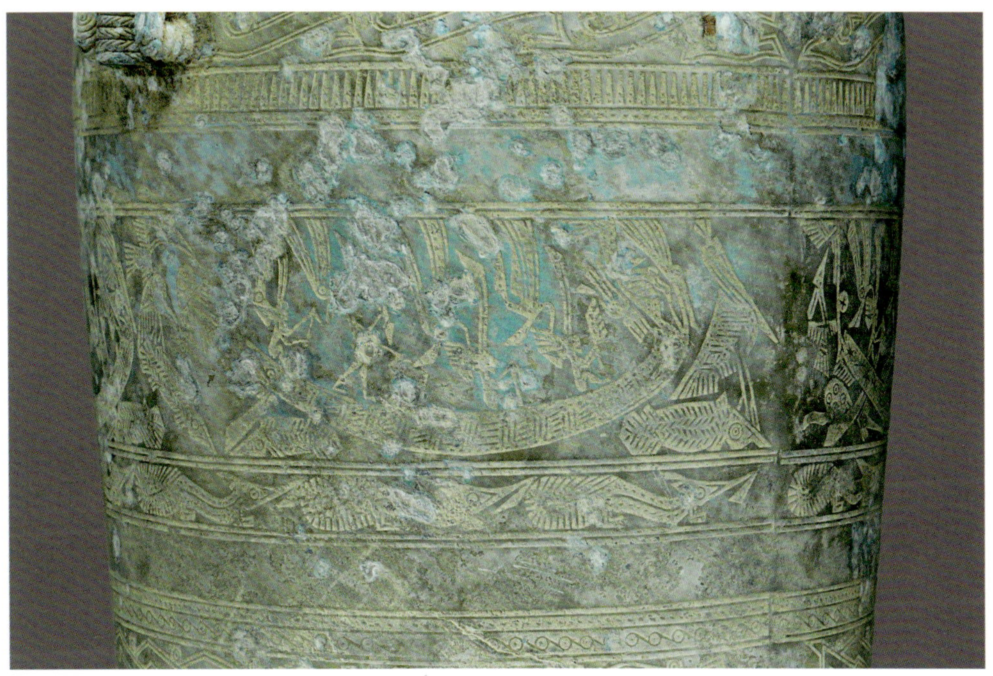

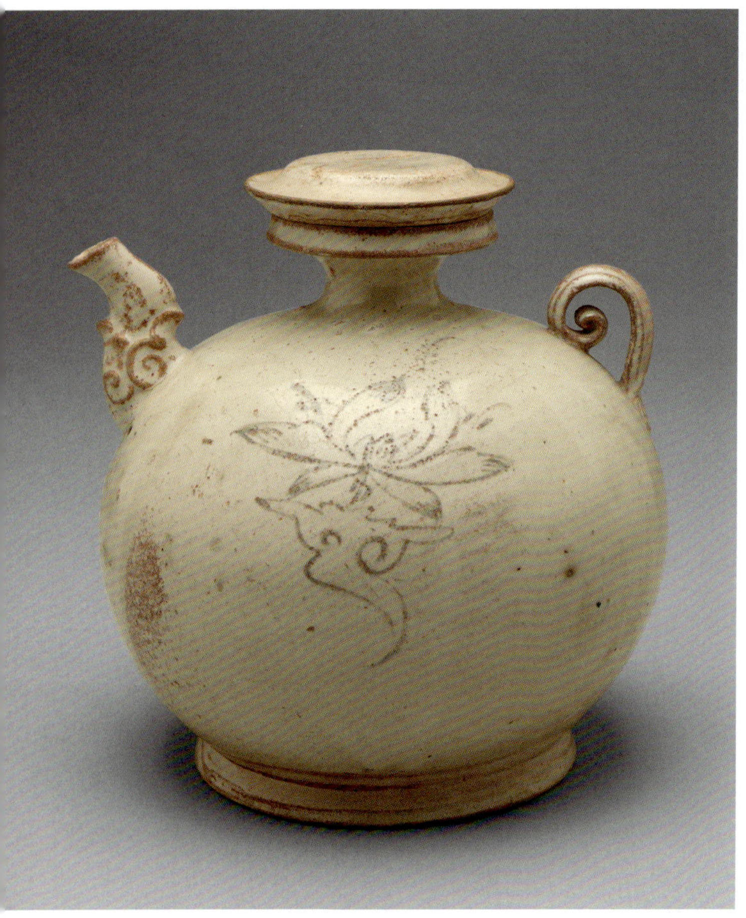

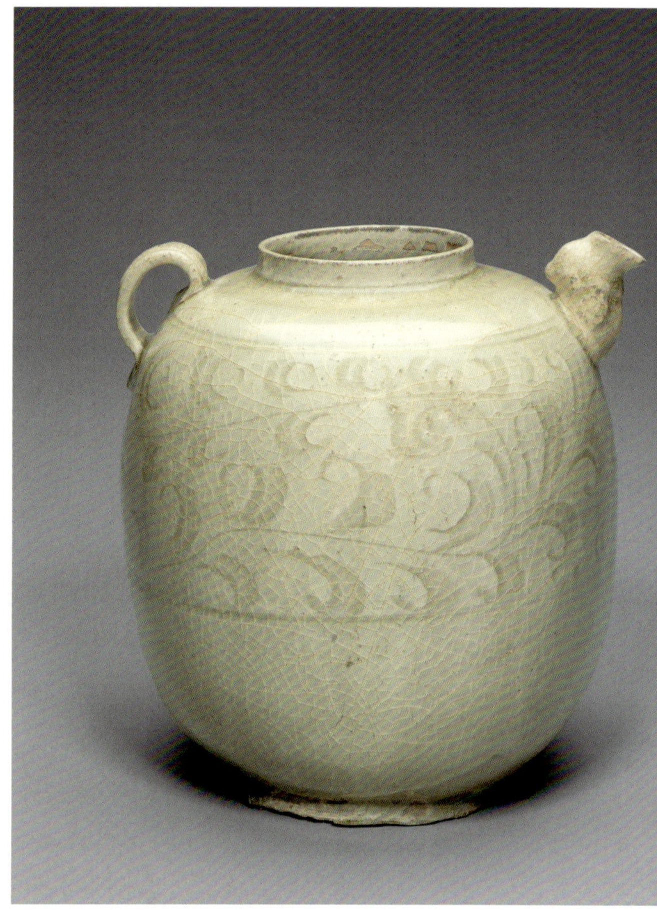

**Fig. 6.7**

*Ewer with a Lotus*, Vietnam, Tran dynasty, 13th–14th century. Stoneware with white slip and iron-brown splashes under glaze, H. 7¾ × DIAM. 7½ in. (19.7 × 19.1 cm). Yale University Art Gallery, Gift of Michael de Havenon, B.A. 1962, and Georgia de Havenon, 2017.53.6a–b

**Fig. 6.8**

*Ewer with a Botanical Design*, Vietnam, Tran dynasty, 13th–14th century. Stoneware with incised decoration under glaze, H. 6¾ × DIAM. 7 in. (17.1 × 17.8 cm). Yale University Art Gallery, Gift of Brian M. Salzberg, B.S. 1963, 2018.140.1

straighter body (fig. 6.8), which was potted from a buff-colored clay and covered with a crackled olive-green glaze. Encircling the body is an incised pattern of lotuses comparable to those inlaid on the more bulbous ewer.

Brown glazes, such as that covering a small bowl (fig. 6.9), were also used in Vietnam. The iron-brown streaks painted over the glaze on this piece echo the painted streaks on northern Chinese wares dating from the twelfth to the fourteenth century.[8] It seems likely that the painting of such streaks on ceramics in north China and Vietnam was spurred by competition with the Jian wares of Fujian, highly prized for their ingenious glaze effects, such as the "hare's-fur" pattern. It is also possible that some kilns in north China and Vietnam did not know the recipes for such glaze effects or have access to the components for producing them. The size and shape of this bowl indicate that it was most likely used for drinking, presumably either wine or tea. While brown-glazed bowls are often presumed to have served tea in China and Japan, Vietnamese examples have not traditionally been discussed or catalogued as tea bowls. Yet, it is worth noting that the cultivation of tea was part of the cultures of Vietnam, Thailand,

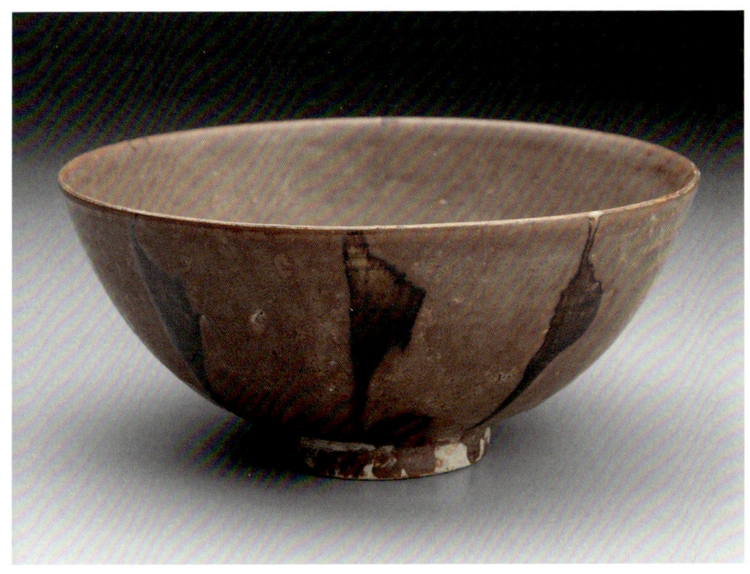

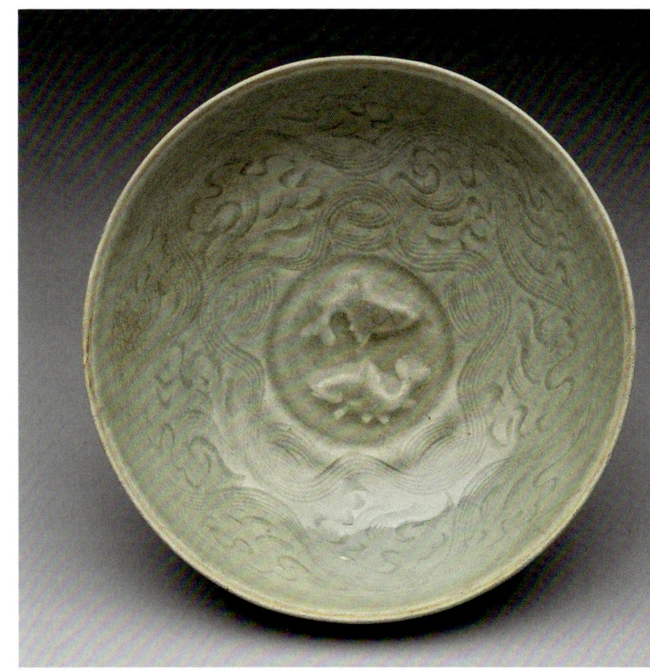

**Fig. 6.9**

*Bowl*, Vietnam, Tran dynasty, 13th–14th century. Stoneware with brown pigment over glaze, H. 2⅞ × DIAM. 6⅝ in. (7.3 × 16.8 cm). Museum of Fine Arts, Boston, Gift of John D. Constable, 1991.994

**Fig. 6.10**

*Bowl with Two Fish among Waves*, Vietnam, Tran dynasty, 14th–15th century. Stoneware with applied, incised, carved, and molded decoration under glaze, H. 3$\frac{1}{16}$ × DIAM. 6$\frac{15}{16}$ in. (7.7 × 17.7 cm). Museum of Fine Arts, Boston, Gift of John D. Constable, 1989.789

and Cambodia, which presupposes the drinking of this beverage there. It seems likely that some Vietnamese pieces in the shape and size of this small bowl might have been used for drinking tea at some point in their histories.

A lovely blue-green-glazed dish with two carp swimming around each other (fig. 6.10) again demonstrates the sharing of shapes and designs in Chinese and Vietnamese ceramics. The two fish, molded into the center of the dish, have counterparts in ceramics produced in Zhejiang, Guangdong, and Fujian. However, they are placed within a central roundel that has no parallel in Chinese fish dishes, and they are surrounded by swirling waves that are more densely carved than is typical in comparable Chinese pieces.

Vietnamese and Thai ceramics dating as far back as the late thirteenth century have been found in sites throughout mainland and island Southeast Asia, in the Philippines, and, in much smaller quantities, in Japan[9] and West Asia. They have also been found in shipwrecks, including the late thirteenth-century Rang Kwien and the fourteenth-century Turiang.[10] Both of these vessels were Chinese-constructed ships discovered in Southeast Asian waters, and both had cargoes that included Longquan and other Chinese wares, as well as Thai ceramics and a small number of Vietnamese works.

It is likely that the competitiveness of Southeast Asian ceramics at this time was driven in part by the economic and other disruptions caused by the transition from the Yuan to the Ming dynasty in China, which temporarily had a negative impact on the production of ceramics throughout China. In addition, unlike the governments of the earlier Southern Song and Yuan dynasties, that of the early Ming dynasty was less interested in interregional trade. The emperor Hongwu (r. 1368–98) issued prohibitions on private trade that diminished maritime activities in the late fourteenth and early fifteenth centuries. Together, the changes in China opened markets, particularly those in Indonesia, to other ceramic makers, such as Vietnam and Thailand.

By the late fourteenth and early fifteenth centuries, in response to the changes in the Chinese industry, Vietnamese kilns began to produce stoneware covered with a white slip and painted with cobalt under a clear glaze. The slip was used to cover the color of the stoneware body and give it the appearance of porcelain. As in China, blue-and-white wares eventually superseded green- and brown-glazed ceramics in Vietnam, as they became the dominant type of ceramic in maritime trade throughout Asia and beyond. Most of the Vietnamese ceramics found in shipwrecks are blue-and-white wares.

### Ceramics in Thailand, Mid-14th to 16th Century

Thai ceramics (including those found in shipwrecks), on the other hand, demonstrate a continued preference for the earlier green- and brown-glazed wares. High-fired, glazed ceramics were first produced in Thailand in the mid-fourteenth century, both for domestic use and to support the independent kingdoms established there as a result of the gradual dissolution of the Khmer Empire. The kingdom of Lan Na (active from the thirteenth to the eighteenth century) was centered around the cities of Chiang Mai and Chiang Saen in the far north, and the kingdoms of Sukhothai (ca. 1240–1348) and Ayutthaya (1356–1767) were farther south.

Kiln complexes in Thailand were also located near rivers and supplies of clay. Like ceramics made in Vietnam, the pieces produced in Thailand ingeniously combine the shapes and designs of Khmer ceramics with those of China; they also sometimes reference the Vietnamese industry. The thin, runny quality of the olive-green glaze covering a jar in the collection of the Asia Society, in New York (fig. 6.11), suggests that the piece was made in the northern part of Thailand, in one of the kiln sites along the Mekong and Chao Phraya Rivers that were active during the Lan Na Kingdom. The glaze resembles those used in some kilns in Guangdong and other southern Chinese provinces, while the tapering body, short neck, and prominent flared lip derive from a Khmer metal form. The closest parallels to the shape of this jar, particularly the wide scoop mouth, are among works produced in the Phayao region of northern Thailand, such as a jar in the Minneapolis Institute of Art (fig. 6.12). The two jars have a similar shape, including the tiny lugs, and a delicate pattern stamped on the shoulder. Stamping decoration on ceramics is a technique with a long history in

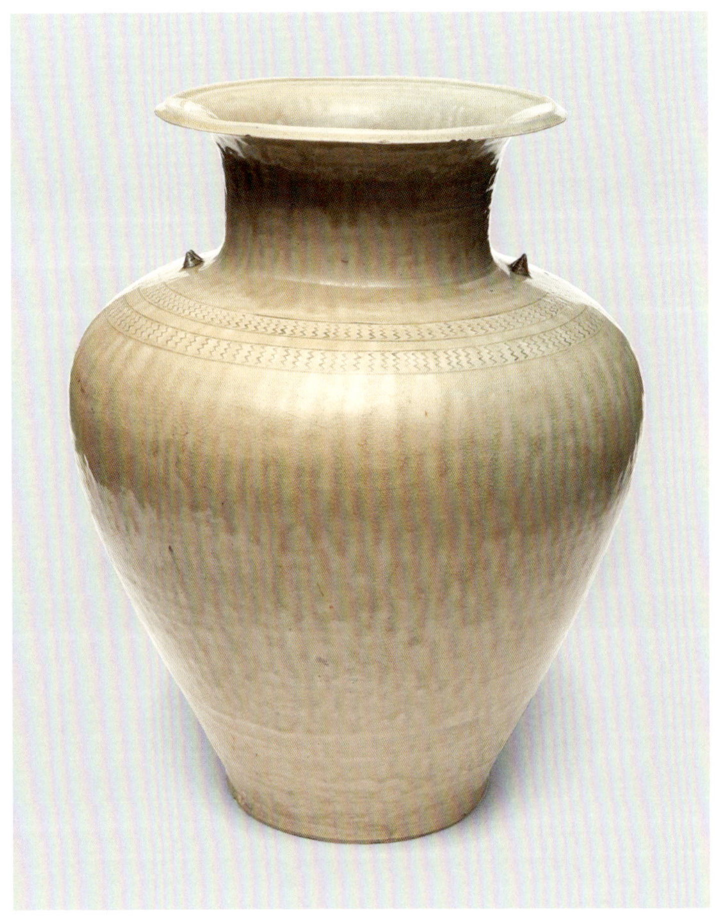

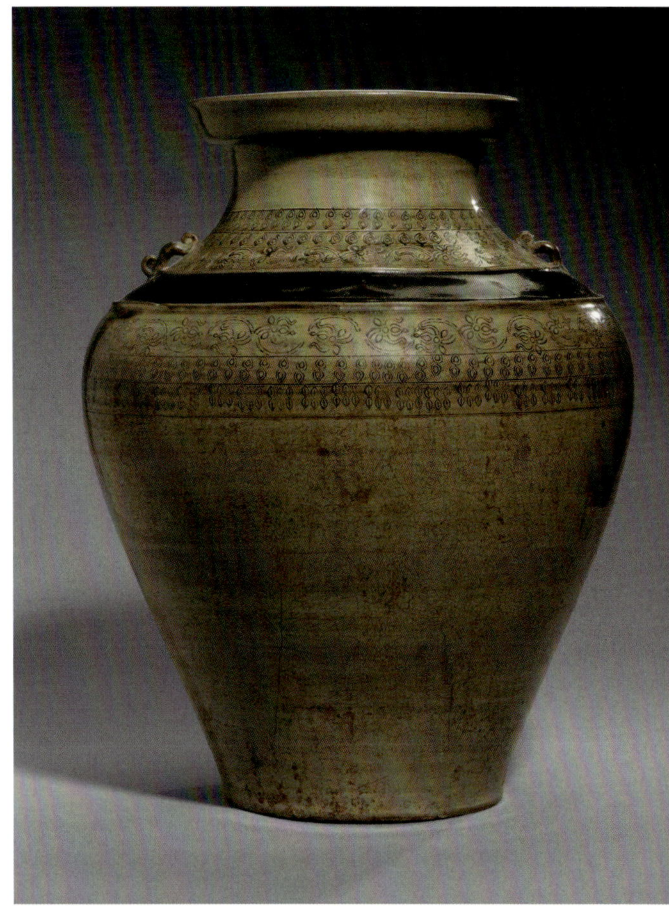

**Fig. 6.11**

*Transport Jar*, Thailand, 14th–15th century. Stoneware with stamped and incised decoration under glaze (Phayao ware), H. 17⅞ × DIAM. 14¼ in. (45.4 × 36.2 cm). Asia Society, New York, Mr. and Mrs. John D. Rockefeller 3rd Collection, 1979.95

**Fig. 6.12**

*Transport Jar*, Thailand, 14th–15th century. Stoneware with stamped and incised decoration under glaze (Phayao ware), H. 18 × DIAM. 14 in. (45.7 × 35.6 cm). Minneapolis Institute of Art, Gift of Funds from Mr. and Mrs. Charles A. Cleveland, 91.29

northern Thailand and neighboring Myanmar. While the green glaze on the jar in Minneapolis is darker than that on the jar in New York, it is similarly mottled or runny. A horizontal band of brown glaze further enhances the shoulder of this jar.

The jar in New York was once intended for storage and transport. When it was unearthed under a Buddhist pagoda in the north-central city of Kamphaeng Phet, south of the Phayao kilns, it was filled with a large number of metal and ceramic votive tablets, probably offerings to the temple.[11] It seems likely that the jar had been repurposed to present these offerings, possibly during a ceremony, as a means of earning the religious merit required for favorable rebirth—a significant concern in all Buddhist practices. The jar in Minneapolis was also found at a site some distance from where it was manufactured. It was one of eight similar jars among seventeen ceramics unearthed in a cave in the Kalong region of northern Thailand in 1990.[12] Why these ceramics were stored in a cave remains unknown, but it is possible that they were part of a hoard that had been hidden to preserve them, suggesting that Phayao wares were treasured at some point in time.

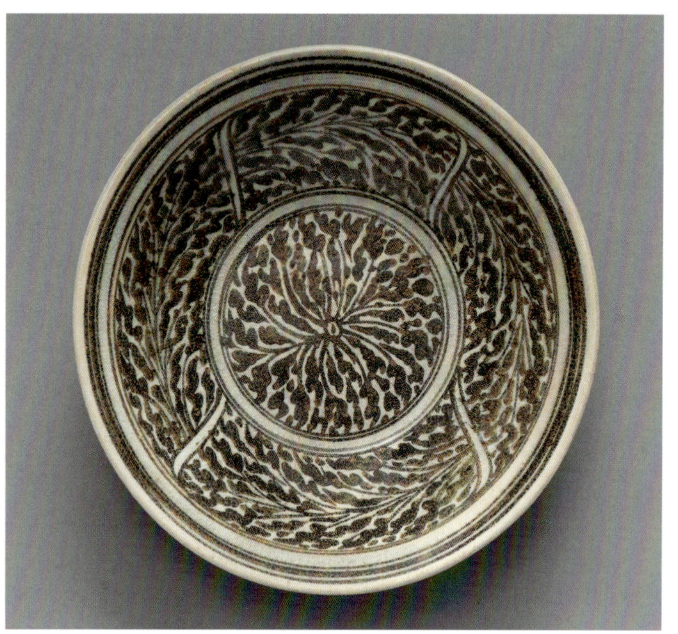

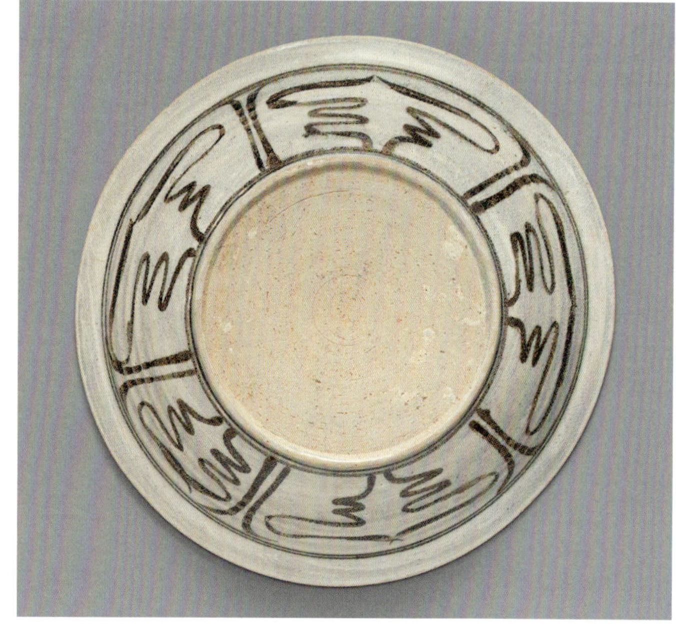

**Fig. 6.13**

*Dish with Seaweed*, Thailand, late 14th–16th century. Stoneware with iron-brown pigment under glaze (Kalong ware), H. 2⅜ × DIAM. 10¼ in. (6 × 26 cm). Yale University Art Gallery, Yung G. Wang Family Endowment Fund, 2021.45.1

**Fig. 6.14**

Base of fig. 6.13

The small number of kilns producing Phayao wares ceased operation around the sixteenth century. In the Kalong region, near the Mae Lo River, however, more than two hundred kilns operated from the late fourteenth to the sixteenth century. Kalong wares are potted with refined clay, which has a high percentage of kaolin, and have thin bodies. Although they also produced green-glazed pieces, the Kalong kilns are noted for their painted ceramics—pieces with buff-colored bodies, white slip, and distinctive, boldly painted designs that do not always have counterparts in Chinese or Vietnamese ceramics. One example is a dish with pieces of seaweed that appear to be moving in water (figs. 6.13–.14). The use of painted lines to separate the seaweed patterns from one another is typical of Kalong ware and is possibly a reference to the role played by molding in other ceramic pieces.

The Si Satchanalai complex—which had over one thousand kilns—dominated the Thai ceramic industry from the late fourteenth to the late sixteenth century. Located farther south, to the north of the town of Sawankhalok, in Sukhothai Province, this complex produced ceramics that were transported along the Chao Phraya River to the port city of Ayutthaya. Examples have been found at sites throughout Southeast Asia as well as in shipwrecks. The terminology used to catalogue the ceramics made in this vast complex can be confusing. In earlier scholarship, the terms "Sukhothai" and "Sawankhalok" were often used to distinguish Si Satchanalai products with different styles of decoration: "Sukhothai" described multicolored works, many with painted decoration, while "Sawankhalok" typically referred to green-glazed ceramics; however, neither

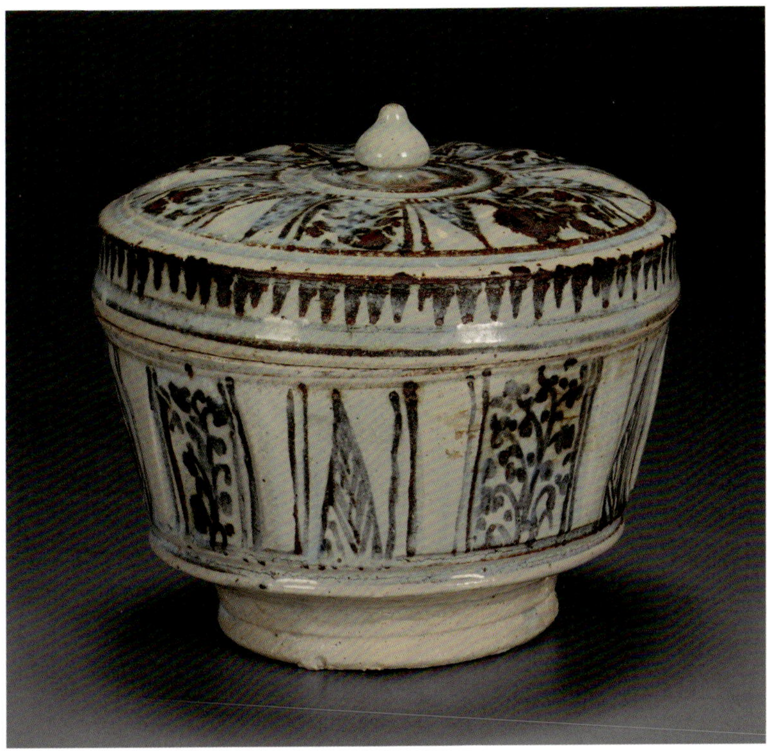

**Fig. 6.15**

*Box with Leaves and Branches*, Thailand, late 14th–16th century. Stoneware with brown, blue, and red pigment under glaze (Si Satchanalai ware, Sukhothai type), H. 4¾ × DIAM. 5¼ in. (12.1 × 13.3 cm). Yale University Art Gallery, Gift of Ann and Gilbert H. Kinney, B.A. 1953, M.A. 1954, 1999.133.7

term was used consistently. Currently, ceramics produced at Si Satchanalai are commonly defined as "Si Satchanalai wares."

A charming box made in one of the Si Satchanalai kilns near the city of Sukhothai (fig. 6.15) illustrates the type of ceramic previously classified as Sukhothai ware. The box—which could have been used to store items such as cosmetics, spices, or tea—was potted with a high-fired light gray clay, covered with a white glaze, and painted with brown, blue, and red pigments. It has alternating segments with designs of leaves and branches, divided from one another by vertical lines. Although the decoration shares the sense of spontaneity seen in the painting of Kalong wares, it is less precisely rendered. The use of blue and red is unusual—brown is the most common pigment in Sukhotai-type wares. Moreover, the use of blue as a pigment suggests that, even though Thai ceramic centers did not produce blue-and-white wares, the potters working there were aware of the growing prominence of cobalt and blue-and-white wares in Chinese and Vietnamese ceramics.

The Si Satchanalai complex also produced ceramics with white or very light gray glazes, although it is noted for its green-glazed wares that often echo shapes and designs found in Chinese celadons. Sawankhalok-type Si Satchanalai wares were potted with a buff clay that sometimes turned red during firing, and they were glazed green. Many have a blue-green hue reminiscent of the

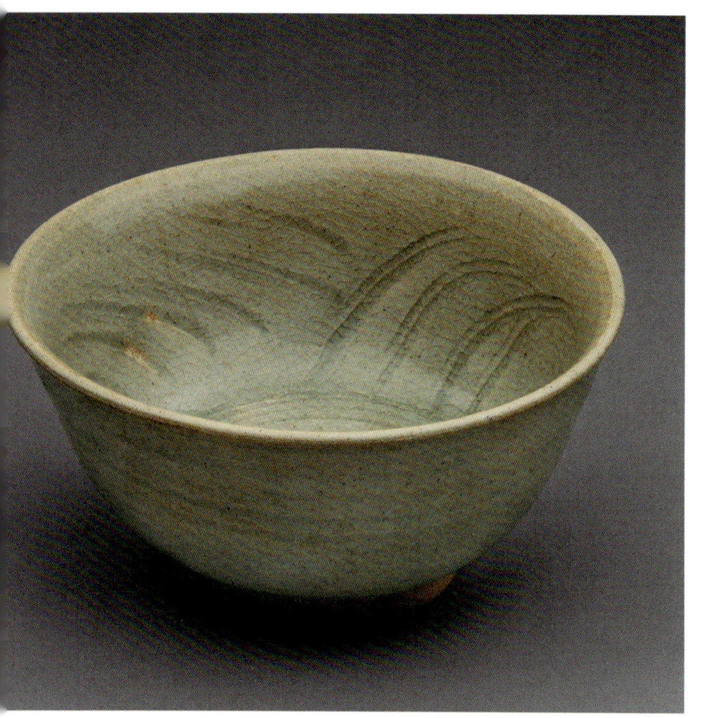

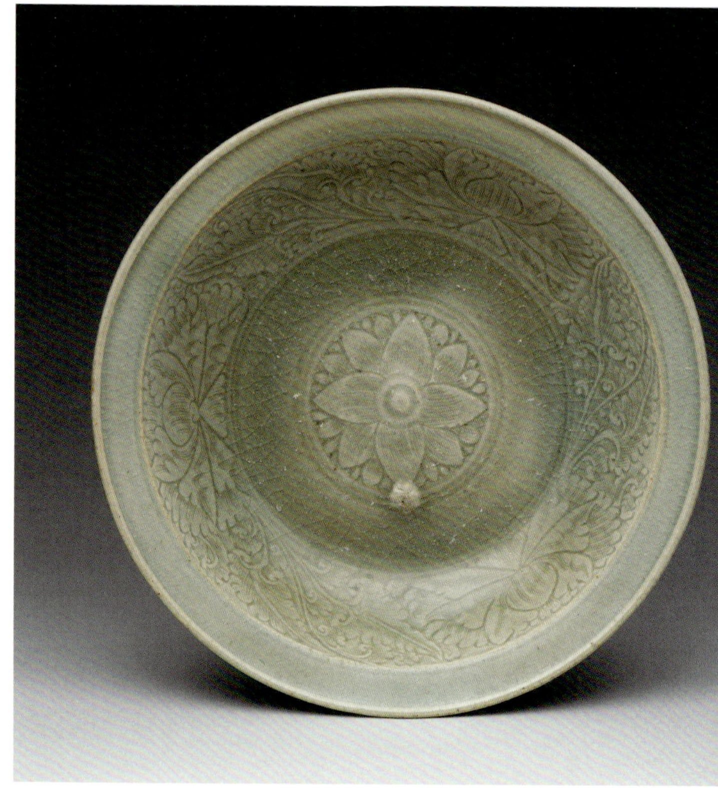

**Fig. 6.16**

*Bowl with a Botanical Design*, Thailand, late 14th–16th century. Stoneware with incised decoration under glaze (Si Satchanalai ware, Sawankhalok type), H. 2⅜ × DIAM. 4 15/16 in. (6 × 12.5 cm). Yale University Art Gallery, Gift of Ann and Gilbert H. Kinney, B.A. 1953, M.A. 1954, 1999.133.5

**Fig. 6.17**

*Dish with a Lotus Flower and Scroll*, Thailand, late 14th–16th century. Stoneware with incised decoration under glaze (Si Satchanalai ware, Sawankhalok type), DIAM. 11½ in. (29.2 cm). Metropolitan Museum of Art, New York, Purchase, Gifts of friends of Jim Thompson, in his memory, 1989, 1989.238.51

renowned Qingbai and certain Longquan wares, which in Thai is referred to as a "crow's-egg" color. A glaze of this hue covers a lovely bowl (fig. 6.16) with an unadorned exterior and an interior with an abstract botanical pattern like those found on earlier pieces from southern Chinese kilns, particularly in Guangdong and Fujian. This blue-green glaze also embellishes a dish (fig. 6.17) with denser floral decoration on the interior, where it has similarly pooled and darkened. The lotus blossom in the center of the dish is encircled by two lines and an open area with no decoration; a lush lotus scroll fills the cavetto, and the rim and exterior are undecorated.

The Sawankhalok blue-green glaze color also enhances a delightful *kendi* (fig. 6.18) in the shape of a sacred goose (*hamsa*, in Sanskrit) with a rider, probably a celestial being (*apsara*). Incisions made before the piece was glazed define the feathers, wings, and tail of the bird, as well as the clothing of the celestial being, which flutters along the goose's neck. Divine geese symbolize purity in Buddhist and Hindu traditions, and the combination of the goose and a celestial figure on this *kendi* suggest that the vessel was for religious or ceremonial use.

Examples of the ceramics produced in the Si Satchanalai region, including both Sawankhalok-type green-glazed pieces and Sukhothai-type painted works, have been found in shipwrecks, such as the fifteenth-century Nanyang

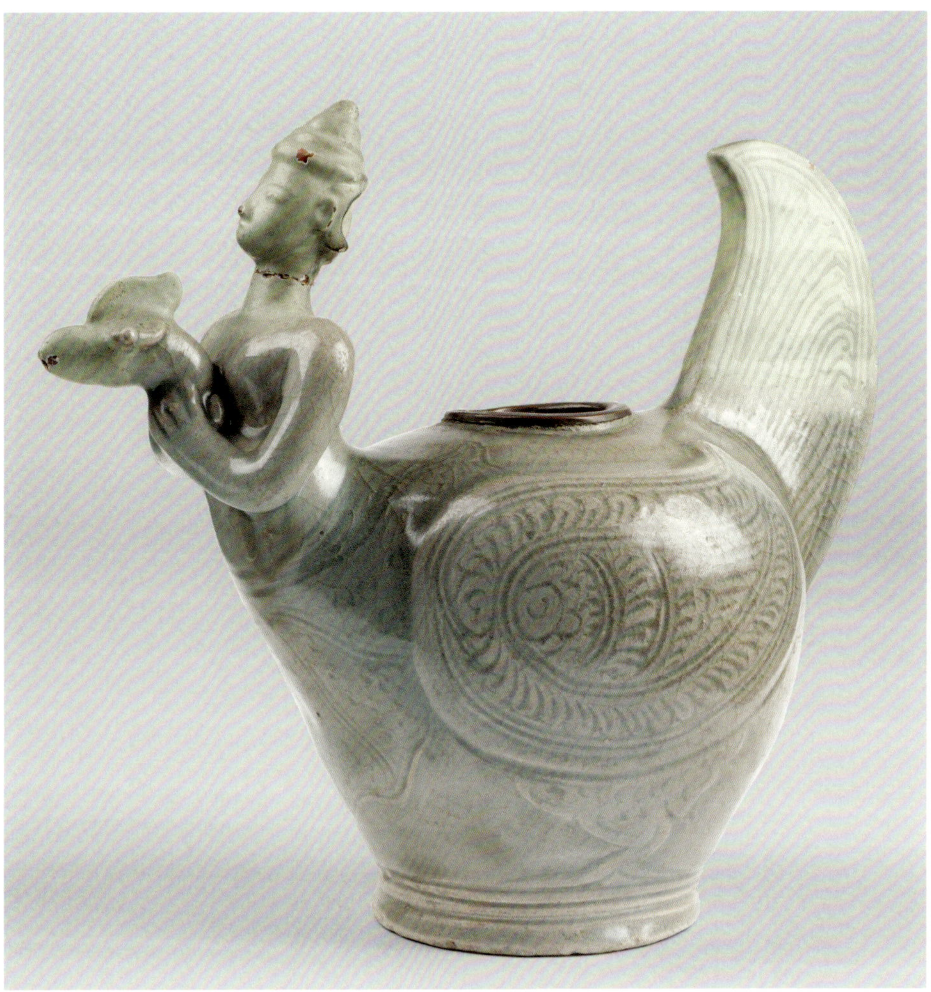

**Fig. 6.18**

*Pouring Vessel (Kendi) in the Shape of a Goose with a Rider*, Thailand, 15th–16th century. Stoneware with incised decoration under glaze (Si Satchanalai ware, Sawankhalok type), 8 × 9½ in. (20.3 × 24.1 cm). Victoria and Albert Museum, London, c.233-1927

and the mid-fifteenth-century Royal Nanhai, both located in Malaysian waters. Discovered in 1995, the Nanyang, a hybrid Southeast Asian–Chinese vessel that was constructed with wooden pegs and iron nails, held a cargo of about ten to fifteen thousand ceramic pieces, primarily works from the Si Satchanalai kilns, and a few Chinese works.[13] The Royal Nanhai, also of hybrid construction, was excavated between 1995 and 1998 and had an equally large percentage of Si Satchanalai wares in its cargo, as well as a few of the Chinese and Vietnamese blue-and-white bowls that would eventually replace celadons and dominate the Asian maritime trade in ceramics.[14]

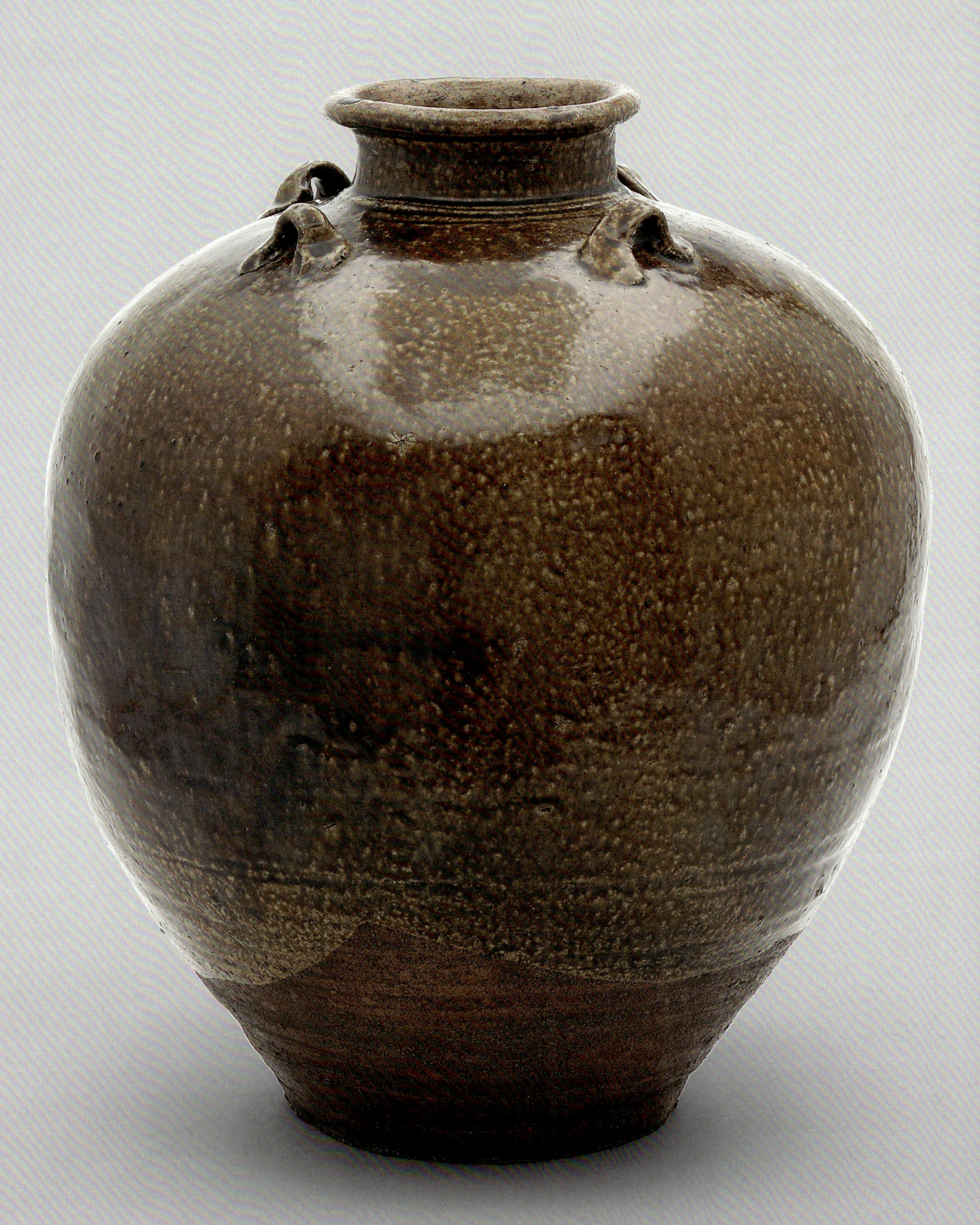

## CHAPTER 7

# Korea and Japan: Reinventing and Repurposing Chinese Ceramics

By the Tang dynasty, when Chinese ceramics began to be valued for their high-fired bodies, glaze colors, and artistry—and when maritime trade first began to flourish—China, Korea, and Japan had been interacting diplomatically, economically, and culturally for centuries. The three countries shared city planning coordinates, governmental and bureaucratic structures, Buddhist practices and imagery, artistic and literary themes, the use of Chinese characters, and more. China traded with Korea by both land and sea, and it traded with Japan either directly overseas or via Korea.

The same types of Chinese wares that have been found in Southeast and West Asia have also been found in Korea and Japan (though they have been preserved in greater numbers in Japan). White wares, such as the Ding and Xing wares made in the northern kilns, and the delicately green-glazed Yue wares from the south first appeared in Korea and Japan in the ninth and tenth centuries, followed by ceramics with Qingbai glazes in the tenth and eleventh centuries. By the twelfth and thirteenth centuries, when trade expanded considerably due to the patronage of the Southern Song and Yuan courts, the darker green Longquan wares and related pieces from Fujian and Guangdong Provinces reached Korea and Japan in significant numbers, largely as trade goods but also as diplomatic and personal gifts brought by travelers, including envoys, merchants, and monks.

### Korea

The Chinese court calligrapher and painter Xu Jing's account of his journey as part of a group of envoys sent to Korea for a month in 1123 provides a fascinating glimpse of the perils of travel along the waterways linking the Chinese port of Ningbo to the Korean port near Gaeseong, the capital of the Goryeo dynasty (918–1392).[1] His forty-chapter treatise *Records of the Chinese Embassy to the Goryeo Court during the Xuanhe Era* (*Xuanhe fengshi gaoli tujiang*) describes the different types of waters—white, yellow, and black—found in the Yellow Sea, as well as over forty islands, channels, and shoals between China and Korea. Xu's mission, which included eight ships, moved up the east coast of China to the mouth of the Huai River (located between the Yellow and Yangzi Rivers) and then crossed the sea to a harbor on the Ryesŏng River (near present-day Inchon) in Korea, before moving up the west coast of Korea to Gaeseong. While this journey took only eight days, weather and other factors extended the return trip to forty-two days. This path was presumably taken by many other ships before and after Xu recorded his mission, and trade goods—including Chinese ceramics—undoubtedly followed the same route.

In his detailed account of life in the Korean capital, Xu discussed Goryeo celadons several times. He equated the green-glazed Korean ceramics to Yue

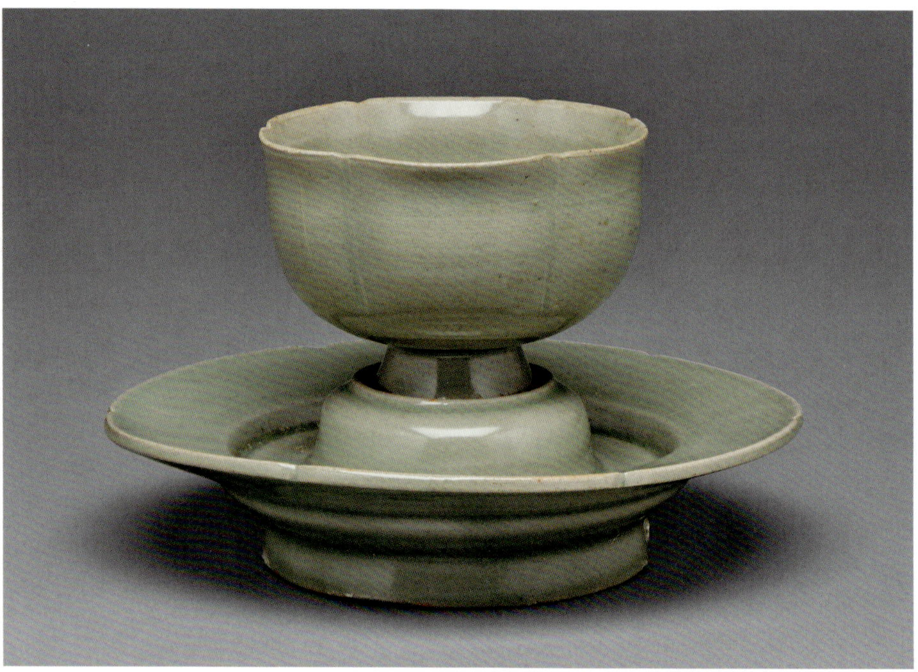

**Fig. 7.1**

*Cup and Stand with a Foliated Lip*, Korea, Goryeo dynasty, 12th century. Stoneware with glaze, H. 3$\frac{9}{16}$ × DIAM. 6$\frac{1}{8}$ in. (9 × 15.5 cm). Yale University Art Gallery, Gift of Robert D. Mowry in honor of Namhi Kim Wagner and in memory of Edward W. Wagner, 2017.154.1a–b

wares—the first green-glazed ceramics celebrated throughout East Asia—and to the imperial Ru wares of the Northern Song court. He compared the delicate gray-green color of Goryeo glazes to the "radiance of jade and the clarity of water" and noted that Korean ceramics with these glazes were as highly valued as silver and gold pieces.[2] Writing slightly later, during the Southern Song dynasty, an author known only by the soubriquet Taiping Laoren (Old Man of Great Peace) included Korean celadons in *Brocaded Sleeves* (*Xiu zhong jin*), a discussion of the items esteemed in China at the time. He described Korean celadons as "first under the heavens."[3]

In addition to sharing the gray-green hue of Yue wares, Korean celadons used comparable clays and glaze compositions—a reflection of the geographic proximity of the two regions and the long-standing cultural impact of Yue wares.[4] Korea had been producing glazed ceramics for centuries before it began to make green-glazed wares in the tenth century, when small numbers were made in Gaeseong. Excavations at kilns in the region demonstrate that, by the eleventh century, production had expanded considerably and was centered in South Jeolla Province, in the southwest. An elegant cup with delicately articulated lobes and a matching stand (fig. 7.1), used for drinking wine or tea, typifies the shapes and gray-green glazes of Goryeo-period celadons. Introduced to Korea from China during the Tang dynasty, tea drinking became an important tradition during the Goryeo dynasty, when the royal court established a special bureau for serving the beverage during ceremonies and as part of daily life. Tea

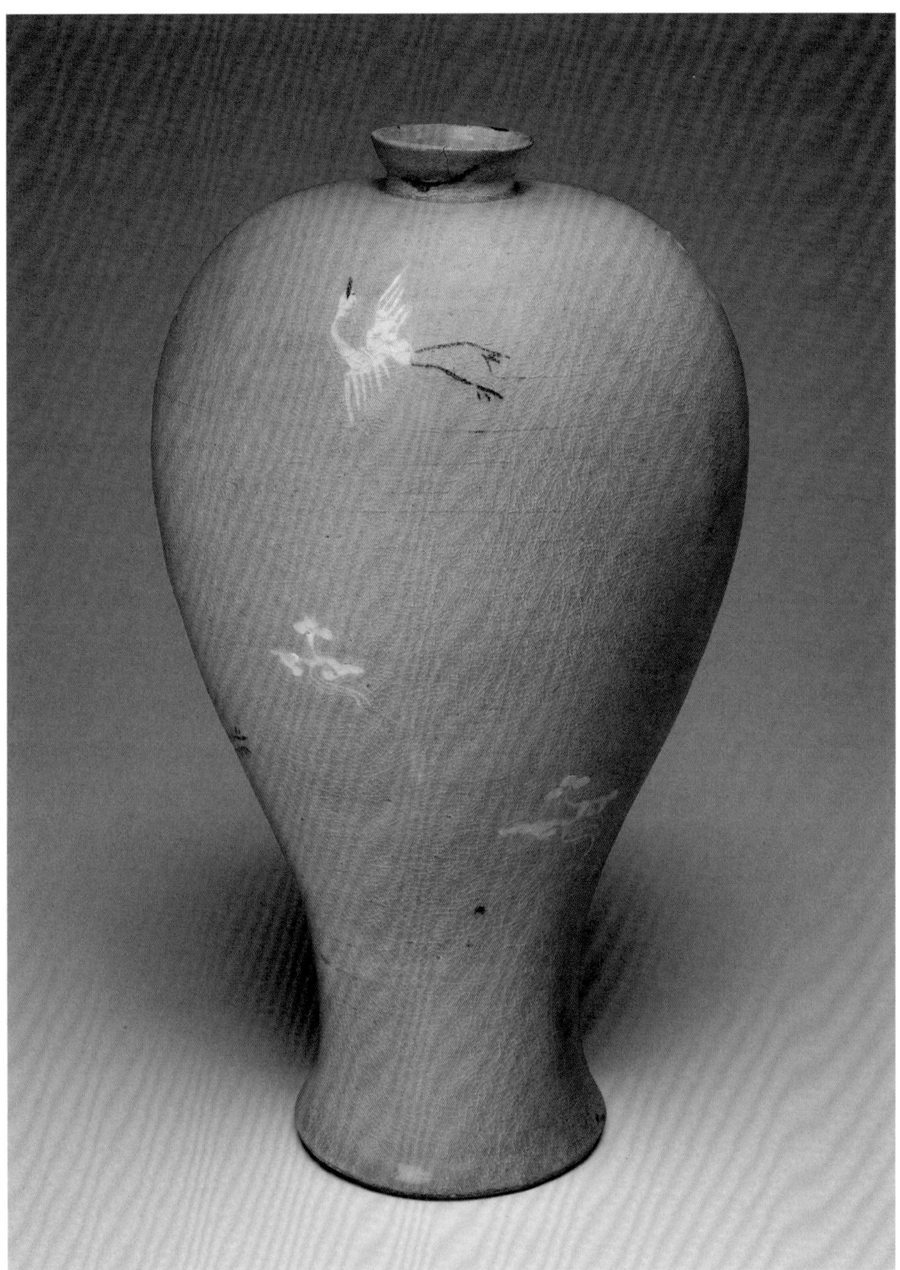

**Fig. 7.2**

*Bottle with Cranes and Clouds*, Korea, Goryeo dynasty, 12th century. Stoneware with inlaid slip under glaze, H. 13 × DIAM. 7¼ in. (33 × 18.4 cm). Yale University Art Gallery, Leonard C. Hanna, Jr., Class of 1913, Fund, 2008.129.1

was given as a gift to retainers at the court, and, as in China and Japan, Buddhist monks drank tea as a stimulant to bolster meditation and used it as an offering to other officiants and to supplicants during rituals.

A bottle (fig. 7.2) in the Chinese *meiping*, or "plum flower vase," shape (known in Korean as *maebyong*) displays three lively cranes flitting among clouds. The bottle has a broad shoulder, typical of Korean wares, that tapers to a much thinner base. Both the cranes and clouds were carved into the clay body when it was partially hardened, or leather hard; they were then filled with one or more layers of slip—the bodies of the cranes and the clouds in white, and the beaks and legs of the birds in black. The piece would have been fired after the inlay was applied. It was then covered with a slip, which was scraped off the inlaid areas, and glazed, before being fired a second time. The use of an inlay on green-glazed ceramics is not found in China or Japan at the time, but it does appear in Vietnamese ceramics (as discussed in the previous chapter). Decorative inlay is often found in metal and lacquer works from the Goryeo period, and it seems likely that its use in ceramics developed in tandem with these other artistic traditions. Although there is some evidence for inlay in Korean ceramics in the eleventh century, such decoration flourished in the mid-twelfth century and was popular until the fourteenth century, when green-glazed wares were gradually replaced by other types of ceramics.

Cranes, symbols of longevity in East Asia, were important in the decoration of Korean ceramics in the late twelfth and thirteenth centuries, due in part to a growing interest in Chinese Daoist practices, many of which were intended to promote long life. During this period, both Buddhist and Daoist rituals were held at the court in an effort to protect Korea from the Mongols, who had established the Yuan dynasty in China and were actively threatening Korea and Japan.[5] Frequent Mongol incursions into Korea beginning in 1231 ultimately led the court to flee to Ganghwa Island, off the western coast, which was not invaded, although the court officially submitted to the Mongols in 1259. (The Mongol attempts to invade Japan in 1271 and 1284 were hindered by unfavorable winds, spurring the Japanese notion of a sacred wind, or *kamikaze*, a term applied to the Japanese military's air attacks in the twentieth century.)

The delicate copper-red accents at the center of the chrysanthemum blossoms inlaid in the surface of a small jar (fig. 7.3) represent another Korean innovation in green-glazed wares of the mid-twelfth century. Red pigment derived from copper is notoriously unstable during firing, and its successful use here attests to the skills of the Goryeo potters. Like the cranes on the *meiping*-shaped bottle, the four carefully but not symmetrically placed flowers are inlaid with slip—white for the blossoms and black for the leaves. The delicate crackle in the glaze, which may have been an intentional response to the contemporaneous interest in such surface patterning in China, adds depth to the rich surface of this tiny but luxurious jar. This piece is another example of the small multipurpose jars made in China, Korea, and Southeast Asia. Unlike those produced elsewhere, however, Korean examples were sometimes preserved as part of larger cosmetic sets; in that context, they held oil for women's hair.

Green-glazed wares were the most important Goryeo ceramics, and they remain the most well known. However, smaller quantities of brown-glazed wares

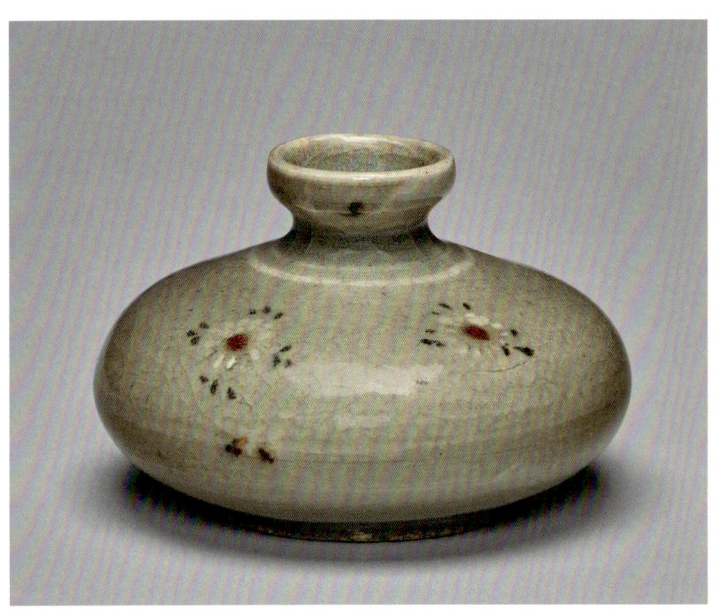

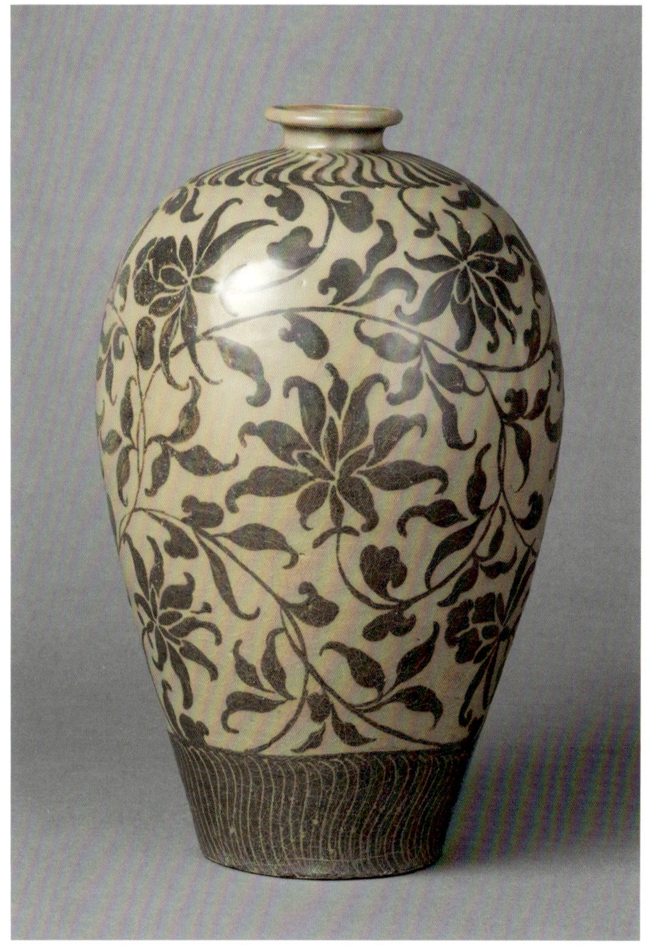

**Fig. 7.3**

*Jar with Chrysanthemums*, Korea, Goryeo dynasty, late 12th–early 13th century. Stoneware with inlaid white slip and copper-red pigment under glaze, H. 2 × DIAM. 2⅜ in. (5.1 × 6 cm). Yale University Art Gallery, Gift of Mr. and Mrs. Sidney N. Morse, Jr., 1992.59.15

**Fig. 7.4**

*Bottle with an Auspicious Blossom Scroll*, Korea, Goryeo dynasty, 12th century. Stoneware with iron-brown pigment under glaze, H. 11⅛ × DIAM. 7 in. (28.2 × 17.8 cm). Museum of Oriental Ceramics, Osaka, Japan, Gift of the SUMITOMO Group, the ATAKA Collection, 00788

and pieces painted with brown pigment were also produced in Korea at this time. Excavations at Korean kiln sites, which have yielded both full objects and fragments, have shown that ceramics painted with brown were produced in kilns that also made green wares, such as those at Sadang-ri and Yongun-ri, in South Jeolla Province. On the surface of another bottle in the *meiping* (*maebyong*) shape (fig. 7.4), painted blossom scrolls illustrate a composite auspicious flower derived from the Buddhist lotus, symbolic of majesty and beauty. Backward-S-shaped lines appear at the shoulder, where they are painted, and at the base, where they are denser and were scratched into the surface using a ceramic technique often described using the Italian word *sgraffito*. Iron brown was also used to paint ceramics in China, in the Cizhou kilns in the north and in the Xicun and Cizao kilns in the south—another example of the long-standing exchanges in East Asian ceramics.

Despite the fact that they were not (or, at least, not overtly) intended for trade, Korean ceramics have been found in both China and Japan. Over twenty examples have been excavated at archaeological sites throughout China.[6] One of the most spectacular is a bottle in the *meiping* shape decorated with inlaid peonies, found in 1994 in Shijiazhuang City, in Hebei Province, in the tomb of Shi Tianzi, an official at the Yuan court who died in 1275.[7] It seems likely that this piece was initially a diplomatic gift. Goryeo celadons have also been found in Japan, particularly in Kyushu, the southernmost island of the Japanese archipelago and home to the port of Hakata, the most significant trading center from the ninth to the fourteenth century.[8] In addition, seven Korean celadons (as well as a single Japanese piece from the kilns in the Seto region) were found in the Sinan shipwreck, suggesting either that individuals traveling on the ship owned these pieces or that the merchants who were moving large cargoes were also trading specific goods in response to individual requests. The ceramics and other items on the Sinan wreck were part of a joint venture between a Chinese trader and several Japanese partners, including three Buddhist establishments. The sale of the cargo of this ship, one of several commissioned specifically to raise funds to support and repair Buddhist temples, was intended to underwrite the restoration of the Tofukuji Temple in Kyoto and two other Japanese temples.

## Japan

Like the ship in the Sinan wreck, ships traveling from China to Japan often departed from Ningbo and then skirted the southern tip of the Korean peninsula before reaching the port of Hakata. From there, Chinese ceramics circulated to palaces, aristocratic homes, and Buddhist establishments in urban centers such as Kyoto and Tokyo, and ultimately throughout all of Japan. The city of Daizafu served as an administrative center for Kyushu and was responsible for managing trade between Japan and the East Asian mainland and for maintaining the Kōrokan, guest quarters for visiting dignitaries and merchants. In addition to Korean ceramics, Chinese ceramics have been found in significant numbers in excavations near these centers,[9] as have pieces from Thailand and Vietnam, particularly after the sixteenth century.

The green-glazed pieces depicted in a scene from a fourteenth-century handscroll (fig. 7.5) attest to the widespread availability of Chinese ceramics in Japan by that time. The scroll is part of a set illustrating the biography of the Buddhist monk Kakunyo. He is shown seated, wearing a gray robe, engaged in a poetry contest with monks and laity. At the top, a portrait of the great poet Kakinomoto Hitomaro hangs on a wall behind a celadon incense burner imported from either Zhejiang or Fujian and two metal flowerpots. Scrolls with paintings or calligraphy that could be unrolled and shown during the event are placed on a red lacquer table. In the kitchen scene at the left, large

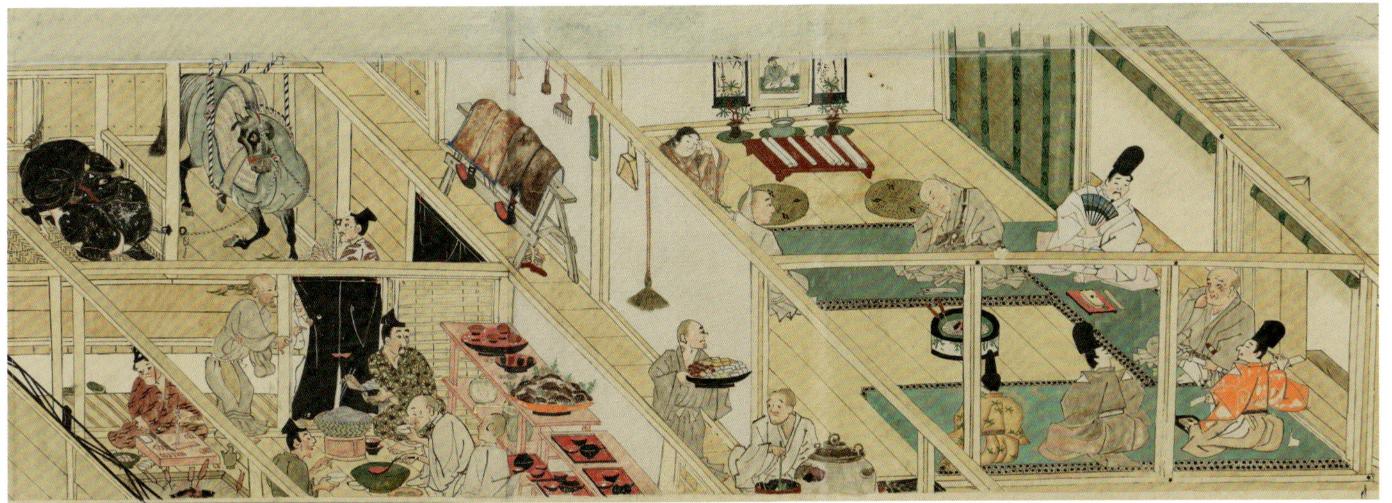

**Fig. 7.5**

Nagia Jo'un and others, *Boki-e (Biographical Stories about Priest Kakunyo)* (detail), Japan, Nanbokucho period, dated 1351. Handscroll; ink and colors on silk. Tokyo National Museum, A-6866_5

green-glazed bowls and jars, as well as red and black lacquer trays and cups, are stored on shelves, while food and tea are prepared for Kakunyo and his guests.

Japanese awareness and appreciation of Korean ceramics, which were imported as early as the fifth century C.E., helped spur the development in the late eighth century of the Sanage kiln complex near Nagoya, in Aichi Prefecture. Supported by the Heian government (794–1185), this center produced the first glazed ceramics in Japan, some green and others brown (fig. 7.6). At its peak, the Sanage complex operated over one thousand kilns; however, its wares were not widely distributed and instead were used in governmental bureaus, palaces, elite homes, and important temples, primarily from the tenth to the twelfth century. By the thirteenth century, when production at Sanage ceased, the city of Seto, also in Aichi, had become an important center for making glazed ceramics. The Seto kilns continued the techniques for potting and glazing that had initially been developed at Sanage, including the use of green and brown glazes. They benefited from proximity to deposits of high-quality clays, including some with a high percentage of kaolin, which enhanced the clay's plasticity. The shape and runny olive-green glaze of a large jar produced in Seto (fig. 7.7), now designated as Japanese Important Cultural Property, reflects the appearance of imported Chinese green wares, particularly those with lushly streaked glazes from Guangdong and Fujian. The lively peony scroll that fills the surface of the jar is a motif shared throughout East Asia.

By the fifteenth and sixteenth centuries, due in part to the widespread practice of the tea ceremony, tea bowls had become significant products of the Seto kilns. Bowls from Seto had shapes and glazes that creatively responded to ceramics imported from kilns in both northern and southern China. The low, open shape of a tea bowl with a black glaze (fig. 7.8) has parallels in green-glazed

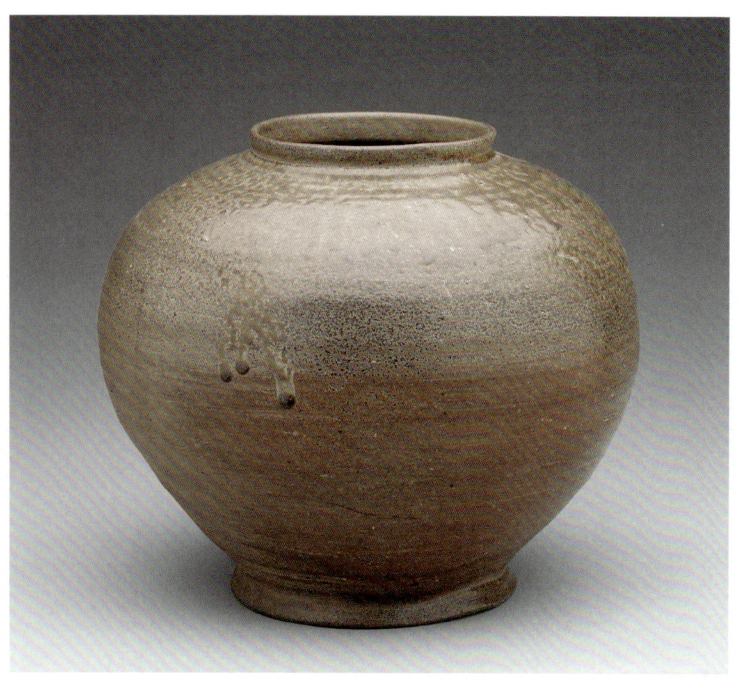

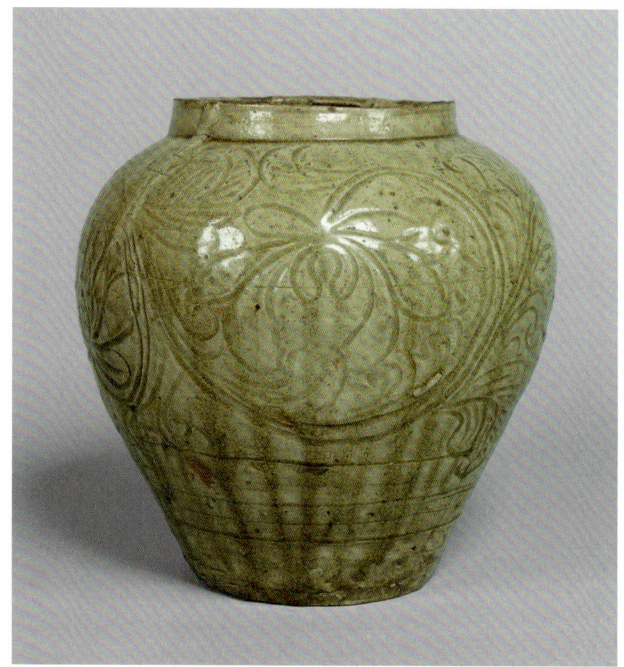

**Fig. 7.6**

*Jar*, Japan, Heian period, 10th century. Stoneware with ash glaze (Sanage ware), H. 10 × DIAM. 11%16 in. (25.4 × 29.4 cm). Yale University Art Gallery, Anonymous gift in memory of Pauline H. Lee, 1971.24

**Fig. 7.7**

*Jar with Vines and Peonies*, Japan, Kamakura period, 14th century. Stoneware with incised decoration under glaze (Seto ware), H. 10 11/16 × DIAM. (mouth) 6 9/16 in. (27.1 × 16.7 cm). Tokyo National Museum, G344. Important Cultural Property

Longquan wares. While the tortoiseshell effect of the spots produced by ash on the iron glaze alludes to the effect seen on brown- and black-glazed Jizhou bowls from Jiangxi, the dark wash evokes the color of Jian wares from Fujian. The delicate gold-lacquer repair at the center of this bowl (fig. 7.9) is an example of *kintsugi* (gold joinery), a Japanese conservation method used as early as the fifteenth century to preserve highly valued ceramics, including pieces from China and Korea. One part of the rim has been further repaired, probably in the nineteenth or twentieth century, with a sprinkled gold-lacquer pattern of blossoming cherries over a dark, possibly silver, ground. The commissioner of the latter repair may have chosen this floral motif as an allusion to their reading of the appearance of the iron spots in the glaze.[10]

Because a high number of Chinese ceramic pieces have been found in Japan—presumably only a minuscule portion of the total number of pieces that traveled there between the twelfth and the fourteenth century—more historical documentation about the use and reuse of Chinese ceramics is available in Japan than in other parts of the Asian maritime world. Some ceramics, such as a cylindrical container (fig. 7.10) used to store a Buddhist text, or sutra, were made to order in China for the Japanese market. The sutra that was once written on paper and rolled for storage in this container has disappeared over time. The piece is coated with a thin gray-green glaze and has a cover in the shape of a pagoda, and broad lotus petals encircle the foot. It was probably made near the port city of Fuzhou, in Fujian.

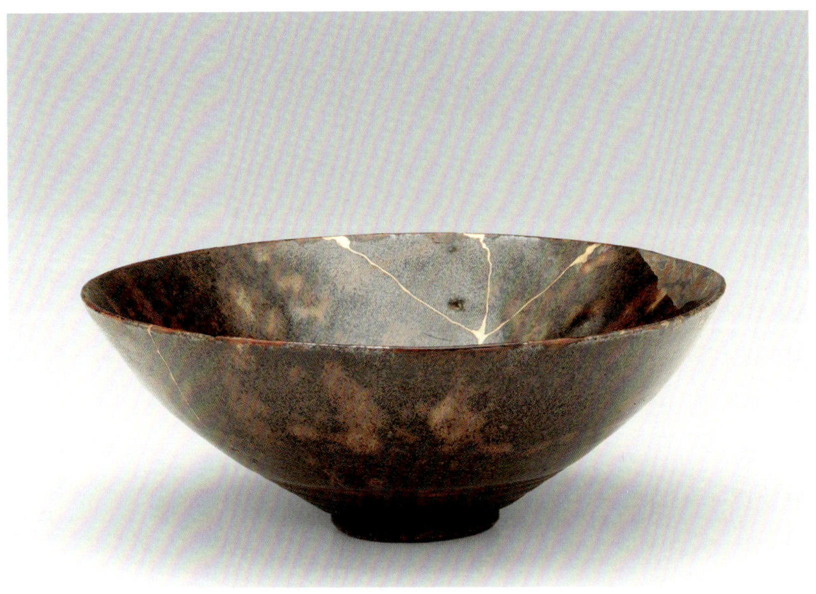

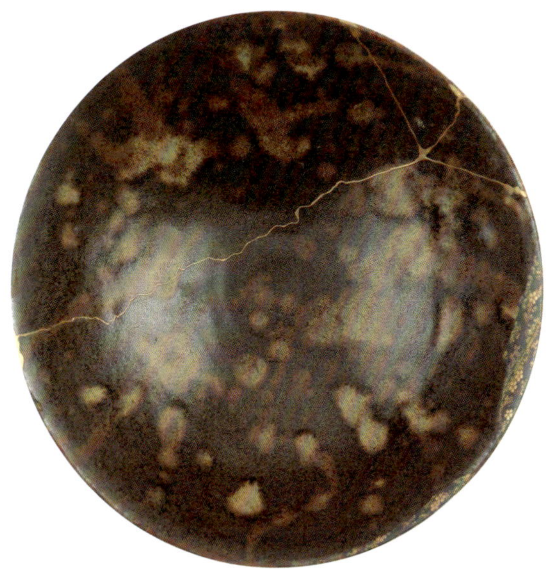

**Fig. 7.8**

*Tea Bowl*, Japan, Muromachi period, early 16th century. Stoneware with iron-oxide and brown glaze (Seto ware), with later gold-lacquer repair, H. 2½ × DIAM. 6⅝ in. (6.3 × 16.8 cm). National Museum of Asian Art, Smithsonian Institution, Washington, D.C., Freer Collection, Gift of Charles Lang Freer, F1900.53

**Fig. 7.9**

Interior of fig. 7.8

**Fig. 7.10**

*Sutra Container*, China, Southern Song dynasty, 12th–13th century. Stoneware with molded and incised decoration under glaze (from a Fujian kiln), H. 13½ × DIAM. 6⅞ in. (34.4 × 17.5 cm). Minneapolis Institute of Art, The Ruth Ann Dayton Chinese Room Endowment Fund, 2016.78a,b

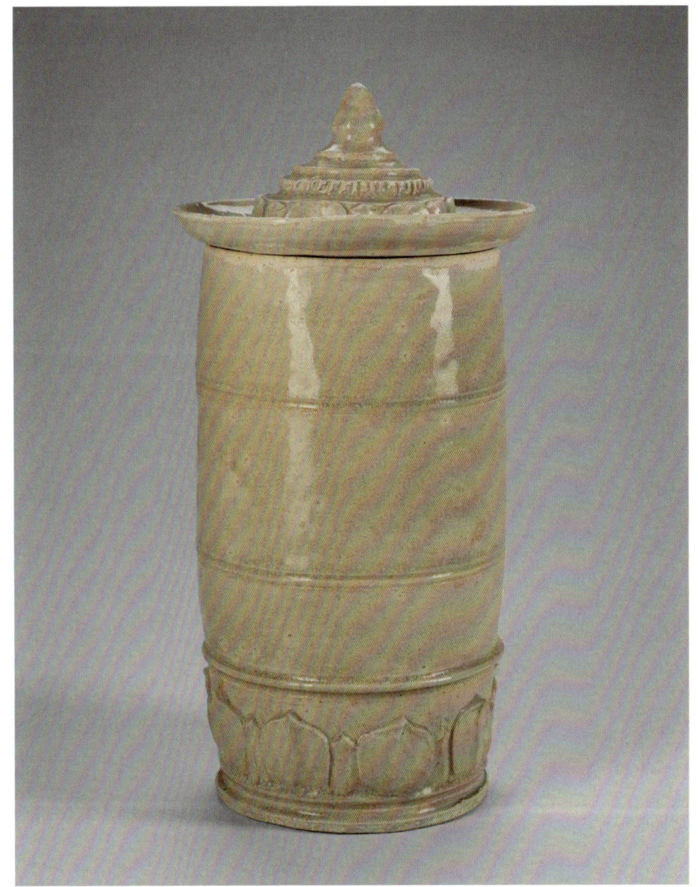

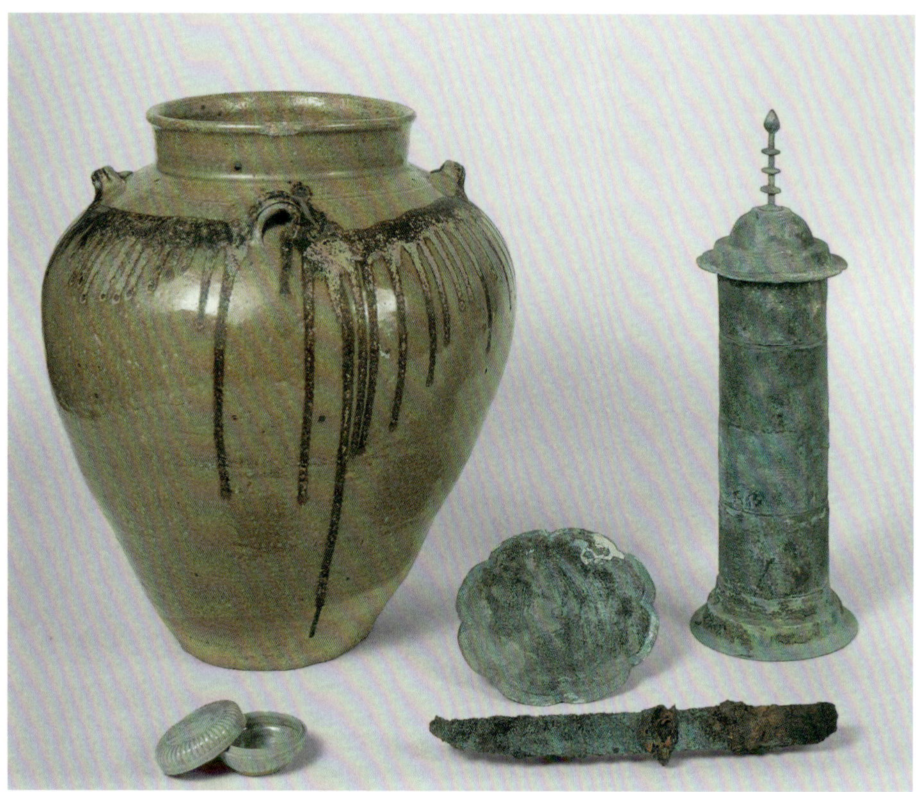

**Fig. 7.11**

Chinese transport jar and other objects (all 12th century), excavated from Sutra Mound K at Hakusan-jinka, Fukuoka, Japan. Kyushu Historical Museum, Japan

Sutra containers made of either bronze or clay are preserved in northern China, particularly at sites supported by the Qidan Liao dynasty, as well as in Japan. In China the containers were often stored in pagodas, but in Japan they were buried, usually in chambers (some lined with stones and charcoal), and covered with the types of earth mounds that had long played a role in funerary practices in India and Central and East Asia.[11] A bronze sutra container was part of an assemblage of goods in a Chinese ceramic transport jar, probably from Guangdong, found buried under a mound in Fukuoka, now the capital of Kyushu (fig. 7.11).[12] While the sutra container and the knife in this group were made in Japan, the bronze mirror and the small ceramic box with a Qingbai glaze were Chinese imports. Typically made in China but sometimes in Indonesia, bronze mirrors were valued for their protective and symbolic functions as well as their use in daily life. Those made in Huzhou, in Zhejiang, were popular trade items from the twelfth to the fourteenth century, and mirrors are often found in shipwrecks, including the Belitung and Cirebon. The Qingbai-glazed box in this group, initially used for cosmetics, had been transformed into a reliquary containing the tiny glass beads that served as symbolic relics in East Asian Buddhist practices.

A Longquan piece in the distinctive shape of a sprinkler (fig. 7.12) is an example of another type of Chinese ceramic that was ordered by Japanese

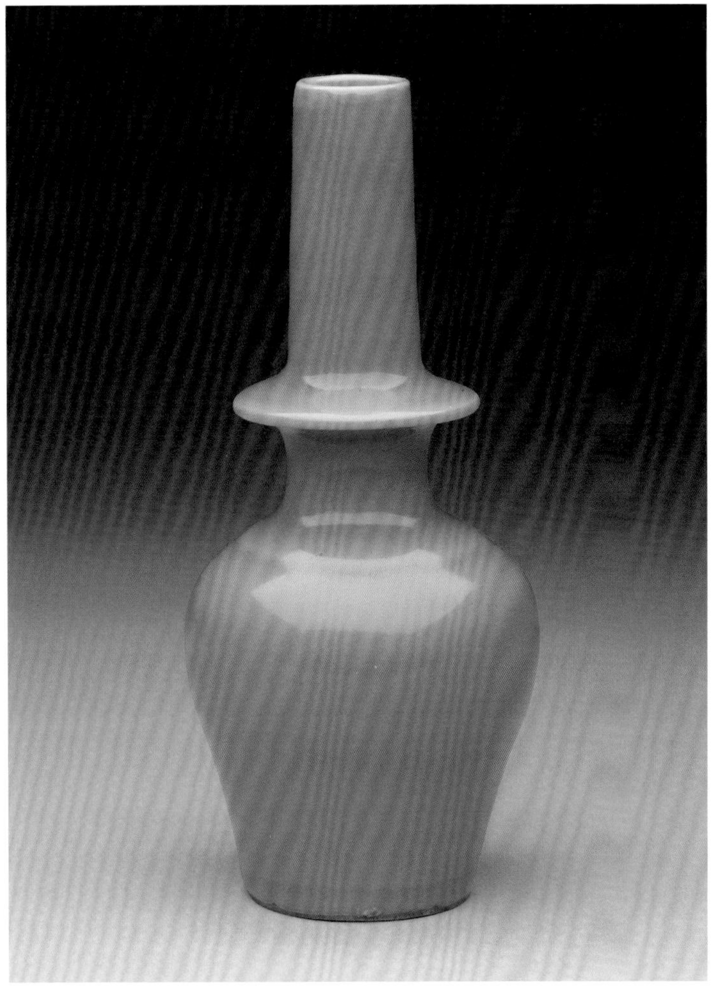

**Fig. 7.12**

*Sprinkler*, China, Yuan dynasty, 14th century. Stoneware with glaze (Longquan ware), H. 6⅛ × DIAM. 1¾ in. (15.6 × 4.5 cm). Collection of Peggy and Richard M. Danziger, LL.B. 1963

clients. As previously mentioned, sprinklers of this type, some of which have spouts, were imported from India to China with Buddhist practices as early as the eighth or ninth century C.E. While the Indian prototypes (known by the Sanskrit word *kundika*) are generally metal, Chinese sprinklers are ceramic. The rigid collar at the base of the neck of this example is evidence of the metal precursor. Originally intended for ritual use, this sprinkler was later repurposed as a flower vase in the Japanese tea ceremony.

The tea ceremony prompted the study, appreciation, repurposing, and preservation of Chinese ceramics in Japan, many of which are still in public and private Japanese collections. Tea drinking was introduced to Japan in the eighth and ninth centuries by Buddhist monks who had traveled to China, particularly individuals associated with Chan, or Zen, practices. It was often part of a monk's daily activities, rituals, and meditation, and it became important at the court in the twelfth century. By the fifteenth century, tea was widely cultivated and

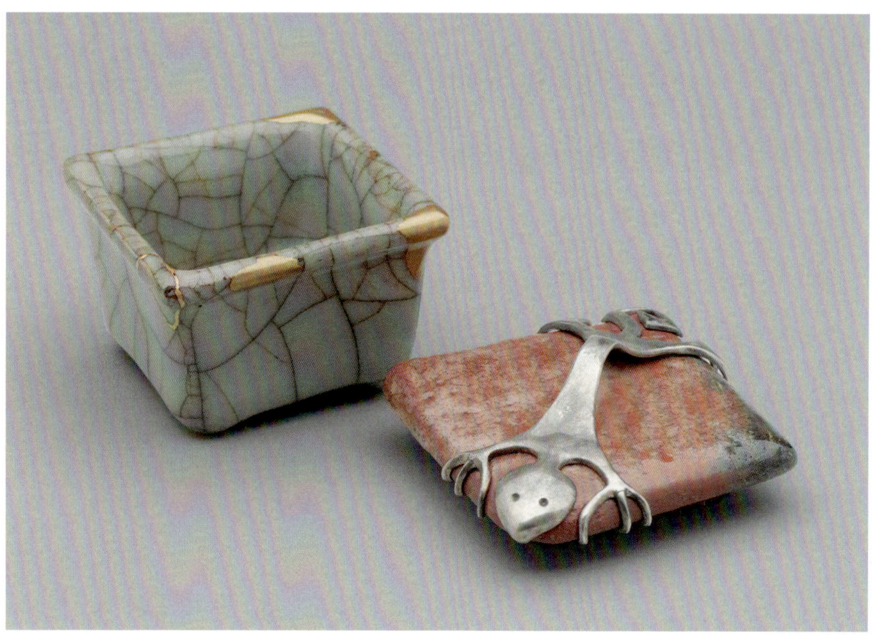

**Fig. 7.13**

*Incense Box with a Handle in the Shape of a Dragon*. Box: China, Southern Song dynasty, 13th century. Stoneware with glaze (Longquan Guan ware), with later Japanese gold-lacquer repair. Lid: Raku Ryōnyū, Japan, late 18th century. Earthenware with glaze. Handle: United States, 20th century. Pewter. Overall 1⅞ × 2 5⁄16 × 2⅜ in. (4.8 × 5.8 × 6 cm). Collection of Peggy and Richard M. Danziger, LL.B. 1963

consumed, and the tea ceremony—a performative version of the preparation and drinking of tea that could include poetry and other arts and featured imported Chinese goods—was held in Buddhist temples, palaces, and wealthy homes, as were tea tastings. In the late fifteenth and sixteenth centuries, masters such as Murata Jukō (previously mentioned for his interest in certain types of ceramics from Fujian) and Sen no Rikyū developed the style of tea ceremony known as "frugal" or "withered" tea (*wabi cha*) and as "grass hut" tea (*sōan cha*). It was practiced in small, specially designed rooms or huts and highlighted objects made in Japan, often works from local or regional kilns that were not necessarily highly valued. The objects for these ceremonies were carefully selected to create a special moment in reference to a season, historical event, or personal transition or celebration. During a ceremony, the knowledge of an object's history—including its prior owners and earlier events in which it was used—added depth to the appreciation of it. By the sixteenth century, as tea masters and adherents began to record the connoisseurship underlying the selection of specific objects for a ceremony, they sometimes gave evocative personal names to the most cherished tea bowls, caddies, jars, and other implements.

A delightful square box (fig. 7.13) is an example of a Chinese work with a fascinating history that was used in Japanese tea ceremonies. Made in the Longquan kilns, the box has the distinctive glaze crackling inspired by the imperial Guan wares of the Southern Song dynasty and could have served many purposes before it reached Japan and was incorporated into the tea ceremony. An inscription on the wooden box for this piece indicates that it was used in Japan as a tea caddy. It also states that the potter Raku Ryōnyū, who inscribed and stamped the bottom of the lid, added the red lid to the box in the late eighteenth century. Ryōnyū was the ninth-generation master of the Raku family of potters in Kyoto, which made works seen as unpretentious and approachable. Beginning in the sixteenth century, Raku wares were often created specifically for the tea ceremony. At some point, probably after it had been chosen for use in ceremonies, the box received a *kintsugi* repair: thick gold-lacquer inserts were applied to some parts of the rim, and thinner slivers were added to the body. The dragon-shaped pewter handle was made by an American artist in the twentieth century and was recently attached to the lid by the current owner of the box.

Since 1951, the Japanese Agency for Cultural Affairs (Bunkachō) has awarded the designations "National Treasure" and "Important Cultural Property" to works of art in public and private collections that are noted for their high level of technical skill and historical and scholarly importance. In addition to three Longquan celadons, five tea bowls from Fujian and one tea bowl from Korea are Japanese National Treasures. The Fujian tea bowls are rare and wonderful examples of Jian wares celebrated for their gracefully balanced shapes, beautifully patterned glazes, and historical importance in Japanese culture.[13] One of the bowls is named *Inaba Tenmoku* (fig. 7.14). As mentioned, *tenmoku* is a term used for both Chinese and Japanese black- and brown-glazed wares. *Inaba* is the name of the family or clan that received this bowl as a gift from the ruling Tokugawa shoguns in the seventeenth century. In the early twentieth century, the piece was acquired by a member of the Iwasaki family of warrior nobility. It is one of three known works, all located in Japan, that are categorized as *yohen tenmoku*. *Yohen*, meaning "iridescent spotted," describes the blue-tinged starlike shapes that appeared during firing.

The purple-tinged silvery spots on another Chinese Jian tea bowl (fig. 7.15), also a Japanese National Treasure, are known as *yuteki*, or "oil spots." This term first appeared in late fourteenth-century Japanese writings that classified and rated Chinese tea bowls; those described as *yohen* or *yuteki* were listed as the most valued.[14] This bowl has a long provenance: it reached Japan during the Kamakura period (1185–1333) and was owned by the chancellor Toyotomi Hidetsugu before it entered the collection of the Nishi Honganji Temple in Kyoto, then a private collection, and ultimately the Museum of Oriental Ceramics, Osaka. Recent testing has shown that the high-quality gold band covering the rim of the bowl was not added in China but in Japan, possibly as a replacement for another metal band[15] and presumably because the contrast of the gold intensified the glaze color. This extraordinary tea bowl is preserved together with red lacquer stands from either China or Japan, which would have

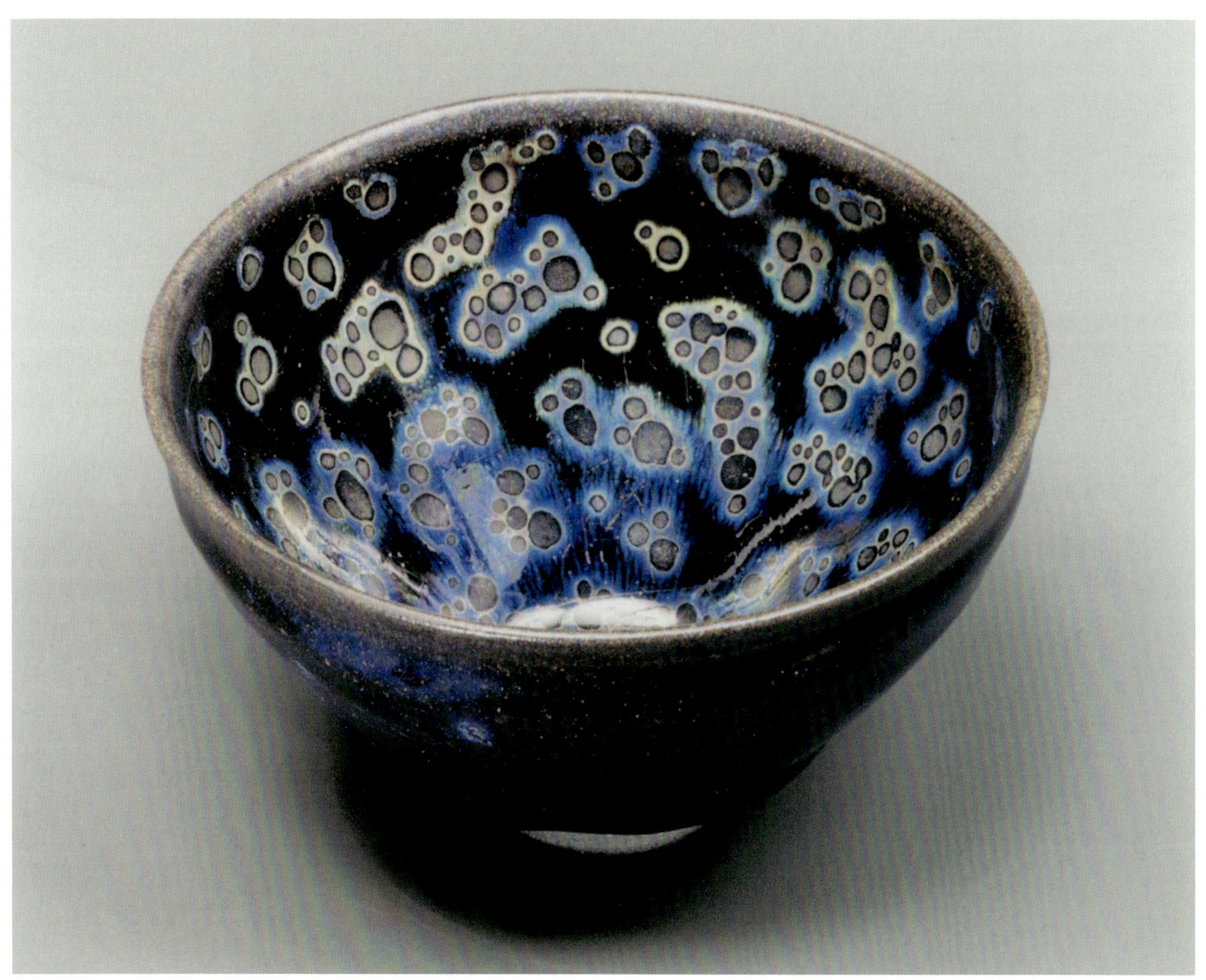

**Fig. 7.14**

*Tea Bowl with Iridescent Spots, named "Inaba Tenmoku,"* China, Southern Song dynasty, 12th–13th century. Stoneware with glaze (Jian ware), DIAM. 4¾ in. (12 cm). Seikado Bunko Museum, Tokyo. Japanese National Treasure

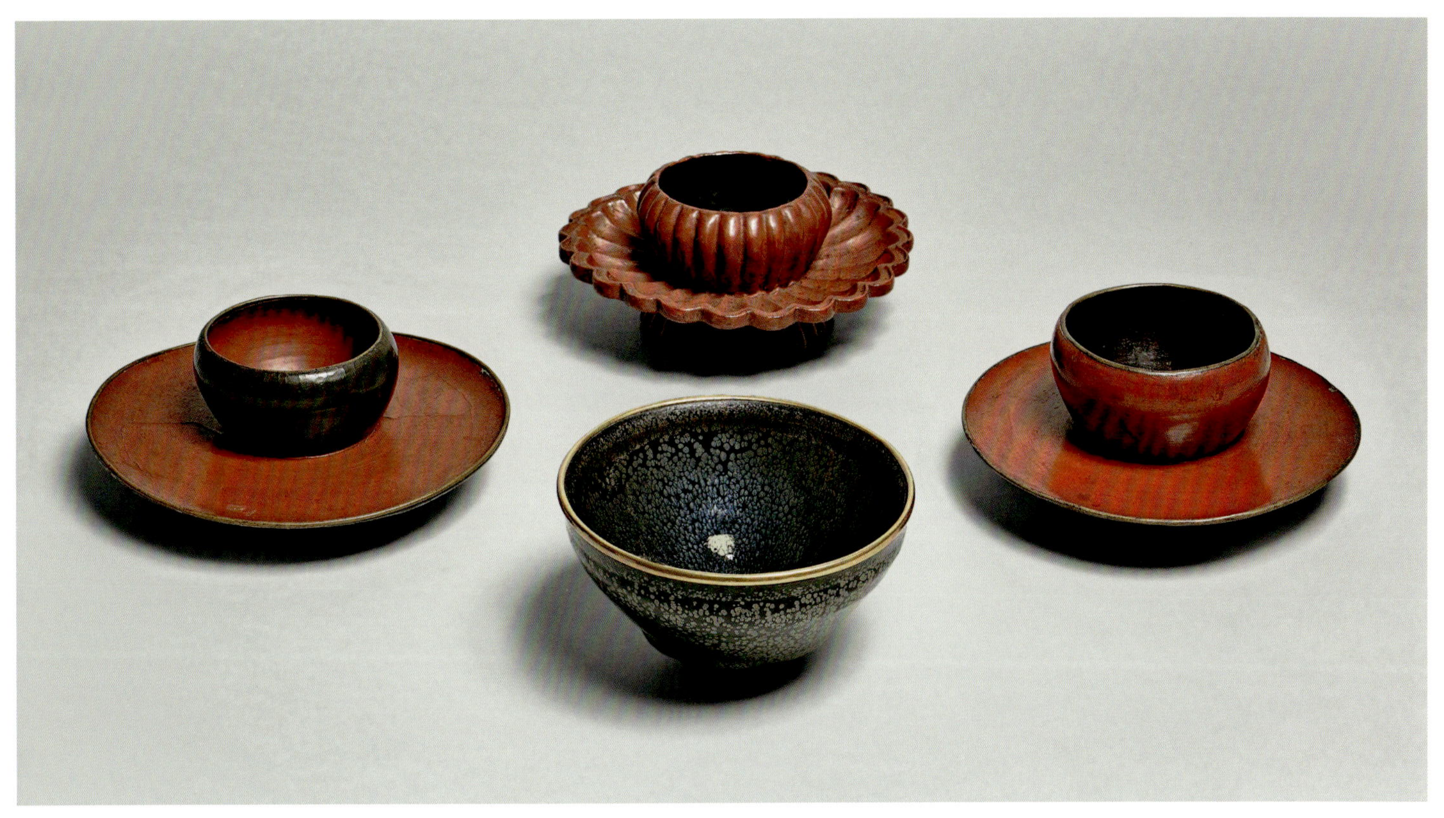

**Fig. 7.15**

(center) *Tea Bowl with Iron Spots*, China, Southern Song dynasty, 12th–13th century. Stoneware with glaze (Jian ware), with gold rim added later, H. $2\frac{15}{16}$ × DIAM. $4\frac{13}{16}$ in. (7.5 × 12.2 cm). Museum of Oriental Ceramics, Osaka, Japan, Gift of SUMITOMO Group, the ATAKA Collection, 00559. Japanese National Treasure

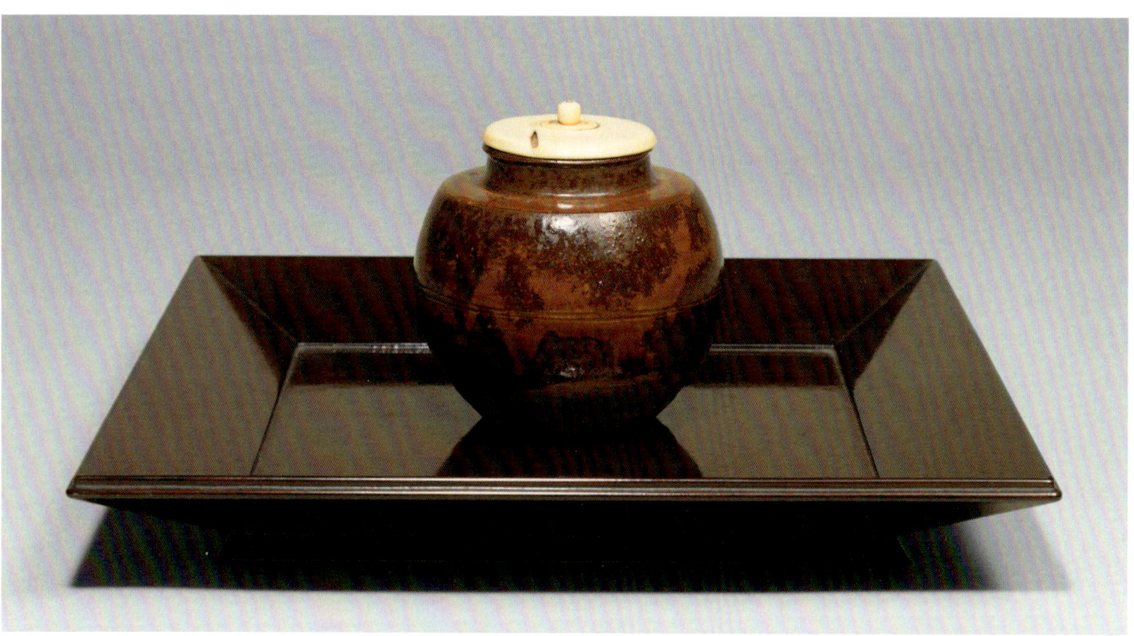

**Fig. 7.16**

*Tea Caddy, named "Matsuya Katatsuki,"* China, Southern Song or Yuan dynasty, 13th–14th century. Stoneware with glaze (possibly from a Fuzhou kiln, Fujian), with ivory lid, H. 3 1/16 × DIAM. 1 7/8 in. (7.7 × 4.7 cm). Nezu Museum, Tokyo, 40091

been selected for use with the bowl during different tea ceremonies or different moments within a ceremony.

Lacquer trays, either imported from China or made in Japan, were also used to present tea caddies, which, like the bowls, were carefully selected for specific ceremonies. The caddies are typically small jars with a brown or black glaze. On a Yuan-dynasty Chinese caddy (fig. 7.16), made at an unidentified kiln in Fujian, possibly near Fuzhou, a richly mottled brown glaze articulates the vessel's strong shape. This caddy is named *Matsuya Katatsuki*, after the Matsuya family who once owned it; *katatsuki*, or "protruding shoulder" (a description of the shape), is one of many terms used in Japan to define and distinguish tea caddies from one another. This caddy may have initially been used as a jar for various goods before it was imported to Japan, where it acquired a lid made of imported ivory and was repurposed as a tea caddy.

The exquisite care with which items were selected for inclusion in tea ceremonies, which included an awareness of their histories, is evident in the fascinating travels of a thirteenth- or fourteenth-century Chinese transport jar (fig. 7.17) that was most likely produced at a kiln in Guangdong or Fujian and used to store other goods during its journey to Japan.[16] This jar may have reached Japan as early as the fourteenth century; by the sixteenth century, it was named *Chigusa*—a reference to Japanese poetry meaning "myriad plants" or "thousand grasses." It is one of the first recorded examples of a tea vessel acquiring a personal name. Used in Japan for storing tea leaves, the jar was also occasionally displayed during tea ceremonies, particularly those held in late

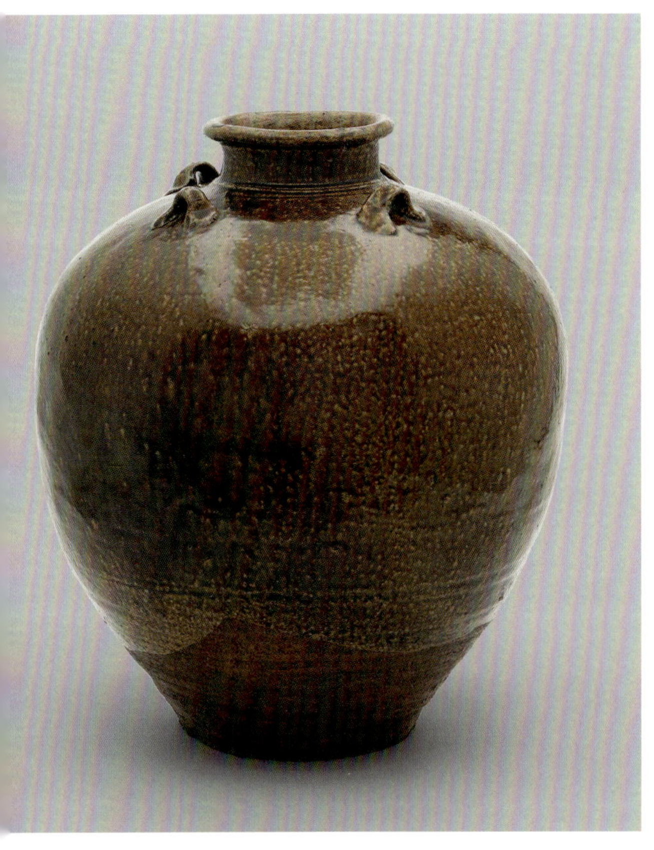

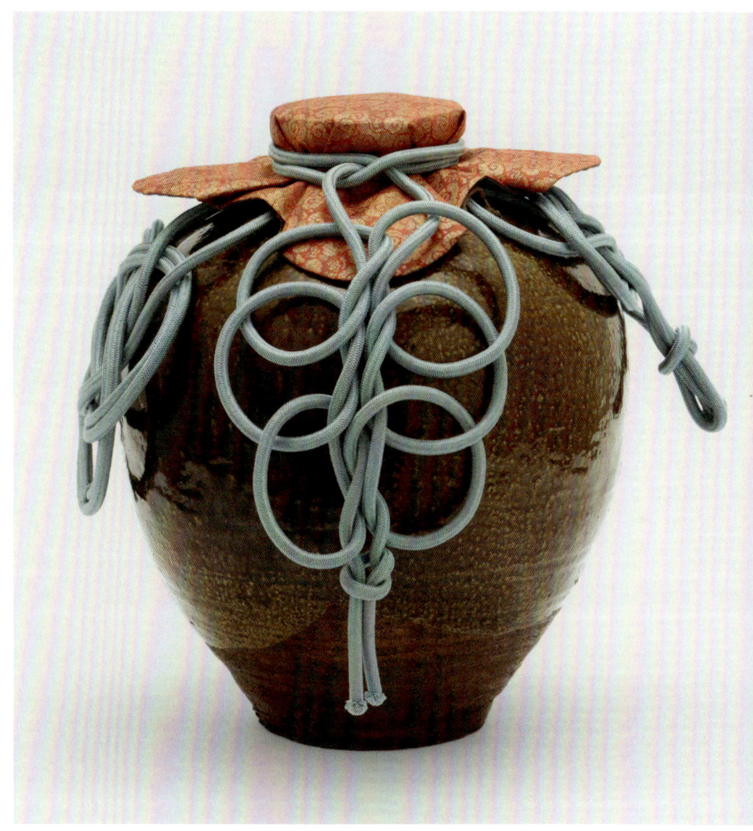

**Fig. 7.17**

*Tea Leaf Storage Jar, named "Chigusa,"* China, Southern Song or Yuan dynasty, 13th–14th century. Stoneware with glaze (probably from a Guangdong kiln), H. 16⅜ × DIAM. 14⁷⁄₁₆ in. (41.6 × 36.6 cm). National Museum of Asian Art, Smithsonian Institution, Washington, D.C., Freer Collection, Purchase—Charles Lang Freer Endowment, F2016.20.1

**Fig. 7.18**

*Chigusa* (fig. 7.17), shown with decorative silk cover and cords

autumn, when such jars—which would previously have been sealed—were opened to highlight the new tea that had become available. Over time, *Chigusa* acquired a range of documents explaining its beauty, history, and importance. These documents are stored in a tray in one of the three nested wooden boxes that house the jar. In addition, *Chigusa* has two sets of special ornaments (fig. 7.18), including covers and cords, a net, and a display mat—all of which are made of Chinese silk.

The selection of a humble thirteenth- or fourteenth-century Chinese transport jar for use in a Japanese tea ceremony in the sixteenth century, and the jar's long record of study and appreciation, offers a superb illustration of the global importance of ceramics made in China. First appreciated for their artistry and beauty in the eighth and ninth centuries, Chinese ceramics—particularly the southern green-glazed, or celadon, wares—became highly treasured and emulated goods throughout maritime Asia from the twelfth to the fourteenth century. Today, they continue to serve as visual mementos of the transformative and vibrant cultural exchanges that characterized the ninth to the fourteenth century throughout East, West, South, and Southeast Asia.

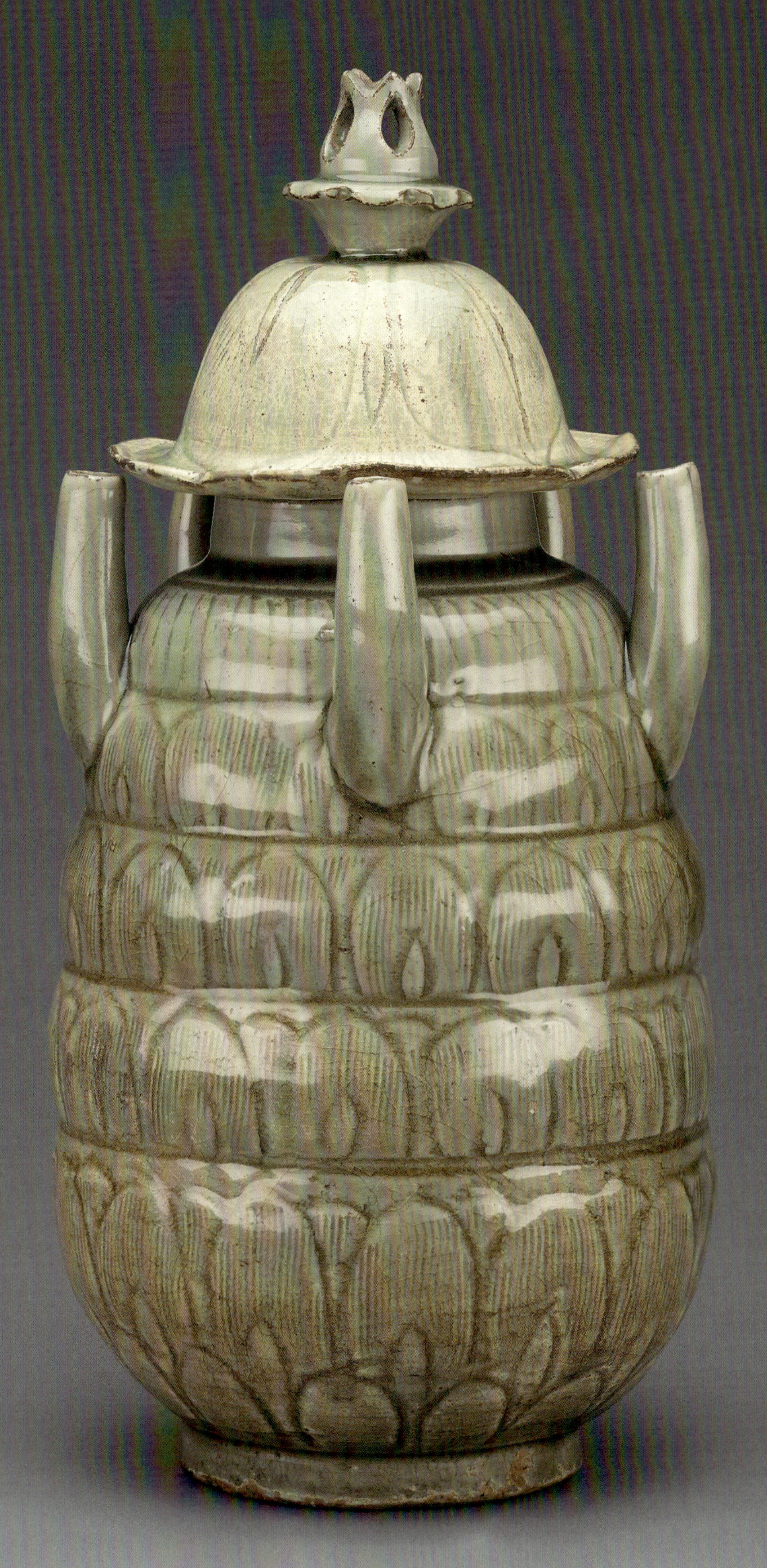

APPENDIX

# The Production of Chinese Ceramics from the 9th to the 14th Century

Amreet Kular and Katherine Peters

In the ninth to the fourteenth century, expert knowledge of the properties of clay and glazes and the evolution of kilns facilitated the rapid development of the ceramic industry of southern China, which produced works that traveled primarily by sea throughout the greater Asian world and beyond. While celadon wares required the same basic materials and manufacturing techniques as other types of ceramics, their unique colors arose from the Chinese potters' mastery of clay and glaze components and kiln firing, developed over time through tradition, study, and experimentation. This appendix presents an overview of the production of ceramics—from shaping and firing the clay to applying and firing the glaze—to enable a better understanding of these works of art.

## Shaping the Clay

"Ceramic" is a term used to define any object made of clay; the word "clay" refers to a certain type of earth composed of both fine-grain minerals with a platelet structure and additional organic material. After it is sourced, clay often undergoes a process to make it usable for being shaped into a ceramic body. It must first be levigated, or worked and washed, to remove impurities. Due to physical and chemical characteristics of the mineral component, clay becomes sticky and malleable when wet; the presence of impurities would affect not only its malleability but also its workability and general qualities, as well as the resulting ceramic body.[1] Once the clay is sourced and processed, it can be used to make a ceramic piece.

The ceramics in this volume were primarily made with a potter's wheel, a tool used in China as early as the Neolithic period.[2] A potter's wheel is essentially a horizontal rotating disk (app. 1.1). After placing a lump of wet clay onto the wheel, the ceramist forms the lump into the desired shape while spinning the wheel by hand or by using a pedal with their foot. As a result of the rotation, objects made on a wheel—such as a bowl from the Huanxiu kilns in Fujian Province (app. 1.2)—have concentric rings stemming from a central point that are usually most visible on the base (app. 1.3). While bowls or cups are typically thrown, or shaped, from a single lump of clay, more complex pieces, such as vases, are thrown in separate pieces that are then assembled. Joining two or more pieces requires significant skill: a difference in the moisture levels in two pieces of clay will result in cracks along the joins when the vessel is fired, because the wetter piece will shrink more than the drier one.

Molds were used to create decorative elements, or appliqués, that were then applied to a vessel's surface. Molds could be either a single piece (app. 1.4) or multiple pieces and were also made of clay. The two fish swimming around one another on a dish produced in the Longquan kiln complex in Zhejiang Province (see fig. 1.24) were molded and applied to the dish before it was fired.

**App. 1.1**

Potter's wheel, 21st century

**App. 1.2**

*Bowl*, China, Yuan dynasty, 13th–14th century. Stoneware with glaze (from a Huanxiu kiln, Fujian), H. 3½ × DIAM. 5 in. (8.9 × 12.7 cm). Yale University Art Gallery, Gift of John Crockett, 2008.222.48

**App. 1.3**

Base of app. 1.2

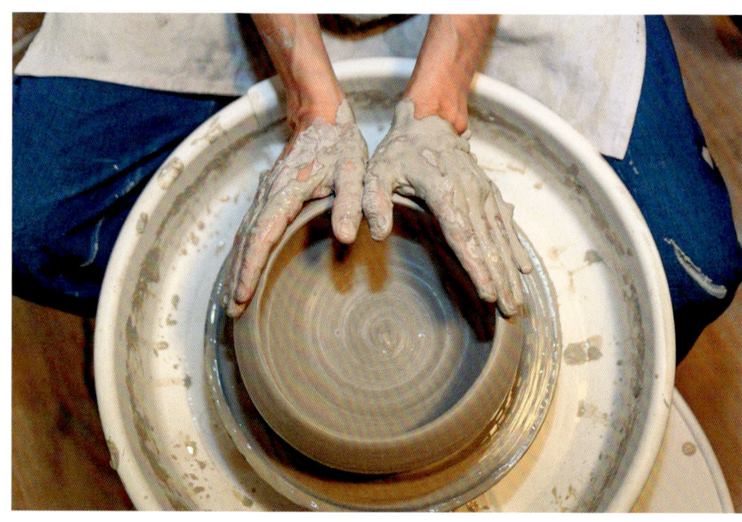

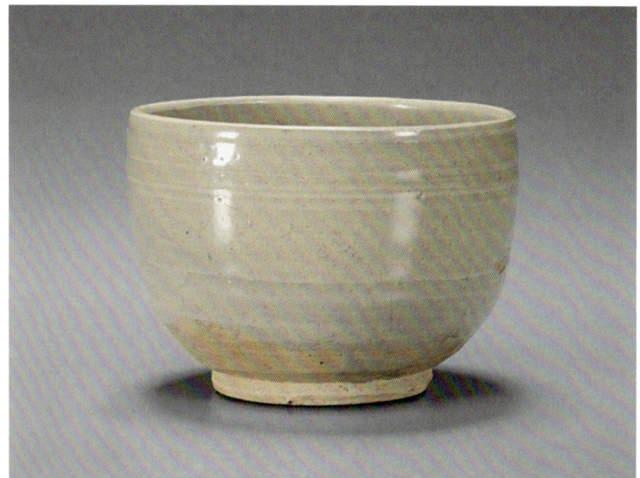

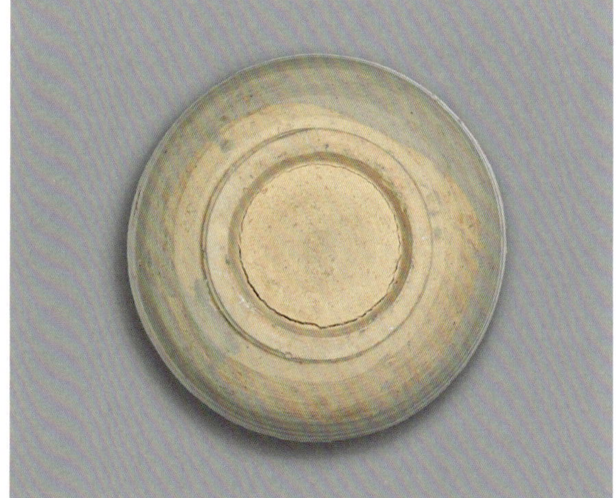

**App. 1.4**

(left) *Mold for a Bowl, with* (right) *a Modern Bowl Made from the Mold*. Mold: China, Northern Song dynasty, 11th–12th century. Stoneware with carved decoration, DIAM. 5½ in. (14 cm). Metropolitan Museum of Art, New York, Gift of C. T. Loo, 1916, 16.149.1

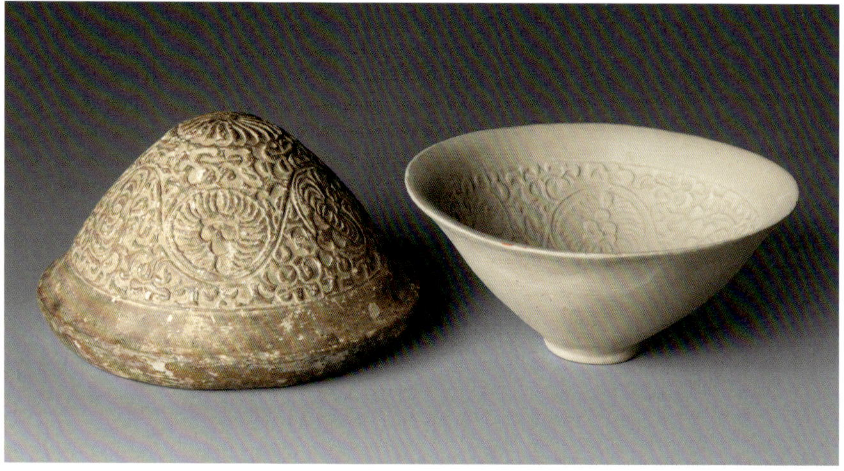

Interestingly, the two fish are seemingly identical—each one may have been made from the same mold before being applied to the dish. Given the scale of production and the importance of dishes with fish in the Longquan trade repertoire, it is also possible that a large number of molds were used to make a variety of fish appliqués that would have been readily available during the production process.

After a clay form has been shaped, the surface can be carved or incised to add decorative elements. A delicate green-glazed bowl from Guangdong Province (see fig. 4.13) is decorated with overlapping plantain leaves that were defined using two different implements: a larger tool was used to carve the outlines of the leaves, and a smaller tool was used for the interior veins of each leaf. These incisions add a sense of depth to the leaves, similar to the use of lines for creating shadows in a drawing. On the exterior of the bowl are narrow lines (see fig. 4.14); their size indicates that they were likely carved with the same smaller tool.

A dramatic funerary jar from Fujian Province (see fig. 5.4) illustrates the use of multiple processes or techniques to shape a ceramic piece. The concentric rings on the interior of the neck and body and a horizontal join line across the body indicate that the jar was made in two pieces (the rounded body and the narrower neck), which were thrown separately on a wheel and then joined together before firing. Incised geometric patterns fill the lower part of the jar. The bird, dragon, child, and other elements—made either by hand or with a mold—were attached to the upper part of the jar before firing.

## Firing the Clay

Firing introduces physical and chemical changes to the clay that transform it from a soft, soluble, malleable material into a hardened, crystalline ceramic. The initial firing of the clay piece before glaze application is called the "bisque firing." Celadons are high-fired ceramics, meaning that they are fired at high kiln temperatures in order for them to become more durable and water-resistant than the more porous and delicate earthenwares. The potters would fire the celadons at 1,200 to 1,300 degrees Celsius.[3]

One of the key factors that contributed to the large-scale production of celadons in southern China was the ingenious design of the kilns in that region. Southern Chinese celadons were fired in dragon, or *long*, kilns—long, narrow kilns built up gently sloping hills with a firebox at the bottom—which had evolved from cave kilns during the Warring States period (475–221 B.C.E.).[4] During the same period, *mantou* kilns were developed in northern China and became the dominant kiln type for firing northern celadons. *Mantou* kilns had a low dome over a horseshoe-shaped ground plan and were on average two meters in diameter—much smaller than the southern dragon kilns, which could reach 140 meters in length.[5] Because of their size, dragon kilns were far more efficient

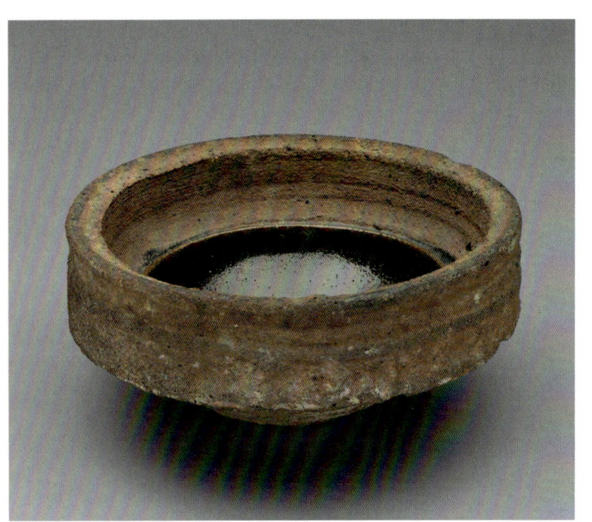

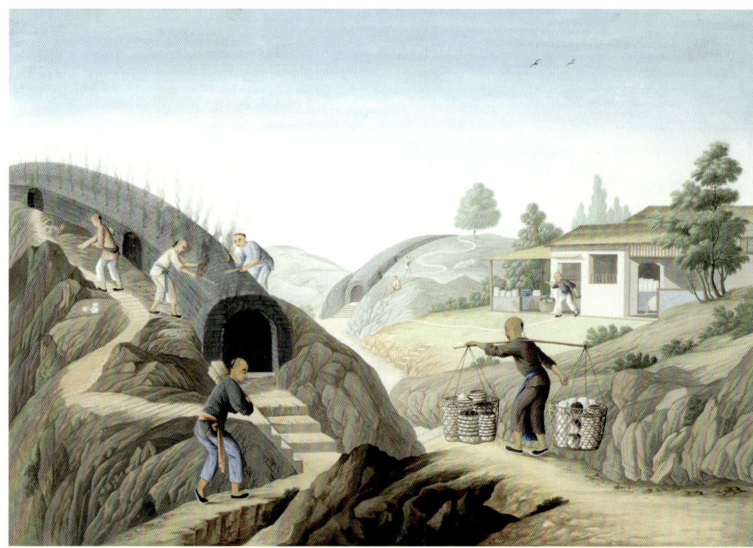

**App. 1.5**

*Tea Bowl in a Saggar*, China, Southern Song dynasty, 10th–13th century. Tea bowl: stoneware with glaze (Jian ware), overall H. 4⅝ × DIAM. 9¼ in. (11.8 × 23.5 cm). Yale University Art Gallery, Gift of Peter and Louise Rosenberg, 1982.119

**App. 1.6**

*Firing the Dragon Kiln*, China, Qing dynasty, ca. 1825. Gouache on paper, 15⅜ × 20⅞ in. (39.1 × 53 cm). Peabody Essex Museum, Salem, Mass., Purchased with funds donated anonymously, 1983, E81592.14

at firing a large number of ceramics at once: while a *mantou* kiln could produce hundreds of ceramics in one firing, a dragon kiln could produce tens of thousands.[6] This extraordinary rate likely contributed to the increase of southern Chinese ceramics in trade.

Inside a dragon kiln, the clay vessels closest to the firebox reached the desired temperature range first. Along the sides of the kiln, there were multiple fire holes through which fuel (wood and brush) were added and stoked to raise and maintain the temperature of each kiln section. The upper part of the kiln served as a chimney, drawing warm air up and over the vessels to preheat the pieces that were placed higher up the hill, thus increasing the kiln's efficiency.[7]

Within the dragon kiln, some vessels were held by saggars (app. 1.5), protective refractory clay containers that could withstand repeated high-temperature firings. A saggar enclosed the clay vessel, protecting it from direct heat, and was tightly sealed to help create an environment with low oxygen levels. Saggars could be stacked on top of one another to maximize space in the kiln, and they were sometimes used to create walls between kiln sections to enable each section to reach the proper temperature.[8] Eventually, the dragon kiln was refined into a multichambered structure that had walls with holes in strategic locations to control the draft (app. 1.6).

## Applying the Glaze

Chinese ceramics are usually covered with a glaze, a glasslike substance that enhances the object's beauty and strengthens the ceramic body, often making it impermeable to water and other liquids. A glaze is applied after the bisque firing transforms the clay vessel into a ceramic, and its components are essential to its

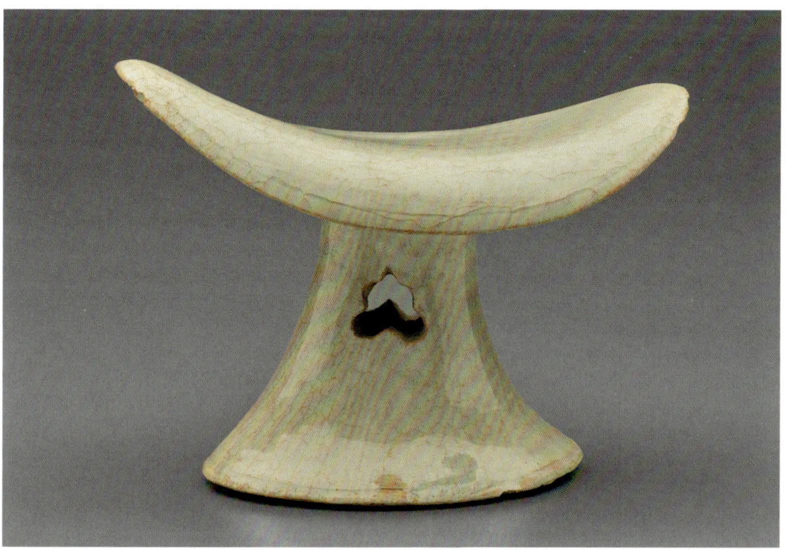

**App. 1.7**

*Pillow in the Shape of a Crescent*, China, Northern Song dynasty, 10th–11th century. Stoneware with glaze (Hunan Qingbai ware), 4¾ × 6½ in. (12.1 × 16.5 cm). Yale University Art Gallery, Gift of John Hadley Cox, B.A. 1935, 1940.371

final appearance. The main component of a glaze is silica, and various fluxes—principally calcium, lead, potassium, or sodium—are added to lower the melting point. Alumina can be added to stiffen the glaze so it does not run off the surface of the vessel. Other metal elements are added to alter the color: in the case of green glazes, this is often copper, which helps to create both greens and blues. Titanium dioxide is an inorganic compound that can be added to alter the color of green glazes, producing a range of hues, including blue, blue-green, gray-green, and olive; the more titanium in a glaze, the more yellow it will look. Glazes can also be formulated to appear either transparent or opaque after the chemical and physical transformations that occur during firing.

The physical application of the glaze can also influence its final appearance. Southern Chinese celadon ceramics display a variety of application techniques, including dipping, pouring, and brushing. In some cases, the thickness of the glaze application can make a piece look as if it has multiple colors. The glaze on a five-spouted jar (see fig. 1.10), for example, emphasizes its incised decoration. On the sides of the body, where it was thinly applied, the glaze appears to be yellow-green, while on the low areas of the design, where it was thickly applied and has pooled, it is darker. Despite this significant variation in hue, there is only one glaze on the piece.

Some glazes have cracks in the surface, known as "crazing" or "crackle," an effect that was highly valued at certain times throughout Chinese history. Crazing is created deliberately by formulating the glaze to shrink more than the clay body during firing. As the glaze shrinks, the resulting tension in the ceramic is released through the formation of fine cracks in the glaze layer. A crescent-shaped pillow (app. 1.7) has a typical Qingbai glaze that displays crazing.

## Firing the Glaze

Once the glaze has been applied, the ceramic piece is fired again to transform the glaze into a hard, vitreous layer. The elements of the firing process have just as much influence on the ultimate visual qualities of the glaze as its composition and its application. During firing, the glaze color can be affected by temperature, duration in the kiln, the kiln atmosphere, the type of fuel, and the position of the object in the kiln.

The kiln atmosphere is crucial for producing the desired glaze color, and skilled ceramists tightly control the atmosphere to attain the right firing temperature. The atmosphere can be "reducing," "oxidizing," or "intermediate." Inside the kiln, carbon atoms from the smoke readily combine with oxygen atoms to produce carbon monoxide. When a smoky fire consumes all of the oxygen in the kiln, the atmosphere is described as "reducing." In this environment, oxygen atoms are prevented from bonding with metal elements in the glaze, and the resulting glaze color is that of the pure metal. In contrast, a brightly burning fire with plenty of air (and thus plenty of oxygen) in the kiln creates an "oxidizing" atmosphere. The oxygen in the air reacts with the metal elements in the glaze, thereby oxidizing the glaze and producing the color of a metal oxide. In an "intermediate" atmosphere, there is a small amount of free oxygen, which may combine with the metallic compounds to produce metal oxides with fewer oxygen atoms. Metal oxides differ in color depending on whether or not they have been fully oxidized. If three identical ceramics with the same metal elements in their glazes were fired in three different atmospheres, they would all look different at the end of the process: each would be a different color, because the metal components in the glazes would have achieved different oxidation states.

Differences in the kiln atmosphere account for the great variation in celadon glazes. The main colorant found in traditional celadon wares is iron oxide, as it can yield various shades of green and blue glazes.[9] Iron oxide is usually found in its ferric, or iron (III), oxide form, and this is added to the glaze recipe. If a glaze containing ferric oxide were fired in reducing conditions, it would become reduced to ferrous, or iron (II), oxide and thus would appear as the quintessential green or blue-green color associated with celadons. However, if the environment in the kiln were intermediate or oxidizing, the resulting glaze color could vary from light yellow to olive green or even dark brown (app. 1.8).[10] The proportions of iron oxide, sodium, potassium oxide, lime, or lead oxide in the glaze will also have an impact on its final color. The kiln atmosphere can likewise contribute to variations in the clay color. Stoneware bodies that were fired in reducing conditions tend to be gray, while many vessels fired in slightly oxidizing conditions have tan or buff-colored bodies.

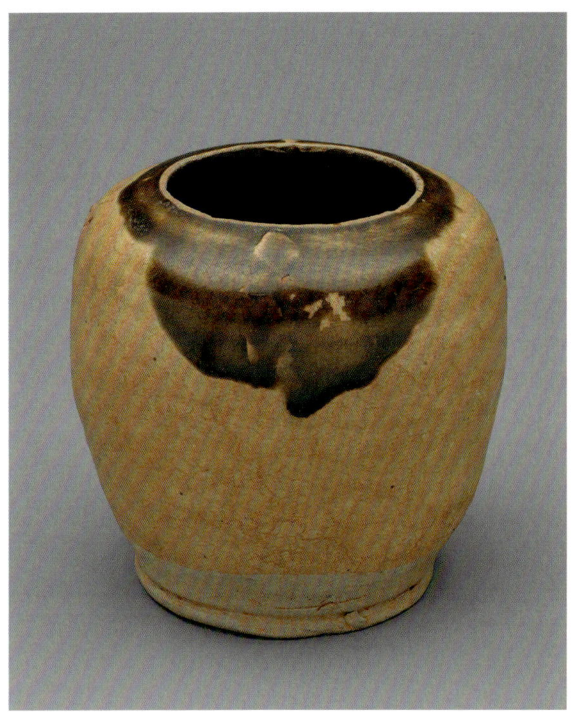

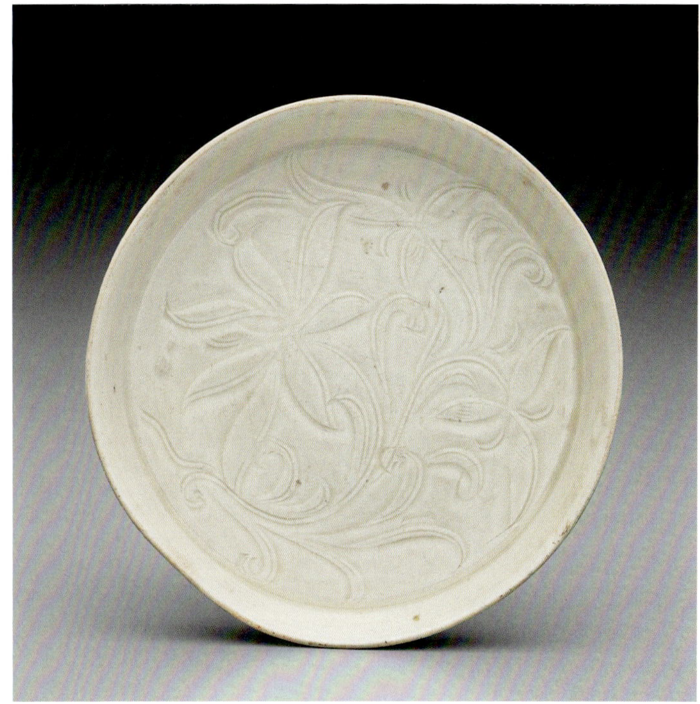

**App. 1.8**

*Jar*, China, Tang dynasty, 9th–10th century. Stoneware with splashed brown glaze over green glaze (Changsha ware), H. 3⅞ × DIAM. 4 in. (9.8 × 10.2 cm). Yale University Art Gallery, Gift of John Hadley Cox, B.A. 1935, 1940.365

**App. 1.9**

*Brush Washer with a Lotus*, China, Northern Song dynasty, 10th–11th century. Porcelain with incised decoration under glaze (Ding ware), H. ¾ × DIAM. 4$\frac{9}{16}$ in. (1.91 × 11.5 cm). Yale University Art Gallery, Wayland Wells Williams, B.A. 1910, Collection, Gift of Mrs. Frances Wayland Williams, 1947.74

The kiln atmosphere and ceramics were also affected by the type of fuel. Wood was commonly burned as fuel, and it could produce a reducing atmosphere relatively easily. Yet the use of wood in ceramic and other manufacturing industries in north China around the tenth century led to a shortage of trees there. The northern coalfields provided Chinese potters in the region with an accessible alternative fuel source, and the use of coal as kiln fuel became prevalent in the north during the tenth and eleventh centuries.[11] Although coal made it easier to reach a high temperature, it made it much harder to achieve a fully reducing atmosphere. Oftentimes, ceramics that were intended to be blue-green came out of the kiln as olive or yellow-green, because pollutants from the coal had prevented a fully reducing atmosphere. Unlike wood ash, which was smooth and did not harm the ceramics, the gritty ash produced from coal could easily damage the glazes; the vessels were therefore placed in saggars for protection. Northern Chinese potters used the new fuel source to their advantage and created wares that varied in glaze color. For example, the Ding wares of northern China, which became popular around the time that green-glazed ceramics did in the south, were made in coal kilns and usually have warm, ivory-colored glazes due to the oxidizing environment (app. 1.9).[12]

Coal was rarely used in the south, as there was not a significant natural supply in southern China. In addition, the dragon kilns needed resinous woods, brushwood, or reeds to produce the long flames necessary for successful reduction firings.

Coal would have made it very difficult to produce the fine blue-green celadon pieces, such as Longquan wares, for which the southern kilns were renowned.

Finally, because different areas of the kiln had slightly different atmospheres, despite the potters' skills at controlling the overall environment, a vessel's position in the kiln also affected its appearance. Ceramics for important clients, such as those made for the court, were placed near the bottom of the kiln, where the correct atmosphere could be easily maintained. To avoid firing losses, small wares were also placed at the bottom of the kiln, because they required less preheating time.[13] Since it was difficult to control the reduction near the chimney, at the top of the kiln, less important wares were placed there. The rest of the kiln was filled with other such wares to maximize efficiency.

The production of ceramics was a complex art that required many technical skills at every step, from the shaping of the clay to the firing of the glaze. From the ninth to the fourteenth century, these objects were cherished and traded far beyond China. Today, they are evidence of extraordinary scientific and artistic knowledge.

# Notes

## Introduction

1. The distinction between stoneware and porcelain—critical in Western ceramic scholarship—is not as important in Chinese writings, which more often characterize ceramics as either low-fired or high-fired. Both stoneware and porcelain are high-fired.

2. For an overview of the production of Chinese ceramics, see the appendix in the present volume.

3. Ray 2012, fig. 2.

4. Guy 2019, fig. 6.27.

5. Lu 2009.

6. Hallett 2009.

7. Gompertz 1968, 21.

8. Savage and Newman 1974, 67–68.

9. Hansen 1996.

10. Whitehouse 1973.

11. Rougeulle 1991.

12. Lo 2002, 31.

13. Li 2020.

## Chapter 1

1. Wood 2007; and Wood and Kerr 2008.

2. For an overview of ceramic production, including a discussion of the conditions required for altering glaze colors, see the appendix in the present volume.

3. Krahl et al. 2010, 49.

4. Mino and Tsiang 1987, 13.

5. Shi and Han 1989; and Wang et al. 2014.

6. Sharf 2011; and Karetzky 1994.

7. Zhejiang Sheng Wenwu Kaogu Yanjiusuo 2017, 3.

8. Lin 1994.

9. Ruan 1994.

10. Flecker 2002.

11. Liebner 2014.

12. This information appears in a discussion of a famous Yue ewer in the collection of the Kyoto National Museum (inv. no. GK161), which is classified in Japan as Important Cultural Property; see Yoshihiro Ono, trans. Melissa M. Rinne, "The 'Secret Colored' Celedon [*sic*] Ewer," Kyoto National Museum, January 11, 1997, https://www.kyohaku.go.jp/eng/learn/home/dictio/touji/seiji/.

13. Yang 2018, 4–17.

14. Du 2002; and *Maboroshi no meiyō* 2010.

15. Krahl 2021, 60.

16. Wang 1969, 637.

17. Wang 1998, 43–57.

18. Lo 2002, 195–98.

19. Ts'ai 1996, 116–17.

20. Needell 2018.

21. The eleventh-century Serçe Limani shipwreck, excavated off the coast of Turkey between 1977 and 1979, is known as the "Glass Wreck" because of the unusually large amount of glass in the cargo.

22. Shen 2002.

23. Li 1993, fig. 16.

24. An 1991, fig. 12.

25. Li 1993.

26. Lin 2006, pls. 47–48.

27. *Maboroshi no meiyō* 2010, pl. 6.

28. Itō and Mino 1991, fig. 7.

29. National Museum of Korea 2017.

30. Nezu Museum 2010, pl. 18.

31. Ibid., 17–25.

32. Derek Heng, "Ships, Shipwrecks, and Archaeological Recoveries as Sources of Southeast Asian History," Oxford Research Encyclopedia for Asian History, September 26, 2019, https://oxfordre.com/asianhistory/display/10.1093/acrefore/9780190277727.001.0001/acrefore-9780190277727-e-97.

33. An 1987, fig. 31.

34. Ströber 2013, pls. 26–28.

## Chapter 2

1. Yang 2010.

2. Shanghai Museum 2005.

3. Krahl 2010. For an example of Ding ware, see appendix image 1.9 in the present volume.

4. Wood 1978; and Wood and Rastelli 2014.

5. Pierson 2000, 7.

6. Sun et al. 2017, nos. 27 and 32.

7. Pierson 2000, 7.

8. Ibid., nos. 107–15.

9. Cai 2010.

10. Chengdu Wenwu Kaogu Yanjiusuo and Suining City Museum 2012, vol. 2, pls. 183–87.

11. Leidy 2016–17.

12. Teo 2000.

13. Li 2010.

14. Feng 1998, 137.

15. Watson and Wilson 2000.

16. It is possible that another such vase was also in Europe at the time, in the collection of Jean, Duc de Berry, the brother of King Charles V of France; see Arnold 1999, 132.

## Chapter 3

1. The difference between "Yue ware" and "Yuezhou ware" is less confusing in Chinese, in which the characters differ: Yue ware made in Zhejiang is written 越, and Yuezhou from Hunan is 岳.

2. Zhang 2008, vol. 13, pl. 137.

3. Lam 1999, figs. 207–549.

4. Mai 1998, 103–4; and Chong and Murphy 2013, fig. 1.

5. Hunan Sheng Wenwu Kaogu Yanjiusuo 1996, 141.

6. Chong and Murphy 2013, 69.

7. Wilkinson 1973, 213–26.

8. George 2015.

9. Watt and Wardwell 1998, nos. 2–5.

10. Juliano and Lerner 1997.

11. Shen 2014.

12. Zhou 2007, figs. 37–38, 141, 231, 266, and 282.

13. Huang, Xiong, and Zhao 2014.

14. Xiong 2014, fig. 11.

15. Priestman 2016.

16. FPM 1975.

17. Qi 1999.

18. Hsieh 2010.

19. Lam 1999, 143.

20. Ibid., 153–54.

21. Zhang 2008, vol. 13, pls. 213–14 and 219.

22. Zhang 2008, vol. 8, pls. 205–6.

23. Zhou and Zheng 2012.

24. Truong 2007, figs. 75 and 86–87.

## Chapter 4

1. Xiong 2014.

2. McLaughlin 2020, 187–98.

3. Fong 2014, 482–84.

4. Schottenhammer 2016, 135.

5. It has intriguingly been suggested that the rulers of the Southern Han, whose family name was Liu, may have been of West Asian descent, possibly Arab or Persian, because *Liu* can be a Chinese reading of the name Ali; see Schottenhammer 2015, 3.

6. Li and Li 2014, fig. 5.

7. GPM and University of Hong Kong Art Gallery 1985, figs. 86–90 and 102.

8. Brown 1989, pls. 1–8.

9. Ridho and McKinnon 1998.

10. Watt 1989, 39.

11. Fanchang Xian Bowuguan 2013, figs. 6–8.

12. Tan et al. 2017, pl. 74.

13. Li 2004, figs. 1–2.

14. Norell, Leidy, and Ross 2011, 122–23.

15. Lam 1985, figs. 60–61 and 65.

16. Ridho and McKinnon 1998, figs. 4–5.

17. Li 2017, fig. 8.17.

18. For a full transcription of this inscription, see Zhang 2008, vol. 10, pl. 40.

## Chapter 5

1. Zhao 1911.

2. Clark 1995.

3. Chaffee 2018.

4. Guy 2010.

5. Lieu 2012.

6. Xu, Niziolek, and Feinman 2019.

7. Tan et al. 2017, fig. 11.

8. Ho 2001.

9. Ludwig 1981.

10. For more on the use of Chinese ceramics in Japanese tea ceremonies, see chapter 7 in the present volume.

11. Tan et al. 2017, 41–47, 51–52.

12. National Museum of Korea 2017, fig. 68.

13. Lin and Ran 2018.

14. Sadō Shiryōkan and FPM 1994.

15. Mowry 1995.

16. FPM, Fujian Cultural Relics Research Institute, and Wuyishan Museum 2015.

17. Fan and Li 2021.

18. For more on the Seto and other kilns in Japan, see chapter 7 in the present volume.

19. Rousmaniere 1995.

20. FPM and Jinjiang Museum 2011.

21. Wong 2016.

22. Zhang 2008, vol. 4, pl. 216.

## Chapter 6

1. Weiyan and Shiung 2014.

2. Rooney 2010, figs. 52–54, 57, and 64–70.

3. Ibid., 108.

4. Yao 2017.

5. Stevenson and Guy 1997, 114 and 206.

6. Ibid., fig. 64.

7. Ibid., 117.

8. Mowry 1995, nos. 42, 45, and 52.

9. Cort 1993; and Cort 1997.

10. Brown 2009, pls. 1–12 and 17–22.

11. Leidy 1994, 122.

12. "Storage Jar," Minneapolis Institute of Art, accessed July 23, 2024, https://collections.artsmia.org/art/4234/storage-jar-thailand.

13. Brown 2009, 41.

14. Ibid., 43.

## Chapter 7

1. Church 2006.

2. Itō and Mino 1991, 27.

3. Mintz 2020.

4. Wood 1994.

5. Seo 2018.

6. Lee 2016.

7. Zhang 2008, vol. 3, pl. 202. The bottle is now in the Hebei Institute of Cultural Relics and Archaeology, in Shijiazhuang, China.

8. *Ilbon Saga Hyŏllip* 2012, nos. 5–30.

9. Saeki 2009.

10. Cort 1992, 74.

11. The placing of Buddhist texts in pagodas in China and the burying of them in Japan, which was particularly important from the eleventh to the thirteenth century, were intended to preserve the words and teachings of the Historical Buddha Shakyamuni during a period when practitioners in East Asia believed that the end of Buddhism was imminent. Such ideas can be found in the writings of Chinese monks as early as the sixth century and led to the development of a tradition known as Pure Land Buddhism, which stressed the desire for rebirth in a perfect realm, or "pure land," known as the Western Paradise, that was presided over by the celestial Buddha Amitabha (Amida, in Japanese). Rebirth in such a paradise provided an ideal environment in which to pursue enlightenment or to await the coming of Maitreya (Miroku), the teaching Buddha of the next cosmic era, who would usher in a new age and reinstate Buddhism. Interestingly, the sutras found in this context include works featuring Buddhas Amitabha and Maitreya as well as the *Lotus Sutra* and the *Sutra of the Benevolent Kings*, which were understood to protect the state, individuals, and adherents but were not necessarily associated with Pure Land practices.

12. Li 2017.

13. Chen and Chen 1991.

14. Kobayashi 2021.

15. Ibid.

16. Cort and Watsky 2014.

## Appendix

1. Bergaya and Lagaly 2013, 1–18.

2. Wood and Kerr 2008, 381–82.

3. Wood 2007, 30.

4. Kingery and Vandiver 1986, 69–91.

5. Wood 2007, 95.

6. Wood and Kerr 2008, 348.

7. Kingery and Vandiver 1986, 76–77.

8. Ibid., 77.

9. Hetherington 1948, 23.

10. Ibid., 24.

11. Wood 2007, 102.

12. Ibid.

13. Kingery and Vandiver 1986, 77.

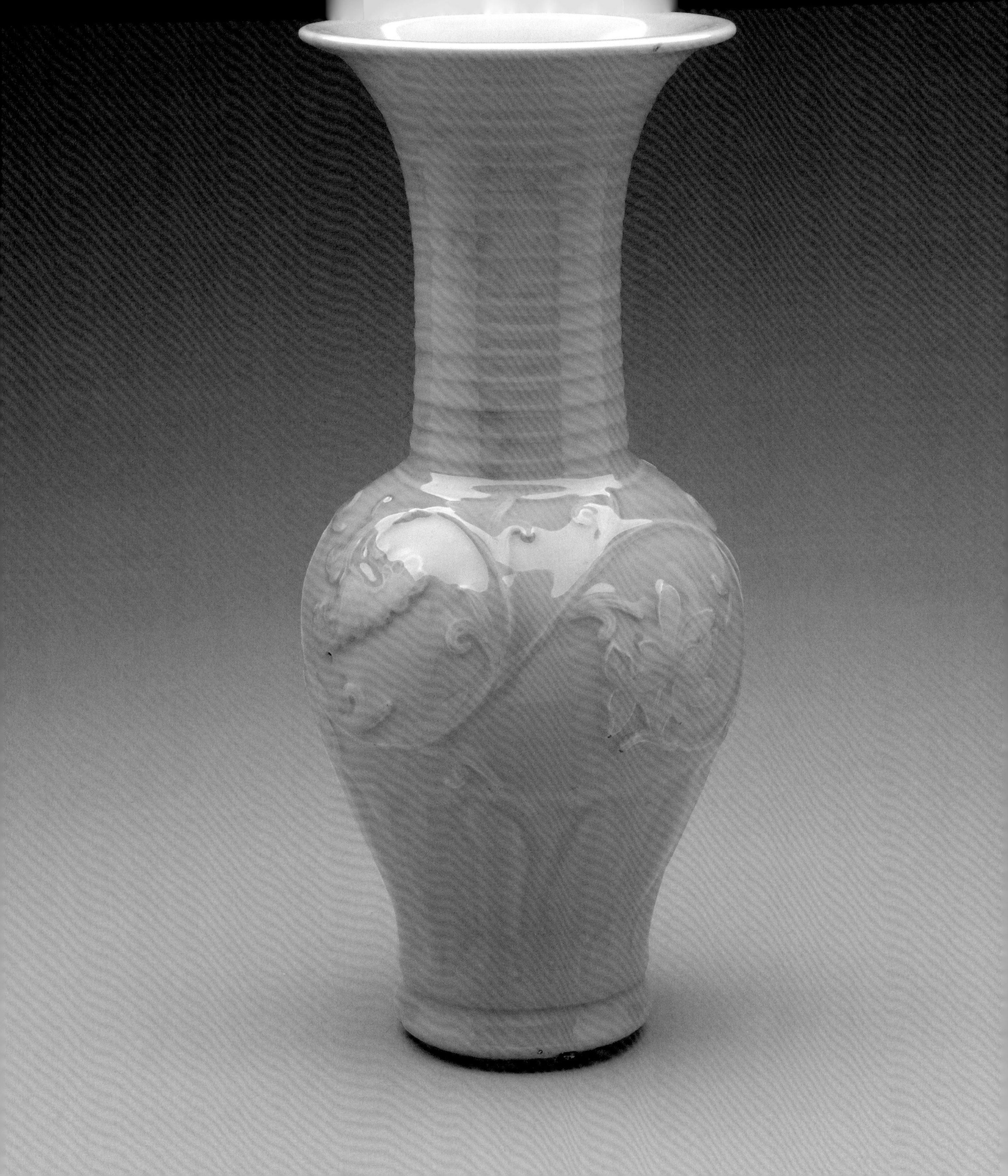

# Bibliography


**An 1987.** An Jiayao. *Early Chinese Glassware*. Trans. Matthew Henderson. Hong Kong: Millennia, 1987.

**An 1991.** An Jiayao. "Dated Islamic Glass in China." *Bulletin of the Asia Institute*, n.s., 5 (1991): 123–37.

**Antony and Schottenhammer 2017.** Antony, Robert J., and Angela Schottenhammer, eds. *Beyond the Silk Roads: New Discourses on China's Role in East Asian Maritime History*. Wiesbaden, Germany: Harrassowitz, 2017.

**Anxi Wenhuaguan 1977.** Anxi Wenhuaguan. "Fujian Anxi gu yaozhi diaocha" [Investigation of the ancient kilns at Anxi of Fujian]. *Wenwu* 7 (1977): 58–65.

**Arnold 1999.** Arnold, Lauren. *Princely Gifts and Papal Treasures: The Franciscan Mission to China and Its Influence on the Art of the West, 1250–1350*. San Francisco: Desiderata, 1999.

**Beijing Art Museum 2015.** Beijing Art Museum. *Zhongguo Chaozhou yao* [Chaozhou kilns of China]. Beijing: Zhongguo Huaqiao Chubanshe, 2015.

**Bergaya and Lagaly 2013.** Bergaya, Faïza, and Gerhard Lagaly. "General Introduction: Clays, Clay Minerals, and Clay Science." In *Handbook of Clay Science*, ed. Faïza Bergaya, Benny K. G. Theng, and Gerhard Lagaly, 1–19. Amsterdam: Elsevier, 2013.

**Brown 1989.** Brown, Roxanna M., ed. *Guangdong Ceramics from Butuan and Other Philippine Sites*. Exh. cat. Singapore: Oxford University Press, 1989.

**Brown 2009.** Brown, Roxanna M. *The Ming Gap and Shipwreck Ceramics in Southeast Asia: Towards a Chronology of Thai Trade Ware*. Bangkok, Thailand: Siam Society, 2009.

**Cai 2010.** Cai Xiaohui. "Jiaocang chutu Song Yuan shiqi Longquan yao qingci de xiangguan yanjiu" [The relevant research of Song and Yuan celadon hoards]. *Dong Fang Bo Wu* 35 (2010): 39–50.

**Chaffee 2006.** Chaffee, John W. "Diasporic Identities in the Historical Development of the Maritime Muslim Communities of Song-Yuan China." *Journal of the Economic and Social History of the Orient* 49, no. 4 (2006): 395–420.

**Chaffee 2018.** Chaffee, John W. *The Muslim Merchants of Premodern China: The History of a Maritime Asian Trade Diaspora, 750–1400*. Cambridge: Cambridge University Press, 2018.

**Chaudhuri 1985.** Chaudhuri, K. N. *Trade and Civilisation in the Indian Ocean: An Economic History from the Rise of Islam to 1750*. Cambridge: Cambridge University Press, 1985.

**Chen and Chen 1991.** Chen Xianqui and Chen Shiping. "Jian yao zhenpin de yanjiu" [The study on masterpieces of Jian tenmoku]. *Journal of the Jingdezhen Ceramic Institute* 22 (1991): 25–32.

**Chengdu Wenwu Kaogu Yanjiusuo and Suining City Museum 2012.** Chengdu Wenwu Kaogu Yanjiusuo and Suining City Museum. *Suining Jinyuncun Nan Song jiaocang* [Jinyuncun hoard of the Southern Song dynasty in Suining]. 2 vols. Beijing: Wenwu Chubanshe, 2012.

**Chong and Murphy 2013.** Chong, Alan, and Stephen A. Murphy, eds. *The Tang Shipwreck: Art and Exchange in the 9th Century*. Exh. cat. Singapore: Asian Civilisations Museum, 2013.

**Church 2006.** Church, Sally K. "Conceptions of Maritime Space in Xu Jing's *Xuanhe fengshi gaoli tujiang*." In *The Perception of Maritime Space in Traditional Chinese Sources*, ed. Angela Schottenhammer and Roderich Ptak, 79–108. Wiesbaden, Germany: Harrassowitz, 2006.

**Clark 1991.** Clark, Hugh R. *Community, Trade, and Networks: Southern Fujian Province from the Third to the Thirteenth Century*. Cambridge: Cambridge University Press, 1991.

**Clark 1995.** Clark, Hugh R. "Muslims and Hindus in the Culture and Morphology of Quanzhou from the Tenth to the Thirteenth Century." *Journal of World History* 6, no. 1 (Spring 1995): 49–74.

**Cobbing 2013.** Cobbing, Andrew, ed. *Hakata: The Cultural Worlds of Northern Kyushu*. Leiden, the Netherlands: Brill, 2013.

**Cort 1992.** Cort, Louise Allison. *Seto and Mino Ceramics: Japanese Collections in the Freer Gallery of Art*. Exh. cat. Washington, D.C.: Freer Gallery of Art, Smithsonian Institution, 1992.

**Cort 1993.** Cort, Louise Allison. "Buried and Treasured in Japan: Another Source for Thai Ceramic History." In Asian Art Museum of San Francisco, *Thai Ceramics: The James and Elaine Connell Collection*, 27–44. Exh. cat. Kuala Lumpur, Malaysia: Oxford University Press, 1993.

**Cort 1997.** Cort, Louise Allison. "Vietnamese Ceramics in Japanese Contexts." In *Vietnamese Ceramics: A Separate Tradition*, ed. John Stevenson and John Guy, 64–83. Chicago: Avery, 1997.

**Cort and Watsky 2014.** Cort, Louise Allison, and Andrew M. Watsky, eds. *Chigusa and the Art of Tea*. Exh. cat. Washington, D.C.: Freer Gallery of Art and Arthur M. Sackler Gallery, Smithsonian Institution, 2014.

**Du 2002.** Du Zhengxian. *Hangzhou Laohudong Yaozhi ciqi jingxuan* [Selected masterpieces from the Laohudong kiln site in Hangzhou]. Beijing: Wenwu Chubanshe, 2002.

**Du and Qin 2004.** Du Zhengxian and Qin Dashu. *Nan Song guan yao yu ge yao: Hangzhou Nan Song guan yao Laohudong yaozhi guoji xueshu yantao huilun wen ji* [Guan and Ge wares of the Southern Song: Symposium of the international conference on Southern Song official ware of the Laohudong kiln site in Hangzhou]. Hangzhou, China: Daxue Chubanshe, 2004.

**Ebrey and Huang 2017.** Ebrey, Patricia Buckley, and Shih-shan Susan Huang, eds. *Visual and Material Cultures in Middle Period China*. Leiden, the Netherlands: Brill, 2017.

**Fan and Li 2020.** Fan Jianan and Li Haichao. "A Study on the Departure Port of the Sinan Shipwreck—A Perspective Based on the Chinese Ceramic Cargo." *Archaeological Research in Asia* 23 (2020): 1–14.

**Fan and Li 2021.** Fan Jianan and Li Haichao. "On-Demand Maritime Trade: A Case Study on the Loading of Cargo and the Packaged Goods on the Sinan Shipwreck." *Journal of Maritime Archaeology* 16 (2021): 163–86.

**Fanchang Xian Bowuguan 2013.** Fanchang Xian Bowuguan. *Fanchang Yao Qingbaici Jicui* [Treasury of Qingbai wares from Fanchang]. Beijing: Wenwu Chubanshe, 2013.

**Feng 1998.** Feng Xianming. *Zhongguo gu taoci tudian* [Dictionary of ancient Chinese ceramics]. Beijing: Wenwu Chubanshe, 1998.

**Finlay 2010.** Finlay, Robert. *The Pilgrim Art: Cultures of Porcelain in World History*. Berkeley: University of California Press, 2010.

**Flecker 2002.** Flecker, Michael. *The Archaeological Excavation of the 10th-Century Intan Shipwreck*. London: British Museum Archaeological Reports, 2002.

**Flecker 2003.** Flecker, Michael. "The Thirteenth-Century *Java Sea Wreck*: A Chinese Cargo in an Indonesian Ship." *Mariner's Mirror* 89, no. 4 (November 2003): 388–404.

**Fong 2014.** Fong, Adam C. "'Together They Might Make Trouble': Cross-Cultural Interactions in Tang Dynasty Guangzhou, 618–907 C.E." *Journal of World History* 25, no. 4 (December 2014): 475–92.

**Frasché 1976.** Frasché, Dean F. *Southeast Asian Ceramics: Ninth through Seventeenth Centuries*. New York: Asia Society, 1976.

**Fuchs 2014.** Fuchs, Ronald W., II. "A History of Chinese Export Porcelain in Ten Objects." *Ceramics in America* (2014): 41–60.

**FPM 1975.** Fujian Provincial Museum (FPM). "Wudai Minguo Liu Hua Mu Fajue Baogao" [Report on the excavation of the burial of Liu Hua of the Min Kingdom of the Five Dynasties period]. *Wenwu* 1 (1975): 62–73.

**FPM 1990.** Fujian Provincial Museum (FPM). *Dehua yao* [Dehua kilns]. Beijing: Wenwu Chubanshe, 1990.

**FPM and Jinjiang Museum 2011.** Fujian Provincial Museum (FPM) and Jinjiang Museum. *Cizao yaozhi* [Cizao kiln]. Beijing: Kexue Chubanshe, 2011.

**FPM, Fujian Cultural Relics Research Institute, and Wuyishan Museum 2015.** Fujian Provincial Museum (FPM), Fujian Cultural Relics Research Institute, and Wuyishan Museum. *Wuyi gu yaozhi* [Ancient kiln site of Wuyi Shan]. Beijing: Kexue Chubanshe, 2015.

**Fung Ping Shan Museum 1985.** Fung Ping Shan Museum. *Ceramic Finds from Tang and Song Kilns in Guangdong.* Hong Kong: Fung Ping Shan Museum, 1985.

**George 2015.** George, Alain. "Direct Sea Trade between Early Islamic Iraq and Tang China: From the Exchange of Goods to the Transmission of Ideas." *Journal of the Royal Asiatic Society*, 3rd ser., 25, no. 4 (October 2015): 579–624.

**Gerritsen 2009.** Gerritsen, Anne. "Fragments of a Global Past: Ceramics Manufacture in Song-Yuan-Ming Jingdezhen." *Journal of the Economic and Social History of the Orient* 52 (2009): 117–52.

**Gerritsen 2020.** Gerritsen, Anne. *The City of Blue and White: Chinese Porcelain and the Early Modern World.* Cambridge: Cambridge University Press, 2020.

**Goble, Robinson, and Wakabayashi 2009.** Goble, Andrew Edmund, Kenneth R. Robinson, and Haruko Wakabayashi, eds. *Tools of Culture: Japan's Cultural, Intellectual, Medical, and Technological Contacts in East Asia, 1000s–1500s.* Ann Arbor, Mich.: Association for Asian Studies, 2009.

**Gompertz 1968.** Gompertz, G. St. G. M. *Celadon Wares*. London: Faber and Faber, 1968.

**GPM and Fung Ping Shan Museum 1985.** Guangdong Provincial Museum (GPM) and Fung Ping Shan Museum. *Ceramic Finds from Tang and Song Kilns in Guangdong*. Hong Kong: University of Hong Kong, 1985.

**GPM and University of Hong Kong Art Gallery 1985.** Guangdong Provincial Museum (GPM) and University of Hong Kong Art Gallery. *Archaeological Finds from the Kilns of the Jing to Tang Periods in Guangdong.* Hong Kong: University of Hong Kong, 1985.

**GPM and University of Hong Kong Art Gallery 1989.** Guangdong Provincial Museum (GPM) and University of Hong Kong Art Gallery. *Archaeological Finds from the Five Dynasties to Qing Periods in Guangdong*. Hong Kong: University of Hong Kong, 1989.

**Guangdong Province Cultural Management Committee and Chinese University of Hong Kong 1987.** Guangdong Province Cultural Management Committee and Chinese University of Hong Kong. *Guangzhou Xicun yao* [Xicun kiln site in Guangzhou]. Hong Kong: Xianggang Zhongwen Daxue Zhongguo Kaogu Yishu Yanjiu Zhong xin, 1987.

**Guy 1986.** Guy, John. *Oriental Trade Ceramics in South-East Asia, Ninth to Sixteenth Centuries*. Singapore: Oxford University Press, 1986.

**Guy 2010.** Guy, John. "Quanzhou: Cosmopolitan City of Faiths." In *The World of Khubilai Khan: Chinese Art in the Yuan Dynasty*, ed. James C. Y. Watt, 159–78. Exh. cat. New York: Metropolitan Museum of Art, 2010.

**Guy 2019.** Guy, John. "Shipwrecks in Late First-Millennium Southeast Asia: Southern China's Maritime Trade and the Emerging Role of Arab Merchants." In *Early Global Interconnectivity across the Indian Ocean World*, ed. Angela Schottenhammer, 1:121–63. London: Palgrave Macmillan, 2019.

**Hall 1985.** Hall, Kenneth R. *Maritime Trade and State Development in Early Southeast Asia*. Honolulu: University of Hawaii Press, 1985.

**Hallett 2009.** Hallett, Jessica. "Pearl Cups Like the Moon: The Abbasid Reception of Chinese Ceramics." In *Shipwrecked: Tang Treasures and Monsoon Winds*, ed. Regina Krahl, John Guy, J. Keith Wilson, and Julian Raby, 75–81. Washington, D.C.: Smithsonian Institution, 2010.

**Hansen 1996.** Hansen, Valerie. "The Mystery of the Qingming Scroll and Its Subject: The Case against Kaifeng." *Journal of Song-Yuan Studies* 26 (1996): 183–200.

**Hartwell 1982.** Hartwell, Robert. "Demographic, Political, and Social Transformations of China, 750–1550." *Harvard Journal of Asiatic Studies* 42, no. 2 (December 1982): 365–442.

**Hebei Sheng Wenwu Yanjiusuo 2001.** Hebei Sheng Wenwu Yanjiusuo. *Xuanhua Liao mu bihua* [Murals from Liao-dynasty tombs in Xuanhua]. Beijing: Wenwu Chubanshe, 2001.

**Heng 2008.** Heng, Derek. "Shipping, Customs Procedures, and the Foreign Community: The 'Pingzhou Ketan' on Aspects of Guangzhou's Maritime Economy in the Late Eleventh Century." *Journal of Song-Yuan Studies* 38 (2008): 1–38.

**Hetherington 1948.** Hetherington, Arthur. *Chinese Ceramic Glazes*. 2nd ed. South Pasadena, Calif.: P. D. and Ione Perkins, 1948.

**Hinsch 2016.** Hinsch, Bret. *The Rise of Tea Culture in Japan: The Invention of the Individual*. New York: Rowman and Littlefield, 2016.

**Ho 1995.** Ho Chuimei. "Turquoise Jars and Other West Asian Ceramics in China." *Bulletin of the Asia Institute*, n.s., 9 (1995): 19–39.

**Ho 2001.** Ho Chuimei. "The Ceramic Boom in Minnan during Song and Yuan Times." In *The Emporium of the World: Maritime Quanzhou, 1000–1400*, ed. Angela Schottenhammer, 237–81. Leiden, the Netherlands: Brill, 2001.

**Honda and Shimazu 1993.** Honda, Hiromu, and Noriki Shimazu. *Vietnamese and Chinese Ceramics Used in the Japanese Tea Ceremony*. Singapore: Oxford University Press, 1993.

**Hsieh 1988.** Hsieh Ming-liang. "Ru yao zhi juping" [The Discussion of Two Ju Ware Mallet-Shaped Vases in the National Palace Museum]. *National Palace Museum Monthly of Chinese Art* 58 (1988): 58–63.

**Hsieh 2010.** Hsieh Ming-liang. "White Wares with Green Décor." In *Shipwrecked: Tang Treasures and Monsoon Winds*, ed. Regina Krahl, John Guy, J. Keith Wilson, and Julian Raby, 161–76. Washington, D.C.: Smithsonian Institution, 2010.

**Huang, Xiong, and Zhao 2014.** Huang, Shan, Zhaoming Xiong, and Chunyan Zhao. "On the Greenish-Blue Glazed Pottery Jug Unearthed from the Eastern Han Tombs at Liaowei in Hepu County, Guangxi." *Chinese Archaeology* 14, no. 1 (November 2014): 182–88.

**Hunan Sheng Wenwu Kaogu Yanjiusuo 1996.** Hunan Sheng Wenwu Kaogu Yanjiusuo. *Changsha yao* [Changsha kilns]. Beijing: Zijincheng Chubanshe, 1996.

***Ilbon Saga Hyŏllip* 2012.** *Ilbon Saga Hyŏllip Kyusyu Toja Munhwagwan sojang Han'guk munhwajae* [Korean art collection in the Kyushu Ceramic Museum, Japan]. Seoul: Kungnip Munhwajae Yon'guso, 2012.

**Itō 2000.** Itō, Ikutarō. *Korean Ceramics from the Museum of Oriental Ceramics, Osaka*. Ed. Judith G. Smith. Exh. cat. New York: Metropolitan Museum of Art, 2000.

**Itō and Mino 1991.** Itō, Ikutarō, and Yukata Mino. *The Radiance of Jade and the Clarity of Water: Korean Ceramics from the Ataka Collection*. Exh. cat. New York: Hudson Hills, 1991.

**Jacques 1979.** Jacques, Claude. "Funan, Zhenla: The Reality Concealed by the Chinese Views of Indochina." In *Early South East Asia: Essays in Archaeology, History, and Historical Geography*, ed. R. B. Smith and William Watson, 371–79. New York: Oxford University Press, 1979.

**Jacques 2007.** Jacques, Claude. "Funan, A Major Early Southeast Asia State." In *The Khmer Empire: Cities and Sanctuaries from the 5th to 14th Century*, 43–63. Trans. Tom White. Bangkok, Thailand: River Books, 2007.

**Jingdezhen Sheng Kaogusuo 2007.** Jingdezhen Sheng Kaogusuo. *Jinggdezhen Hutian Yaozhou* [Jingdezhen Hutian kiln]. Beijing: Wenwu Chubanshe, 2007.

**Juliano and Lerner 1997.** Juliano, Annette L., and Judith Lerner. "Cultural Crossroads: Central Asian and Chinese Entertainers on the Miho Funerary Couch." *Orientations* 28 (October 1997): 72–78.

**Kamei 1986.** Kamei Meitoku. *Nihon bōeki tōjishi no kenkyū* [The historical study of trade ceramics found in Japan]. Kyoto: Dōbōsha Shuppan, 1986.

**Karashima 2004.** Karashima, Noboru. *In Search of Chinese Ceramic-Sherds in South India and Sri Lanka*. Tokyo: Taisho University Press, 2004.

**Karetzky 1994.** Karetzky, Patricia Eichenbaum. "Esoteric Buddhism and the Famensi Finds." *Archives of Asian Art* 47 (1994): 78–85.

**Kauz 2010.** Kauz, Ralph, ed. *Aspects of the Maritime Silk Road: From the Persian Gulf to the East China Sea*. Wiesbaden, Germany: Harrassowitz, 2010.

**Khoo 2003.** Khoo, James C. M., ed. *Art and Archaeology of Fu Nan: Pre-Khmer Kingdom of the Lower Mekong Valley*. Bangkok, Thailand: Southeast Asian Ceramic Society, 2003.

**Kimura 2015.** Kimura, Jun. "Maritime Archaeological Perspectives on Seaborne Trade in the South China Sea and East China Sea between the Seventh and the Thirteenth Centuries." *Crossroads: Studies on the History of Exchange Relations in the East Asian World* 11 (2015): 47–61.

**Kimura 2016.** Kimura, Jun. *Archaeology of East Asian Shipbuilding*. Gainesville: University of Florida Press, 2016.

**Kingery and Vandiver 1986.** Kingery, William D., and Pamela B. Vandiver. *Ceramic Masterpieces: Art, Structure, and Technology*. New York: Free Press, 1986.

**Kobayashi 2021.** Kobayashi, Hitoshi. "Culmination of Beauty: The National Treasure Yuteki Tenmoku Tea Bowl in the Collection of the Museum of Oriental Ceramics, Osaka." *Orientations* 52, no. 6 (November–December 2021): 69–73.

**Krahl 2010.** Krahl, Regina. "White Wares in Northern China." In *Shipwrecked: Tang Treasures and Monsoon Winds*, ed. Regina Krahl, John Guy, J. Keith Wilson, and Julian Raby, 201–7. Washington, D.C.: Smithsonian Institution, 2010.

**Krahl et al. 2010.** Krahl, Regina, John Guy, J. Keith Wilson, and Julian Raby, eds. *Shipwrecked: Tang Treasures and Monsoon Winds*. Washington, D.C.: Smithsonian Institution, 2010.

**Krahl 2021.** Krahl, Regina. "Ruyao No. 88 Resides in Dresden, Germany, and Another Chance Discovery." *Arts of Asia* (Spring 2021): 60–65.

**Kyushu National Museum 2007.** Kyushu National Museum. *Mirai-e no okurimono: Chūgoku taizan sekkei to Jōdokyō bijutsu tokubetsuken* [Eternal presence: Buddhism treasures]. Seibu, Japan: Yomiura Shinbun, 2007.

**Lam 1985.** Lam, Peter K., ed. *A Ceramic Legacy of Asia's Maritime Trade: Song Dynasty Guangdong Wares and Other 11th to 19th Century Trade Ceramics Found on Tioman Island, Malaysia*. Exh. cat. Singapore: Oxford University Press, 1985.

**Lam 1999.** Lam, Timothy See-Yiu. *Tang Ceramics: Changsha Kilns*. Hong Kong: Lammett Arts, 1999.

**Lee 2016.** Lee Jongmin. "Goryeo sidai sanggam cheongja simundeon unhakmum yeonggu" [A study on the type of meaning of the excavated Goryeo celadon in China]. *Misulsa Yeongu* 31 (2016): 59–84.

**Lee 2021.** Lee Myoung-ok. "Korai jidai no iseki kara shutsudo suru Chūgoku tōjiki no jōtai to tokuchō: Kankoku shutsudohin chūshin toshite" [The conditions and characteristics of Chinese ceramics excavated from sites of the Goryeo dynasty: A study focused on the archaeological findings from South Korea]. Trans. Araki Kazunori. *Bulletin of the National Museum of Japanese History* 223 (2021): 313–38.

**Leidy 1994.** Leidy, Denise Patry. *Treasures of Asian Art: The Asia Society's Mr. and Mrs. John D. Rockefeller 3rd Collection*. New York: Abbeville, 1994.

**Leidy 2015.** Leidy, Denise Patry. *How to Read Chinese Ceramics*. New York: Metropolitan Museum of Art, 2015.

**Leidy 2016–17.** Leidy, Denise Patry. "Qingbai Buddhist Sculpture." *Transactions of the Oriental Ceramic Society* 81 (2016–17): 111–22.

**Li 2012.** Li Baoping. "Inscribed Chinese Stoneware Storage Jars from the 14th Century Sinan Wreck in Korea: The Context of Asian Ceramic Trade and Japanese Tea Culture." *National Museum of Korea Museum Network Fellowship Research Papers* (2012): 88–103.

**Li and Li 2014.** Li Baoping and Li Jianan. "Chinese Storage Jars in China and Beyond." In *Chigusa and the Art of Tea*, ed. Louise Allison Cort and Andrew M. Watsky, 73–85. Exh. cat. Washington, D.C.: Freer Gallery of Art and Arthur M. Sackler Gallery, Smithsonian Institution, 2014.

**Li 2004.** Li Bingyan. *Song dai Bijiashan Chaozhou yao* [Ceramics from the Song period kiln in Bijiashan, Chaozhou]. Shantou, China: Shantou Daxue Chubanshe, 2004.

**Li 2020.** Li Peining. "The Trade Patterns of the South China Sea during the Song Period." *Asian Archaeology* 3 (2020): 83–93.

**Li 2010.** Li Qingxin. *Nanhai yihao yu Haishang sichou zhilu* [Nanhai I and the Maritime Silk Road]. Beijing: Wuzhou Chuanbo Chubanshe, 2010.

**Li 2017.** Li Yiwen. "Chinese Objects Recovered from Sutra Mounds in Japan, 1000–1300." In *Visual and Material Cultures in Middle Period China*, ed. Patricia Buckley Ebrey and Shih-shan Susan Huang, 284–317. Leiden, the Netherlands: Brill, 2017.

**Li 1993.** Li Zhengshi. *Liao Chenguo gongzhu mu* [The tomb of the Liao Princess of Chen]. Beijing: Wenwu Chubanshe, 1993.

**Liebner 2014.** Liebner, Horst Hubertus. "The Siren of Cirebon: A Tenth-Century Trading Vessel Lost in the Java Sea." Ph.D. diss., University of Leeds, 2014.

**Lieu 2012.** Lieu, Samuel N. C. *Medieval Christian and Manichaean Remains from Quanzhou*. Turnhout, Belgium: Brepols, 2012.

**Lin 2006.** Lin Boting. *Da Guan: Bei Song Ru yao tezhan* [Grand view: Special exhibition of Ju wares from the Northern Song]. Exh. cat. Taipei, Taiwan: Palace Museum, 2006.

**Lin and Ran 2018.** Lin Meicun and Ran Zhang. "A Chinese Porcelain Jar Associated with Marco Polo: A Discussion from an Archaeological Perspective." *European Journal of Archaeology* 21, no. 1 (February 2018): 39–56.

**Lin 1994.** Lin Shimin. "Zhejiang Export Green Glazed Wares: Ningbo Data." In *New Light on Chinese Yue and Longquan Wares: Archaeological Ceramics Found in Eastern and Southern Asia, A.D. 800–1400*, ed. Ho Chuimei, 141–68. Hong Kong: Centre of Asian Studies, University of Hong Kong, 1994.

**Lin and Zhang 1993.** Lin Zhongan and Wenyin Zhang. "Fujian Song Yuan Qingbaici gaolun" [Outline of the Song Yuan Qingbai porcelains in Fujian]. *Jingdezhen Taoci* 3 (1993): 6–10.

**Liu 2013.** Liu Xinping. "Fujian Song Yuan shiqi de qingbaici he" [The Qingbai boxes of the Song and Yuan periods in Fujian]. *Fujian Wenbo* 2 (2013): 75–77.

**Liu 1988.** Liu Xinru. *Silk and Religion: An Exploration of Material Life and the Thought of the People, A.D. 600–1200*. Delhi, India: Oxford University Press, 1988.

**Lo 2002.** Lo Jung-pang. *China as a Sea Power, 1127–1368: A Preliminary Survey of the Maritime Expansion and Naval Exploits of the Chinese People during the Southern Song and Yuan Periods*. Ed. and with commentary by Bruce A. Elleman. Singapore: National University of Singapore Press, 2002.

**Long 1994.** Long, So Kee. "The Trade Ceramics Industry in Southern Fukien during the Sung." *Journal of Song-Yuan Studies* 24 (1994): 1–19.

**Lu 2009.** Lu Yu. *The Classic of Tea* [Chajing]. Trans. Jiang Xin. Changsha, China: Hunan Renmin Chubanshe, 2009.

**Ludwig 1981.** Ludwig, Theodore M. "Before Rikyū: Religious and Aesthetic Influences in the Early History of the Tea Ceremony." *Monumenta Nipponica* 36, no. 4 (Winter 1981): 367–90.

***Maboroshi no meiyō* 2010.** *Maboroshi no meiyō: Nansō Shunaishi kan'yō: Kōshū Rōkodō yōshi hakkutsu seikaten: Kokusai kōryū kikakuten* [Temporary exhibition: Southern Song Xiunesi Guan ware: Archaeological findings from the kiln site at Laohudong, Hangzhou]. Exh. cat. Osaka, Japan: Osaka Hakubutsukan Kyōkaim, 2010.

**Mai 1998.** Mai Yaoxiang. *Xiangcai tianxia: Hunan gudai taoci* [Hunan colors: Ancient ceramics of Hunan Province]. Hong Kong: University of Hong Kong Press, 1998.

**McCarthy and Chase 2009.** McCarthy, Blythe, and Ellen Chase, eds. *Scientific Research on Historic Asian Ceramics: Proceedings of the Fourth Forbes Symposium at the Freer Gallery of Art*. Washington, D.C.: Freer Gallery of Art, Smithsonian Institution, 2009.

**McLaughlin 2020.** McLaughlin, Raoul. *The Roman Empire and the Silk Routes: The Ancient World Economy and the Empires of Parthia, Central Asia, and Han China*. Yorkshire, England: Pen and Sword History, 2020.

**Mino and Tsiang 1987.** Mino, Yutaka, and Katherine R. Tsiang. *Ice and Green Clouds: Traditions of Chinese Celadon*. Exh. cat. Indianapolis: Indianapolis Museum of Art, 1987.

**Mintz 2020.** Mintz, Robert. "Bringing Life to the Galleries of the Asian Art Museum of San Francisco." *Orientations* (March–April 2020): 44–51.

**Mori 2015.** Mori Testuya. *Chūgoku seiji no kenkyū* [Research on Chinese celadon]. Tokyo: Kyūuko Shoin, 2015.

**Mowry 1995.** Mowry, Robert D. *Hare's Fur, Tortoiseshell, and Partridge Feathers: Chinese Brown- and Black-Glazed Ceramics, 400–1400.* With contributions by Eugene Farrell and Nicole Coolidge Rousmaniere. Exh. cat. Cambridge, Mass.: Harvard University Art Museums, 1995.

**Museum of Oriental Ceramics, Osaka, 2015.** Museum of Oriental Ceramics, Osaka. *Shinhakken no korai seiji: Kankoku suichū kōkogaku seikaten nikkan hokkō seijōka gojisshūnnen kien kokusai kōryū tokubetsuten* [Newly discovered Goryeo celadon and the achievements of underwater archaeology]. Osaka, Japan: Museum of Oriental Ceramics, Osaka, 2015.

**National Museum of History 2010.** National Museum of History. *Sheng shihuang chao mi bu: Famensi digong yu Tang wenwu tezhan* [Imperial treasures: Relics of the Famensi underground pagoda and the flourishing Tang]. Taipei, Taiwan: National Museum of History, 2010.

**National Museum of Korea 2017.** National Museum of Korea. *Sinan haejŏsŏn esŏ ch'ajanaen kŏttŭl* [Discoveries from the Sinan Shipwreck]. Seoul: National Museum of Korea, 2017.

**Needell 2018.** Needell, Carolyn Swan. "*Cirebon*: Islamic Glass from a 10th-Century Shipwreck in the Java Sea." *Journal of Glass Studies* 60 (2018): 69–114.

**Neill 1982.** Neill, Mary Gardner. *The Communion of Scholars: Chinese Art at Yale.* Exh. cat. New York: China House Gallery, 1982.

**Nezu Museum 2010.** Nezu Museum. *Nansō no seiji: Sara was utsusuutsuwa* [Heavenly blue: Southern Song celadons]. Tokyo: Nezu Museum, 2010.

**Nezu Museum 2013.** Nezu Museum. *Hyakka sen: Nezu Bijutsukan* [Selected masterpieces from the Nezu Museum collection]. Tokyo: Nezu Museum, 2013.

**Norell, Leidy, and Ross 2011.** Norell, Mark, Denise Patry Leidy, and Laura Ross. *Traveling the Silk Road: Ancient Pathway to the Modern World.* Exh. cat. New York: American Museum of Natural History, 2011.

**Ohki 2009.** Ohki, Sadako. *Tea Culture of Japan.* With a contribution by Takeshi Watanabe. New Haven, Conn.: Yale University Art Gallery, 2009.

**Oka et al. 2009.** Oka, Rahul, Laure Dussubieux, Chapurukha M. Kusimba, and Vishwas D. Gogte. "The Impact of Imitation Ceramic Industries and Internal Political Restrictions on Chinese Commercial Ceramic Exports in the Indian Ocean Maritime Exchange, ca. 1200–1700." In *Scientific Research on Historic Asian Ceramics: Proceedings of the Fourth Forbes Symposium at the Freer Gallery of Art*, ed. Blythe McCarthy and Ellen Chase, 175–85. Washington, D.C.: Freer Gallery of Art, Smithsonian Institution, 2009.

**Oriental Ceramic Society of the Philippines 1993.** Oriental Ceramic Society of the Philippines. *Chinese and South-East Asian White Ware Found in the Philippines.* Singapore: Oxford University Press, 1993.

**Pierson 2000.** Pierson, Stacey, ed. *Qingbai Ware: Chinese Porcelain of the Song and Yuan Dynasties.* London: Percival David Foundation of Chinese Art, 2000.

**Prematilleke 1990.** Prematilleke, P. L. "Chinese Ceramics Discovered in Sri Lanka: An Overview." In *Sri Lanka and the Silk Roads of the Sea*, ed. Senake Bandaranayake, 233–44. Colombo: Sri Lanka National Commission for UNESCO and the Central Cultural Fund, 1990.

**Priestman 2016.** Priestman, Seth. "The Silk Road or the Sea? Sasanian and Islamic Exports to Japan." *Journal of Islamic Archaeology* 3, no. 1 (2016): 1–35.

**Priestman 2021.** Priestman, Seth. *Ceramic Exchange and the Indian Ocean Economy (AD 400–1275).* London: British Museum, 2021.

**Qi 1999.** Qi Dongfang. *Tang dai jinyinqi yanjiu* [Research on Tang gold and silver]. Beijing: Zhongguo Shehui Kexue Chubanshe, 1999.

**Qin and Xiang 2011.** Qin Dashu and Xiang Kunpeng. "Sri Vijaya as the Entrepôt for Circum-Indian Ocean Trade: Evidence from Documentary Records and Materials from Shipwrecks of the 9th–10th Centuries." *Études Océan Indien* 46–47 (2011): 308–36.

**Qin, Chang, and Yu 2017.** Qin Dashu, Chang Jung Jung, and Yu Shan. "Early Results of an Investigation into Ancient Kiln Sites Producing Ceramic Storage Jars and Some Related Issues." *Bulletin de l'École francaise d'Extrême-Orient* 103 (2017): 359–84.

**Rawson 1989.** Rawson, Jessica. "Chinese Silver and Its Influence on Porcelain Development." In *Cross-Craft and Cross-Cultural Interactions in Ceramics*, ed. Patrick E. McGovern, 275–99. Columbus, Ohio: American Ceramic Society, 1989.

**Rawson 1991.** Rawson, Jessica. "Central Asian Silver and Its Influence on Chinese Ceramics." *Bulletin of the Asia Institute*, n.s., 5 (1991): 139–51.

**Rawson 1993.** Rawson, Jessica. "Sets or Singletons? Uses of Chinese Ceramics: 10th–14th Centuries." *Journal of Song-Yuan Studies* 23 (1993): 71–94.

**Ray 2012.** Ray, Himanshu Prabha. "Narratives of Travel and Shipwrecks." In *Buddhist Narrative in Asia and Beyond: In Honour of HRH Princess Maha Chakri Sirindhorn on Her Fifty-Fifth Birth Anniversary*, ed. Peter Skilling and Justin McDaniel, 2:47–65. Bangkok, Thailand: Institute of Thai Studies, 2012.

**Ridho and McKinnon 1998.** Ridho, Abu, and E. Edwards McKinnon. *The Pulau Buaya Wreck: Finds from the Song Period.* Jakarta: Indonesian Ceramic Society, 1998.

**Rooney 2010.** Rooney, Dawn F. *Khmer Ceramics: Beauty and Meaning.* Bangkok, Thailand: River Books, 2010.

**Rougeulle 1991.** Rougeulle, Axelle. "Les importations des céramiques chinoises dans le Golfe arabo-persique (VIIIe–XIe siècles)." *Archaéologie islamique* 2 (1991): 5–46.

**Rougeulle 1996.** Rougeulle, Axelle. "Medieval Trade Networks in the Western Indian Ocean (8th–14th Centuries): Some Reflections from the Distribution Patterns of Chinese Imports in the Islamic World." In *Tradition and Archaeology: Early Maritime Contacts in the Indian Ocean*, ed. Himanshu Prabha Ray and Jean-François Salles, 159–80. New Delhi: Manohar, 1996.

**Rousmaniere 1995.** Rousmaniere, Nicole Coolidge. "Defining Temmoku: Jian Ware Tea Bowls Imported into Japan." In Robert D. Mowry, with contributions by Eugene Farrell and Nicole Coolidge Rousmaniere, *Hare's Fur, Tortoiseshell, and Partridge Feathers: Chinese Brown- and Black-Glazed Ceramics, 400–1400*, 43–58. Exh. cat. Cambridge, Mass.: Harvard University Art Museums, 1995.

**Ruan 1994.** Ruan, Pinger. "The Distribution of Manufacturing Sites and Markets." In *New Light on Chinese Yue and Longquan Wares: Archaeological Ceramics Found in Eastern and Southern Asia, A.D. 800–1400*, ed. Ho Chuimei, 3–20. Hong Kong: Centre of Asian Studies, University of Hong Kong, 1994.

**Sadō Shiryōkan and FPM 1994.** Sadō Shiryōkan and Fujian Provincial Museum (FPM). *Kankoku Shin'an kaitei ibutsu: Kesan to kokuyūwan* [Relics from the sea floor at Sinan, Korea: Jian tea bowls and black-glazed bowls]. Kyoto: Sadō Shiryōkan, 1994.

**Saeki 2009.** Saeki Kōji. "Chinese Trade Ceramics in Medieval Japan." Trans. and adapted by Peter Shapinsky. In *Tools of Culture: Japan's Cultural, Intellectual, Medical, and Technological Contacts in East Asia, 1000s–1500s*, ed. Andrew Edmund Goble, Kenneth R. Robinson, and Haruko Wakabayashi, 163–84. Ann Arbor, Mich.: Association for Asian Studies, 2009.

**Sato and Mikasa 2018.** Sato, Sarah, and Keiko Mikasa. *Shoki hakuji* [Early white porcelain]. Tokyo: Tokiyama Bunko Foundation, 2018.

**Savage and Newman 1974.** Savage, George, and Harold Newman. *An Illustrated Dictionary of Ceramics*. New York: Van Nostrand Reinhold, 1974.

**Schottenhammer 1999.** Schottenhammer, Angela. "Local Politico-Economic Particulars of the Quanzhou Region during the Tenth Century." *Journal of Song-Yuan Studies* 29 (1999): 1–41.

**Schottenhammer 2001.** Schottenhammer, Angela, ed. *The Emporium of the World: Maritime Quanzhou, 1000–1400*. Leiden, the Netherlands: Brill, 2001.

**Schottenhammer 2015.** Schottenhammer, Angela. "China's Gate to the South: Iranian and Arab Merchant Networks in Guangzhou during the Tang–Song Transition (c. 750–1050), Part II: 900–c. 1050." *Austrian Academy of Sciences Working Papers in Social Anthropology* 29 (2015): 1–30.

**Schottenhammer 2016.** Schottenhammer, Angela. "China's Gate to the Indian Ocean: Iranian and Arab Long-Distance Traders." *Harvard Journal of Asiatic Studies* 76, nos. 1–2 (June–December 2016): 135–79.

**Schottenhammer 2019.** Schottenhammer, Angela, ed. *Early Global Interconnectivity across the Indian Ocean World*. 2 vols. London: Palgrave Macmillan, 2019.

**Schottenhammer and Ptak 2006.** Schottenhammer, Angela, and Roderich Ptak, eds. *The Perception of Maritime Space in Traditional Chinese Sources*. Wiesbaden, Germany: Harrassowitz, 2006.

**Seikado Foundation 2013.** Seikado Foundation. *Seikadō 120-sen* [120 Seikado masterpieces]. Tokyo: Seikado, 2013.

**Sen 2003.** Sen, Tansen. *Buddhism, Diplomacy, and Trade: The Realignment of Sino-Indian Relations, 600–1400*. Honolulu: University of Hawaii Press, 2003.

**Sen 2006.** Sen, Tansen. "The Formation of Chinese Maritime Networks to Southern Asia, 1200–1450." *Journal of the Economic and Social History of the Orient* 49, no. 4 (2006): 421–53.

**Sen 2010.** Sen, Tansen. "The Intricacies of Premodern Asian Connections." *Journal of Asian Studies* 69, no. 4 (December 2010): 991–99.

**Sen 2011.** Sen, Tansen. "Maritime Interactions between China and India: Coastal India and the Ascendancy of Chinese Maritime Power in the Indian Ocean." *Journal of Central Eurasian Studies* 2 (May 2011): 41–82.

**Seo 2018.** Seo Hye-eun. "Jungguk chulto Goryeo cheongja ui yu hyeonggwa uimi" [A study on inlaid celadon decorated with cloud and crane pattern in the Goryeo Dynasty]. *Art History and Cultural Heritage* 7 (2018): 39–70.

**Shanghai Museum 2005**. Shanghai Museum. *Zhongguo gudai baici guoji xueshu yan taohui luwen ji* [Symposium of Ancient Chinese White Porcelain proceedings]. Shanghai: Shanghai Museum, 2005.

**Sharf 2011.** Sharf, Robert H. "The Buddha's Finger Bones at Famensi and the Art of Chinese Esoteric Buddhism." *Art Bulletin* 93, no. 1 (March 2011): 38–59.

**Shen 2002.** Shen, Hsueh-man. "Luxury of Necessity: Glassware in 'Sarira' Relic Pagodas of the Tang and Northern Song Periods." In *Chinese Glass: Archaeological Studies on the Uses and Social Context of Glass Artefacts from the Warring States to the Northern Song Period, Fifth Century B.C.E.–Twelfth Century A.D.*, ed. Cecilia Braghin, 7–110. Florence: Leo. S. Olschi, 2002.

**Shen 2014.** Shen, Hsueh-man. "Familiar Differences: Chinese Polychromes in the Indian Ocean Trade during the Ninth Century." In *Beiträge zur islamischen Kunst und Archäologie*, ed. Julia Gonnella and Rania Abdellatiff, 4:107–22. Wiesbaden, Germany: Reichert, 2014.

**Shi and Han 1989.** Shi Xingbang and Han Wei. *Famensi digong zhenbao* [Precious cultural relics in the crypt of the Famen Temple]. Shanxi, China: Shanxi Renmin Chubanshe, 1989.

**Song 2012.** Song Donglin. "Bei Song Jin Dai jiacang ciqi gaosu" [Ceramics from Northern Song and Jin hoards]. *Gugong Xuekan* 8 (2012): 8–54.

**Stevenson and Guy 1997.** Stevenson, John, and John Guy. *Vietnamese Ceramics: A Separate Tradition*. Chicago: Avery, 1997.

**Ströber 2013.** Ströber, Eva. *Ming: Porcelain for a Globalised Trade*. Stuttgart, Germany: Arnoldsche Art Publishers, 2013.

**Subbarayalu 1996.** Subbarayalu, Y. "Chinese Ceramics of the Tamilnadu and Kerala Coasts." In *Tradition and Archaeology: Early Maritime Contact in the Indian Ocean*, ed. Himanshu Prabha Ray and Jean-François Salles, 109–14. New Delhi: Manohar, 1996.

**Sun et al. 2017.** Sun, Jason Zhixin. *Age of Empires: Art of the Qin and Han Dynasties*. Exh. cat. New York: Metropolitan Museum of Art, 2017.

**Tan et al. 2017.** Tan, Rita C., Li Jian'an, Go Bon Juan, Purissima Benitez-Johannot, and Gilbert Fournier. *Fujian Ware Found in the Philippines: Song–Yuan Period, 11th–14th Century*. Exh. cat. Makati City: Oriental Ceramic Society of the Philippines, 2017.

**Teo 2000.** Teo, Catherine. "Qingbai Wares for Export." In *Qingbai Ware: Chinese Porcelain of the Song and Yuan Dynasties*, ed. Stacey Pierson, 111–22. London: Percival David Foundation of Chinese Art, 2000.

**Tite, Freestone, and Bimson 1984.** Tite, M. S., I. C. Freestone, and M. Bimson. "A Technological Study of Chinese Porcelain of the Yuan Dynasty." *Archaeometry* 26, no. 2 (1984): 139–54.

**Truong 2007.** Truong, Philippe. *The Elephant and the Lotus: Vietnamese Ceramics from the Collection of the Museum of Fine Arts, Boston*. Boston: Museum of Fine Arts, Boston, 2007.

**Ts'ai 1996.** Ts'ai, Mei-fen. "A Discussion of Ting Ware with Unglazed Rims and Related Twelfth-Century Official Porcelain." In *Arts of the Sung and Yüan*, ed. Maxwell K. Hearn and Judith G. Smith, 109–31. New York: Metropolitan Museum of Art, 1996.

**Vermeersch 2016.** Vermeersch, Sem. *A Chinese Traveler in Medieval Korea: Xu Jing's "Illustrated Account of the Xuanhe Embassy to Koryŏ."* Honolulu: University of Hawai'i Press, 2016.

**von Verschuer 2006.** von Verschuer, Charlotte. *Across the Perilous Seas: Japanese Trade with China and Korea from the Seventh to the Sixteenth Centuries*. Trans. Kristen Lee Hunter. Ithaca, N.Y.: Cornell University Press, 2006.

**Wang et al. 2014.** Wang, Eugene Y., Tansen Sen, Chong Wang Shen, Conan Cheong, Kan Shuyi, Libby Lai-pik Chan, and Pedro Moura Carvalho. *Secrets of the Fallen Pagoda: The Famen Temple and Tang Court Culture*. Exh. cat. Singapore: Asian Civilisations Museum, 2014.

**Wang 1969.** Wang Fu. *Xuanhe bogu tu* [Illustrated catalogue of a wide range of antiquities during the Xuanhe period]. Reprint, Taipei, Taiwan: Xinxing shuji, 1969.

**Wang 1998.** Wang Gungwu. *The Nanhai Trade: The Early History of Chinese Trade in the South China Sea*. Singapore: Times Academic Press, 1998.

**Wang 2020.** Wang Qiang. *Legendary Port of the Maritime Silk Routes: Zayton (Quanzhou)*. New York: Peter Lang, 2020.

**Wang 1996.** Wang Qingzheng, ed. *Yue yao: Mise ci* [Yue ware: Mise porcelain]. Shanghai: Shanghai Guji Chubanshe, 1996.

**Watson and Wilson 2000.** Watson, F. J. B., and Gillian Wilson. *Mounted Oriental Porcelain in the J. Paul Getty Museum*. Rev. ed. Oxford: Oxford University Press, 2000.

**Watt 1989.** Watt, James C. Y. "His-Ts'un, Chao'an and Other Ceramic Wares of Kwangtung in the Northern Song Period." In *Guangdong Ceramics from Butuan and Other Philippine Sites*, ed. Roxanna M. Brown, 35–44. Exh. cat. Singapore: Oxford University Press, 1989.

**Watt 2004.** Watt, James C. Y., ed. *China: Dawn of a Golden Age, 200–750 A.D.* Exh. cat. New York: Metropolitan Museum of Art, 2004.

**Watt 2010.** Watt, James C. Y., ed. *The World of Khubilai Khan: Chinese Art in the Yuan Dynasty*. Exh. cat. New York: Metropolitan Museum of Art, 2010.

**Watt and Wardwell 1998.** Watt, James C. Y., and Anne E. Wardwell. *When Silk Was Gold: Central Asian and Chinese Textiles*. With an essay by Morris Rossabi. Exh. cat. New York: Metropolitan Museum of Art, 1998.

**Weiyan and Shiung 2014.** Weiyan Wei and Shiung Chung-ching. "Viet Khe Burial 2: Identifying the Exotic Bronze Wares and Assessing Cultural Contact between the Dong Son and Yue Cultures." *Asian Archaeology* 2 (2014): 77–92.

**Whitehouse 1972.** Whitehouse, David. "Chinese Porcelain in Medieval Europe." *Medieval Archaeology* 16, no. 1 (1972): 63–78.

**Whitehouse 1973.** Whitehouse, David. "Chinese Stoneware from Siraf: The Earliest Finds." In *Southeast Asian Archaeology*, ed. Norman Hammond, 242–55. Leiden, the Netherlands: Brill, 1973.

**Wilkinson 1973.** Wilkinson, Charles K. *Nishapur: Pottery of the Early Islamic Period*. New York: Metropolitan Museum of Art, 1973.

**Wong 2016.** Wong, Sharon Wai-yee. "A Case Report on the Function(s) of the 'Mercury Jar': Fort Canning, Singapore, in the 14th Century." *Archaeological Research in Asia* 7 (July 2016): 10–17.

**Wong 2017.** Wong, Sharon Wai-yee. "Rethinking Storage Jars Found in the 9th to 20th Centuries Archaeological Sites in Guangdong, Hong Kong, and Macau." *Bulletin de l'École française d'Extrême-Orient* 103 (2017): 333–58.

**Wood 1978.** Wood, Nigel. "Chinese Porcelain." *Pottery Quarterly* 12, no. 47 (1978): 101–28.

**Wood 1994.** Wood, Nigel. "Technological Parallels between Chinese Yue Wares and Korean Celadons." *Papers of the British Association for Korean Studies* 5 (1994): 39–64.

**Wood 2007.** Wood, Nigel. *Chinese Glazes: Their Origins, Chemistry, and Recreation*. Reprint, London: A & C Black, 2007.

**Wood and Kerr 2008.** Wood, Nigel, and Rose Kerr. *Ceramic Technology*. Vol. 5, pt. 12 of *Science and Civilisation in China*, ed. Joseph Needham. Cambridge: Cambridge University Press, 2008.

**Wood and Rastelli 2014.** Wood, Nigel, and Sabrina Rastelli. "Parallel Developments in Chinese Porcelain Technology in the 13th–14th Centuries A.D." In *Craft and Science: International Perspectives on Archaeological Ceramics*, ed. Marcos Martinón-Torres, 225–33. Doha: Bloomsbury Qatar Foundation, 2014.

**Wu 2016.** Wu, Chunming, ed. *Early Navigation in the Asian-Pacific Region: A Maritime Archaeological Perspective*. Singapore: Springer, 2016.

**Xiong 2014.** Xiong, Zhaoming. "The Hepu Han Tombs and the Maritime Silk Road of the Han Dynasty." *Antiquity* 88, no. 342 (December 2014): 1229–43.

**Xu, Niziolek, and Feinman 2019.** Xu, Wenpeng, Lisa C. Niziolek, and Gary M. Feinman. "Sourcing *Qingbai* Porcelains from the *Java Sea Shipwreck*: Compositional Analysis Using Portable XRF." *Journal of Archaeological Science* 103 (March 2019): 57–71.

**Yamaguchi Kenritsu Hagi Bijustukan 2012.** Yamaguchi Kenritsu Hagi Bijustukan. *Ryūsen'yō seiji ten: Nihonjin no aishita Chūgoku tōji* [Longquan ware: Chinese celadon beloved by the Japanese]. Yamaguchi, Japan: Yamaguchi Kenritsu Hagi Bijutsukan, 2012.

**Yang 2018.** Yang, Meili. *The Circulation of Elite Longquan Celadon Ceramics from China to Japan: An Interdisciplinary and Cross-Cultural Study*. Eastborne, England: Sussex Academic Press, 2018.

**Yang 2010.** Yang Yuzhang. *Anhui Fanchang yao yizhi fajue yu yanjiu* [Discovery and research of the Fanchang kiln in Anhui]. Beijing: Zhongguo Shehu Kexue Chubanshe, 2010.

**Yao 2017.** Yao, Alice. "The Dian and Dong Son Cultures." In *Handbook of East and Southeast Asian Archaeology*, ed. Junko Habu, Peter V. Lape, and John W. Olsen, 503–12. Berlin: Springer, 2017.

**Zeng, Xu, and Wang 1996.** Zeng Gan, Xu Benzhang, and Wang Conghui. *Fujian taoci* [Fujian ceramics]. Shanghai: Shanghai Renmin Meishu Chubanshe, 1996.

**Zhang 2008.** Zhang Bai, ed. *Zhongguo chutu ciqi quanji* [Complete collection of ceramic art unearthed in China]. 16 vols. Beijing: Kexue Chubanshe, 2008.

**Zhao 2017.** Zhao Bing. "The Production of Storage Jars in China and Southeast Asia: A Vibrant but Little-Known Artisanal Practice." *Bulletin de l'École française d'Extrême-Orient* 103 (2017): 259–65.

**Zhao 1911.** Zhao Rugua. *Chau Ju-kua: His Work on the Chinese and Arab Trade in the Twelfth and Thirteenth Centuries*. Trans. and annotated by Friedrich Hirth and William Woodville Rockhill. Saint Petersburg: Imperial Academy of Sciences, 1911.

**Zhejiang Sheng Wenwu Kaogu Yanjiusuo 2017.** Zhejiang Sheng Wenwu Kaogu Yanjiusuo. *Mise Yueqi: Shanglinghu Housi'ao yaozhi chutu Tangdai mise ciqi* [Yue mise wares: Tang dynasty mise ceramics excavated from the Housiao kiln]. Beijing: Wenwu Chubanshe, 2017.

**Zhou 2007.** Zhou Shirong. *Hunan gumu yu yaozhi* [Ancient tombs and kilns in Hunan Province]. Changsha, China: Yuelushu Shi, 2007.

**Zhou and Zheng 2012.** Zhou Shirong and Zheng Junsheng. *Hengzhou yu Hengshan yao* [Hengzhou wares and Hengshan wares]. Changsha, China: Hunan Meishu Chubanshe, 2012.

**Zhuzhou 1991.** Zhuzhou Shi Wenwu Guanli Chu. "Hunan Xiaoxian chutu Longquan qingci" [Longguan greenwares unearthed in Xiaoxian, Hunan]. *Hunan Kaogu Jikan* 7 (1991): 150–52.

## Photo Credits

Every effort has been made to credit the artists and the sources; if there are errors or omissions, please contact the Yale University Art Gallery so that corrections can be made in any subsequent editions. All images courtesy Visual Resources Department, Yale University Art Gallery, unless otherwise noted.

© Art Gallery of New South Wales: fig. 3.10

The Art Institute of Chicago/Art Resource, N.Y.: fig. 2.3

Courtesy Asia Society New York: fig. 6.11

© Asian Art Museum of San Francisco: fig. 6.2

Asian Civilisations Museum, Tang Shipwreck Collection. Photo: John Tsantes and Robert Harrell, Arthur M. Sackler Gallery: fig. 3.7

Davide Bonaldo/Alamy Stock Photo: app. 1.1

From: Chengdu Wenwu Kaogu Yanjiusuo and Suining City Museum, *Suining Jinyuncun Nan Song jiaocang* [Jinyuncun hoard of the Southern Song dynasty in Suining], vol. 1 (Beijing: Wenwu Chubanshe, 2012), fig. 5: fig. 2.8

From: Chengdu Wenwu Kaogu Yanjiusuo and Suining City Museum, *Suining Jinyuncun Nan Song jiaocang* [Jinyuncun hoard of the Southern Song dynasty in Suining], vol. 2 (Beijing: Wenwu Chubanshe, 2012), pl. 106: fig. 2.6

The Cleveland Museum of Art (CC0): figs. 1.12, 4.12; p. 74

CPA Media Pte Ltd/Alamy Stock Photo: fig. 0.2

Detroit Institute of Arts: fig. 5.21

From: Fan Jianan and Li Haichao, "On-Demand Maritime Trade: A Case Study on the Loading of Cargo and the Packaged Goods on the Sinan Shipwreck," *Journal of Maritime Archaeology* 16 (2021): 163–86, fig. 8.2: fig. 5.19

© Dr. Michael Flecker: figs. 0.4–.5, 4.2–.3

© Fondation Baur Genève/Photo: Marian Gérard: fig. 4.8

From: Ronald W. Fuchs II, "A History of Chinese Export Porcelain in Ten Objects," *Ceramics in America* (2014): 41–60, fig. 1: fig. 2.12

From: Hebei Sheng Wenwu Yanjiusuo, *Xuanhua Liao mu bihua* [Murals from Liao-dynasty tombs in Xuanhua] (Beijing: Wenwu Chubanshe, 2001), fig. 60: fig. 2.7

Image courtesy the Johnson Museum: fig. 6.3

Adrian Kitzinger: pp. 8–10

From: Regina Krahl, John Guy, J. Keith Wilson, and Julian Raby, eds., *Shipwrecked: Tang Treasures and Monsoon Winds* (Washington, D.C.: Smithsonian Institution, 2010), fig. 106: fig. 3.8

From: Kyushu National Museum, *Mirai-e no okurimono: Chūgoku taizan sekkei to Jōdokyō bijutsu tokubetsuken* [Eternal presence: Buddhism treasures] (Seibu, Japan: Yomiura Shinbun, 2007), pl. 112: fig. 7.11

Photo: leochen66: fig. 0.3

From: Li Peining, "The Trade Patterns of the South China Sea during the Song Period," *Asian Archaeology* 3 (2020): 83–93, fig. 3: fig. 0.6

© The Metropolitan Museum of Art. Image source: Art Resource, N.Y.: figs. 1.16, 1.18, 2.2, 3.12, 6.1, 6.17; app. 1.4

Minneapolis Institute of Art: figs. 6.12, 7.10

Photo: MUDA Tomohiro: fig. 7.15

Photograph © 2024 Museum of Fine Arts, Boston: figs. 3.21, 6.9–.10

From: National Museum of History, *Sheng shihuang chao mi bu: Famensi digong yu Tang wenwu tezhan* [Imperial treasures: Relics of the Famensi underground pagoda and the flourishing Tang] (Taipei, Taiwan: National Museum of History, 2010), pls. 13, 16: figs. 1.3, 3.9

Collection of the National Museum of Korea: fig. 1.17; p. 22

© National Palace Museum: fig. 0.1

Nezu Museum: fig. 7.16

Photo: NISHIKAWA Shigeru: fig. 7.4

Photo: Neal Oshima. From: Rita C. Tan, Li Jian'an, Go Bon Juan, Purissima Benitez-Johannot, and Gilbert Fournier, *Fujian Ware Found in the Philippines: Song–Yuan Period, 11th–14th Century*, exh. cat. (Makati City: Oriental Ceramic Society of the Philippines, 2017), no. 11: fig. 5.1

Courtesy the Peabody Essex Museum. Photo: Jeffrey R. Dykes/PEM: app. 1.6

Photo © President and Fellows of Harvard College: fig. 5.16

Princeton University Art Museum/Art Resource, N.Y.: fig. 3.2

© Qin Dashu. From Qin Dashu and Xiang Kunpeng, "Sri Vijaya as the Entrepôt for Circum-Indian Ocean Trade: Evidence from Documentary Records and Materials from Shipwrecks of the 9th–10th Centuries," *Études Océan Indien* 46–47 (2011): 308–36, fig. 13: fig. 1.19

From: Seikado Foundation, *Seikadō 120-sen* [120 Seikado masterpieces] (Tokyo: Seikado, 2013), no. 91: fig. 7.14

TNM Image Archives: figs. 7.5, 7.7

© The Trustees of the British Museum: figs. 1.14–.15

Courtesy the Trustees of the Sir Percival David Foundation; © The Trustees of the British Museum: fig. 1.11

© Victoria and Albert Museum, London: figs. 2.11, 6.18

From: Wang Qiang, *Legendary Port of the Maritime Silk Routes: Zayton (Quanzhou)* (New York: Peter Lang, 2020), fig. 2.1: fig. 0.7

Werner Forman/Universal Images Group/Getty Images: fig. 5.13

From: Zhang Bai, ed., *Zhongguo chutu ciqi quanji* [Complete collection of ceramic art unearthed in China], vol. 7 (Beijing: Kexue Chubanshe, 2008), pl. 76: fig. 3.13

From: Zhang Bai, ed., *Zhongguo chutu ciqi quanji* [Complete collection of ceramic art unearthed in China], vol. 10 (Beijing: Kexue Chubanshe, 2008), pls. 51, 40, 215, 216, 219: figs. 4.16, 4.17, 5.8, 5.9, 5.11